W9-DBV-136

ARCTIC JUSTICE

McGILL-QUEEN'S NATIVE AND NORTHERN SERIES
BRUCE G. TRIGGER, EDITOR

Arctic Justice
On Trial for Murder, Pond Inlet, 1923

SHELAGH D. GRANT

McGill-Queen's University Press
Montreal & Kingston · London · Ithaca

WLU DISCARD

© McGill-Queen's University Press 2002
ISBN 0-7735-2337-5 (cloth)
ISBN 0-7735-2929-2 (paper)

Legal deposit fourth quarter 2002
Bibliothèque nationale du Québec

Printed in Canada on acid-free paper.
First paperback edition 2005

This book was first published with the help of a
grant from the Humanities and Social Sciences
Federation of Canada, using funds provided by the
Social Sciences and Humanities Research Council
of Canada.

McGill-Queen's University Press acknowledges the
support of the Canada Council for the Arts for our
publishing program. We also acknowledge the financial support of the Government of Canada
through the Book Publishing Industry Development
Program (BPIDP) for our publishing activities.

**National Library of Canada Cataloguing in
Publication**

Grant, Shelagh D. (Shelagh Dawn), 1938–
    Arctic justice: on trial for murder, Pond Inlet, 1923/
Shelagh D. Grant

    Includes bibliographical references and index.
ISBN 0-7735-2337-5 bnd
ISBN 0-7735-2929-2 pbk

    1. Janes, Robert – Relations with Inuit. 2. Murder –
Nunavut – Baffin Island. 3. Trials (Murder) –
Nunavut – Pond Inlet. 4. Criminal justice, Adminis-
tration of – Nunavut – Pond Inlet – History. 5. Pond
Inlet (Nunavut) – Ethnic relations. I. Title.

HV6535.C33P63 2002   364.15′23′0971952
C2002-901291-0

This book was typeset by Dynagram Inc.
in 10/12.5 Palatino.

This book is dedicated
to the memory of

ANNA ATAGUTTIAQ

Contents

Maps

Photographs and Illustrations

Preface

My fascination with Eclipse Sound began in 1984 when I first visited Pond
Inlet as part of a study group tour of the Arctic with the Canadian Institute
of International Affairs. Our stopover was brief, but it was a sunny day –
not a cloud in the sky. Standing on the hill above the tiny hamlet, I was
spellbound by the mystical panorama of glaciers and mountain peaks on
Bylot Island. Intuitively I knew that I would be back.

Seven years later I returned, this time on a holiday with my husband.
There had been a fierce storm the night before, and as we walked to our
campsite near the mouth of Salmon Creek, I spotted a wooden plank in
the debris tossed on the shore. I picked it up, turned it over, and was
surprised to read "In Memory of R.S. Janes" carved on the underside.
Looking around, we realized there were two piles of stones nearby. A
wooden cross bearing the name "Hector Pitchforth" was set on one pile,
so we carefully planted the Janes marker on the other. Curious as to why
these two men were buried here and not in one of the two graveyards on
top of the hill, I stopped at the library the next day to ask for more
information.

After reading the file on Robert Janes and the murder trial, I realized that
a decade earlier in Inuvik I had interviewed the widow of one of the police
officers stationed at Pond Inlet at the time. Although our discussion had focused on her experiences in the Mackenzie Delta during the Second World
War, she was eager to show me a large trunk of papers and photographs
belonging to her husband. I recalled urging her to donate the collection to
an archive or similar institution, but Maria McInnes shook her head. She
explained that she wanted to keep them with her until she died, at which
time it would be up to her granddaughter to dispose of them.

Fate again intervened when I told the story to Philippa Ootoowak, the librarian at Pond Inlet. She had learned of Maria's death and happened to

have the granddaughter's name and phone number on file. Within minutes I was on the phone to Yellowknife, talking to Andrea Zupko, now Andrea Williams.

Two months later the postman delivered a large cardboard box that had once contained boxes of Sunlight detergent. Now it was filled with the diaries, notebooks, audiotapes, newspaper clippings, Inuit drawings, and over five hundred photographs that had belonged to former Corporal Finley McInnes of the Royal Canadian Mounted Police. In return for access to the material, I arranged to have the collection catalogued, properly stored in archival folders, and deposited in the Trent University Archives until their final disposition was decided. I also agreed to have negatives and working copies made of the photographs, including a set for the family.

The diary and tapes describing the years McInnes spent at Pond Inlet suggested the possibility of a far more interesting account of early police work than described in government records. Much has been written about the missionaries and the Hudson's Bay Company in the eastern Arctic, but little about the activities of the mounted police. The idea of adding an Inuit perspective was compelling, especially if there were elders still living who had witnessed the trial or were directly related to the key participants. The archival research was well under way when I learned that I had been awarded a three-year grant from the Social Sciences and Humanities Research Council (SSHRC) to undertake oral history interviews at Pond Inlet and Pangnirtung. Now, there was no turning back.

By design, *Arctic Justice* is an interdisciplinary study, combining legal and social history with a good measure of cultural anthropology, criminology, and public policy. In essence, the circumstances surrounding Janes' death and the trial are used as a framework to examine the social interaction between Inuit and *qallunaat** in northern Baffin Island, during the years between the First and Second World Wars. The story is set within the context of environmental determinants, Inuit cultural traditions, and the politics of Arctic sovereignty. As such, the narrative provides insight into a variety of interrelated issues such as: partisan priorities and the origins of the Eastern Arctic Patrol, infectious diseases and starvation, law enforcement and the administration of justice, vignettes of life in a southern penitentiary, the outbreak of tuberculosis in North Baffin, government censorship, and the early use of documentary films as propaganda. Although *Arctic Justice* might be described as a hybrid socio-legal history, it will likely appeal to anyone interested in the Arctic and its indigenous peoples.

At one time, histories of the Arctic could be divided into two types: the oral version passed down through generations by Inuit elders, and the

---

* *Qallunaat* (singular, *qallunaaq*) is the Inuktitut word for a white person.

written narratives of the western world. Each in its own way was influenced by the perceptions and societal values of one's cultural origins.
Misconceptions that arise as a result of these differing thought processes
are universal and at the core of studies on colonialism. For this reason,
Inuit oral history is included here alongside the *qallunaat* interpretation to
show the conflicting values and mechanisms that created fear and
misunderstanding.

Out of respect for the Inuit people and their language, I have elected to
use contemporary Inuktitut spelling in North Baffin dialect for names of
people and places. Since current spelling differs significantly from that
used by the police in the 1920s, at the first reference the Inuktitut spelling of
the name is followed in parentheses, with the original phonetic form found
in the historical documents. Thereafter, contemporary names are used except in the case of direct quotations, where the original spelling is retained
with reference to the present form in square brackets. A glossary of Inuktitut names and terminology is located in the appendix for reference. In a few
cases the current spelling may be open to debate as standardization is still
evolving and may differ in each community. In hopes of avoiding confusion, the glossary was submitted to Nunavut's Language Commissioner for
verification or correction. Except in direct quotations which contain terms
such as Native, Eskimo, or Esquimaux, the terms "Inuit"and "Inuk" are
used throughout.

For decades, the most reliable sources of information on the Janes' case
were the *Annual Reports of the Royal Canadian Mounted Police* and a book by
RCMP historian Harwood Steele, *Policing the Arctic: The Story of the Conquest of the Arctic by the Royal Canadian (Formerly North-West) Mounted
Police*. Both were relatively accurate, but important segments of the story
were missing. Shorter accounts appear in a number of anthropological
studies and popular histories, many with factual errors and inaccurate
assumptions.

Arctic Justice, on the other hand, benefited from the recent availability of
relevant police records. Apart from identifying the evidence and assumptions upon which the case was prosecuted, these files offered new insight
into the motivations driving both the investigation and the trial. Of particular significance were the statements of numerous witnesses who described the circumstances leading to Janes' death and the event itself.
When combined with elders' stories, the Inuit perspective brings the scene
to life with details not found in official reports.

In one sense *Arctic Justice* is a story about protecting Arctic sovereignty
through the introduction of Canadian law and justice to the Inuit of Baffin
Island. Yet it is also the story of Nuqallaq, an Inuk who acted according to
his cultural traditions to protect his people from harm, but who happened

to be in the wrong place at the wrong time. From a broader perspective, this is a study of contact relationships during the initiation of colonial rule over the indigenous peoples of Baffin Island. This window on the past may also provide clues to why violent crimes in Nunavut today, while they vary with each community, are overall six times the national average.

ACKNOWLEDGMENTS

The multi-disciplinary character of the research and the use of Inuit oral history required assistance from an unusually large number of individuals and institutions. First and foremost, my sincerest appreciation goes to Andrea (McInnes) Williams who kindly loaned me the diaries, photographs, audiotapes, and miscellaneous papers belonging to her grandfather, former RCMP Corporal Finley McInnes. Special thanks also go to Michael Cullin of Trent Photographics, who worked on approximately four hundred of the original photographs to create a quality set of negatives and working copies.

In the early stages of my research, Glenn Wright, at the time with the historical division at RCMP headquarters in Ottawa, was particularly helpful in providing access to their photo collection and annual reports and compiling information on staffing at the Arctic detachments. Doug Whyte, in charge of the Northern Affairs Records at the National Archives of Canada, was adept in directing me to the appropriate sources for elusive documents, as was Philip Goldring of Parks Canada. I am also indebted to the staff of various photographic divisions, notably of the National Archives in Ottawa, the Northwest Territories Archives in Yellowknife, the Roman Catholic Diocese of Churchill-Hudson Bay Archives, the McManus Galleries in Dundee, Scotland, and the Manitoba Provincial Archives in Winnipeg. In addition, a number of individuals kindly provided photographs from their private collections: former RCMP Constable Robert Christy (now deceased) who was at Pond Inlet during the early 1930s; Malcolm MacGregor, son of former RCMP Constable William MacGregor (Pond Inlet 1922–23); Philippa Ootoowak, librarian at the Rebecca Idlout Library in Pond Inlet; and Stéphane Cloutier in Iqaluit. Stéphane, who is currently working on a major project on Captain J.E. Bernier, was also an invaluable source for information on geneology.

My sincere thanks go to the many individuals who assisted in the Pond Inlet oral history project, including Bruce Rigby, then superintendent of Parks Canada for the eastern Arctic, for facilitating the coordination of this study with the department's own oral history interviews; Lynn Cousins, who organized the elders' interviews, ran the video camera, and edited the English translations; the interviewers and transcribers who worked on the project; Philippa Ootoowak, the librarian at Pond Inlet, for her ongoing interest and assistance over the past ten years; the staff at the Nattinnalik Visitor's Centre for providing space for meetings with school groups and elders; and John MacDonald of the Igloolik Research Centre for providing access to specific transcripts from the Igloolik Inullariit Society's oral history collection.

The participating elders at Pond Inlet will always hold a very special place in my memories – Martha Akumalik, Samuel Arnakallak, Joanasie Arreak, Timothy Kadloo, Ningiuk Killiktee, Letia Kyak, Cornelius Nutarak, and Elisapee Ootoova. Their stories were invaluable and the follow-up discussions a delight, but it was their enthusiasm and encouragement that provided the incentive to complete this manuscript. Philip Paneak, who provided simultaneous translation during our discussions, offered additional insight into Inuit customs and relationships. Others were generous with their assistance in the final stages: Eva Aariak, Nunavut's language commissioner, who proofread and corrected the Inuktitut spelling in the text and glossary, as well as Martha Kyak and Elisapee Ootoova, who both worked on the Inuktitut version of my research notes for use by the community. I am grateful to the entire Kyak family, and most especially to Letia, with whom I stayed at Pond Inlet, for welcoming me into their homes and making me feel a part of the community.

At Trent University, I am grateful to my colleagues for their interest and support; to the Frost Centre for Canadian Heritage and Development Studies for the seed money to begin work on the McInnes Collection; to the Fred Roots Endowment Fund for partial funding to translate my research notes into Inuktitut, and to former student Sheri Feldman who worked on the McInnes collection as a research assistant. I am particularly appreciative of the advice from two professors emeriti in history from Trent University: Alan Wilson, now living in Nova Scotia, who proofread and commented on earlier drafts of the social history manuscript, and Bruce Hodgins, who read the final draft of this book for content and analysis.

Because of the interdisciplinary nature of this study, I consulted a number of experts, including Robert McGhee and Doug Stenton for archaeology; W. Gillies Ross for the whaling era; Christopher Trott for Inuit spiritual traditions and transition to Christianity; Norman Hallendy, director of the Tukilik Project, for interpretation of Inuit practices in controlling social behaviour; and Alan MacEachern, historian at the University of Western Ontario, with regard to the 1910 government expedition. A very special vote of thanks goes to Graham Price – lawyer, legal historian, and a former acting deputy court judge for the Northwest Territories – for his advice on judicial questions and terminology.

In the final stages, it was editor Aurèle Parisien, coordinating editor Joan McGilvray, copy editor Maureen Garvie, cartographer Eric Leinberger, and the staff at McGill-Queen's Press who deserve high honours for guiding the manuscript through to publication. And on a more personal note, I am eternally grateful for the ongoing support of my husband and family.

Overall, I cannot think of a research project that brought so much pure enjoyment through contact with so many wonderful people.

Shelagh D. Grant
2 November 2001

NOTE TO 2005 REPRINT

Less than a year after the publication of *Arctic Justice*, the comment by an Inuit elder – "we all know that the white man does not always tell the truth" – would come back to haunt me. In a couple of instances, where I had relied upon secondary sources for information peripheral to the main story, I unwittingly duplicated their original errors. For example, during recent research on the Fifth Thule Expedition, I found that the official report by Therkel Mathiassen clearly refutes the story about a mass starvation related by Peter Freuchen in two of his most popular books. The event did not happen as Freuchen claimed: it was a fabrication, the work of an avid story-teller with a vivid imagination. As a result, two paragraphs on page 209 have been rewritten in this edition. Similarly, Alfred Tremblay's description of how Nuqallaq had mistakenly returned Alexander Elder's grave marker to Pond Inlet was queried by Eric Mitchell, a former Hudson's Bay manager at Arctic Bay. According to stories told Mitchell by Inuit elders, it was an Inuk by the name of Kalluk who had mistakenly brought the stone marker to Pond Inlet.

Some captions in the archival photo albums were also misleading. As an example, the photograph (first edition, page 113) identified by first-hand observer W.H. Grant as the "AGES post" is not of the post at Button Point but of Captain Bernier's former post at Igarjuaq near Mount Herodier. The correct photograph has been substituted in this edition. To someone who has never been there, the two photographs look very similar – except for the skyline, as Inuit familiar with the area were quick to point out. Once alerted, I sent copies of the correct photo to Pond Inlet, first for verification and then for distribution to previous and future purchasers.

Where possible, photographs in this edition have been digitally modified to eliminate streaks and watermarks. There are a few other minor revisions and clarifications, none central to the story. I am indebted to Philip Goldring, Philippa Ootoowak, Eric Manning, and Ian R. Stone for bringing them to my attention.

Shelagh D. Grant
September 2004

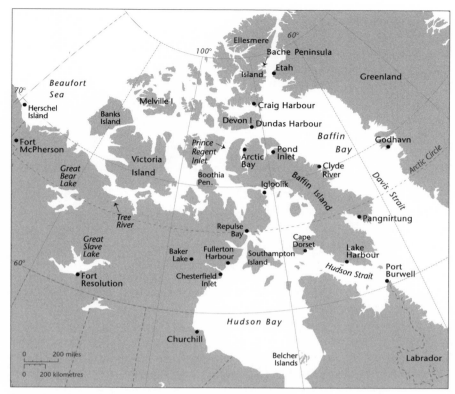

Arctic Canada, circa 1930s.

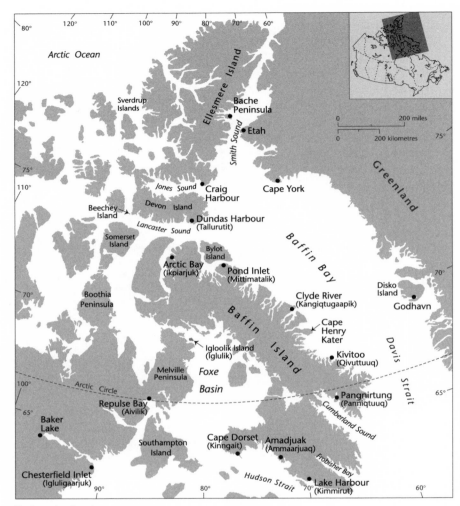

Eastern Arctic, circa 1930s.

ARCTIC JUSTICE

Prologue

The evening twilight cast eerie shadows over the snow-covered ice of Admiralty Inlet, outlining the igloos of an Inuit hunting camp huddled in a semi-circle, the light from stone lamps barely showing through the blocks of snow. A silence hung over the scene, creating an atmosphere pregnant with anticipation. Several figures could be seen half-hidden in the shadows, but there was little movement. Suddenly from one of the snow houses a tall figure emerged, a *qallunaaq* clad in caribou pants and a dark vest that barely covered tattered red wool underwear. He paused, perhaps letting his eyes become accustomed to the semi-darkness, then groped his way forward as if looking for someone. An Inuk in a caribou parka followed him – ever so slowly. A rifle shot pierced the air. The *qallunaaq* paused, then tentatively took a few more steps. A second shot stopped him in his tracks, but then he staggered on. A slight figure emerged from the shadows and grabbed him from behind, pushing him along until he tripped over a sled and fell to the ground.

At first he did not move. Then, attempting to raise his head, he muttered something about foxes. The words were barely audible – something about "never mind the foxes." He seemed to summon his strength and feebly called out "Ululijarnaat – help me!" Other figures emerged from behind the snow houses, keeping a safe distance. An Inuk with a rifle stood up from behind a *qamutiik* placed on its side and ran to a nearby igloo.

The onlookers inched their way forward, their eyes rivetted on the figure lying on the snow. The Inuk reappeared from the snow house, rifle still in hand, his face taut with determination. Cautiously he approached the wounded man. There was slight movement and somebody shouted, "Watch out – he is trying to get up." A moment of silence was followed by a panic cry, "Shoot him again." The Inuk with the rifle was now only five or six feet away. He slowly raised his gun and took aim. This time his shot struck the fallen man on the side of the head. It was over. And so life passed away from the body of the fur trader from Newfoundland, his crimson blood oozing from the head wound onto the pristine snow. The silence was broken by the shuffling of feet as the Inuit hunters moved closer. Then there were whispers and in the background the panting and whimpering of the dogs, as their masters tried to hold them back.

Following Inuit custom, the hunters carefully put mitts and boots on the dead man's hands and feet before wrapping the body in caribou skins and transporting it by *qamutiik* to the mainland. Someone had suggested leaving the body on the ice, so it would disappear with the spring thaw. Others disagreed, saying that the white man's family might come to claim the body. In accordance with their traditional law, everyone remained at the camp for three days out of respect for the dead man's spirit. Several hunters gave fox skins to the Inuk who had shot him, in gratitude for having killed the man who had threatened to kill them and their dogs.

Then everyone departed. Those responsible for the shooting accompanied Janes' former guide to return the deceased's effects to Eclipse Sound. When told what had happened, the trader at Igarjuaq seemed neither surprised nor concerned but thanked the Inuit and locked away the dead man's furs and belongings.[1] It was up to the owner of the trading post to decide what to do, and he would not arrive by ship for another four months.

Some days later several hunters from Igloolik arrived at Admiralty Inlet to put the frozen body in a box, then stow it high on a cliff in a rock crevice where it would not be disturbed by animals. They believed that they had treated the body with respect, in a manner appropriate for a white man so that his soul would rest in peace. A few feared that *qallanaat* might come to avenge his death, but no one believed that they had done anything wrong. The Inuit hunters had followed the dictates of their customary law. No police or missionaries had ever visited North Baffin to tell them otherwise.

The incident took place in the late evening of 15 March 1920, at a hunting camp on the ice of Admiralty Inlet, not far from Cape Crauford. The victim was Robert S. Janes, a Caucasian of British heritage, approximately six feet tall, with a large frame, a scraggy beard, and greying hair. For the past four years he had operated a trading post at Tulukkaat, near the mouth of the Patricia River on Eclipse Sound. He left behind a wife and children in St John's, Newfoundland, and at his former trading post an Inuit woman pregnant with his child. The man who shot him was Nuqallaq,* sometimes called Qiugaarjuk, an Inuk in his forties, of average height, with dark skin, brown eyes, and shoulder-length black hair. He originally came from the Igloolik area, the son of a shaman.

---

* In government documents of the period, Nuqallaq's name appears as "Nukudlah" or sometimes "Nookudlah," his alias written as "Kiwatsoo."

  Henceforth, at the first reference the current spelling of an Inuit name is followed by the original phonetic spelling in parentheses. In quotations the current spelling in square brackets follows the original.

On the day before the shooting the white trader had become angry when the Inuit refused to hand over their fox skins, which he claimed were owed to him. In a fit of rage that left him visibly shaking, he threatened to kill their dogs and perhaps one of the hunters if they refused his requests. The Inuit took his threats seriously, and a respected elder suggested that someone should kill him before he killed one of them. After much discussion, Nuqallaq was selected to terminate his life because the trader had previously threatened him and had also attacked his father with a snow-knife. The Inuk consented, but only if Janes became angry again. The next day the trader informed his guide that he intended to meet with Inuit hunters that night and press them even harder to turn over their furs. Unwittingly, he had sealed his own fate. At least three others helped plan his execution, but only one Inuk fired the shot that killed Robert Janes.

Although Nuqallaq had acted in accordance with Inuit tradition, the consequences of his actions would be dictated by the British code of justice. A lone police officer was sent eighteen months later to investigate reports of Janes' death. He presided as coroner over an inquest that recommended that three Inuit be arrested and held for questioning. Several months later the investigating officer, now acting as justice of the peace with powers of two, conducted preliminary hearings that led to the three suspects being committed to trial on charges of murder. They would be held under "house arrest" at Pond Inlet for over a year, waiting for the arrival of a court party to try the case. By Canadian law the planned execution was considered premeditated murder, yet by Inuit tradition the individuals were held blameless because the decision to end his life was supported by consensual agreement of the hunters.[2]

In the end the charge would be reduced to manslaughter with a plea for clemency. In a trial by jury, but not one of his peers, Nuqallaq would be convicted and sentenced by the judge to ten years hard labour at Stony Mountain Penitentiary in Manitoba. Ululijarnaat (Oorooreungnak) would serve two years "hard labour" at the Pond Inlet detachment, where he was provided with flour and tea, along with a gun and ammunition. Aatitaaq (Ahteetah) was acquitted for lack of evidence.

Nuqallaq served less than eighteen months of his sentence before he contracted tuberculosis. At the request of senior officials, including the commissioner of the Royal Canadian Mounted Police, the prisoner was released on a "ticket of leave" and returned to Pond Inlet where he was reunited with his wife. Canadian officials had acted out of compassion, believing the cold air would put the disease into remission. Nuqallaq, however, was a very sick man and died within a few months. Sadly, the story does not end there, for it appears that he left behind a legacy – an outbreak of tuberculosis that spread throughout the North Baffin hunting camps that winter and the next spring, and as far south as Clyde River.[3]

The following is the story of the circumstances leading to Janes' death, the political influences driving the decision to try the accused at Pond Inlet, and the consequences for those held responsible and for others residing on Baffin Island. In one sense *Arctic Justice* is a story of an Inuk who killed an abusive white man at the request of those who feared for their lives. Yet it is also about the introduction of Canadian law and justice to the Inuit of North Baffin where there had been no previous attempt to enforce colonial rule. The narrative gives rise to stark contrasts of imagery, ranging from images of diplomats debating the finer points of international law to fisti-cuffs between angry, knife-wielding fur traders. There are also stories within stories, as they relate to various sovereignty issues, competition for gold and furs, the use of film as propaganda, government censorship, and prison life at Stony Mountain Penitentiary, and to the neglect of an out-break of tuberculosis in North Baffin.

Throughout each story runs a common theme of fear – collectively or individually – in response to the unknown. Among the Inuit, fear of the *qallunaat* was ever present, but in this case was initially focused on an irra-tional white trader who threatened to kill their dogs and possibly those who refused his demands. After he was shot and no longer a threat, a more pervasive fear that the *qallunaat* might seek revenge spread among those who had witnessed the incident. Fear was also prevalent in *qallunaat* minds, as evident in the government's reaction to perceived threats to Arc-tic sovereignty and in a white trader's concern of being abandoned with-out sufficient furs to pay for his way home. For both Inuit and *qallunaat* there was the constant fear of starvation and other perils associated with life in the high Arctic.

The objective here is not to establish whether there was a miscarriage of justice but to provide insight into the motivations and frustrations of enforc-ing law and order on the Arctic frontier. Even then, *Arctic Justice* is ultimately a much broader study about human response to an alien culture. As such, it is a story about truths and untruths, perceptions and realities, and the conse-quences – in the short and long term – for the Inuit of North Baffin.

1

North Baffin Prior to 1905

The Arctic environment – its weather extremes and unique landforms – exerted a dominant influence on the lives of its indigenous peoples to produce a culture distinct from other hunters and gatherers in North America.[1] Over time, regional differences in wildlife resources created more subtle variations, as did migration patterns and climate change. The nature and timing of early contact with the Europeans would generate further distinctions. Yet with the exception of climate-induced changes during the Little Ice Age, the physical environment of the Arctic has remained relatively unchanged since the arrival of the first migrants from Siberia over four thousand years ago.

In sharp contrast to the lowlands in the south, the highland rim of the Canadian Shield along the northeastern coast of Baffin Island is characterized by peaked mountains, active glaciers, trough valleys, broad peninsulas, and deep fiords carved out of sedimentary rock by glacial erosion. Bylot Island, lying to the northeast, is separated from the larger island by Eclipse Sound, with access from Davis Strait by way of Pond's Inlet and from Lancaster Sound through Navy Board Inlet. The domed icecap on Bylot Island rises approximately six thousand feet above sea level, surrounded by snow-capped peaks and glaciers – an impressive site when viewed from across the sound. To the southwest lie the Tununiq Mountains at the head of Milne Inlet with the highest peak rising four thousand feet above sea level.[2]

For millennia the protected waters of Eclipse Sound and surrounding lands provided Inuit with an abundance of wildlife resources, including narwhal, seal, walrus, polar bear, fish, and a variety of migratory birds. Caribou, although at one time more numerous, can still be found feeding on the lichen-covered rocks of nearby hills.[3] There were other advantages. From August to October, icebergs frequently drift into Eclipse Sound, carried by the prevailing current from Greenland until caught in the winter

Aerial view of the mountain peaks, glaciers, and snowfields of northeastern Baffin Island.
S. Grant, 1997.

freeze-up. Grounded each year on the shallow sand bars near the present-day settlement of Pond Inlet, they provided, and continue to provide, a ready source of fresh drinking water, a factor that may explain the number of ancient campsites at Mittimatalik and further west along the beach at Qilalukkan.[4] In summer the melting snow uncovers a profusion of vegetation ranging from the Arctic willow, only a few inches high, to a colourful array of tundra plants and perennial wildflowers. The season is short, but the intensity of the summer sun accelerates growth at a much faster rate than in southern climes, allowing the hardy vegetation to play a key role in the food chain of the precariously balanced high Arctic ecosystem.

Moving westward across the top of North Baffin, the jagged peaks give way to a more rounded landscape of undulating plateaus dissected by dried-up river valleys leading into Admiralty Inlet. On the east side, several bays probe inland like long fingers, the largest being Strathcona Sound to the north, then Adams Sound and Moffat Inlet to the south. At various points, glacial erosion created high cliffs marked horizontally with red and orange layers of rock stained by iron oxide. The other side of the Brodeur Peninsula slopes gradually to the shores of Prince Regent Inlet.[5] The height of land also diminishes southward towards the head of Admiralty Inlet until reaching the Foxe Basin lowlands and the camps of the Igloolik Inuit.

Since many Iglulingmiut are central to this story, the North Baffin region is defined here to include their camps in the vicinity of Aggu on Baffin Island and Igloolik Island. As was the case in Eclipse Sound, the abundance of wildlife resources in this area sustained a relatively large population over a very long period of time.

Migrants from the shores of Siberia by way of Alaska – the Palaeo-Eskimos – occupied sites in the vicinity of both Eclipse Sound and Igloolik, dating back to around 2000 BC. Today, Inuit elders refer to these Inuit as Tuniit* to distinguish them from their own ancestors, the Thule people or Tunijjuat, who arrived at North Baffin around 900 AD. The latter were smaller in stature but possessed more sophisticated tools and weapons.[6] The Tuniit were displaced from their traditional hunting grounds and eventually disappeared. That the two cultures actually lived together or adjacent to each other at any time is considered unlikely by most archaeologists, but elders' stories about Tuniit around Eclipse Sound suggest there was contact and that it was somewhat more than fleeting.[7] While in some areas the Little Ice Age caused the Thule people to migrate southward, archaeological evidence uncovered by the Danish Fifth Thule Expedition (1921–24) suggested that many living in the vicinity of Igloolik and Eclipse Sound did not leave the area but instead underwent a more gradual transition from the Thule culture to the present day.[8]

The Inuit living on Eclipse Sound call themselves Tununirmiut, meaning the people of Tununiq, "the land that faces away from the sun" or the "shaded place," in reference to the mountains at the head of Milne Inlet off Eclipse Sound. By similar definition, Tununirusiq, meaning the "lesser shaded place," refers to an area with smaller mountains in the vicinity of Arctic Bay off Admiralty Inlet, and the Tununirusirmiut as the people living there.[9] The leader of the Fifth Thule Expedition, Knud Rasmussen, suggested that these people belonged to a larger cultural grouping that included those residing in the vicinity of Igloolik Island. Father Guy Mary-Rousselière, an amateur archaeologist and long-time resident at Pond Inlet, believed the Tununirmiut were also closely related to the Adkudnirmiut of the Clyde River area because of similarities in their language and clothing.[10] How much interaction took place in the years prior to contact with Europeans is unknown, but trade with the whalers undoubtedly created closer ties between Inuit groups throughout North Baffin.

Cultural adaptations to the environment continued long after Inuit contact with the Europeans.[11] The sun, or its absence, for example, dictated a seasonal routine in their lives, differing in some regions according to the

* Tuniit is the Inuktitut name used by Inuit elders for the people who occupied their lands before the arrival of their ancestors, the Tunijjuat – or in anthropological terms, the late Dorset culture and Thule people, respectively.

length of time without sunlight during the winter months and to the availability of certain species of wildlife. In North Baffin, located well above the
Arctic Circle, the sun slipped below the horizon around mid-November
and did not return until mid-February. As a consequence, Inuit would
spend the winter months of darkness in quasi-hibernation, moving out of
their insulated winter homes only to obtain seal oil for their lamps and
food from their caches. The return of sunlight in late February was understandably cause for celebration. Children ventured outdoors to play, their
laughter filling the air, while hunters headed out on the sea ice in search of
seal (*nattiq*) and polar bear (*nanuq*). Later, they moved their entire families
to spring hunting camps on the ice or near the floe edge. As the sun's
warmth began to melt the snow and ice around Eclipse Sound, the Inuit
moved again, this time to fish at the mouths of rivers, and later to climb the
well-worn paths along the banks to harvest those caught in shallow pools
or man-made dams. In the Igloolik area the sea ice melted earlier, allowing
the men to head out in their kayaks (*qajait*) in search of walrus (*aiviq*) or
narwhal (*qilalugaq*). Once the snow disappeared from the hills, the hunters
headed inland in search of caribou (*tuktuit*). Women and children, meanwhile, collected eggs and picked berries.

Inuit travelled great distances in the spring to visit friends and trade,
but by late summer and early fall, activities were geared to preparing for
winter. Hunters filled their food caches and the women sewed warmer
outfits for the months ahead. Gradually families drifted back to their winter camps, where they rebuilt the stone foundations that were sunk into
the ground for warmth. Skins were placed over whale ribs to form the
roof, followed by a layer of heather for insulation, then a second layer of
skins. A skin tent was attached on the inside to protect against frost build-
up, and snow was packed around the outside for warmth. The pace of
physical activities slowed dramatically as the sun slid below the horizon
and once again everyone waited for spring.[12] During the winter months
Inuit families were more vulnerable to hunger and disease, especially if
there was a shortage of food or insufficient seal oil to keep the stone lamps
(*qulliit*) lit for heat and light. For the more fortunate, it was just a matter
of awaiting the return of the sun. Patience was not a virtue – it was a
necessity.

The climate also dictated the mode for long-distance travel. For carrying
heavy loads, the obvious choice was by *qamutiik* over hard-packed snow or
sea ice. In summer, hunters might travel overland on foot for short distances, with their dogs carrying packs on their backs. Once the sea ice had
melted, an *umiaq* (a large boat made of skins stretched over whale bone and
rowed by the women) might be used to move families to a new campsite.
Whatever the season, their dogs were critical to the hunters' ability to
travel in search of food.

Travelling on snow and sea ice in winter or on the land during summer, Inuit were dependent upon their dogs. McInnes Collection.

Sudden changes in the weather could be disastrous. An unusually early breakup of sea ice could strand entire families on the wrong side of a large body of water. Similarly, an unexpected warm spell in spring could turn hard snow into heavy wet mush, making travel overland difficult, sometimes impossible. The cold air could be brutal if accompanied by strong winds. At Pond Inlet the average low temperature in February is roughly

−37 degrees Celsius, but known to fall as low as −59° c. Although the accumulation of snow is less than in more southerly regions, blizzard conditions are frequent.[13] There are many stories of hunters who became disoriented during intense storms and were later found frozen to death not far from their camp. Some elders maintain that the Inuktitut name for Pond Inlet − Mittimatalik, meaning the place where Mittima died − is derived from just such a story.[14]

According to history texts, the first European ship to reach Lancaster Sound was the British ship *Discovery* in 1616, commanded by Captain Robert Bylot. A recent discovery of handspun Viking yarn suggests that they may have been preceded in the early fourteenth century by Norsemen, sailing from their colony on southwest Greenland.[15] Nonetheless, the names of Bylot Island and the larger island called after his pilot, William Baffin, remain as a testament to the first British expedition to reach the northern-most tip of Baffin Island.[16] Owing to impenetrable ice in Davis Strait during the Little Ice Age, another two hundred years passed before explorers again ventured as far north as Lancaster Sound. The first was a British Admiralty Expedition in 1818, led by Captain John Ross. He landed briefly on Bylot Island and named the entrance to what appeared to be a large bay Pond's Inlet, after John Pond, the Astronomer Royal. The following year Captain William Edward Parry led yet another expedition into Lancaster Sound, this time naming Devon and Somerset Islands, as well as Admiralty and Navy Board Inlets. Parry was the first to provide a detailed description of Inuit from this region after visiting a small camp near Clyde River just south of the entrance to Pond's Inlet.[17]

That same year several whalers from Scotland and England reached the shores of North Baffin, and reports of their success brought many more. Over the next decade roughly 750 vessels were reported to have fished the waters, with the average catch amounting to more than ten whales per ship.[18] Meanwhile the whaling captains mapped the coast and gave names to every unnamed landmark. More were added as they penetrated into Lancaster Sound and Hudson Bay. Eclipse Sound, as an example, was named by Captain John Gray after his ship. Likewise, Adams Sound and Arctic Bay were named after Captain William Adams Sr and his ship *Arctic I*, the first to anchor in the sheltered bay off Admiralty Inlet.

By mid-century, whale stocks in the northern waters had declined from over-fishing, causing most ships to move southward to Cumberland Sound and later into Hudson Bay. At both locations, American and Scottish whalers began to winter over, utilizing Inuit to man the small whale boats, assist in rendering the whale blubber, and provide the ship's crew with country food and skin clothing. Intense social interaction was inevitable and resulted in a proliferation of children with mixed blood, all of whom were proudly raised as Inuit, either by their natural mother or adoptive families. Whalers were quite willing to take advantage of the fact that a

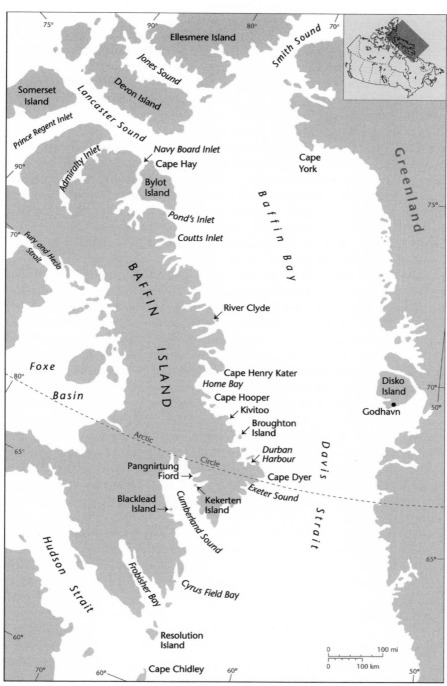

Nineteenth century map of Baffin Island an vicinity.

husband, instead of expressing jealousy, often seemed pleased that his wife was appreciated.[19]

By the late 1800s most sailing ships were fitted with auxiliary steam engines, allowing them to arrive earlier, penetrate deeper into ice-strewn waters, and depart later in the season. A few whalers continued to fish off the North Baffin coast, nearly all from Peterhead or Dundee, Scotland. The technique they employed was called "rock-nosing," whereby a ship would anchor in a protected harbour or just off-shore, while its small whale boats searched for whales migrating to winter quarters off southern Greenland and Labrador. The ships were self-sufficient, carrying crews of forty or more to man the boats that brought the carcass alongside the ship. Here they removed the baleen and flensed the blubber. The baleen was tied into bundles and the whale blubber stored in large wooden casks for rendering back in Scotland. Although Inuit assistance was not required by the "rock-nose whalers," they were nevertheless welcomed aboard to trade their ivory and furs for European goods.[20]

Although a few ships were reported to have ventured into Prince Regent Inlet, the Iglulingmiut generally travelled to Eclipse Sound or Repulse Bay to trade with the whalers. Some reportedly were hired to work on the whaling ships in Hudson Bay. The trading sessions developed into social occasions that included tea and biscuits, musical entertainment, and square dances.[21] Inevitably the Inuit of North Baffin became dependent upon a trade economy over which they had little control, apart from their ability to negotiate. Favoured items were tobacco, guns, and ammunition, but the Inuit also valued knives, fox traps, saws, hatchets, clothing items, telescopes, tea, kettles, pots, and later, musical instruments and sewing machines.[22] Over time Inuit culture underwent subtle changes that included addiction to tobacco, new dietary preferences, use of *qallunaat* clothing, and loss of traditional hunting techniques. In addition to trade goods, the Europeans also brought infectious diseases such as measles, influenza, and venereal disease, all of which took their toll in deaths and disabilities.[23]

For the most part, relations between the Inuit of North Baffin and the whalers were peaceful – with a notable exception occurring in the late nineteenth century. According to elders' stories told to Father Guy Mary-Rousselière, several Inuit families had crossed over Lancaster Sound to hunt polar bears on Devon Island. When a whaling ship anchored near their camp, several hunters boarded the ship to trade. One Inuk, known to be a thief, stole a telescope and other items. In anger the ship's crew suddenly opened fire, killing all Inuit on board save one who was thought to have been taken a prisoner.[24] Those who witnessed the incident from the shore fled in fear that the whalers would come ashore and kill them as well. The fact that three elders were able to recall the story of the massacre almost a hundred years later reflects a deep and lasting impression.

Eclipse II in the pack ice of Davis Strait. Dundee City Council, Arts and Heritage, DUNMG 1975–2–4 (14).

With whale stocks almost depleted at the end of the nineteenth century, some shipowners maintained their former whaling stations in Cumberland Sound as trading centres for ivory, sealskin, furs, and fish, thus moderating the disruption in Inuit lives during the transition to a fur-trapping economy. At least two companies attempted to set up trading stations along the Baffin coast, but the supply system proved unstable.

The Hudson's Bay Company (HBC), which began establishing posts in the Ungava region in the mid-nineteenth century, moved slowly northward, to Lake Harbour in 1911, Cape Dorset in 1913, and as far as Repulse Bay in 1916. Further expansion halted during the Great War and did not resume until 1920.[25] Although the Iglulingmiut continued to trade at the HBC post at Repulse Bay, the Tununirmiut would have been without ammunition had it not been for the arrival of free traders at Eclipse Sound.[26]

There were inherent risks as Inuit moved further afield in search of whalers and trade goods. Family groups travelling through unfamiliar territory were sometimes caught by bad weather and lost their way. Some died of starvation, a fate feared worse than death itself. One story tells of thirteen Inuit in the 1870s who were beset by bad weather en route from Igloolik to Pond Inlet. Only two survived by eating the deceased and managed to make their way on foot to Eclipse Sound.[27] Around 1893 a group from a camp on Admiralty Inlet went over to Elwyn Bay on Somerset Island, apparently looking for whales or possibly whalers who sometimes visited that location. When the whaling ship *Baleana* arrived the next summer, they found their corpses, victims of starvation. It was reported that they had first eaten their dogs, then the dead, until the last succumbed sometime during the winter. Given the valuables left behind, it was believed that there had been no survivors.[28] Eating the flesh of a deceased human was a taboo in Inuit culture, just as in western societies, but acute starvation was claimed to cause one to lose all reason.

Unlike the Indian policies that evolved in British North America after the Royal Proclamation of 1763, no official Inuit policy – neither British nor later Canadian – existed until after the Second World War. Although recognized as "Natives," the Inuit were not included in the Indian Act, nor was legislation passed making them wards of the federal government.[29] As a consequence, they were technically full-fledged Canadian citizens without any privileges – no access to health or educational services, and no vote. As residents of the Northwest Territories, they fell under the general authority of the Department of the Interior until 1924, when the responsibility for Inuit policy was temporarily transferred to the Department of Indian Affairs by an amendment to a sub-section of the Indian Act. The RCMP were mandated to supervise their health and welfare in the field.[30]

Without a permanent government or police presence on Baffin Island, a mutually acceptable form of "frontier justice" prevailed in the nineteenth century, allowing for relatively easy coexistence between whalers and the Inuit. If a *qallunaaq* became angry, an Inuk might go out of his way to appease him,[31] a reaction that was likely responsible for the image of the Inuit as "a friendly, peaceful race." Most Inuit relationships with the *qallunaat* were influenced by a response known as *ilira*, which resulted in a show of deference or subservience to frightening or intimidating individuals. By

Hugh Brody's interpretation, that response was at the core of all early contact relationships: "The word *ilira* goes to the heart of colonial relationships, and it helps to explain the many times that Inuit, and so many other peoples, say yes when they want to say no, or say yes and reveal, later, that they never meant it at all. *Ilira* is a word that speaks to the subtle but pervasive result of inequality. Through the inequality it reveals, the word shapes the whole tenor of interpersonal behaviour, creating many forms of misunderstanding, mistrust, and bad faith. It is the fear that colonialism instils and evokes, which then distorts meanings, social life and politics."[32]

Inuit/whaler relationships also involved a natural co-dependency. Just as an Inuk would not wish to alienate those who supplied European goods, a ship's captain would not want to cut off his access to furs and ivory, particularly in light of the declining whale fishery. Even so, certain ground rules were established. According to one elder from Arctic Bay, it was understood that trouble would follow if they killed a white man.[33] Apparently such views were not understood in terms of "right or wrong" or Canadian laws but in terms of their own cultural traditions that allowed the family of a murdered man to take revenge on his killer.[34]

Similarly, most Europeans were mindful that it was not in their best interests to alienate the Inuit. As an example, the story of how shipwrecked sailors on Akpatok Island were killed by their Inuit hosts – because of food shortages and their unreasonable demands – was well known in the whaling fraternity.[35] As Commander A.P. Low of Canada's 1903–04 expedition to the Arctic explained, the Inuit as a people were "very hospitable and kind; but like other savages would probably soon tire of continuous efforts to support helpless whites cast upon them, especially when the guests assume a superiority over their hosts."[36]

In the nineteenth century, reports of violence among the Inuit were generally ignored. Whalers preferred not to get involved. This was not necessarily the case with the Hudson's Bay Company, as outbreaks of violence tended to have an adverse effect on their trade. In the Ungava region, for instance, it was reported that HBC traders supported the Inuit custom of execution as it was in their interest to be rid of a potential menace in their midst.[37] Yet prior to 1911 there were no HBC posts on Baffin Island. Nor was there a police presence before 1921, except for a very brief visit by the North West Mounted Police (NWMP) who had accompanied the 1897 and 1903 expeditions to Cumberland Sound. Significantly, there were no police officers on board in 1904 when the A.P. Low expedition first visited Eclipse Sound. Nor were there any on the expeditions led by Captain Bernier from 1906 to 1911. Thus, while there was a fleeting government presence of sorts on Baffin Island between 1897 and 1911, there was no effective means of enforcing law and order in the region during the forty years following Britain's transfer of the territory to Canada. Likewise, except for a visit to

Cumberland Sound by a Moravian brother in 1856, Baffin Island had no permanent missionary presence until 1894.[38] As a result, the Inuit were portrayed in nineteenth-century literature and art as an uncivilized pagan race who dressed in animal skins and carried Stone Age weapons but somehow managed to survive the most inhospitable environment known to western man. This stereotype prevailed well into the twentieth century.

The advance of Christianity in the eastern Arctic that began with the Moravians in Labrador in 1776 continued into the mid-nineteenth century with the establishment of an Anglican mission at Moose River on James Bay and later at Great Whale River on the east coast of Hudson Bay. In 1876 Reverend Edmund Peck founded a mission at Little Whale River on Ungava Bay, where he began working on a syllabic alphabet to represent Inuktitut, based on one created by Reverend James Evans for use with the Cree Indians. In 1894, armed with syllabic prayer books and Bibles, Peck established the first Christian mission on Baffin Island, at a whaling station on Blacklead Island in Cumberland Sound. A rudimentary school was set up as well as a one-room mission hospital.[39]

Peck's travels and those of his assistants were generally limited to nearby camps, although one year he visited camps along the coast as far north as Qivittuuq while returning home to England on a whaling ship. A number of lay preachers travelled further afield, distributing Bibles and spreading word about the new religion.[40] Several families from Cumberland Sound were reported to have migrated to Igloolik with their Bibles. In this manner, many Iglulingmiut learned to read and write in syllabics without ever having met a *qallunaat* missionary.[41] Understanding the biblical passages was more difficult.

Literacy grew at an astonishing rate, but the meaning of the words was not always understood. This gave rise to a number of "syncretic movements" that combined traditional spiritual beliefs of shamanism with those of Christianity. Occasionally there were bouts of religious frenzy and in a few cases tragic deaths. Peter Pitseolak described two such occasions near Lake Harbour which he described as "over-doing religion." There were similar incidents reported near Sugluk in the Ungava region of Quebec and near Pangnirtung.[42] Although another Anglican mission opened at Lake Harbour in 1909, it was not until 1928 that a European missionary visited Pond Inlet, and then only briefly during a stop by the HBC supply ship. In other words, there was no supervised teaching of Christianity north of Cumberland Sound until 1928.[43]

Inuit of North Baffin, like those elsewhere in the Arctic, had their own spiritual convictions as set out in the legends and teachings of the shamans. These beliefs were largely driven by fear and maintained by an elaborate network of taboos that governed their everyday life. There was no "one supreme being," although Sedna, the sea goddess, also known as

Nuliajuk or Sanna, was considered to be the giver or taker of life because of her powerful influence over the fish and mammals. A number of lesser spirits were thought to have control over such things as the weather, health, fertility, and even one's happiness. Only the shamans possessed the ability to communicate with the spirits. Some had "great powers" to travel to the moon or to the depths of the sea. Some had special healing powers, while others were skilled at knowing where to look for caribou or marine mammals. Disease and starvation were believed to be caused by someone having broken a taboo. If anyone behaved badly, a shaman might encourage a public confession to help that person overcome the problem. There were good shamans and bad, the latter greatly feared because of their power to do evil.[44]

Commander A.P. Low appeared knowledgeable about Inuit spiritual beliefs and shamanism when he visited North Baffin in the summer of 1904.[45] In his book describing the expedition, he referred to Inuit rules governing social behaviour, including the criteria for executing an individual. By his understanding, "if an individual becomes dangerously obnoxious, or insane, a consultation of the men of the band is held, and one or more of them are deputed to remove the criminal or lunatic; in such a case the individuals acting are held blameless in the matter."[46]

Yet some government officials would argue that because the Inuit travelled in small groups, they did not possess a formal system of justice or governance. Zebedee Nungak, speaking as chairman of the Inuit Justice Task Force in Nunavik, strongly disagreed, claiming that not only did Inuit know right from wrong by their own standards but they also had a system to deal with serious offenders: "The overriding concern was the sustenance of the collective. Any dispute among the people was settled by the elders and/or leaders, who always had the respect and high regard of the group."[47] Inuit also employed various means such as counselling, derision, gossip, and public confession to modify unacceptable behaviour. Granted, there were regional differences, but only as a last resort did elders advise banishment or execution.[48] In spite of the many cultural differences, the tradition of consensual agreement and the goal of restoring harmony in the community were two traits Inuit shared with the Dogrib Indians of the Dene Nation.[49]

If an Inuk's actions became deviant and menaced others, and if that individual did not respond to other means of control, then he or she was considered to be or insane, providing just cause that his or her life be terminated.[50] In such cases execution required careful planning to catch the victim when most vulnerable. By British standards such actions were clear evidence of premeditated murder, yet by Inuit customary law, consensual agreement legitimized the action. Equally at odds with British justice was the Inuit belief that "insanity" provided a justifiable reason for killing a person, compared to the *qallunaat* practice of pleading insanity to avoid responsibility for one's crime. Even the objectives of social control differed in the two societies. When Inuit were confronted with a serious crime such as persistent thieving, assault, or murder, the aim was to resolve the conflict, if possible, so as not to lose an able-bodied hunter. By British tradition a criminal was severely punished to deter others from contemplating similar acts.

Although the Inuit traditions in dealing with violence appear to have been understood by an informed white elite at the turn of the century, few were aware of the subtle regional differences in process.[51] In the southwest corner of Baffin Island, for example, discussion about a criminal act was formalized and involved a gathering of leaders and shamans in what Norman Hallendy describes as a "Great Council," which "questioned witnesses and the accused, heard confessions, listened to pleas, attempted to resolve conflicts, and decided punishments."[52] In North Baffin the procedure was far less formal and required only the consent of elders or camp leaders.[53]

Not all Inuit killings were planned in advance. As historian William R. Morrison explains, "in aboriginal Inuit groups, even temper was prized, and bad temper was regarded as a serious threat, not only to the individual, but to the whole band." In this context, "if a man spoke harshly to you, he had it in his mind to kill you, and it was thus entirely reasonable to defend yourself by killing him first."[54] In North Baffin an adult was expected to refrain from showing anger and instead show *isuma*, meaning "the capacity for a sense of reason." The loss of *isuma*, which might be evidenced by a flushed face or aggressive gestures, was equated with the loss of reason or insanity.[55] When the death of an Inuk was the result of an impulsive act without consensual agreement, a member of the victim's family possessed the right to retaliate and seek revenge. This often led to "blood feuds" if a killer was unable to convince the victim's family of the necessity of his act.[56]

Taking another's life without prior consent or provocation – *inuaqsiniq* – was considered the worst of all crimes because of the adverse effect it would have on a group with close kinship ties. But self-defence was an exception, according to Emile Imaruittuq, an elder from Igloolik. "If someone was attacking you, trying to kill you, you would be justified in defending yourself. If you killed the person before he killed you, that would be justified. But if a killing was committed without a provocation, that was terrible. We are on this Earth to try to live. We have to protect ourselves, if someone is trying to kill us."[57] In other words, self-defence was an acceptable motive.

In some cases murderers might be forgiven if they regretted their actions and showed a willingness to change. Even then, they tended to be feared, as it was thought that "once an individual has killed someone, the desire to kill again would return." Those most feared were individuals who claimed that they "heard voices" or were thought to be losing their minds.[58] Prior to 1912 there had been no reports of an Inuk killing a white man, and thus no attempts to interfere in what were perceived as domestic matters. Moreover, on Baffin Island, there were no police to receive such a report.

After 1904, trade improved for the Tununirmiut because of a new land-based whaling station established on Eclipse Sound by the Dundee Whaling Company. Captain James Mutch, a veteran whaler, accompanied by William Duval and several Inuit families from Cumberland Sound, was sent to establish a post in the vicinity of Pond Inlet.

According to Mutch, he had been unable to encourage families from Qivittuuq to join him because "they were afraid of the Ponds Bay Eskimos, as there were so many murders up there." John Matthiasson, an anthropologist who lived at Pond Inlet during the 1960s, was also told about "a very bad man" who had lived there many years ago, and who began to kill all the people who lived with him."[59] The Inuk in question may have been Qillaq, the leader of the Qitdlarssuaq migration to Greenland. According to several stories told by Inuit elders, this group appeared to be the primary cause of violence in the region.[60]

After spending one winter at Erik Harbour in the winter of 1903–04, Mutch moved to a permanent location at Igarjuaq in Albert Harbour, several miles east of the present-day site of Pond Inlet. Although the station was equipped to render whale blubber, it primarily operated as a trading post. Here Mutch employed a number of hunters to assist in harvesting seals and narwhals, and women to render the fat into oil. In summer the families lived in skin tents surrounding the main building. In the winter months they were paid "a scant weekly allowance of biscuits, tea, molasses and tobacco … to keep them on hand until the spring arrived," at which time, the small whale boats were pulled to floe edge to hunt seals, whales, narwhals, and polar bears.[61] Occasionally these boats were given to Inuit as payment for services or goods and were considered prize possessions.

Duval, a German-born American called Sivutiksaq, meaning "the harpooner," remained at the station for three years along with his Inuit wife and two daughters.[62] In 1923 he would return to Pond Inlet as the interpreter for the first jury trial held in the eastern Arctic.

Inuit living in vicinity of the whaling station enjoyed a few years of relative prosperity, as did those who came from Arctic Bay and Igloolik to trade. As Mutch* observed, the Tununirmiut had become shrewd

---

* known to the Inuit as Jimmi Mutchie.

Igarjuaq whaling station near Albert Harbour operated from 1904 to 1910 as a trading post for furs and ivory. Philippe Brodeur Collection, G.R. Lancefield, photographer. NAC – PA 139395.

bargainers after eighty-five years of trade with the whalers: "The real Ponds Bay Eskimo had been coming and going all winter, trading a fox-skin when they had one, but always wanting nearly home value for it or for anything they might bring ... When a bear-skin was brought, though it was small, a telescope or a gun was asked for it. They are much like those who said, 'If one never asks, one never gets.' They all charged well for their goods, and had been accustomed to getting full value for seal-skins or for any other skins they ever took on board the whalers when they were there."[63]

Over the years, it appears, the Tununirmiut had learned the fair value of their trade items. Although increasingly dependent upon European goods, they were not easily intimidated or duped into handing over their furs and ivory for less than their worth. Inuit from Admiralty Inlet and Clyde River also travelled more often to Igarjuaq to trade. The Iglulingmiut, on the other hand, tended to alternate their travels between Eclipse Sound and Repulse Bay.[64] Social contact increased, and literacy also spread as a result of the syllabic Bibles brought to Igarjuaq by the Inuit families from Cumberland Sound.[65]

Although the physical environment was once the dominant influence on the culture and activities of the North Baffin Inuit, contact with the Scottish whalers caused many changes in food preferences, clothing, and hunting techniques. These would become even more pronounced in the twentieth century, but because the transition from a whaling economy to a fur trading economy took place gradually over a period of many years, the Inuit

Inuit family who worked at the Igarjuaq station in 1906, their relative prosperity evidenced by European clothing and cooking pots. Philippe Brodeur Collection, G.R. Lancefield, photographer. NAC – PA 165673.

neither noticed nor feared. Likely their greatest concern was that some day the ships might disappear altogether. Since many of the ancient hunting skills were abandoned after the introduction of rifles, such an event could have been disastrous.

2

Sovereignty and Justice, 1874–1920

Britain's offer to transfer the Arctic Islands to Canada came less than seven years after Confederation and only four years after the acquisition of Rupert's Land and the remaining mainland territory to the northwest. The overture in 1874 took Canadian politicians by surprise, as many had assumed the Arctic Archipelago was part of the Hudson's Bay Company lands acquired earlier. Yet the vision of a nation bounded by three oceans had a unifying appeal that seemed to obscure potential liabilities. No one would question the vague wording of the 1880 Imperial Order-in-Council transferring the Arctic Islands, nor did anyone suspect that Canada might have inherited an "imperfect title."

The idea of transferring the Arctic Islands arose after the British Colonial Office received two inquiries regarding purchase of land in Cumberland Sound, one from Lieutenant Mintzer, formerly of the United States Navy Engineer Corps, who wished to extract minerals for export.[1] Lord Carnarvon as under-secretary of the British Foreign Office sent a secret despatch to Canada's governor general, Lord Dufferin, outlining the proposed transfer. In his opinion, it was not desirable for "Her Majesty's Government to authorize settlement in any unoccupied British territory near Canada, unless the Dominion Government and Legislature were prepared to assume the responsibility of exercising such surveillance over it as may be required to prevent the occurrence of lawless acts or other abuses ..."[2] In the words of an official of the Colonial Office, the objective of turning over the islands was "to prevent the United States from claiming them, not from the likelihood of their being of any value to Canada."[3]

Ignoring the fact that Canada had no navy or coastguard to patrol the Arctic waters, Lord Dufferin graciously accepted the offer on behalf of the Canadian government.[4] During the interval between the proposal and the actual transfer in 1880, the American engineer had already extracted quantities of mica and graphite from the site and had long since departed – without prior knowledge of British authorities.[5] The Admiralty, it appeared, had no intention of committing its prestigious navy to regular patrols of Arctic waters, but they did send the Nares expedition to northern Ellesmere in 1875 to ensure that Britain held discovery claims to the most northerly portion of the island.

Until they requested specific boundary definitions for the land transfer, the Colonial Office was unaware of any potential weakness in the British title. Much to their astonishment, the chief hydrographer reported the existence of claims by the United States to portions of Baffin and Ellesmere Islands and advised that the wording of any imperial order-in-council should be kept as vague as possible.[6] No one, it appears, informed the Canadian government of this anomaly.

Following official transfer in 1880, the Canadian government decided that no steps would be taken to govern the newly acquired territory until such time it was deemed necessary. Nor was it incumbent to consult or inform the Inuit of the change. In Britain's view, indigenous people had no sovereignty over claimed territory, only "the right to use the land, which could be transferred only to the Crown."[7] Since there was no urgency to acquire large tracts of the Arctic tundra for settlement, as was the case with Indian lands to the south, there was no need to establish rules of governance or negotiate treaties with the Inuit. Thus another fifteen years passed before Canada passed an order-in-council in 1895, formally accepting the transferred lands and incorporating them into the newly created District of Franklin.[8] In the interim the Canadian government had sent several expeditions to Hudson Bay between 1884 and 1886, primarily to assess the navigability of Hudson Strait and the mineral potential of Rupert's Land.[9]

Responsibility for surveillance of the Arctic Islands seemed irrelevant until reports that American whalers were wintering over in Hudson Bay and Cumberland Sound finally caught the attention of Department of Marine and Fisheries. Thus in 1897, Captain William Wakeham led a government expedition north on the chartered ss *Diana*. The ship was unable to enter Hudson Bay owing to heavy pack ice and rough weather, but it did manage to reach the Scottish whaling station on Kekerten Island in Cumberland Sound. There Wakeham and his party raised the Union Jack, claimed the territory in the name of the Dominion of Canada, and took photographs to record the event. They also paid a brief visit to a station on Blacklead Island, owned by the Noble Company of Aberdeen, Scotland.[10] No American ships were encountered – understandably so, since they had sold out their interests to the Scots three years earlier.[11] Instead, their activities were now concentrated in Hudson Bay and the Beaufort Sea in the western Arctic.

For the next five years, concerns about Arctic sovereignty took backstage to more urgent matters related to the Klondike Gold Rush and the dispute over the boundary between Alaska and Canada. Following the rejection of Canada's claims by the Alaska Boundary Tribunal in 1903, Clifford Sifton, as minister of the Interior, looked at the American whaling activities with renewed concern. This time the government decided that the symbolic gesture of "raising the flag" was insufficient and ordered the establishment of North West Mounted Police (NWMP) detachments at Fort MacMurray and Herschel Island in the western Arctic and at Fullerton Harbour on Hudson Bay, with a mandate to collect customs duties and issue whaling licences. Sovereignty concerns were downplayed. Instead, the public were told that police were required to prevent exploitation of "Canadian" Inuit by foreign whalers.

When the federal force was created in 1873 to enforce law and order in the northwest, it was essentially an independent agency reporting to the prime minister and Parliament through the Privy Council Office, but linked to the Ministry of Justice for matters related criminal activities. When gold was first discovered in the Klondike region, a NWMP contingent was dispatched to protect Canadian interests in the Yukon against an anticipated influx of foreign prospectors. By maintaining law and order among a predominately American population, the police became the active agents in protecting Canada's sovereignty. Now they were expected to protect the nation's claims to the Arctic against any possible challenge by American whalers. Although the NWMP comptroller argued vehemently against the detachment planned for the eastern Arctic, his concerns fell on deaf ears.[12] After their success in the Yukon, no one considered that the mounted police might be inadequately trained and poorly equipped to fulfil a similar mandate in the Arctic. As it happened, the first years at Fullerton and later at Churchill were plagued by accidents, cases of insanity, and at least two drownings. Officers in the western Arctic were equally challenged.[13]

Thus in 1903 Albert P. Low of the Canadian Geological Survey was placed in command of an expedition aboard a chartered sealing vessel, the SS *Neptune,* under the authority of the Department of Marine and Fisheries. His orders were to monitor the whaling activities along the Baffin coast and to assist in establishing a police detachment at Fullerton Harbour. With NWMP Superintendent Major J.D. Moodie and five other members of the police force on board, the ship headed first for Cumberland Sound, where the party visited three whaling stations and informed them of Canada's intention to exert its authority over the region. Low noted that there were roughly five hundred Inuit in the area and "many would perish should the whaling stations be closed without other provision being made for the accustomed supplies."[14] Reverend Edmund Peck, on the other hand, urged Moodie to bring the immoral practices of the whalers to the government's attention.[15] Little did he realize that any attempt to place restrictions on their behaviour would likely cause an even more rapid decline in an already dying industry.

Leaving Cumberland Sound, the ship then sailed south and westward through Hudson Strait to Fullerton Harbour, where a police post was built near the anchorage of the *Era*, the sole American whaling ship in Hudson Bay that year.[16] Moodie's attempts to exert his authority were resented by Captain Comer of the *Era*, and it appears from his diary that the police officer had ignored his instructions to avoid any "any harsh or hurried enforcement of the laws."[17] Moodie, on the other hand, complained that the whalers were not giving proper value for Inuit furs, but he was powerless to do anything. Although the police presence may have been more symbolic than intended, government officials publicly declared the project a great success.[18]

Some would have disagreed. Citing a journal entry by the *Neptune's* surgeon, Dr L.E. Borden, W. Gillies Ross relates how Moodie had talked to a gathering of Inuit about "the big chief ... who had many tribes of different colours" and "wanted them all to do what was right and good." He then questioned them "about their practices of infanticide, parricide and cannibalism" before presenting each of the adults with a set of woollen underwear.

The irony of the situation, although apparently not to Moodie, was abundantly clear to Borden, Comer, and most certainly to the Eskimos. Here were a people who had maintained intimate ties with foreign whalers for more than forty years being treated as simple, helpless, credulous savages. Here were men who possessed whaleboats, darting guns, shoulder guns ... and who hunted with telescopes and powerful repeating rifles ... Here were women who used manufactured domestic implements and containers, who made up clothes on sewing machines, who attended shipboard dances in imported dresses, and who bore children sired by the whalemen. To these people an officious, uniformed stranger was distributing underwear as if it were a priceless treasure and lecturing them on morals and their allegiance to a big white chief.[19]

After witnessing the incident, Captain Comer was convinced that the Canadian government intended to put an end to all American whaling in the region.[20] His suspicions were not entirely unfounded.

Although Moodie had been expected to accompany Commander Low north that summer, he instead disembarked at Port Burwell and took passage on a supply ship heading south. On arrival, he allegedly told reporters that he hoped to open two more detachments and would require thirty men and two ships. He also wrote to the NWMP comptroller recommending that he should be given the "rank and title of Lt. Governor" and that his detachment should be provided "with a patrol ship mounting two rapid-fire guns." None of these requests was granted, but Moodie did gain overall command of the 1904–05 expedition.[21]

The *Neptune,* meanwhile, sailed northward to Eclipse Sound to observe the whaling activities along the Baffin coast. By now, unfortunately, there was little to observe as the industry was virtually at an end. Only three ships were anchored in Albert Harbour, all from Scotland, with another reported in Erik Harbour south of Pond's Inlet. At Button Point on Bylot Island, Low found an Inuit camp of skin and canvas tents, with many "sick with a disease resembling typhoid-pneumonia." But it was just an observation, with no suggestion that the government was in any way responsible for these people. He also obtained a rough estimate of the native population: approximately 140 men, women, and children around Eclipse Sound, another forty reported to be living on Admiralty Inlet, sixty more in the Igloolik area, and ninety in the vicinity of Clyde River and Home Bay. Compared to the Inuit population in Cumberland Sound, they were fewer in number and more widely scattered.[22] Stopping at Port Burwell on the homeward leg of the voyage, Low met Captain Joseph-Elzéar Bernier at the helm of the CGS *Arctic* on his way to Fullerton Harbour.[23]

For years Bernier had dreamed of leading an expedition to the Arctic. His grandfather and uncle had been ships' masters, and he himself spent many years at sea before earning his papers. Intrigued with the American C.F. Hall's explorations, he began to amass a large library of maps and books on polar exploration. While governor of the Quebec gaol (1895–96), he devised a plan whereby he hoped to be the first to reach the North Pole by drifting with the polar ice northeastward from the Bering Strait. He began giving public lectures and lobbying senior government officials in hopes of gaining support for his scheme.[24]

In the spring of 1904 Bernier's vision seemed tenable when Prime Minister Wilfred Laurier tentatively agreed to fund a polar expedition and sent him to Germany to purchase the three-year-old *Gauss,* a sturdy wooden ship that had been built specifically for exploration in Antarctica. Renamed the CGS *Arctic,* the 165-foot vessel was described as a three-masted top sail schooner, with square fore mast and a 275-horsepower auxiliary engine. The dining saloon was elegantly wood panelled, but otherwise the quarters below were described as "cramped."[25] Bernier had hoped to sail the ship south around the Horn, then north through the Bering Strait to enter the pack ice. Much to his dismay, his expedition was abruptly cancelled and instead he was sent to Hudson Bay – in his words, "to ascertain whether a certain well known and highly respected ship's captain was engaged in selling liquor to the natives."[26] There was no mistaking his anger and disgust. Instead of earning honours for his country by being the first to reach the North Pole, he now reported to Superintendent Moodie, who had brought along his wife and son for company.[27]

The *Gauss*, originally built in Germany for sailing in Antarctica, was purchased by the Canadian government in 1904 and renamed the CGS *Arctic*. Photograph by J.E. Bernier, McInnes Collection.

By the time Bernier returned home in 1905, a number of changes had taken place that affected the administration of the Arctic region. With the creation of the new provinces of Alberta and Saskatchewan, an amendment to the Northwest Territories Act abolished the former legislature and replaced it with a commissioner and an appointed four-member council. Taking effect immediately, the comptroller of the Royal North West Mounted Police* (RNWMP), Lieutenant Colonel Frederick White, was appointed

---

* On 24 June 1904 King Edward VII decreed that "Royal" be prefixed to their name in honour of their outstanding contribution in assisting settlement of the Canadian West and the Yukon.

commissioner of the Northwest Territories, a position he held until his death
in September 1918. No council members were appointed until 1921, with the
result that no new legislation was passed for a period of sixteen years. Instead White relied upon the existing ordinances and outdated provisions of
the Northwest Territories Act, as amended in 1905. With RNWMP headquarters located in Regina, all reports from the commissioner to the government
were funnelled through the comptroller's office in Ottawa, inadvertently
giving White more visibility and influence than he otherwise deserved. By
comparison, his responsibilities as commissioner of the Northwest Territories seemed almost perfunctory in nature.[28] Nonetheless, the dual appoint-
ments created an impression that the Arctic was run as a police state.[29] In
point of fact no agency had been assigned responsibility for the Inuit, although Indian Affairs responded occasionally to appeals from Reverend
Peck to purchase food for the destitute.[30]

In 1905 the RNWMP increased their enrolment to service the new provinces. By comparison, positions at the Arctic detachments were relatively
few in number, but eagerly sought by younger recruits who yearned for
adventure and challenge.[31] Only existing members could apply for northern service, with the successful candidates hand-picked for their physical
strength, strong character, and specific skills such as canoeing, carpentry,
and chopping wood.[32] Even then, some proved to be inadequate to the
challenge.

The creation of the new western provinces also brought about changes
in the judicial system. The infrastructure and jurisdiction of the former territorial courts underwent major downsizing with some of their functions
transferred to the police. In 1907, for example, Inspector Jarvis of the
Mackenzie District was granted the "powers of two" justices of the peace,
allowing him to try all but the most serious crimes.[33] That same year
RNWMP Commissioner A. Bowen Perry was named a stipendiary judge
for the NWT, and replaced two years later by E.C. Senkler, a former Yukon
gold commissioner. After the boundary extensions of Manitoba, Ontario,
and Quebec were finalized in 1912, it was decided that there was no immediate need for a magistrate, and the position lay vacant.[34] Also in 1912
White retired as comptroller of the RNWMP but continued to hold the office of commissioner of the NWT for another six years.[35] Initially responsibility for Arctic sovereignty was shared by the Department of the Interior,
the RNWMP, and the Department of Marine and Fisheries, with the governor general providing the link to the Foreign Office in Great Britain on
matters of international diplomacy. In 1909 the latter function was transferred to Canada's newly formed Department of External Affairs.[36]

A published report by Chief Astronomer W.F. King in 1905 had warned
that Canadian sovereignty over the Arctic Islands was not secure. Based on
his study of British documents and maps, King argued that while Canada's

title to the northern islands was based on Great Britain's claims of discovery and possession, "these Acts were never, prior to the transfer to Canada, ratified by state authority, or confirmed by exercise of jurisdiction." As a consequence he believed that "Canada's assumption of authority in 1895 may not have full international force" but that it might be "perfected by exercise of jurisdiction where any settlement exists."[37] The debatable question in 1905 was whether a trading post constituted a settlement.

A number of foreign explorers gave further cause for concern, notably Americans Robert Peary and Donald Macmillan, as well as Norwegians Otto Sverdrup and Roald Amundsen. Although Sverdrup's discovery of several islands west of Ellesmere had not been officially ratified by the Norwegian government, the possibility of a direct challenge to Canada's title seemed imminent.[38]

Thus in 1906 Bernier was placed in command of an expedition with the expressed purpose of affirming sovereignty over the Arctic Archipelago, but with explicit instructions to avoid any international incident. Deputy Minister Gourdeau informed him, "By the Minister's instructions, I am to impress upon you the necessity of being most careful in all your actions not to take any course which might result in international complications with any Foreign country. When action on your part would seem likely to give rise to any such contingency, you will hold your hand but fully report the facts on your return."[39] Significantly, there were no police aboard the ship when it headed north towards Lancaster Sound. Although Bernier had been appointed a justice of the peace with "broad authority to uphold the Fisheries Act with respect to foreign vessels," his ship was not armed for combat and he had no means to exert his authority if challenged. Similarly, he was given no written instructions concerning relations with the Inuit.

On reaching Eclipse Sound, Bernier purchased dogs for use on overland treks and hired two Inuuk guides, Miqqusaaq (Monkeyshaw) and Qaumauq (Cameo), before heading northwest to Melville Island by way of Lancaster Sound. Bernier would later claim that he had hired Inuit guides to allow them to become better "acquainted with government officials" and get "used to the notion that they were now wards of the government, and must accordingly begin to adopt the ways of white men." He also believed that the two Inuuk would gain esteem among their people for having worked for the *qallunaat* and be able to provide future support for law enforcement.[40] Such statements seem retrospectively self-serving, as Bernier was far more dependent upon the Inuit than he admitted. Moreover, the Inuit were not "wards of the government," as he suggested. Nor did his authority as a justice of the peace include the powers required to try a person for an indictable criminal offence. Thus, while he claimed to have explained "the laws of the country" to the Inuit people, he did not have legal authority to enforce them.[41] In this respect his attempts to "educate" the Inuit may have been a personal initiative rather than official policy.

Bernier had explicit orders to "formally annex all new lands at which you may call, leaving proclamations in cairns at all points."[42] His biographer, Yolande Dorion-Robitaille, described the procedure:

The *Arctic* would anchor as close to shore as possible. Bernier, accompanied by his officers and several of the crew, would make for shore in a longboat. Once ashore, they would make their way to a spot that could be seen from a ship, usually on some point or hill, and erect a cairn, a cone-shaped structure of stone. Bernier would then place inside the cairn a metal box containing a proclamation signed by Bernier and his men declaring that the island had been claimed in the name of Canada. A Canadian flag would then be attached to the end of a pole, and the pole placed in the cairn. After the official photographs were taken, the party returned to the ship.[43]

Bernier also removed any documents left by previous explorers. The only departure from this routine was a flag-raising ceremony photographed with Inuit in attendance, implying their acceptance of Canadian authority over Baffin Island.

After an unsuccessful attempt to reach Banks Island by way of Lancaster Sound, the ship returned to Eclipse Sound and wintered over in Albert Harbour near the new whaling station at Igarjuaq, owned and operated by Robert Kinnes Company of Dundee, Scotland.[44] That winter Bernier hired four more guides: Qanaaqa (Kanaka), Miqutui (Muckatowee), Turngaaluk (Tomallo), and Qattuuq (Kacktoo). The hiring of Miqutui is particularly significant, as he would be a witness to the death of Robert Janes many years later.

That winter the captain and crew lived on the ship, which had been made ready by lowering the masts and covering the open decks with sails to form a tent-like structure. The men followed a regimen that included daily chores and recreation, with church services every Sunday. Inuit were invited to visit the ship on special occasions.[45] Some were sombre events, such as a burial service for the ship's oiler who died of a heart attack, but there were also festive occasions such as Christmas Day:

At 7 pm tea and coffee were served to all the invited, and some candy was given to the children … The natives behaved very well and there were no disturbances of any sort, but perfect good order reigned throughout. During the evening there were different tracks and acts done by the members of the expedition and natives. There were wrestling matches between Canadians and other matches of the same style between Eskimos; the men also performed acrobatic feats, juggling and other acts. Music selections from the pianola and the graphophone [sic] were given during the evening. The Eskimos danced to the music of the accordeon [sic].[46]

Top: Captain Bernier, second on left, formally takes possession of Bylot Island in a flag-raising ceremony at Canada Point, August 1906. The name of the ship, *Arctic*, and the date were chiselled into the stone, with the result that Inuit call this location Titiralik, meaning, "the place where there is writing." Photographer G.R. Lancefield. NAC – PA 139394.

Bottom: Captain Bernier, in the presence of Inuit and officers of the CGS *Arctic* at Albert Harbour, claims all of Baffin Island for the Dominion of Canada, 9 November 1906. Photographer, G.R. Lancefield. NAC – PA 165672.

Bernier reported that he used the occasion to inform the Inuit once again "that they were Canadians and would be treated as such as long as they would do what was right."[47] He did not elaborate on his explanation of "what was right" or how his statements might have been interpreted in Inuktitut. On another occasion he reported the death of an Inuk who had earlier shot and killed another native, saying that "no action" had been taken at the time of the shooting because he was too ill. Again he did not elaborate on what action, if any, could have been taken. Meanwhile, the ship's officers and crew brought new diseases to those visiting the ship. Having little immunity, many became seriously ill, and seven died that winter in spite of medical attention from the ship's doctor.[48]

While Bernier was wintering at Albert Harbour, Senator Pascal Poirier proposed that the government should adopt the concept of a "sector theory" to lay claim to all lands north of its mainland. Although this theory was challenged as having adverse political implications elsewhere in the polar regions, it gained support in some quarters as an answer to Canada's lack of ships to effectively patrol the region.[49] Hence in 1908 Bernier once again set out for the high Arctic, but this time his destination was Winter Harbour on Melville Island. There he erected a plaque that declared "possession for the Dominion of Canada of the whole 'Arctic Archipelago' lying north of America from longitude 60° west to 141° west and on up to latitude 90° north."[50] The extent of scientific work and mapping accomplished in this voyage was exceptional, with two parties sent over the ice to Banks and Victoria Islands. On return, the ship stopped only briefly at Pond Inlet, as the whaling ships had already departed, but licences were issued to several on the way to Cumberland Sound. Here they visited four stations before heading home.

Bernier was popular among the Inuit of North Baffin, and even today, elders at Pond Inlet speak of Kapitaikallak, meaning the "stout, little captain," with warmth and affection. While one might argue that he had earned his high regard by feeding them well, his concern for their well being was genuine. He wrote in his report,

Murders and other crimes comparatively unknown previous to the contact of bad white men, occasionally occur amongst the untaught natives who have not the example of exemplary men. In addition to the natural state of the Eskimo, seeds of immorality and crime have been sown, and the natives are in a worse state than before the introduction of our civilization. Since the white man visited the habitations of these people, death among the children is a common occurrence; the best suited race for the cold inhospitable climes will disappear if some strenuous efforts are not made to preserve them. The missionary with high motives and some medical knowledge is the best instructor to send amongst them. The natives can be made useful assistants in developing the resources of the country and, furthermore, the

Christmas celebrations, 1906, with Captain Bernier at the player piano in the salon of the CGS *Arctic*, medical officer Dr J.R. Pepin standing, left, and expedition historian Fabien Vanasse on the right. Energy Mines and Resources Collection. NAC – PA 149035.

white races owe it to themselves, as well as to the natives, to undo the evil which they have done. I cannot too strongly emphasize the duty of white men, to save a race which they have done so much to destroy.[51]

Although the concept of the "white man's burden" was more commonly associated with colonial rule in Africa, Bernier was not the first to urge a change in government policy. Similar concerns had been expressed by the British explorer Sir Leopold McClintock, a half century earlier.[52] Whaling captains William Penny Jr and William Parker had also petitioned the British government to come to the aid of the Inuit,[53] as did Captain William Adams Sr, who urged support for a permanent settlement on Baffin Island in the belief that "such an act would remove a blot from the flag of Christian England, which was unfurled in Possession Bay by Ross and Parry in 1818."[54] Britain's response had been to transfer the Arctic Islands to Canada.

Bernier also recommended expansion of the local trading economy to include exports of salmon trout (Arctic char) and cod. When the Canadian government showed no interest in his ideas, he apparently decided to take matters into his own hands and purchased the buildings and property at the Igarjuaq whaling station. Obviously aware of his intentions, the government approved a land grant of an additional 960 acres in the vicinity, made out to "J.E. Bernier, Captain of the CGS *Arctic.*"[55]

For his next expedition in 1910 Bernier was given specific instructions to proceed westward through the Northwest Passage if ice conditions permitted. Most of his crew were veterans from previous voyages, including his nephew Wilfred Caron, but this year he hired a new second officer – a Newfoundlander by the name of Robert Janes – and several other anglophones, including a new third officer, Edward Macdonald from Prince Edward Island, Alfred Tremblay as an able seaman, and James Holden, as a boatswain. Macdonald's diary provides a more personal and likely more accurate insight into the daily activities and tensions on board the ship. Before departure, he described stumbling over several drunken crew members lying on the gangway and noted that, in his opinion, "they are a bum lot and not the kind of men that are required on an expedition like this."[56] As it happened, this voyage would be very different from previous expeditions but not because of the crew.

Stopping first at Pond Inlet, Bernier purchased thirty-eight dogs and again hired Miqutui (Macatowee) and Miqqusaaq (Macashaw). Macdonald wrote that the Inuuk were hired to look after the dogs, but described them as "very intelligent" and noted that one could speak some English. Before leaving Eclipse Sound, the crew procured and salted a large quantity of char at the mouth of the Salmon River, while Bernier supervised construction of a government food cache at Albert Harbour to be used by shipwrecked sailors or similar emergencies.[57]

The ship left Eclipse Sound on 13 August 1910, with the intent to traverse the Northwest Passage. Reportedly within two hundred kilometres of the Beaufort Sea, Bernier gave orders to turn back, claiming that a huge ice floe prevented any hope of moving forward. Although Second Officer Janes concurred, others thought the captain had given up too easily.[58] Heading back to Admiralty Inlet, Bernier selected an anchorage in Arctic Bay just two miles from an Inuit camp. Additional hunters were hired that winter and spring: Takijualuk (Tom Coonoon) to act as an interpreter, and three others including Piunngittuq (Peewiktoo) as guides. Bernier sent one of his men to deliver a number of Reverend Peck's syllabic Bibles to Igloolik, with the result that news of the ship spread among the winter camps and more visitors arrived to trade their furs and ivory.[59] Of significance to later events, Bernier reported that Umik (Ooming) and his son (presumably Nuqallaq) arrived in June with "450 pounds of fresh salmon."[60] Similarly, special mention was made of Miqutui's "sterling qualities ... the best type of faithful and kind guide."[61]

As was his practice at Albert Harbour, Bernier claimed to have designated specific dates as "Reception Days" for the Inuit to visit the ship,

CGS *Arctic* in pack ice, Eclipse Sound, July 1910. Bernier Collection. NAC – PA 209060.

although the third officer claimed that the visits were far more frequent and that the captain entertained them in his cabin and fed them well.[62] Geologist J.T.E. Lavoie and Arthur English, meanwhile, spent most of their time collecting ore samples in their search for gold. The assay reports would later show that the specimens contained mostly copper and iron pyrites, except for a small amount of silver from Strathcona Sound and minute traces of gold from Adams Sound.[63]

Unlike the official government report, Macdonald's diary provided explicit details about the captain's activities, with several references to the fact that Bernier was only interested in trading for furs, that it was more of a "fur trading voyage" than a scientific expedition, and that he had no interest in searching for the Northwest Passage. By mid-August Macdonald concluded that "it was all planned before hand. All a game of bluff."[64] Titus Uyarasuk, an elder from Igloolik, seemed to confirm the suspicions, recalling that both Captain Bernier and Wilfred Caron were trading "a lot of things," but that he was "not exactly sure what their mission was."[65]

In mid-December Bernier sent Second Officer Janes to Eclipse Sound, accompanied by three Inuit guides, two heavily laden *qamutiit*, and thirty dogs. According to Macdonald, this followed several confrontations between Janes and crew members who had refused to obey his orders.[66] Upon arrival, Janes found the Tununirmiut to be near starvation. Although

Second Officer Robert S. Janes of Newfoundland, aboard the CGS *Arctic*,
1910. NAC – PA 61749.

the Igarjuaq station was closed, they had remained in the area in hopes that
someone might return. After supplying them with food and ammunition,
Janes had many willing helpers.[67]

As soon as the ice went out, the CGS *Arctic* left Admiralty Inlet and
headed for Eclipse Sound to pick up the second officer. On Janes' advice,
Bernier sent his prospector to the Salmon River to take samples of coal
and ore, but as expected the latter only contained pyrites. He then unloaded all the furs and ivory collected over the winter and stored them in
the attic of the Igarjuaq whaling station. Then heading north through
Navy Board Inlet, they stopped at Canada Point, where they discovered a

number of well-preserved trees embedded in the soil. Portions were cut away for examination by Ottawa's Victoria Museum and samples were taken from a large seam of coal found nearby.[68] After a rather half-hearted attempt to exit by way of Prince Regent Sound, the ship reversed course and sailed southward along the east coast of Baffin Island. The journey home was unremarkable, except that there were no signs of any whaling ships, even in Cumberland Sound where Bernier stopped to deliver the rest of the syllabic Bibles to the mission on Blacklead Island – as per his instructions.[69]

Significant to later events, Robert Janes was reported to have had a major argument with Bernier just prior to departure. Yet when Bernier resigned as captain of the CGS *Arctic* that winter, it was because of Assistant Steward Joseph Mathe, who told a reporter for a Quebec newspaper that Bernier had misappropriated government funds. Although Bernier denied the charges, he could no longer count on the support of the Liberal Party after they lost the December election to the Conservatives. The following spring a public inquiry heard stories about how Bernier had refused to proceed through the Northwest Passage, neglected his sovereignty and scientific responsibilities, forced the crew to rent the ship's fox traps, and then confiscated any furs they caught. Although some of the accusations were verified by Macdonald's diary entries, there was no provision in Bernier's contract forbidding him to trade for personal benefit. He was also accused of providing the crew with inadequate provisions and of attacking the second cook with a potato masher for failing to prepare his peas in a proper fashion, allegations that were apparently confirmed by the expedition's historian, Fabian Vanasse, who had been with Bernier on all his previous voyages.[70]

The purchase of the Igarjuaq property suggests Bernier had already planned to resign. Perhaps he had predicted there would be no further need for his services. Meanwhile, he had built up strong trading ties with the Tununirusirmiut and Iglulingmiut – inadvertently or purposefully. He had also introduced Robert Janes to the Arctic fur trade.

The Conservative government led by Prime Minister Robert Borden had other plans to deal with sovereignty concerns, initially by providing financial support for Vilhjalmur Stefansson's Canadian Arctic Expedition in 1913–18. A policy change was evident in his instructions that stated unequivocally that "members of the party will not engage in any private trading."[71] In spite of dissent among the leaders and loss of the expedition's ship, *Karluk,* Stefansson did find four previously undiscovered islands. Hoping to win support for further expeditions, he named them Borden, Meighen, Lougheed, and Brock in honour of key figures in the Conservative government.[72] To his chagrin, however, the war in Europe had taken priority over any concerns about Arctic sovereignty.

Janes digging coal near Canada Point, Bylot Island, midnight, August 1911. Bernier Expedition Collection. NAC – C 14262.

War or no war, the Department of Justice would be required to address reports of violence on the home front, even among Inuit in the central Arctic. Rumours persisted about the fate of two adventurers, an American, Henry Radford, and a Canadian, George Street, last seen in the summer of 1912 near Bathurst Inlet. In 1914 Sergeant Major T.B. Caulkin reported that a group of "murderous Eskimoes" near Bathurst Inlet had not only killed Radford and Street but earlier another white man, identified as Mr Caldwell, and his two native guides.[73] Prime Minister Borden first consulted with his predecessor, then instructed the police to "establish friendly relations with the tribe" during their inquiry, since it was thought that no jury would convict the Inuit because they had no prior knowledge of Canadian laws.[74] Reports that Fathers Rouvière and Le Roux had met their death in a similar manner were taken more seriously, and the police were dispatched forthwith to arrest the Inuit responsible.[75]

Although the two Oblate priests died near the mouth of the Coppermine river sometime in November 1913, it would take two and a half years for Inspector C.D. La Nauze to locate those responsible. As a justice of the peace "with the powers of two," the officer brought the two Inuuk, Sinnisiak and Uluksuk, to Bernard Harbour, where he heard evidence and committed them to stand trial. In the absence of a stipendiary magistrate, their cases would be heard before the Supreme Court of Alberta, under the "concurrent jurisdiction" arrangement set out in the Criminal Code.[76] This marked the first time an Inuk had ever appeared in a Canadian courtroom. At Edmonton in 1917 Sinnisiak was tried separately for the murder of Father Rouvière and unexpectedly acquitted by a jury who were thought to have been influenced by an overly sympathetic press. The gist of the argument was that Sinnisiak should not be convicted because he had feared for his life when threatened by one of the priests and had acted in accordance with Inuit custom. The fact that the two had cut open the victims' bodies and eaten part of their livers was discounted as ritual. Justice officials dissented, with the result that a second trial was ordered with the venue moved to Calgary. This time Sinnisiak and Uluksuk were tried together for the murder of Father Le Roux. Although they were found guilty, the death sentence was later "commuted to life imprisonment," because they had no prior knowledge of the white man's laws.[77]

Meanwhile Inspector F.H. French was still trying to track down the murderers of Radford and Street, a futile task as they had gone into hiding after La Nauze had taken away the murderers of the Oblate priests. He did report a major difference between various Inuit groups, claiming that some were honest and willing to assist, whereas those living on Coronation Gulf between Bathurst Inlet and the mouth of the Coppermine River were "born thieves and fearful liars and not to be trusted out of one's sight ... I should not be surprised to hear of some of them committing more murders before long as any one of them would sell his soul to possess a rifle, but at present the whole thing hinges on whatever happens to the murderers of the two Roman Catholic Priests. If these two men are turned loose and return to this country it will not be safe for a lone white man to travel amongst them as they would take the first opportunity to murder him to get his outfit."[78]

French's report arrived at headquarters a year after the pair's death sentences were commuted. Moreover, "life imprisonment" proved to be no more than two years "hard labour" at the Fort Resolution police detachment. From an Inuk's perspective, the "punishment" was more like a reward, especially when they were hired by the police to work at the detachment for two more years after their release. When they finally returned home, they reportedly boasted about being given free food, clothing, and a warm place to sleep, and told extraordinary tales, such as how one pushed a button and "the moon came into the room."[79] With cast-off clothing and material goods in lieu of wages, Sinnisiak and Uluksuk were looked upon as wealthy men. In William R. Morrison's words, "the lesson learned was that crime paid."[80]

The expectation that their imprisonment would be sufficient to deter further violence ended when the police received a report that another Inuk had shot and killed a fellow hunter near the mouth of the Coppermine River. This was followed by more rumours of violence at summer camps to

Sinnisiak and Uluksuk after their arrest in 1916 for the murder
of Father Rouvière and Father Le Roux. RCMP Collection.
NAC – PA 210274.

the north. New policies were discussed, including moving the trial location
to the vicinity of the crime and providing police officers with greater authority to conduct an inquest and hold preliminary hearings. When implemented, these changes would mark the beginning of a rudimentary circuit
court system in the North West Territories.

There were a number of reasons for conducting a trial near the site of the
crime. Not only would it provide a stronger deterrent if friends and family
of the accused witnessed the trial proceedings but it was also thought to be
more economical to bring a court party north than to pay for the transport
and accommodation of the prisoner, interpreter, and witnesses at a southern location. Moreover, a trial in the accused's own territory would comply
more closely with the principle of being tried before a jury of one's peers as
set out in the Magna Carta, although the jurors selected for the Inuit mur-

der trials in the 1920s would hardly qualify as peers. Justice officials, on the other hand, believed that a jury of six northern residents would be less sympathetic to native traditions than southerners, who felt no personal threat from Inuit violent behaviour and might favour acquittal. Although implied but not explicitly stated, it was apparent that a court trial in the far North would enhance Arctic sovereignty. The only downside appeared to be the lack of radio communications and difficulty in transporting a court party to remote locations.[81]

In 1920 the primary objective of the Department of Justice was to deter further violence among the Inuit. To accomplish this goal, it was thought that one or two high profile court trials in strategic locations would be sufficient. Thus no provision was made for a court to travel north on an annual basis.[82] The first challenge was to find the appropriate cases to prosecute. In this regard detachment officers exerted a fair degree of influence through the wording of their "crime reports." In one incident a young boy had purposefully shot and killed his father, yet the investigating officer successfully argued that the son's actions were justified. The Department of Justice agreed and no further action was taken.[83]

The case of Ouangwak, who allegedly killed two brothers near Baker Lake, seemed to offer better potential. At the time of his arrest in February 1920 the officer brought the accused to The Pas, Manitoba. Upon learning that the witnesses were still in the Keewatin area, the Department of Justice quashed the coroner's verdict and instructed the officer to return the prisoner to Chesterfield Inlet and await the arrival of a police officer with the proper authority to conduct an inquest and preliminary hearings. Inspector A.E.O. Reames finally arrived in September, but it was early 1921 before he made his way to Baker Lake and the scene of the crime. He exhumed the bodies of the victims and commenced to take evidence at the inquest – the first ever to be held in an igloo. As it happened, there would be no trial. Upon hearing that Reames had gone to Baker Lake, Ouangwak escaped custody and apparently froze to death in a blizzard. The few bones discovered after the snow had melted suggested that wild animals had ravaged the remains.[84]

Another potential case for consideration occurred on the Belcher Islands (Sanikiluaq). Reports of violence in the remote island community in Hudson Bay had come to the attention of the Department of Justice by a rather circuitous route. In April 1919 a clerk at the Great Whale River trading post had written to the Fur Trade Commissioner about rumours of a murder having occurred on the islands.[85] The commissioner passed the information to the RNWMP comptroller's office in Ottawa. On receiving the report, the acting comptroller denied any responsibility, in the belief that the Belcher Islands were part of Quebec, thus outside of federal jurisdiction.[86] He then sent the report to the appropriate provincial authorities. Another

Ouangwak, arrested on suspicion of murder
near Chesterfield Inlet, January 1921. NAC –
C 143424.

month went by before the deputy attorney general of Quebec, Charles
Lanctôt, wrote to Deputy Minister of Justice E.L. Newcombe, reminding
him that the Belcher Islands lay within the boundaries of the Northwest
Territories and were thus a federal responsibility. Likely embarrassed by
the error, the police commissioner directed his staff to prepare for an investigation in the summer of 1920, regardless of cost.[87] By this time, the name
of the federal police force had been changed to the Royal Canadian
Mounted Police (RCMP). The case was not unique in itself, but the decisions
and legal opinions expressed following the inquest created important precedents for future inquiries.

On 6 August 1920 Inspector J.W. Phillips and Sergeant A.H. Joy left
from Haileybury, Ontario, and proceeded by canoe down the Missinaibi
River to Moose Factory. Here they chartered a motor launch and crew to
take them to the Belcher Islands. On arrival they exhumed and examined
the two-year-old remains of a corpse to determine the cause of death,

Coroner's igloo, where Inspector A.O.E. Reames as justice of the peace conducted an inquest into the deaths of two Inuuk at Baker Lake, March 1921. Harwood Steele, *Policing the Arctic*, 1935.

then heard the testimony of ten witnesses. With Inspector Phillips acting as coroner, assisted by Sergeant Joy and the boat crew as the jury, the inquest was reportedly carried out with decorum and solemnity. In summary, an Inuk had forcibly abducted the wife of another hunter and threatened to kill anyone who came after him. Fearing that he would shoot them if they left the camp, the others reportedly went for weeks without fishing or hunting. Threatened by starvation, the hunters discussed the matter, decided the man was insane, and assigned a young Inuk and the aggrieved husband to kill the abductor. At the last moment the husband fled, leaving the youth to carry out the council's decision.[88] The coroner's report noted that the victim "was killed for the common good and safety of the Band, consisting of fifty or more souls." Because it was the decision of a "male council," he recommended that "no criminal charge be laid" but advised that "a responsible representative of the Government be sent amongst these people to instruct them in the laws of the country."[89]

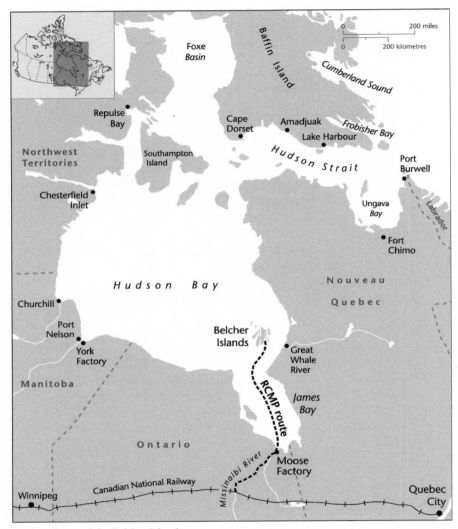

Hudson Bay and the Belcher Islands, 1920.

The story might have ended there had the police not uncovered another death during their investigations. A second inquiry began immediately upon completion of the first. In this case a married man by the name of Kookyauk had run off with his wife's sister. When the abandoned spouse reported that he had threatened to kill anyone who tried to intervene, a small group of hunters met and decided that the errant husband should be tied up and placed alone on a nearby island without food or water until he promised to change his ways. Observing that he had untied himself and was wandering about, the camp leader sent four men to the island see if he was willing to reform. His response was apparently negative for he was retied in such a way that he died within a matter of hours.[90]

This time Phillips came to a different conclusion, after hearing that victim had died "by being wilfully and maliciously tied with seal lines until death came by strangulation, without any just cause or apparent reason." The coroner's report went on to recommend that "the four persons named be directly held responsible," but that from a "humane standpoint," he had decided not to take them into custody, as it would likely result in starvation of their families.[91] Phillips was particularly touched by the poverty of the group: "It is not an uncommon thing for these people to have to resort to mice, roots and berries for many days at a stretch to avoid starvation ... The women and children are clothed in a combination garb of cotton, purchased in years when fur was plentiful, patched up with skins of everything procurable, and in many cases not enough to cover their bodies ... Their real condition is inconceivable to one who has not seen."[92] As a result, he suggested that a judicial party be sent the next spring, with contingency plans for the families should the verdict demand removal of the hunters from the islands.

In both cases Phillips noted that several witnesses had explained how the missionaries at Great Whale River taught them that it was "insane" to cohabit with a woman other than one's wife. Although the word "insane" may have been confused with "in sin," the Inuit still maintained that it was by "God's right" that these men were killed. Phillips believed that "the question of morality ... [was] impressed upon them too strongly by their spiritual advisors," implying that the blame for the crimes rested with the missionary.[93] Responding to the police inspector's accusations, Reverend W.G. Walton wrote to explain that the church was not to blame and that such violence was common among these people. As proof, he cited three incidents that had occurred during his tenure – "On one occasion, nine persons were murdered, on another seventeen, and on a third, thirteen" – but he made no distinction as to whether they were Inuit or Cree Indians. A hospital and doctor were seriously needed, he argued, along with a "duly qualified Magistrate" and a chief constable.[94] His argument was valid, but neither the federal nor Quebec governments would be willing to fund such initiatives.

Meanwhile, Deputy Minister Newcombe had written to RCMP Commissioner Perry to say that he was "afraid the Eskimos who were responsible" for the Inuk's death "will have to be charged and tried for murder," and asked for suggestions with regard to arrangements for the trial.[95] By the following June, however, Newcombe had changed his mind and Inspector Phillips was asked to prepare a set of recommendations to explain why the Inuit should not be brought to trial. His revised report stressed the disastrous effect upon their families should the hunters be removed from the community and his belief that these Inuit were not "criminals at heart" and

Inuit gathered for the inquests, Belcher Islands, summer 1920. NAC – C 143427.

had truly believed that their victim was deranged. Heeding the suggestions by Rev. Walton, Philips went on to recommend "that if the natives of the Northern Districts of Canada are to be brought to a state of civilization, the only solution is to have a permanent representative from the Indian Department established amongst them, or detachments of the Royal Canadian Mounted Police."[96] If applied to the entire Arctic, the cost would be so horrendous that it was virtually guaranteed that the recommendation would never receive serious consideration.

The significance of this first police investigation in the eastern Arctic rests with the legal opinion set out by Deputy Minister E.L. Newcombe on 9 June 1921, and its subsequent use as advisement in a later case:[97]

I find that it would be a very difficult and expensive matter to send a tribunal with the necessary officials to the Belcher Islands this summer for the purpose of trying the case, and I consider it very doubtful upon the evidence as submitted, that a conviction would result, having regard to the barbarous and primitive conditions in which the natives of Belcher Islands find their livelihood and to all the other circumstances of the case. It is certain I think that if the four natives or any of them charged in the coroner's inquest were found guilty of a capital offence, the sentence of the law would not compatibly with principles of justice be executed, although it would in that event be necessary to imprison these unfortunate men for a long period, at least while the proceedings were in course of transmission and under review ...

If the case were one of deliberate killing for *motives of gain or revenge* or the like, perhaps the prosecution could not well be avoided, notwithstanding the attendant difficulties and inconvenience, but I am impressed with the view that Ko-okyauk was principally himself responsible for his own unfortunate end and that these men who tied him up considered that they were acting in the general interest of the band. There seems to have been no motive for the killing except that Ko-okyauk did not conform to the conditions of life which were considered proper in the community and that he was regarded as a source of danger [emphasis added].[98]

As an alternative, Newcombe suggested that Inspector Phillips visit the island that summer and "explain to them the elementary laws for the protection of life and property by which they are governed."[99] Significant to future cases was the deputy minister's opinion on how Canadian justice might be applied to Inuit violence, with reference to such influences as public opinion and potential costs. Newcombe was prepared to be lenient with crimes committed by Inuit who were ignorant of the law, but only "under certain circumstances," one of which was "perceived insanity," if accompanied by the consensual agreement of the community.[100] Newcombe had also provided clear direction to RCMP Commissioner Perry when he suggested that the criteria required to assure a conviction should include a motive of revenge or material gain.

In the interim a more appropriate case had surfaced in the Mackenzie Valley, involving an Indian trapper accused of killing his wife and newborn child. His motive was clearly identified as revenge for his wife having given birth to a white child. The case would be tried at Fort Providence in June 1921 before an appointed stipendiary magistrate, the Hon. Lucien Dubuc of Alberta. As expected, a six-member jury unanimously convicted Albert Le Beaux of murder, with the judge summarily sentencing the murderer to death by hanging.[101] In spite of his claim to innocence, there was no reprieve. On 1 November 1921 Le Beaux died on a makeshift gallows erected in a field to the west of Fort Smith.[102] The Department of Justice now had a real-life example of a case that resulted in a clear conviction and uncontested death penalty.

In 1920 opinions were still divided about the Inuit and their potential for violent behaviour. Although once they had been considered by the police as "a warm and friendly race," it was recognized that some groups behaved differently than others and that some incidents of "barbarous behaviour" might be explained by their ignorance of qallunaat laws. The challenge facing the police was the difficulty in explaining to Inuit why it was important to abide by Canadian laws, without a visible example of severe punishment to illustrate the consequences of disobedience. The trial of Sinnisiak and Uluksuk was "intended not so much to serve justice, but as an object lesson to the Inuit."[103] The failure to achieve that objective was not a fault of the trial but of the punishment, which was inconsistent with the values and customs of Inuit culture.

Of greater significance to the story of Nuqallaq and the death of Robert Janes was the evolution of legal opinion concerning Inuit violence.

Policy changes followed, as did new attitudes towards the Inuit people. Yet during this period, roughly from 1912 to 1920, there were no reports of Inuit violence on Baffin Island, no police supervision, no visiting representatives of the Canadian government, and in North Baffin, no missionaries to explain the ethics of the sixth commandment, "Thou shall not kill."

3

Traders and Gold-Seekers, 1912–1919

Rumours that gold had been found in North Baffin inspired three men to lead separate excursions to Eclipse Sound in search of wealth and adventure – an Englishman, a French-Canadian, and a Newfoundlander. Two of the three, Captain Bernier and his former second officer, Robert Janes, had been on the 1910–11 government expedition which had just returned from Pond Inlet. The third was an Englishman by the name of Henry Toke Munn who had never been to the Arctic. Eventually all three would establish fur trading posts in the vicinity. Their story is about competition and greed, and how the loss of rationality led to the death of a fortune hunter from Newfoundland.

After resigning from government service in December 1911 Captain Bernier began to prepare for his commercial venture at Pond Inlet. Two other expeditions were also fitted out that spring, both financed by speculators who believed they would strike it rich in northern Baffin Island. Robert Janes had been quoted in Newfoundland papers as saying he had found gold nuggets on the riverbed of the Salmon River on Eclipse Sound. His story convinced a veteran mining promoter known as "Lucky" Scott to charter the SS *Neptune* and organize a prospecting party. The financial backer of this expedition was a New Yorker by the name of Pell. The plan was for Janes to lead them directly to the gold, which they would extract and immediately head back home.[1]

Newspaper stories about Janes' alleged gold discovery and proposed expedition prompted Bernier to take swift action. While it was doubtful that he believed the Newfoundlander's story, he still had hopes of finding a major ore body around Strathcona or Adams Sound off Admiralty Inlet. Three men joined him as "prospectors": Alfred Tremblay, who was on the 1910 expedition as an able seaman, George Wilson, and A.B. Reader. All three were obsessed with dreams of instant riches and exciting adventures, as Reader explained in the introduction to Tremblay's book, *Cruise of the*

North Baffin Region, circa 1920.

Minnie Maud: "it was gold – the sordid lure of gold and the hope of filthy lucre that impelled nine men – six French Canadians, two Englishmen and one New Zealander – to venture forth from the shadow of the ancient embattlements of old historic Quebec in a two masts [sic] schooner and brave the perils and rigours of the Arctic seas and wilds."[2] While Tremblay,

Wilson, and Reader were driven by the lust for gold, Bernier had other plans. For years he had talked about establishing a permanent settlement on Eclipse Sound that would become a commercial centre for exports in ivory, furs, salted fish, coal, and possibly even gold.[3] It was an ambitious dream, but in 1912 it seemed viable.

Of more immediate concern was the safety of the furs and ivory he had stored at Albert Harbour. In light of his quarrel with Janes the previous summer, Bernier could not risk leaving his cache unattended if his former second officer was planning to return. In preparation he purchased the eighty-five-foot fishing schooner *Minnie Maud* and sufficient trade goods and food to last two years. His nephew Wilfred Caron would join the party to take charge of the trading operation in Bernier's absence. According to Noah Piugaattuk, an elder from Igloolik, "Quvviunginnaq [Caron] had lost his father at an early age so Kapitaikallak had started to take him along on voyages to this area. He was in fact being trained and with his ability to learn he quickly ascended to higher rank."[4] If Caron was remembered from the days of the government expeditions, he would become even more popular with the Inuit in the years ahead. Not only did he learn to speak their language, but he played Inuit games, ate country food, performed drum dances, and even sang Inuit songs.[5]

Captain Henry Toke Munn also heard rumours about gold on Baffin Island. Munn was a well-connected Englishman who had come to Canada to seek adventure on the western frontier. His early travels took him to the Mackenzie Valley where he learned about the fur trade and how to drive a dog team. With hordes of others he headed for Dawson City during the Klondike gold rush, returning to England in time to participate in the South African War. It was here that he earned the rank of captain in a British cavalry unit. In 1908 Munn was back in Canada for the Northern Ontario gold rush, where he met George Bartlett, son of famed Newfoundland sea captain John Bartlett. It was a fateful meeting that would forever alter Munn's life.[6]

From young Bartlett, the English adventurer learned of a 1860s map that showed two sites where gold allegedly had been found on the east coast of Baffin Island. According to the story, a cooper on a Scottish whaler had gone ashore to fetch fresh water and found gold nuggets, which he later sold to a Glasgow jeweller. He had returned to Newfoundland in hopes of finding a way back to North Baffin, but without the nuggets no one believed his story. As a result the hapless cooper spent his last years in relative poverty. Just before he died he gave his "treasure map" to a storekeeper who had been kind to him in his old age. The map eventually found its way to Captain Bartlett who, upon reading the newspaper reports of Janes' alleged discovery, immediately contacted his son. Munn had never been to the Arctic but was attracted as much by the idea of the

Wilfred Caron, nephew of Captain Bernier, circa 1909.
Courtesy of Madame Suzanne Audet.

adventure as by the prospect of riches. Offering to help fund the expedition, he accompanied George back to Newfoundland to assist in the final preparations.

On 26 June 1912 Munn's party departed on the ss *Algerine*, a former British gunboat converted for sealing, with Captain John Bartlett at the helm. Two weeks later they arrived at the floe edge near Pond Inlet and were met by Inuit clamouring for tobacco. Munn found two who could speak some English, Takijualuk (Tom Coonoon) who had once worked for Bernier, and an older Inuk named Sanguja (Sangoya). Both agreed to join the party on the *Algerine* as the captain tried to move closer to shore by following a lead in the ice. Their destination was not the Salmon River but a site south of Pond Inlet between Cape Bowen and Coutts Inlet.

When the ship could go no further, Munn and George Bartlett continued on by canoe, then by foot. Takijualuk and Sanguja followed with supplies loaded on their *qamutiit*, then left the *qallunaat* as soon as a base camp was set up on shore. For a week the two gold-seekers searched every stream and river, but without success. The only geological formation of interest was some distance inland near an inactive glacier. When heading back for more supplies, Munn learned that their ship had been holed by ice and sunk. The crew had managed to escape unharmed but with little food or supplies. Munn set out again with the younger Bartlett, this time heading for the government supply depot at Albert Harbour where they helped themselves to food, blankets, and other supplies. Several miles down the shore, they took shelter in the abandoned whaling station at Igarjuaq.

The next day Munn and the younger Bartlett walked to the Salmon River to examine the coal deposits mentioned in the government report and check for any geological features that might suggest the presence of gold. They found coal but nothing else. No sooner had they returned to Igarjuaq but the ss *Neptune* arrived with Robert Janes, Lucky Scott, and their party of prospectors. Assuming that Munn had already staked claims on the Salmon River, Scott angrily threatened to leave them all stranded. When told there was nothing along the river but poor quality coal, the angry speculator threatened to shoot Janes if he failed to lead them to the gold. As Munn anticipated, there was none. He watched with amusement as the teller of tall tales ran for his life across the tundra while Scott and his party fired shots over his head.

At this point it was uncertain who would depart and who would remain, until Janes revealed Bernier's cache of furs and ivory hidden in the attic of the abandoned whaling station. Somewhat mollified that he would not be returning empty-handed, Scott agreed to take Munn and his party south. Quickly loading the goods aboard the *Neptune,* they had no sooner weighed anchor when Bernier's ship, the *Minnie Maud*, was sighted working her way through the ice of the inlet. After a brief explanation about their sunken ship to explain their hurried departure, the *Neptune* sped south with a small fortune in stolen furs and ivory hidden below the deck. There is no record whether Bernier suspected they had taken his furs, but there was little he could do. With so few people on board, an armed confrontation at sea was not an option.

Unlike the gold-seekers, Bernier had come prepared to set up a permanent trading post, then send three of his men to Admiralty Inlet to collect ore samples. Tremblay had been a member of the crew on the last government expedition, but Reader and Wilson were newcomers to the Arctic. Although the Igarjuaq station would be their base, Bernier also built a large storehouse at the mouth of the Salmon River for their fish and coal export trade. In spring and fall his men with Inuit help used large gill nets to catch hundreds of pounds of char at the mouths of nearby rivers. These were salted, then packed into barrels for transport south.[7] As part of his purchase from Robert Kinnes, Bernier had also acquired about thirty acres at Button Point, which included a small stone house used as a depot for spring whaling and sealing operations at the floe edge.[8]

In 1912 the Inuit population of the North Baffin region was estimated to be around 480, with another forty living on Igloolik Island – a number much larger than Low had estimated eight years earlier.[9] The Inuit camp at the Igarjuaq station had also grown, comprising now approximately fifty men, women, and children, living in nineteen sealskin tents or *tupiit.* They

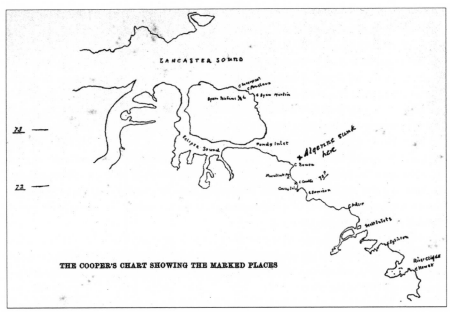

THE COOPER'S CHART SHOWING THE MARKED PLACES

Munn's "treasure map," showing where a cooper on a Scottish whaler allegedly found nuggets of gold. Added notation marks where their chartered ship, the ss *Algerine,* was crushed in the ice and sank. Munn, *Prairie Trails and Arctic By-Ways,* 1932.

had been surprised at the small size of the *Minnie Maud* but delighted that the ship had brought trade goods and intended to stay the winter. No whalers had come that summer, and they had run out of ammunition and tobacco, the two items Inuit were most dependent upon.

An important legacy of this private expedition was Alfred Tremblay's book *Cruise of the Minnie Maud,* which contains a wealth of information about the region's history and its resources. For purposes here, however, its significance lies in the descriptions of Tremblay's experiences with Nuqallaq. The author claimed he had become proficient in Inuktitut while living with the Iglulingmiut so that he was able to converse freely with his guides to gain knowledge not readily shared with transient visitors. To the Inuit he was known as Taamali. Noah Piugaatuk, who was a child at the time, described him as a "good behaviour man" who took many notes because he wanted to find out how "the Inuit were able to survive in hostile environment ... where there were no white people around."[10] Older Inuit would more likely remember his many questions about where to find gold and his large collection of ore samples.

In late August, with Tom Lasso, Takijualuk, and Ululijarnaat as guides, Tremblay and Wilson made their way through Navy Board Inlet and westward to Admiralty Inlet, stopping at camps along the way. They met a number of Inuit who had either worked for Bernier or had visited the government ship during the winter spent in Arctic Bay, including Piungittuq, Qattuuq, Nuqallaq, Aatitaaq, and Iqipiriaq. Wilson returned to Pond Inlet in late January, but Tremblay stayed on to continue the search for gold. His description of an Inuk who had arrived from Repulse Bay was particularly significant, as it showed the distance some hunters had travelled and the communications network that had developed across the Arctic as a result of the whaling activities:

Coggan had come all the way from the native village of Aivilik [Repulse Bay] situated a few miles north of Wager Bay on the west coast of Hudson Bay, where Captain Comer, the commander of the American whaling schooner had made his headquarters for the past 30 years ... Coggan was a fine handy man and spoke some English, which he picked up from Comer's men. [He] is about 35 years of age, very intelligent and a great traveller. He had visited Marble Island, Southampton Island, Wager Inlet, and had crossed from Wager Inlet overland to the Back's River, traversing the same country where Mr. Caldwell, some years ago, disappeared and was never heard of again.[11]

Although the extent of the Inuk's travels may indicate he was a shaman, Tremblay also implied that Coggan sometimes travelled with Iqipiriaq and Nuqallaq, suggesting that at least some families from the Igloolik area may have had far more experience with the American whalers than previously assumed and perhaps had been in contact with the police at Fullerton Harbour. Unlike those living in the vicinity of Eclipse Sound and along Admiralty Inlet, the Iglulingmiut seemed to be less isolated from what was happening in the central Arctic, yet still able to control the degree of contact with the *qallunaat*.

Tremblay's two sections on "Troubles with the Eskimos." were particularly revealing. He is critical of only one Inuk – Nuqallaq – whom he claimed had deliberately told lies about him to the other Inuit, with the result that "the moment that Nookudla [sic] arrived at Igloolik I had trouble with the natives, who from being willing and anxious to accompany and assist me in every way, suddenly became sullen and suspicious and refused to accompany me or to help me in any way."[12] On reviewing the sequence of events, however, there may be a more logical explanation for the sudden change in attitude.

In late March, when Inuit knew that the winter camp at Aggu would be abandoned, Tremblay had insisted on going there because he thought Wilson might have arrived or have sent someone with supplies. Assuming it would be a short trip, he hired a young Inuk named Taqaugak (Takkowah) and his wife to accompany him, but took only one *qamutiik* and minimal food, in the belief they could travel faster and obtain food on the way. They had an extremely difficult time on the way to Aggu, only to find the camp abandoned and no signs of Wilson. On their way back they were unable to find sufficient country food for themselves or their dogs. In a blinding snow storm, Tremblay forced Taqaugak to press on against his wishes, but because of poor visibility, they travelled twelve miles out of their way onto thin ice. Tremblay blamed the near disaster on his young guide who had fallen asleep on the sled from exhaustion. Travelling twenty-eight hours without stopping, they finally reached Igloolik in a state of total collapse and near starvation. In his book Tremblay described how he "knew best," that if he had given in to the Inuk's pleas to stop, they all would have perished.[13] He saw himself as a hero and did not associate his poor judgment with the sudden change of attitude among the Iglulingmiut. Under the circumstances it seemed understandable that both Takijualuk and Nuqallaq might refuse to take him overland to Churchill as he had requested. Nor was it surprising that he found most Inuit reluctant to take him back to Pond Inlet, after he insisted on taking a more difficult route so he would have the distinction of being the first *qallunaaq* to do so. Fortunately for Tremblay, it was also in the Inuit best interests to return him to Bernier before he caused himself or others any serious harm.

His real "troubles with the Eskimos" began when he refused to listen to the guides who had agreed to take him to Pond Inlet. Instead of leaving at once to avoid problems of melting snow, he wanted first to investigate rumours of a gold deposit on the other side of the Melville Peninsula. As he explained in his book, "it was only by a ruse that I induced Takkowah to accompany me ... I knew once we left Igloolik he would go where ever I told him."

Nookudla by his underground work and which was unknown to me at the time, had frightened the rest of the natives of Igloolik from accompanying me, and when I had broached the subject, they had raised all kinds of objection; saying that the ice was too rough, the season was getting late, that their supply of walrus meat was too small, etc., etc. It was a case of 'where there's a will, there's a way' and they did not have the will. Coggan, Peewikto and Nookudla all wished to return to Ponds Inlet as they pretended that the snow would soon vanish from the hills and valleys of Cockburn Land which I knew would last to May. They also told me that several bands of Eskimos had lost their lives when crossing the land, owing to their cartridges giving out and being in consequence unable to kill enough caribou for themselves and their dogs. So I took only young Takkowah, under the pretence of making a short flying trip for a couple of days. But I was secretly determined to visit the great lakes and country that lay 100 miles to the south, as the Eskimos had told me there were many veins of quartz in the rocks.[14]

This time, the two only made it part way across the Melville Peninsula before they ran out of food and were forced to return to Igloolik – as before – exhausted and hungry.[15]

Alfred Tremblay – a self-portrait. *Cruise of the Minnie Maude*, 1921.

Most *qallunaat* living among the Inuit soon learn that it is almost impossible to make experienced Inuit do something they do not think is right.[16] Yet Tremblay was convinced that his knowledge and judgment were superior, an apparent blind spot for a man who claimed to be studying how Inuit had survived with "no white people around." If Nuqallaq was blamed for the Iglulingmiut's sudden lack of cooperation, it may have been that he was less intimidated by *qallunaat* after working for whalers in Hudson Bay, and thus not afraid to speak out against Tremblay's unreasonable demands.

More trouble arose at the entrance to Murray Maxwell Bay, when Tremblay insisted on waiting for an Inuk who was to bring him furs. Nuqallaq wanted to go on ahead, but Tremblay demanded he stay because he "was the only Eskimo with me who knew the trail across Cockburn Land* to Milne Inlet, the others having been in the habit of going by Scheming [Sirmik] Islands and Admiralty Sound."[17] In an attempt to dissuade him

* North Baffin was named Cockburn Land on early maps.

from waiting, Nuqallaq argued that the Inuk in question would not be coming for he had said that Tremblay "was of no account and that only Captain Bernier was of any account." Understandably, this infuriated the stubborn *qallunaaq*, who was sure Nuqallaq was lying, and he threatened to "take them all back to Igloolik … and get at the truth of the story." He was convinced that if he had "done so there would assuredly have been a fight with a probable certainty of blood shed." In the end, they worked out a compromise allowing Coggan to go on ahead, while the others fell back with the heavy load of ore samples.[18]

According to Tremblay, Nuqallaq thought he was on a mission for Bernier to bring back the stone marker from the grave of Alexander Elder, who had died during Parry's 1821–23 expedition. As reported later, Bernier had requested the ice anchor located near the grave, not the stone marker. Some Inuit, however, say it was an Inuk named Kalluk who brought back the marker, even though Tremblay made a point of stating that Nuqallaq was carrying an extra weight of approximately 150 pounds.[19]

Another curious anomaly in Tremblay's story was his repeated references to how the Inuit continually missed or only wounded caribou, compared to his own successes. At first glance this seemed like "bragging rights," as it was surprising that the Inuit hunters could be so inept. Later, when they were short of food, Tremblay reported that he had only four cartridges left and that each one must count to avoid starvation. Was it possible the Inuit purposely let him use up his ammunition to avoid a dangerous situation if he later became irrational? Similarly, it seems more than a coincidence that they would run out of food at the precise location where they earlier had told him about a family dying of starvation because they had run out of cartridges and could not hunt.[20] Or was Tremblay becoming paranoid and imagining that Nuqallaq had masterminded some diabolical plot to prove that he had been right when he warned of possible dangers in delaying their return?

Tremblay reported that while still several miles from Milne Inlet, Nuqallaq had fallen behind, claiming that his dogs were too tired. "He then passed me and reached Ponds inlet [sic] ahead of me and went straight on to Button Point and so I had no opportunity, before sailing home, of giving him a lesson."[21] From that point it was normally only few days travel to Pond Inlet, but Tremblay and the older Inuit family who had stayed with him encountered "deep, heavy snow" which made travel "difficult." After being without food for six days, their dogs were weak and unable to pull their load. According to Tremblay, "we had to keep whipping and shouting at the brutes to make them get up and travel at all."[22] Through inexperience, he had not understood that "the problem of melting snow" was not just the absence of it. Wet, heavy snow could make sled travel extremely difficult, if not impossible.

For the most part, Nuqallaq's actions were consistent with what one might expect of an Inuk having previous experience with *qallunaat*. According to Tremblay, the Inuk had not seemed the least intimidated and showed little signs of *ilira* or deference. On the other hand, he did guide Tremblay safely across the southern route, as promised. The fact that Nuqallaq did not wait around to "be taught a lesson" suggests that he simply wished to avoid further confrontation. He would not consider Tremblay insane or a serious threat to the Inuit, but he may have thought he was an *aqittungajuq* – "someone who does not have much sense."[23] We do not know if Tremblay ever threatened his guides with a gun, but even if he had, they would likely want to get him back to Igarjuaq safely because of his association with Bernier. Certainly, they would not want him to return to Igloolik where he had outlived his welcome.

Tremblay's repeated criticism of Nuqallaq under the same subtitle, "Problems with the Eskimos," is inconsistent with other parts of the book that emphasize his ability to get along with the Inuit. In fact, it seems strange that he would even want to discuss his "problem." Other references to Nuqallaq are benign, such as the fact that he had joined them on the trail, the number of dogs he had, or their hunting trips together, suggesting that the critical sections may have been inserted later, possibly after learning that Nuqallaq was under suspicion for murder. This seems more of a possibility when considering that Tremblay worked for Janes on the 1910 government expedition and that the book was published months, perhaps a year, after the news of his death had reached Ottawa.

There are other inconsistencies. While the author describes the various methods traditionally used by Inuit to control behaviour, the stories that he uses as examples seem to illustrate exceptions to the norm. At Arctic Bay, for instance, he talks about an elder named "Old Lasso," whom he describes as a "stern figure of an Eskimo, a great walrus hunter and greatly feared and respected by the other Eskimos ... He had killed several malefactors, it was said, with very little compunction. One of them was found crawling one night near his igloo, and driving his harpoon through the man's body, who was a well-known thief, he called the other Eskimos out of their igloos, and, pointing to the dead body, said he had taken it for a seal in the darkness. His action was promptly commended."[24] Similarly, Tremblay cites a case near Tuluriaq (Toolooria), where an unrepentant thief was taken by boat to an island, left without food or weapons, and died before the water froze over to allow him to escape his island prison.[25] Intentionally or otherwise, these stories create the impression that the Inuit of northeast Baffin were ruthless and cold-hearted.

Tremblay's views of what should be done for the Inuit are totally inconsistent with those expressed by Bernier, but likely reflective of more pessimistic or cynical points of view at that time. At one point, he describes their relative poverty, along with incidents of starvation and disease, then in the same paragraph states that they were "a magnificent race of people" but "quite unfitted for contact with the white man's civilization." This is followed by an argument that all attempts to civilize them should be stopped, for otherwise they would become weak and corrupt: "give them an idea of real-estate interest and personal property rights in houses and food, and they become as selfish as civilized beings."[26]

Tremblay also writes that the Inuit are like children who "have been taught to fear the White Man, but in their hearts they feel themselves quite as capable."[27] On this point, he was close to the truth, but little did he realize that the Inuit often talked about how some *qallunaat* behaved like children when travelling by dog sled, because they did not know how to look after themselves.[28] The two perceptions of "childlike" speak volumes – one timid yet capable, the other inexperienced and inept.

When two such diverse cultures come into contact, it is to be expected that each would have different interpretations of circumstances and events. Tremblay's opinions were those of a man who had lived with the Inuit for a few months at a time.[29] By comparison, both Henry Toke Munn and Captain Bernier were far more complimentary and appreciative of the Inuit, with both making urgent pleas for government assistance and medical help. Autobiographical accounts often say more about the observer than the observed; yet it is only through comparison that we can piece together the many different *qallunaat* views of the Inuit, and by means of oral history, how various Inuit viewed the *qallunaat*.

Although Bernier's men were unable to find so much as a trace of gold, the trading operation was an unqualified success that first year. Leaving Caron in charge of the station with Takijualuk as his headman, Bernier returned south in the fall of 1913 with a full load of furs, salted char, and ivory. From his profits he purchased a small steamer named the *Guide*. In 1915 he bought two additional properties, thirty acres near Button Point and sixty acres at the mouth of the Salmon River, and obtained a permit to mine coal on the Salmon River. He also expanded his export trade into more exotic fields, such as capturing live polar bears for zoos or selling their skins to museums. Bernier would spend two more winters in Albert Harbour, 1914–15 and 1916–17.[30] "Berniera," as he called his settlement, might have been more successful had he not faced such stiff competition.

After his first misadventure, Henry Toke Munn also planned to return to Pond Inlet. Likely impressed by the quantity of fur and ivory that Bernier had cached in the attic of the whaling station, he too decided to operate a trading post while he continued his search for gold. In 1914 the Englishman convinced his wealthy friends to invest in the Arctic Gold Exploration Syndicate (AGES), with Munn and Lord Lascelles as the principal shareholders and sufficient capital to purchase a ship and supplies.[31] Their vessel was none other than the *Albert*, which had been used for many years to supply the Dundee Whaling Company's station at Igarjuaq, but was now refitted with a modern steam engine. During the syndicate's nine years in operation, it hired veteran whaling masters to sail the vessel – names such as Milne, William Adams Jr, and John Murray.[32]

When Munn first arrived at Pond's Inlet in early September 1914, he discovered Bernier's steamer anchored in Albert Harbour. Changing course, he unloaded his trade goods and building supplies at Button Point (Sannirut). His ship then departed, leaving Munn behind with an assistant by the name of Taylor Cummins. That first year Munn hired Paniluk (Peneloo) and Panikpak (Panikpah), along with Innuja (Inooya), his previous helper, who had proved to be as able a hunter as she was a seamstress. On occasion, her husband Sanguja (Sangoya) would accompany Munn on short trips. Trade was slow at first, owing to the popularity of Bernier's post, but by offering generous goods Munn soon attracted a respectable number of Inuit to his post. They would call him Kapitaikuluk, meaning the kind captain, a tribute to his sensitivity and caring for the Inuit people. To his credit he also learned to speak their language. His relationship with Bernier was described by Munn as "distant," and understandably so, as he was likely viewed as an accomplice in the theft of the furs stored at Igarjuaq. While his first year's profits were substantial, Munn's search for gold was a dismal failure. After an extensive search of every stream and river south of Cape Bowen, he found only lumps of yellow iron pyrite, which he now believed had been mistaken for gold.[33]

On a sled run to Admiralty Inlet next spring, Munn came upon a half-starved German photographer by the name of Franke, who had been stranded without dogs or food after his brother-in-law had wandered off. The dogs were found with their leads frozen in the ice some distance away, but it was not until the snow melted that they found the body of Franke's companion, frozen in an upright sitting position, his pipe still in his mouth. Reportedly the body was buried in the same position, next to Brokenhauser's grave in Albert Harbour.[34] An inexperienced *qallunaaq* setting out alone usually found himself in trouble, yet those who treated the Inuit with respect – and had sufficient goods to pay them – had no difficulty obtaining a guide or dog driver.

For the most part, Inuit took great care to ensure the *qallunaat* were well looked after. There were limits, however, as Bernier explained in his autobiography. "They are good-humoured, willing workers, loving freedom, but cannot be forced to do anything they dislike, or put up with anything that is against their ideas of what is right and proper. The Eskimo is his own master, but nevertheless can be jollied along by those who understand his peculiar psychology."[35] Most Inuit at the time believed that they were superior to the white man, and in terms of knowledge about survival in an

Captain Henry Toke Munn (British Cavalry retired), known to
the Inuit as Kapitaikuluk, the "kind captain." Munn, *Prairie Trails
and Arctic By-Ways*, 1932.

Arctic environment they were. Neither Bernier nor Munn had difficulty
with that perception, but not all *qallunaat* thought alike.

In the summer of 1915 the *Albert* was the first ship to arrive in Eclipse
Sound, bearing news that the war had broken out in Europe. Leaving an
agent in charge, Munn headed for Peterhead, Scotland. Bernier also departed, but for Quebec City. Neither found a meaningful way to participate
in the war effort. Much to his disgust, Munn was told that he was too old
for overseas action. The thought of sitting behind a desk held no allure for
the inveterate adventurer.[36] Bernier, on the other hand, was placed in
charge of an unseaworthy vessel, the *Percassin*, which was sent in a convoy
to Britain. It sank during a storm, with the captain and crew narrowly
escaping drowning.[37] It was hardly surprising that both Bernier and Munn
returned to Pond Inlet the following summer.

Bernier remained at Igarjuaq during the winter of 1916–17 and conducted further geological studies in Admiralty Inlet, this time along Strathcona Sound. He officially registered a claim, only to find out later that the
assays once again failed to find any trace of gold.[38] When Munn returned
to Pond Inlet in 1916, he left an agent by the name of James Florence in
charge and headed south to Durban Harbour to pick up several Inuit fami-

lies and William Duval, formerly employed by the Dundee Whaling Company at Pond Inlet but now working for AGES. Munn's plan was to establish two posts in Hudson Bay, but foul weather forced the entire party ashore at South Bay on Southampton Island. To Munn's despair the *Albert* failed to arrive the following summer. Finally in August 1918, everyone was picked up and brought back to Cumberland Sound, where Munn left Duval and the Inuit to establish a post at Usualuk Harbour. Unfortunately, bad weather prevented the *Albert* from reaching Pond Inlet, leaving Florence to spend a third winter in the Arctic, with no staple foods or goods to trade and no idea when he would be replaced.[39] Bernier as well had not returned, leaving Caron equally uncertain about the future. In the meantime, a third trader had arrived on the scene.

After the debacle in 1912 Robert Janes also planned to return to Pond Inlet but, unlike Bernier and Munn, he had difficulty finding financial support. Initially he sought assistance from Prime Minister Robert Borden and was apparently offered encouragement and references. In 1916 Janes wrote to the prime minister and thanked him for his earlier help. He recounted how he had raised sufficient commitments but they had been withdrawn when the war broke out. His latest proposal was described as an exploration venture, with hopes of meeting up with Vilhjalmar Stefansson on Banks Island. As it turned out, Janes had no plans to explore, nor did he have any experience or qualifications to do so. Like the hoax of finding gold nuggets in the Salmon River, his letter to the prime minister seemed to be based more on his imagination than reality.[40] In the end Kenneth Prowse of St John's, Newfoundland, agreed to be his financial backer, but the two men had a major disagreement before Janes' departure. Prowse, it appears, thought he was funding an expedition in search of gold and was angry to learn that trade goods had been purchased with his money.[41]

Shortly before Munn left for Durban Harbour and Cumberland Sound in the summer of 1916, the ss *Kite* sailed into Eclipse Sound, past Albert Harbour and the Salmon River, and anchored near the mouth of the Patricia River to drop off Janes and his assistant, Thomas Holden, along with supplies and lumber. Unlike when he visited in 1912, Janes brought ample trade goods and food to last for two years and set up operations in a small shack that doubled as living quarters. To attract Inuit to his post at Tulukkaat, he was excessively generous that first year, giving away rifles, provisions, tools, and ammunition as gifts.[42] Not surprisingly, the Inuit enjoyed trading with their generous friend, whom they fondly remembered from the winter of 1910–11 as the *qallunaaq* who gave them food and supplies when they were hungry and starving. Most still called him Sakirmiaq, although some preferred Sakirmiaviniq, meaning, no longer second mate. That winter, Bernier and Caron, as well as Munn's agent, watched helplessly as their share of trade and profits dwindled.

Inuit pulling Janes' qamutiik across the tundra, 1 June 1911. Bernier claimed the Inuit were always eager to assist his second officer because they knew he carried a plentiful supply of biscuits. Arctic Images Album. NAC – C 23202.

During that first winter Janes was reported to have had frequent outbursts of anger and quarrels with his assistant, who had also been on the 1910–11 government expedition. In desperation, Holden tried to escape by swimming across the Salmon River to reach Bernier's ship before it departed; sadly, he died of pneumonia before he reached home port. Janes also alienated the other traders. After Munn's ship failed to arrive in the summer of 1917, Janes refused to share any of his food or supplies with Florence unless he was first paid 50 per cent of the AGES' entire trade. Florence rejected the offer and instead lived mostly on country food, with some supplies obtained on credit at Bernier's post.[43] Although married with a wife and family in Newfoundland, Janes was said to have an Inuit "wife," a woman named Kalluk (Kudloo) who provided him with clothing and other necessities of life. From a white man's perspective, it may seem strange that her husband, Inuutiq, also lived with them, yet prior to the arrival of the missionaries, polyandry was quite common.

In the spring of 1918 Janes became intensely jealous of Nuqallaq, also known as Quigaarjuk, a widower whom he believed was trying to gain Kalluk's affection. On one occasion, Janes was seen beating the woman because she wanted to go to a dance. He warned Nuqallaq to keep away and threatened to shoot him if he ever came near his post. Duly alarmed, the Inuk kept his distance. For no apparent reason Janes boastfully repeated his threat to Inuit and traders alike – once even in writing.[44] When warned that his threats and aggressive manner might alienate the Inuit, Janes declared that "he would shoot any native if he misbehaved," appearing to take pride in the fact that they feared him.[45] By the following summer

Nuqallaq had a new wife, Anna Ataguttiaq, but he still avoided any contact with the jealous trader.

Meanwhile Janes' fortunes took a turn for the worse. In the summer of 1918 he had waited in vain for the ss *Kite* to arrive, unaware that his sponsor in Newfoundland had sold the ship. Prowse, it turned out, was so irate when he learned that Janes had stopped at a Labrador port and bought more trading goods on his sponsor's account that he vowed to leave him in the Arctic to find his own way home.[46] No one, it appears, thought to relay that message to Pond Inlet. The fact that no ships arrived that summer was equally disturbing for everyone.

Later that winter Janes had a fight with the AGES agent in front of a large audience. The story still seems to be a favourite among the elders. "Who won and who lost," however, seems to vary depending on the source. According to the version reported to the police at Chesterfield Inlet, Takijualuk was said to have intervened in the fight and pulled Janes off James Florence just before he was about to kill him with a knife.[47] This story emphasized how dangerous Janes was – a "bad man" – in Takijualuk's opinion. Noah Piugaattuk, an elder from Igloolik, was more precise in his description of the encounter, except that his story had Janes pinned to the floor with the other agent holding a knife to his breast.

Noah Piugaattuk – Igloolik, 16 January 1989

That summer no ships came, so they all ran out of supplies, especially their food. They were expecting a ship but Kapitaikallak [Bernier] was in service elsewhere. The people with the late Sakirmiaq ran out of food so he went to Igarjuaq to buy some food for himself ...

Then Sakirmiaq had to go down and buy food from the other trading post [AGES] with the pelts that he had traded from the trappers. They had a long big argument which soon broke into a fight. This was in the winter towards the spring. Takijualuk, the namesake of Kunukuluk who was known as Kunuk, was our interpreter with Kapitaikallak. He was with these people when the fight broke out. The taller one [Janes] was thrown to the ground and the other one [Florence] who did not appear to be heavily built, in fact he looked meek, turned out to be pretty strong. They both were whites. The other person pinned the other by the arm and took a knife with his left hand which he aimed to the left side of his breast. The Inuk [Takijualuk] yelled for him to stop fighting.

He said that he did not want a white person to be killed in the land of the Inuit. [Florence] stopped for a while but soon gave out a cry "He Eee!" and looked to the direction of the breast where he surely would have struck had not the Inuk stopped him. This was the first time that [Sakirmiaq] was almost killed. The Inuk was saying that he did not want any white man to die of unnatural causes in the land of the

Inuit. [Sakirmiaq] was almost killed by another white person, but was prevented by an Inuk.[48]

This account explains the more sympathetic view held by some Inuit, who recalled the generous trader of earlier times and could only rationalize the change in his behaviour in terms of his being rejected by the other traders. Janes' later threat to kill Takijualuk, however, makes no sense if in fact Florence was the aggressor. Nonetheless, this version of the fight is important to show how the Inuit earnestly tried to make sense of something they could not understand.

Meanwhile, the difficulty in servicing the posts and increased competition was posing a problem for all the traders. In December 1918 Captain Bernier met with Munn in England to discuss the situation and agreed to sell all his goods and properties to the Arctic Gold Exploration Syndicate on the condition that his nephew, Wilfred Caron, was provided free passage home. The purchase included the mineral rights to the land Bernier had claimed on the north side of Strathcona Sound.[49]

Before sailing north the next summer, Munn stopped in Newfoundland and tried to contact Kenneth Prowse. He was informed that Prowse was unwell and unable to see him. Munn's motives for trying to contact Janes' backer are unclear. After purchasing Bernier's operation, he may have hoped to eliminate all competition, but he also could have been just checking as a matter of courtesy. After making further inquiries, he learned that Janes' ship had been sold.[50]

When Munn reached Pond Inlet in the summer of 1919, he passed on the news to Janes and offered to take him home on the *Albert* in return for half his furs – essentially the same offer Janes had made to Florence two years earlier. The price seemed exorbitant, but so was the price Janes had quoted to Munn's agent. The trader refused, swearing that he would never sail with Munn but would take his furs overland to Igloolik, then on to Repulse Bay and Chesterfield Inlet. A fight broke out on the *Albert*, apparently over money that Florence claimed was owed him for supplies purchased on credit. Most elders relate how Janes had attacked Florence, but again Noah Piugaattuk reversed the part played by the two men:

Noah Piugaattuk – Igloolik, 16 January 1989

A ship finally came but Sakirmiaq could not get on it ... He got into argument with the same person [Florence] which soon erupted to a full fight on the deck of the ship. The other person threw Sakirmiaq to the deck, and because he was struggling to get free, his clothing got torn. [Florence] then started to look around to see if he could find a weapon to use against the other person. Because there was a danger that he might grab a weapon, Nakungajuq [Captain John Murray] grabbed him below his arm and lifted him up and carried him aside. At the same time, the captain of the ship told the other person to go to the land.

[Sakirmiaq] who won the fight kept on talking and struggled to get free, while someone was carrying him as if he was a child. His clothing had been torn in the struggle so he tried to straighten them out. The man holding him put him into a small boat even though he was struggling. He then took the oars with both hands to get to the land.

After the ship's boat had started off and covered some distance from the ship, the man on board the ship holding [Florence] let go as he knew that the man would not be able to do anything. But he looked around and found a short thick rod which he took and ran for the gangway where he got ready to strike, then someone grabbed him from behind to prevent him from making a strike. This time it was the captain of the ship that was preventing him making a strike. Sakirmiaq did not get killed at that time either.[51]

Most Inuit recalled that Janes' clothing had been torn, which to them signified the seriousness of the fight. Who was the victor is uncertain, but Janes' refusal to accept Munn's offer was understandable. Because of his initial generosity, he had accumulated only a modest amount of furs and ivory and had found no gold. As a result he had barely enough to pay off his creditors in Newfoundland.[52]

The day of the fight Munn followed Janes ashore to renew his offer to take him out. Once again Janes angrily rejected any assistance. Concerned for his welfare, Captain Murray said he would send Janes' wife a message to say that he intended to leave "by dog team and arrive home the following summer via Churchill," not realizing that it would be the first time anyone in Newfoundland had heard from him in over three years.[53] Munn, meanwhile, left instructions with the new AGES agent, George Diment, to supply the trader with food for his overland trip. Even then Munn was not hopeful of the outcome and wrote in his journal, "I do not think he will get out alive."[54]

That fall Janes became increasingly morose. Initially, he solved his food shortage by breaking into the government cache at Albert Harbour. After exhausting those supplies, he hired a party of Inuit, including Amarualik, Naqitarvik, Aatitaaq, Ijjangiaq, and Kipumii, to take him to the emergency cache on Beechey Island. He removed the food, tobacco, coal oil, and a Ross rifle, then paid the hunters with stolen supplies to haul the goods back to his post. Unaware of Janes' plans to depart overland that spring, Naqitarvik also gave him two years' worth of furs for which he was paid only a small portion of their value, in return for the promise of "a boat, rifle, tent, camera, tobacco and cartridges when the boat came up in the summer."[55] Janes knew his own ship was not coming for him, but even if some arrangement were made for his evacuation, there was no hope of any new supplies. If he was a bully and a braggart, as the other traders claimed, Janes also seemed to have trouble telling the truth. His behaviour was not that of a rational man.

The stranded trader at first tried to entice other Inuit to trade with him by promising to pay them later. He was a large man, which made him all the more intimidating. By now many mistrusted him and avoided his post on their way to trade at Sannirut or Igarjuaq. This seemed to make Janes even more aggressive. He demanded that the Inuit hand over their furs as payment for articles he had given them the first year, declaring that they had not paid enough in previous trades.[56] On one occasion he had an argument with Umik, Nuqallaq's father, and was seen chasing after the elderly shaman with a long-bladed snow knife[57]:

Noah Piugaattuk – Igloolik, 16 January 1989

It was not long when Sakirmiaq started to show signs of restlessness, now that no other ships would be coming to the area. He would not be allowed to get on a ship from the port at Mittimatalik. The only way he could get to a boat was for him to be taken by a dog team through [the Admiralty Bay region]. Then once they had reached that area, they would proceed on to Igluligaarjuuk, and then on to Churchill where he would be able to get on a ship …

He was also getting fidgety. That winter he was getting really restless. Sometimes there is a large build up of snow on the lee side of a house and right up close to the wall is usually a bank. They were outside and the snow bank was now high, about the height of a person. On this spot, Janes started an argument with Umik, the father of Qiugaarjuk [Nuqallaq]. The Inuk was trying to reason with him but he was fidgety. There was danger that he might do harm to others so Umik was trying to calm him down. They really started to argue and so Sakirmiaq took a knife and threatened Umik with it.

When Sakirmiaq threatened him, Umik noticed that he looked to [a spot] and knew right away that he was not just threatening him. So he made an attempt to get on top of the snow bank, which he did, getting away from his reach. Once he was on top he rolled over. Sakirmiaq was not only threatening him, but had intentions of striking him with a knife because he had become so restless. It was from this point on that he became feared.[58]

Later, Janes stopped Aatitaaq on the trail and demanded that he hand over his bag of furs. The Inuk resisted at first but said that he feared for his life when Janes reached for his gun.[59]

By mid-winter the coal oil from Beechey Island had run out and Janes was now using seal oil for heat and light. Even Kalluk and Innutiq were short of country food. According to his diary, Janes had convinced himself that he had been too generous and that many Inuit owed him from previous trade transactions.[60] Although warned by the AGES agent George Diment that his bullying tactics would end in trouble, Janes reportedly shrugged it off, saying he knew how to handle the natives.[61] It never occurred to him that the Inuit might have their own ways of dealing with him.

4

Sakirmiaviniq

After the sun disappeared from the sky around mid-November, Robert Janes, or Sakirmiaq* as he was called by the Inuit, became increasingly irritable and at times irrational.[1] His living quarters at Tulukkaat would do little to lift his spirits, being only eight by fourteen feet and only six feet high, flat-roofed, made from rough lumber, and covered in tar paper. A low lean-to at the rear was used to house Kalluk and Innutiq. Nearby stood a twelve by fifteen foot storehouse for furs and trade supplies. A sooty residue now covered the walls from use of a seal-oil lamp (*qulliq*) for heat and light.[2]

At Christmas time Janes visited the AGES agent George Diment at Sannirut and stayed several days. For no apparent reason he began bragging about what he would do to Nuqallaq if he ever came near his place. Diment later recalled that "he appeared to nurse a great wrath and hatred against him, and he further boasted that the natives were afraid of him. Janes talked wildly during his stay with me, and repeatedly stated he would shoot Nookudlah. I gathered that the trouble was a native woman who was living with Janes and that Nookudlah was also after her. I formed the opinion that he was not quite sound in his mind."[3] In early February, Janes again visited Diment, this time to remind him that Munn had promised to provide supplies for his journey to Repulse Bay. The AGES agent obliged with sufficient food and ammunition for both the trader and his guide.

At first Janes had been unable to find anyone to accompany him. Only when he threatened to shoot the Inuit dogs did Uuttukuttuk (Oo-too-ki-to) offer to take him as far as Repulse Bay.[4] Janes' threat to "shoot the dogs" was used liberally as a way of coercing people to agree to his demands.

---

* After his return in 1916 Sakirmiaq was sometimes called Sakirmiaviniq, meaning he was no longer second mate. After his death the name Sikirmiaviniq signified he was no longer living.

Robert Janes in less formal attire, seen here with stump of an ancient tree he discovered at Canada Point in summer, 1911. Bernier Collection.
NAC – C 10973.

Before setting out, for instance, he explained to Uuttukuttuk that he planned "to borrow some dogs from the natives on Admiralty Inlet, and pay for them when the ship came up. If they would not let him have any, he would shoot their dogs."[5]

Finally on 25 February 1920 Janes and Uuttukuttuk set out with their heavily laden *qamutiik*. Kalluk, who was due to give birth to Janes' child within a few days, was left behind. Arguing that they needed to travel as fast as possible, Janes convinced Uuttukuttuk to leave his wife behind as well. Because the dogs were in poor condition and unfit for overland travel, they took the easiest route by way of Navy Board Inlet and over the ice of Lancaster Sound. They had little dog food and had hoped to pick up some at camps on the way.[6] Continually delayed by high winds, bitter cold, and heavy snow, they made slow progress.

At one point they were overtaken by Kaukuarjuk, who was travelling light, carrying only a few trade goods with which to buy furs for George Diment. Kaukuarjuk stayed two nights in their igloo before taking his leave, then caught up with Nuqallaq and four other families who were hunting walrus and polar bear on the ice floes near Adams Island (Tuujjuk). On learning that Janes was leaving, Nuqallaq remarked that he thought it was a good idea. Kaukuarjuk decided to join their group, but they decided to stay out of sight until Janes had passed by.[7] Uuttukuttuk later claimed that he met Nuqallaq when he was out hunting for food but that he had not told Janes. Curiously, neither Nuqallaq nor anyone else in the group remembered meeting Janes' guide.

When they finally reached the shores of Admiralty Inlet on 9 March, Janes sent Uuttukuttuk toward Strathcona Sound to look for Inuit camps. On that same day, he wrote in his diary about the bad weather and slow progress, saying that they had been out "15 days and not at my destination yet, the longest trip here during my stay in this land."[8] The next morning Uuttukuttuk returned and reported that he had found no sign of Inuit camps. As their dogs were now near starvation, Janes decided to follow the *qamutiit* tracks heading out on the ice in hopes of finding Inuit out seal hunting. Again he complained bitterly about the cold and the fact that he had frozen his nose.

At six that evening, the two arrived at a large camp about ten miles southeast of Cape Crauford.* They took shelter in the snow house belonging to Paumi, with Janes noting in his diary that "fortunately, I picked a warm one."[9] Most Inuit at the camp were from the Arctic Bay or Igloolik area, including Siniqqaq, Qaunaq, Aatitaaq, Ijjangiaq, Ataguttaaluk, Iqaqsaq, Paumi, Maniq, Tupirnngaq, Kunuk (of Arctic Bay), Ivalu, Saittuq, Nutaraarjuk, and their wives and children. Kassak, Kaukuarjuk, Ululijarnaat, Nutarariaq, and Nuqallaq arrived the next day from Pond Inlet.[10] They were surprised to see Janes, having expected him to head straight for Igloolik. Nuqallaq went directly to Paumi's igloo to see if the trader was still angry with him. Janes, however, assured him that "it did not matter anymore" because he was leaving the area.[11]

The Inuit seemed friendly enough the day after the trader's arrival, and he was pleased when he received four fox skins in a trade. The next day, however, they were less accommodating once they realized that the trader

---

* The proper spelling is Crauford, although the RCMP used Crawford in their reports.

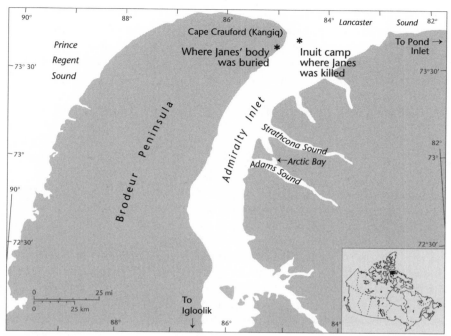

Admiralty Inlet, 1920.

had few goods of any value. Most claimed they had no furs, and others simply refused to trade. Lack of cooperation was also evident when the Inuk sent to pick up the load Janes had cached on the trail returned empty handed.[12]

On 11 March, two more *qamutiit* arrived from Igloolik, bringing Miqutui and Iqipiriaq along with their families. They had intended to stop only briefly, as they were on their way to trade at Pond Inlet. Miqutui had been one of the first guides hired by Bernier and was now a respected leader of his camp. On hearing the trader's plans, he warned that the snow and ice conditions were bad for travelling and that any Inuit intending to go to Repulse Bay had already left Igloolik.[13] Others later testified that Miqutui's statements were untrue, but at the time no one had dared contradict the word of the older Inuk. If he had hoped the misleading information would deter Janes from going to Igloolik and becoming a burden on the community, he succeeded.[14] That night, the dejected trader noted in his diary the disappointing news and his decision to return to Pond Inlet:

They report all the other natives gone from Igloolick [sic] to trade with the Hudson's Bay Company at Fullerton. They left in February and took with them lots of foxes. This is unfortunate for me as some of those natives owed me several skins each. I

loose [sic] these. I am in a quandary now to know what to do. My dogs are of a poor
sort and meat is scarce away yonder. I am afraid I shall not be able to accomplish the
task to and fro. It is useless for me to go and stop at Fullerton if a ship comes here for
me during the summer. I shall be nowhere as far as getting out. I think I had better
retreat and wait the next four months.[15]

That same evening, Janes told Uuttukuttuk that if the Inuit camped at Cape
Crauford did not give him fox skins, he would shoot them if they ever
came to his post at Pond Inlet. When warned that they would shoot back,
he evidently replied that "he did not care, he was getting old, and he
would be hungry if the ship did not come for him."[16]

Janes may have been initially depressed, but he soon began devising a
new strategy. He knew that no ship would be coming for him. Moreover,
now that Bernier had sold his property, the only ship scheduled to come to
Eclipse Sound belonged to AGES. To retain enough furs and ivory to pay off
his creditors, he must somehow acquire more to pay Munn for his passage
home. Without food or ammunition to trade, his only hope was to coerce
the Inuit into handing over their furs, either by saying they had not paid
enough in the past or by promising to pay them when his ship came in.
Janes seemed oblivious to his untruthfulness and unconcerned that he
might be depriving the Inuit from receiving fair value for the furs. Instead,
he had convinced himself that the Inuit had cheated him by not paying
enough for his goods. The Inuit were not so easily deceived. Those who
had fox skins were understandably reluctant to hand them over. They
wanted food or ammunition in return, the two items they knew Janes did
not have in sufficient quantities to trade. Several buried their fox skins in
the snow so he could not find them.

As part of his revised plan Janes asked Nuqallaq to act as an interpreter
to help him get more fox furs. He also said he would need him to trade the
skins for supplies at Munn's station, apparently not wishing to confront
the agent in person. Even more bizarre was his demand that Nuqallaq
should go and find Kalluk and bring her back, with the warning that if she
refused to come, he would kill him.[17] Janes' threats seemed endless, but he
was apparently confident that the Inuit were sufficiently afraid of him that
they would do whatever he asked.

His request to have Nuqallaq act as his interpreter might seem strange,
except that Janes was not particularly fluent in Inuktitut, and some Inuit
had difficulty understanding him. Similarly, in his confused state of mind,
he may have thought that Nuqallaq still feared him and would be willing
to pressure the other Inuit into submitting to his demands. The next day
Janes lost his temper when he discovered that Kunuk's large bag contained only seagull skins. Speaking mostly in English, he threatened to kill
everyone's dogs to prevent them from trading at Munn's post, claiming he

did not care if the Inuit shot him in return. For those who did not understand what he was saying, his angry gestures left no doubt as to his intentions. The tirade, which began inside Kunuk's house, continued outside. He demanded to see Kaukuarjuk and accused him of turning the Inuit against him. The elderly Inuk was frightened as he knew Janes would be angry if it was known that he had come to Admiralty Inlet to trade on behalf of Munn's post. At one point, Aatitaaq tried to calm Janes down, but he stalked off to his igloo and began looking for his gun, saying "never mind if I kill some of the people and afterwards their dogs." Fortunately, Uuttukuttuk had borrowed the trader's rifle to go walrus hunting that day.[18]

Others witnessed the scene, including Miqutui, the leader from Igloolik. Later he admitted to the police that he had told those gathered "that if somebody wants to kill Janes, to go ahead and kill him" before he shot somebody.[19] Several Inuit also described how the white trader visibly shook when he was angry, giving the appearance that he was out of control. In time Janes quietened down and invited Nuqallaq and Ijjangiaq to eat with him in Paumi's igloo. Once inside, however, Nuqallaq reported, he became angry again and declared that when he got back to Eclipse Sound, he would "watch Tom [Takijualuk] when he was sleeping then shoot him because he was getting short of grub, then do the same with Florence,"[20] apparently forgetting that Florence had been replaced by George Diment. Ijjangiaq knew Janes was angry, but did not know what he had said until Nuqallaq told him.[21]

That evening Janes told Uuttukuttuk how he had threatened to kill the dogs that day, saying that he would also kill the Inuit if they still refused to give him any furs.[22] Later, he recorded the day's events in his diary:

Saturday, March 14th.

Light NE wind fine + clear. All natives hunting today few got seals. Twome paid me for goods delivered last year. One other fellow whom I interviewed told me he had no foxes but I told him I knew better + he had better pay up. If not he would never get to the other white fellow, for I would shoot his and the others dogs as sure as the sun rises + I will too. I guess they will pay up later on + save trouble. I have given myself a lot of trouble by issuing those fellows credit. It's a bad policy in this land. Night very fine 7pm day light NNW. All well Thero 22 below.[23]

Although Nuqallaq assured everyone that Janes was no longer angry, the hunters continued to talk among themselves. It seemed natural that Nuqallaq would become the central figure in these discussions and assume a leadership role, given his command of English and the fact that Janes had trusted him to act as his interpreter. He instructed Uuttukuttuk "to stay in the igloo all the time and watch Janes, and if he was going to shoot the

Takijualuk (Tom Coonoon) on the CGS *Arctic*, 1922, worked for Bernier as
an interpreter and then as head man for the AGES post at Sannirut and later
at Igarjuaq. W.H. Grant Collection. NAC – PA 170152.

people, to take away everything he could kill the people with."[24] Others
hid their guns so Janes could not use them. The general feeling was that the
trader should be killed before he killed one of them.

Nuqallaq discussed the situation with his wife, Ataguttiaq. He told her
that he wanted to leave the camp but was afraid lest Janes become angry
over losing his interpreter and kill someone.[25] Although there was no formal meeting with everyone present, Nuqallaq talked with Kunuk, Ijjangiaq, and Miqutui about Janes' threats, and then to a number of others.
Most agreed that Janes should be killed, but no one wanted to do it. They
all gave reasons why Nuqallaq should be the one, primarily because Janes
had threatened to kill him on numerous occasions and had physically

attacked his father. One Inuk suggested that perhaps Aatitaaq should kill him, because Janes had stolen furs from him. At some point Nuqallaq told everyone that as long as Janes remained "happy," he would do nothing, but he assured them that he would kill the trader if he became angry again.

That evening and the next morning several hunters brought Janes foxes in hopes of keeping him "happy." Iqipiriaq told Paumi that he wanted his skins back if Janes was killed, saying that he thought "somebody would do it before long."[26] Iqaqsaq brought five foxes to trade but Janes became angry and insisted they were owed to him. Iqaqsaq protested that he had always paid the full amount for any goods he obtained, but finally gave in to avoid further argument.[27]

Most of the men left the camp the next day to hunt seals, except for Paumi who remained behind because his wife was afraid to be alone with the *qallunaaq*. Perhaps buoyed by the apparent success of his threats the day before, Janes confided to Paumi that he intended to gather them all together that evening and "put them more afraid." Reports of this new threat spread among the women left at the camp and they were terrified. Kunuk's wife was particularly upset because Janes had focused so much of his anger on her husband. With a child in her *amauti*, she left the camp to find the hunters. Nuqallaq's wife ran out after her, and they both followed the *qamutiit* tracks to warn the men that Janes was "mad" again.

When Nuqallaq heard the news, he calmly exchanged his gun for Kaukuarjuk's newer rifle and headed for the camp. Discussion took place in one igloo, then another. Later that afternoon Paumi's wife watched as Janes began dancing about the igloo and whistling. He called for someone to get Nuqallaq, but was told that he was busy feeding his dogs.

Meanwhile, believing that Miqutui and other senior hunters had agreed that Janes should be killed, Nuqallaq and several others began to plan their strategy. It was important to catch the *qallunaaq* unawares so he would not kill anyone.[28] Three years later, Miqutui would tell the police that he had warned Nuqallaq that there might be trouble in future if Janes were shot. Given his inaccurate stories about the condition of the trail and the Inuit traders having left Igloolik, this statement may have been equally self-serving.

Kaukuarjuk had been so terrified after Janes had accused him of turning the other Inuit against him that he talked Siniqqaq into going back out on the ice, where they built a small snow house for shelter. As they had no oil lamp for heat, they nearly froze to death. Kunuk was also frightened and stayed out on the ice until after dark, so he could slip into his igloo without Janes seeing him. Paumi's wife, who was scared that Janes would escape and kill them all, ran to Kunuk's place to hide. Ataguttiaq had wanted to go with her, but Nuqallaq said that she must not in case Janes suspected something was afoot. Thus, she remained alone in her igloo, sobbing, until she was joined by Kassak. Ululijarnaat agreed to help lure the white trader out of Paumi's igloo. Maniq placed a *qamutiik* on its side for Nuqallaq to hide behind. Aatitaaq and Ijjangiaq stood watching from behind the snow houses.

When Ululijarnaat first went to Paumi's igloo, he discovered Janes was still eating, so he left. Returning some time later, he told the trader "to come outside, there are some foxes that the natives have to sell you."[29] Janes emerged from the igloo and began walking towards Nuqallaq's place. Nuqallaq held his fire until he came closer, then took aim – and missed. He tried again and this time shot the fur trader in the mid-section. Janes remained upright, then staggered, until Aatitaaq came from behind and pushed him to the ground. The wounded man seemed unable to move his lower body but raised his head and said something most Inuit could not understand. One person thought he might have spoken the word "foxes," perhaps "never mind the foxes." Janes then called for Ululijarnaat to come and help him. The others remained silent, watching and waiting.

After going back to his igloo for another cartridge, Nuqallaq approached the wounded man. He seemed to move, and everyone began talking at once. Aatitaaq claimed that he heard Miqutui say, "Watch out, he is getting up – shoot him." This time Nuqallaq shot him in the head at close range, killing him instantly. Some stood around while others grabbed their dogs to keep them away from the body. Uuttuquttuk went to get Janes' clothes and blankets to cover him; Nuqallaq and the others went to fetch his *qamutiik*.

Aatitaaq's son Uujukuluk would never forget that night. Half a century later he could still recall how frightened he had been.

Uujukuluk – Arctic Bay, 1974

My memories began in Kangiq [Cape Crauford] when someone killed a *qallunaaq*. I could not forget it because I was very frightened. The man's name was Sakirmiaviniq. I can still remember it. It happened at dusk. We heard two shots and because we were children, we went running over when we saw the people gathered around. My mother called me back, but I wanted to see. When I got there, the *qallunaaq* was lying on the ground and I realized that he had been shot.[30]

Miqutui and his son stayed with the body to keep the dogs away until the others returned. Nuqallaq, Aatitaaq, and Ululijarnaat watched as Uuttukuttuk put mitts on the dead man's hands and his deerskin *kamiik* on his feet, then wrapped him in his blankets. They placed him on his *qamutiik* and took it to the mainland. Respectful of the Inuit tradition that required everyone to remain at the site for three days following a death, no one left the camp until the appropriate time had elapsed.

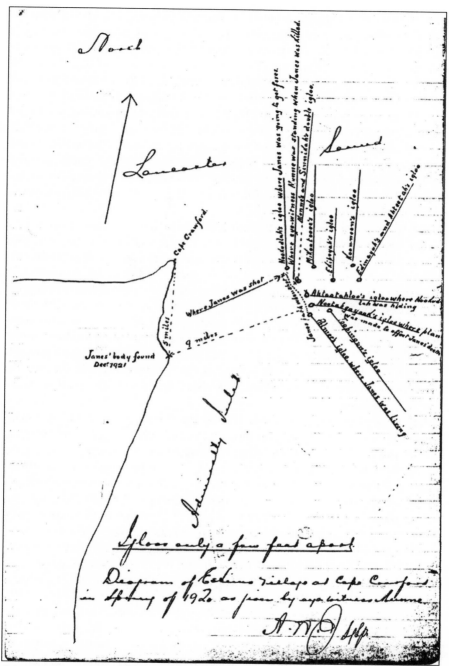

Crime scene, drawn by Staff-Sergeant Joy. NAC – RG 18/3280/1920–HQ–681–G–4(2).

In appreciation for killing Janes, six hunters presented Nuqallaq with fox skins. Another gave him a bear skin. For the moment, everyone was happy that Janes was dead and no longer a threat. Those who had given Janes furs the previous day went to Paumi's igloo to collect them and found his wife packing up the fur trader's belongings. Aatitaaq helped himself to Janes' rifle and some of his furs, claiming they were owed to him. Nuqallaq had already given a pocket knife to Ululijarnaat and later distributed half the tobacco and a portion of the cartridges to Aatitaaq and Ijjangiaq, keeping the remaining tobacco and a few cartridges for himself. The rest of Janes' belongings – his fox furs, the remaining cartridges, his notebooks and diaries, personal clothing, eating utensils, food supplies, two coins, a medal, and the keys to his store – were delivered by Uuttukuttuk to George Diment at Eclipse Sound.

The AGES agent instructed them to take everything to Janes' post, where he personally locked the boxes and furs in the storage shed to await further instructions when the *Albert* returned next summer.[31] Uuttukuttuk explained "that Janes had gone out of his mind and that the natives were afraid of him." In a signed statement, Diment later claimed that Nuqallaq had feared for his own life, so he had "shot him to save himself."[32] Since this latter statement was not confirmed by any of the Inuit who were present at the camp, this may have been Diment's own idea, perhaps in the belief that the authorities would look more leniently upon a shooting in self defence. He did not appear upset about the incident, nor did he criticize Nuqallaq's actions. No one at Pond Inlet mourned the death of Robert Janes – or so it appeared.

Aaluluuq, a young boy at the time of the shooting, recalled his cousin Nuqallaq and his wife approaching his father where they were hunting seal on the ice. Upon learning what had happened, the uncle reprimanded his nephew for killing a *qallunaaq*, saying "now he would see another." Aaluluuq and his father then crossed to the mainland and found the body "lying on a caribou blanket with his face covered." Other Iglulingmiut helped them build a wooden box for a proper Christian burial and to "placate his soul." They covered the box with canvas and set it on a rock ledge on the west side of Admiralty Sound, where no person or animals would find it.[33] Later, they told Peter Freuchen that the box was twelve feet long because Janes "was as bad as two ordinary men and therefore needed a coffin twice the size."[34]

Some Inuit began to have second thoughts. Iqaqsaq claimed that his father warned him that the white man might make trouble. Tupirnnagaq voiced similar concerns, as did others – or so they said, when questioned two years later by the police. Those who had admired Sakirmiaviniq because of his earlier generosity believed that he had become irrational after he was abandoned by his ship and the other traders. According to their traditions, they were justified in killing an insane person if he or she posed a serious threat to the lives of others. Nuqallaq believed he had done no wrong. He had accepted the responsibility conferred on him by the other hunters and believed that he had saved the camp from possible starvation. There was only one problem: Robert Janes was a *qallunaaq*.

When Henry Toke Munn arrived at Eclipse Sound the next summer, he saw his flag flying at half mast and knew instinctively that Janes had not survived the winter. Nuqallaq and other witnesses to the shooting were on hand to meet the AGES ship and report to Kapitaikuluk what had happened. Munn's original plan had been to leave Wilfred Caron in charge of the post and return to England with the furs traded that year,[35] but the death of his former competitor changed everything. Instead, he decided to remain at the post with Caron to make sure that the situation was stable. At the beginning of September, before his ship departed, Munn wrote a short report to the Canadian authorities, describing what he had learned from Janes' driver, George Diment, and Nuqallaq himself.

According to native reports, confirmed by documentary evidence which Wilfred Caron will send you, Janes had often threatened the native who committed the deed, a man named Noo-kud-lah. Natives tell me the trouble was over a native woman who was living with Janes ... Natives further report Janes had started overland to Hudson Bay in March. Meeting certain Igloolik natives, they told him the journey was impossible at that season. Janes returned toward ... Cape Crawford and there met some Ponds Inlet Natives, amongst them Noo-kud-lah. Janes is said to have behaved in a very strange manner, threatening them, in particular Noo-kud-lah, saying he would shoot all their dogs and later kill those natives he did not like. The natives are stated to have been afraid to remain in their own igloos and for some nights to have all crowded together in one or two igloos, a native of this party was abused by Janes and very much frightened.[36]

Unfortunately this report was not consistent with later statements by witnesses to the shooting. There had been no problem about "a woman," nor did Janes single out Nuqallaq in his threats. The errors seemed to be derived from Diment's account of events, likely coloured by the stories he had heard from Florence the summer before. Munn also described a confrontation on the trail between Nuqallaq and Janes on the way to Cape Crawford, an incident that did not occur. Janes' diary verified that the only Inuk he met was Kaukuarjuk (Kowkwatsoo).

In a hurry to get the report written before the ship left, Munn appears to have learned only part of the story and attempted to fill in the rest from Diment's report.* For example, he claimed that Nuqallaq had said that "Janes has said for a long time he was going to kill me; he has told many

---

* This assumption is based on the fact that Diment's signed statement, which was sent from England, was almost identical to Munn's first report.

natives so; I was afraid and so I shot him first."[37] Considering his previous reactions to Janes, and to Tremblay as well, Nuqallaq would more likely have run away to avoid any personal confrontation.

Like Diment, Munn may also have thought Nuqallaq would stand a better chance of avoiding punishment if he could prove self defence. The reference to a dispute over a woman was also misrepresented. On the other hand, for a *qallunaaq* a crime of passion may have seemed like a more logical motive – certainly more exciting – than simply defending one's family against the threats of an irrational man. Although Munn thought he was being helpful, his initial report suggested a possible motive of revenge, which would fit with the Department of Justice's criteria that assured a conviction.

Since Nuqallaq had made no attempt to run away and had not stolen any of Janes' furs or belongings, Munn suggested that the Canadian authorities "may not wish to incur the great expense of arresting and trying this native." Instead he promised to investigate the incident more fully that winter and graciously offered his services to assist the government in any way he could.[38] Meanwhile, he had asked each of his agents – Caron, Florence, and Diment – to make statements under oath and forward them to the Canadian government. Caron also wrote a letter to Bernier before the *Albert* departed:

8 septembre 1920

J'ai à vous apprendre que R. Janes a été tiré à Admiralty par Nookudloo. Moi, ça ne ma'a pas surpris parce qu'il a fait le [barbeu] après qu'on été parti l'an dernier. Je demand de travailler pour Nookudloo, parce que il est un Esquimaux, un de nos bons travaillants et il y a une autre affair. Je ne veux pas de police ici l'année prochaine parce que le capitaine Munn et moi nous restons cette année et je va rester l'année prochaine si je le satisfait.[39]

In his written statement to the police, Caron also described the letter Janes had written him in October 1918, threatening to kill "Kiwakyou."*

A year later, Munn sent the police a portion of a letter found in Janes' effects, written by Florence to warn Janes that some of the Inuit were "down on" him for attacking Umik with a knife, and that they might try to shoot him.[40] In his signed statement Florence also emphasized the self-defence motive: "I knew that Noo-kad-lah was afraid of Janes, and was in constant dread that he would shoot him. Noo-kad-lah told me this on several occasions in my own house. I often heard Janes say that he would shoot any native if he misbehaved. Janes frequently boasted to me that he knew the natives were afraid of him, and he appeared proud of it. I was not

_____

* Janes' spelling of Nuqallaq's alias, Qiugaarjuk.

astonished that Noo-kad-lah had shot Janes, as Janes did everything to bring this about by his treatment of him."[41] All three of Munn's agents, Florence included, suggested that the earlier confrontation over Kalluk was somehow responsible for the Inuk's action.

After receiving Munn's report and the statements from his agents, RCMP Commissioner Perry reported the incident to Deputy Minister of Justice Newcombe, explaining that it was "impossible to take any action at the present time," as there were no police stationed anywhere near the scene of the crime. Nor did he seem overly concerned about the shooting, noting that "Janes' attitude toward the Natives generally and Noo-kud-lah in particular was very overbearing." He did suggest that the police might be able to investigate the following summer, in conjunction with the proposed government expedition to Ellesmere Island.[42]

Munn also wrote to Janes' widow, saying only that her husband had died during his attempt to reach Fort Churchill. He did not give the cause of death, but stated that because of the weather, his "party must have suffered great hardship." His letter was the subject of an article in a Newfoundland newspaper, which in turn elicited more stories from crew members of the *Albert* on their return to St John's.

Questions were raised about the possibility of foul play.[43] Arthur English and Emile Lavoie, who had been with Janes on the 1910–11 government expedition, believed he was killed for his furs, which they thought would be worth at least $100,000, or possibly for his notes, which might have contained information about gold discoveries. Lavoie wrote to the police, suggesting that these were likely the reasons for Janes' death and that he and Arthur English intended to make their own inquiries. Captain Bernier, in reply to a letter from Lavoie, said he knew little about Janes' activities, except that he had been ill in the fall of 1917, that his trading was poor, and that he was in need of new supplies. Ambrose Janes, the victim's father, at first thought Captain Munn was likely responsible for his son's death, then later accused Wilfred Caron of inciting the Inuit against his son.[44] Neither family nor friends were willing to believe that Janes might have been responsible for his own demise.

Arthur English, the geologist who had collected ore samples for the government in 1911, interviewed Janes' financial backer and found that Prowse "was certainly sore with poor Janes," having invested more than $10,000 in the venture and provided his wife with a free house. He also discovered that no one had heard from Janes since he had left Newfoundland in 1916, except for the message from Captain Murray a year before. From the crew of the *Albert*, English learned of the fight aboard the ship and Janes' avowal that he would see Munn "in hell before he would give him 50% of his fur value for passage." English was now convinced that Munn's report was "a well-laid plan to cover up the theft of Janes' furs."[45]

Unaware that he was being accused of foul play, Munn obtained statements from five witnesses that winter, using his head man, Takijualuk (Tom Coonoon), as the interpreter. Munn claimed that these new statements were read over and verified as accurate by each witness. In his concluding remarks Munn also explained that he was "able to understand enough Esquimaux to check up most of it" and that he "did not find the interpreter saying anything other than the witness said at any time." Although his methods were by no means as thorough and professional as a police investigation, the stories told by five witnesses, Uuttukuttuk, Nuqullaq, Qaunaq, Kaukuarjuk, and Kunuk, are important in that they were freely told to "the kind captain" and Takijualuk, both of whom they trusted. Moreover, the incident was still fresh in their memories as only six months had passed since the shooting. Munn then wrote a second report, portions of it in a question and answer format.[46]

Uuttukuttuk – Eclipse Sound, Spring 1921

Janes asked me to go with him to Igluliut [sic]. I was to return here (Pond's Inlet). I was to get a small boat at his station for pay. We went up Navy Board Inlet to go by Admiralty Inlet to Igluliut. Near Adams Island Nu-kud-lah overtook us. I told him Janes was going to Hudson's Bay [sic]. He did not stop with us nor camp near us.

We were at Cape Crawford three days before Nu-kud-lah came there. Nu-kud-lah was surprised to see us and said he thought we had gone down Admiralty Inlet to Igluliut. The day before Nu-kud-lah shot Janes, I went away with a sled after walrus; I took Janes' rifle (Government Ross 303) as it was better than my rifle to obtain walrus. Janes had been very angry with the Natives because they did not give [him] fox skins and had said he would shoot some of them. I hid my own rifle that day before going to hunt walrus.

When I returned, Janes was angry with me because I took his rifle. He said "If I had had a rifle to-day, I would have shot some Natives." The Natives had hidden their rifles also. Some Natives were very frightened and left their Igloos and slept out on the ice without any blankets. Janes would walk about with his book in his hand, calling to the Natives to bring him fox skins … The Natives were all afraid. Nu-kud-lah shot Janes when he was going from our Igloo to a Native Igloo; I was in my Igloo then.

He was dead at once; I closed his eyes. Nu-kud-lah said "take everything belonging to Janes down to George." [Diment] I did this; there were six Boxes, three Bags, a Rifle, an Iron Oil Drum, and a Saw. Later I gave to "George" a bag with some fox skins Janes had traded, which had been left to be thawed out.

Nuqallaq – Eclipse Sound, Spring 1921

A Native told me at Navy Board Inlet that Janes was going to Igluliut when I overtook him.

Q. Did you hear Janes say he would shoot some of the Natives when at Cape Crawford and shoot their dogs?

A. I heard Janes say many times he would shoot some Natives; he was angry because they did not give him any fox skins, he also said he would shoot their dogs.

Q. The day before you shot Janes did you go to his igloo and why?

A. Janes was outside his igloo and very angry he said he would shoot some Natives and went to his porch to get his rifle. I ran to the porch to stop him. I had no rifle with me. I intended to hold him inside the porch if he tried to come outside with his rifle but he could not find it as Oo-tooki-took had taken it to hunt walrus that day. I went inside the igloo with Janes and we talked. He became less angry and did not shout at me. He took some cartridges from his pocket and showed them to me saying "If I had found my rifle I would have shot you or some Natives with these."

Q. Did you believe he meant to do this?

A. Yes I am sure he would have killed someone if he had had his rifle when he was angry.

Q. What had the Natives who were not hunting done with their Rifles?

A. They were hidden in the snow.

Q. If Janes had killed the dogs what would have happened to the Natives?

A. There would be great danger of the children or women starving.

Kunuk – Eclipse Sound, Spring 1921

Q. What do you know of this affair?

A. Janes came to my Igloo with Nu-Kud-Lah who acted as interpreter. Janes asked me if I had the Foxes he said I owed him. I said I had none of my own; Janes became angry and talked loudly and angerily [sic]. The next day most of the men went away to the floe edge hunting; I also went. While I was away my old wife became very frightened by Janes who was angry and talking, so she ran away from the Igloos far out on the Ice taking my child on her back; I met her as I was returning from hunting. She wanted to sleep out on the ice but it was too cold. I waited until nearly dark and came back to my Igloo by a round about way.

Q. Did you hear Janes say he would kill anyone?

A. I heard Janes say that if the Natives did not pay him the Foxes he said they owed him, he would shoot their dogs so that they would not be able to go away hunting and if the Natives got angry at this, he would shoot them.

Q. Where were you when Janes was shot?

A. I was in my Igloo. I was very afraid and did not leave it after I arrived there but kept watch through the window all night. I did not hear Janes outside. My igloo was not near his.

Qaunaq – Eclipse Sound, Spring 1921

Q. Were you at Cape Crawford? When Janes was there?

A. I was at Cape Crawford before Janes arrived. I have never had any debt from Janes. He often wanted to give me debt but I would not take any.

Q. Did you hear Janes say he would shoot anybody?

A. I heard Janes say outside his igloo to all the Natives who were there that if they would not give him foxes, it would be better they should be killed and he would kill them. When he said this he was angry and all the Natives were afraid. I was afraid too.

Q. Where were you the day Janes was killed?

A. I went out hunting the day before Janes was shot and when I returned late at night I found two women far out on the ice. It was dangerous for the women to be so far away alone without any dogs or a rifle on account of the bears. The women said Janes was angry and they were afraid to stay in their igloos. They had a child with them. I took them on my sled back to the igloos. When I had returned to my igloo, I stepped inside and did not go out again that night because I was very afraid. I heard nothing more till I heard the rifle shot which killed Janes.

Kaukuarjuk – Eclipse Sound, Spring 1921

Q. What do you know about this affair?

A. I arrived at Cape Crawford the day after Janes arrived. I did not know he was there. I had been sent by "George" to try and trade for him. Janes came to my sled and looked at my fox skins and asked if I had come to try and buy more. I said Yes! as I had bought for Captain Bernier before. Janes said to me "Quaquajuk, you cannot buy foxes here. I have come here to do that myself. The next day Janes was angry. I was in my igloo and the Natives called to me to come outside as they thought Janes was going to shoot my dogs. I came outside and Janes said to me "Natives cannot kill me, Quaquajuk. They would have to put two bullets in there [sic] rifles to shoot me. I am able to shoot all the dogs and all the Natives and I will do so if they do not give me their Fox Skins." I was very afraid when he was angry like this. I went away at once on a sled belonging to another Native who was going hunting. I went far out on the ice and built a small igloo and stayed there all day and all night. I had no food or blankets and because I was very afraid, my nose bled greatly and my heart became weak, and I thought I was going to die. It was very cold, but I was afraid to go back to my igloo at the village. The second night I returned late and heard that Nu-Kud-Lah had shot Janes the previous night.

In his concluding remarks Munn corrected his earlier statement that suggested the shooting was related to a confrontation over a woman. He now claimed that if Nuqallaq had once thought of enticing Kalluk away from Janes, he had long ago abandoned the idea – "if he ever had it." Unfortunately, the damage was already done. The investigating officer would never receive the second report, nor would it be submitted as evidence at the trial.

Munn also provided information about Nuqallaq's background and character – details not found in any police report:

Some years ago, Nu-kud-lah had been a Boat-man* for the Scotch Whalers in Hudson's Bay for two or three seasons; he was also a Boat-man for Captain Bernier at Ponds Inlet for some seasons; he understood English but did not speak it intelligibly; he is apparently between thirty and thirty-five years of age; he is above the average height of an Esquimaux and the strongest Native I have seen.

He is inclined to be moody, is impulsive, and I do not consider him quite as mentally as well balanced as most of the Natives I have met. This is not meant to suggest he is in any way insane ... From my personal knowledge of Nu-kud-lah, I think it would be dangerous for one man to attempt to arrest him single handed unless it was at a Station where other White men were. If he was arrested far away, entailing a long over land journey with him as prisoner, he should be watched very carefully for I think he might be dangerous to travel with under these conditions.

Munn's purpose in adding the last statements is not known. Nuqallaq had worked for and travelled with Caron that winter and was said to be trustworthy. Moreover, in a book written sometime later, Munn refers to Nuqallaq as "my friend." Yet his description here suggests that there may have been something about the Inuk that inspired respect in some but fear in others. In the same report Munn stated that after Kalluk gave birth to Janes' child, she and Inuutiq moved to Button Point for a short time, then left to live with her husband's family at Durban Harbour just north of Cumberland Sound.

Munn and Caron stayed at Sannirut that winter, having insulated the building with blocks of snow. There was an outer room twenty by eighteen feet that served as a workshop, meeting room, and dance hall. The two men lived in the back rooms, which were heated by a stove using coal from the Salmon River. Munn did all the cooking, and they always ate alone. In addition to Takijualuk as his head man, he hired the Inuk's sister to sew and to help clean the post. She also happened to be the wife of Akumalik, who was described as "an excellent native and very intelligent." He had been converted to Christianity at Cumberland Sound and was now preaching the new religion at Pond Inlet. Among his converts to Christianity were Umik, the former shaman, and his son Nuqallaq.[47] Curiously, Munn made no mention of this fact in his report to the Canadian authorities.

As soon as the ice set on Eclipse Sound, Munn and his men set out for Janes' station to collect his furs and personal belongings. They carried out a full inventory, then sorted, cleaned, and re-packed the furs. After Christ-

---

* "Boatman" or "sailor" were terms used to describe Inuit who were employed on ships or at whaling stations.

mas celebrations, Munn sent Takijualuk to Admiralty Inlet, and Caron with Nuqallaq to Igloolik. On his return trip Caron was accompanied by eleven *qamutiit* belonging to the Iglulingmiut. Munn was particularly impressed by their appearance, believing their apparent prosperity was because of the excellent resources in the area and the fact that they had little direct contact with the whalers.[48] He seemed unaware that the Iglulingmiut might have had as much, if not more, interaction with the American whalers at Repulse Bay and with Scottish ships in Hudson Bay and Hudson Strait. "These people were by far the best Eskimos, collectively, I had seen," claimed Munn, "They were very clean in their clothes, straightforward and independent in their trading, and altogether a very superior type."[49] Caron reported that Nuqallaq had served him"faithfully"on the eight-hundred mile trek.[50]

In his second report to Canadian authorities, Munn explained that Nuqallaq had left in the spring with a party of Inuit, although he had first asked if the trader had any objections. Unexpectedly, the Inuk had a difficult time finding his way overland to Igloolik. The party had lost their way, then run short of food. Nuqallaq's wife, Ataguttiaq, later described the ordeal to Father Mary-Rousselière.

Ataguttiaq – Pond Inlet, circa 1971

We set up camp and leaving our companions there, my husband and I headed for the sea. It was understood that if we killed seal, we would come back. When we reached the coast, we set up camp and my husband got three seals.

After sleeping, we found we had to remain there another day because our dogs, having eaten, had gone astray. When we arrived at our companions' camp, we found that they had no meat nor fat, with only a few biscuits and some tea and a bit of flour. They were especially hungry for meat.

We arrived in complete darkness and peeked through the door, and when my husband announced we had killed some seals, they all began shouting with joy … I put fat in the lamps and lit them. The igloo was quite smoky because they had a gas heater. After cooking the meat and washing off the soot, we left them for Aukarnirjuaq. From that time on we did not lack seal or caribou, hunger was forgotten. We took off for Igloolik and spent the summer there.[51]

At Igloolik they joined up with Umik and began to preach a syncretic form of Christianity to the Iglulingmiut.[52]

That next spring, members of the Danish Fifth Thule Expedition observed the former shaman and his son preaching, apparently with great enthusiasm. Peter Freuchen described how Umik proudly told him how his son had killed a white man because of his "dreadful temper." Nuqallaq, it appears, mistook the Dane for a policeman and presented him with a letter written in syllabics to explain why he had killed Janes. Another year passed before Freuchen had an opportunity to report the incident to the RCMP. By then he had lost Nuqallaq's letter and was recalling the contents from memory. Even then, the explanation was consistent with the story told earlier to Munn.

Nuqallaq's story, as told to Peter Freuchen – Igloolik, May 1921

When I came close to the house I saw several men talking loud and I saw him too. He said that the natives were thinking of their food and themselves only. Another day he said that the best thing would be if all the dogs were shot, and he said that he would not mind if all the natives died. Therefore, we thought we had better kill him, and — and —* said it would be better to kill him, so when he came out of his house, I shot him. The natives said it was just as well, and the white men said that they did not care.[53]

When asked whether he feared "the white man's law," Nuqallaq was said to have replied that "no one should do him harm for that, but even though they would, he was not afraid because he would be taken to the white men's country before being punished."[54] It is not known where he got the idea of going south – possibly from an explanation provided by Captain Munn, or perhaps he was privy to the stories told by Sinnisiak and Uluksuk. The fact that Nuqallaq's brother was living in Chesterfield Inlet suggests he may have learned about the enjoyable time the two murderers had "in prison." Chronologically, however he could not have heard about their release before the time of Janes' death, but later information might explain his lack of fear about being sent south.

Freuchen seemed more concerned about the influence that the alleged murderer and his father were having over the people of Igloolik. He claimed that their preaching had "made them both rather big men amongst the natives in the settlement." Reportedly, they no longer hunted but "had all the game killed by the natives brought to them and divided according to their views." Freuchen was particularly distressed that one of his own natives had given his watch to Nuqallaq and was told to "say nothing about it" while still in Igloolik.[55] Although his report would not reach police headquarters until after the trial, it no doubt provided assurances that the eventual outcome was appropriate – at least according to Freuchen's interpretation.

News of Janes' death also travelled as far as Chesterfield when Miqutui and his party travelled south. RCMP Constable Paquet, who met the hunter at Wager Bay, reported his story to Sergeant W.O. Douglas of the Chester-

* Freuchen left the names of the accomplices blank in his report to the police.

field detachment, who passed it on to Inspector Albert E. Reames. Parts of Miqutui's account seem to have become confused and distorted in the telling, but the story line that Janes was a bad man and had threatened to kill the Inuit and their dogs was consistent.

Early in the spring of 1920, Mik-ku-te-ek left his hunting grounds at Igloolik, Melville Peninsula, and travelled with the intention of reaching Pond's Bay, accompanied by his son E-kas-nok. About six days' travel this side of Pond's Bay they came to a camp of natives living on the ice, seal hunting. Also at this camp there was a white man with a trading outfit from the trading post at Pond's Bay.

Mik-ku-te-ek stated that the white man had traded all of his trade outfit to the natives for fur, and that the natives still had fur which the white man wanted to take back to the post with him, and to pay the natives for same at some future date. These furs the natives refused to give him, as they had done the same thing some time previous and had never received payment. Not being able to get the furs from the natives, the white man became very angry and said that he would get his rifle and shoot all the natives and their dogs. After saying this, he went to his igloo, and when he came out, native Kai-o-ga-ke-uk [Qiugaarjuk, an alias for Nuqallaq] shot him through the body. The white man, however, could still walk and he told the natives that his native had got his rifle away seal hunting, but that when he came back with it, he would kill them all for shooting him. At this, native Kai-o-ga-ke-uk shot him again, this time in the head, killing him dead.

Kai-o-ga-ke-uk told Mik-ku-to-ek that he knew that the white man was a bad man, as some time previous the white man had tried to kill his father. Knowing this, he was afraid to take any chances with him.

Mik-ku-to-ek stated that he did not go to Pond's Bay after this but after a six days' stay in the said camp, he returned to Igloolik. Some days after leaving the camp, he states that he heard that the white man had been buried in a box. He does not know if by white men or natives.[56]

Miqutui also told the policeman that the people at Pond Inlet knew Janes was a "bad man" and told the story of how Takijualuk had broken up a fight just as Janes was about to kill the other trader with a knife. Miqutui appeared to fully support Nuqallaq's actions, saying that the Inuit had no other choice but to rid themselves of the white trader who was threatening to kill them and their dogs.

Inspector Reames also heard a similar story from an Inuk by the name of Albert who came from the Aivilik region, and who had heard the story from Miqutui and Iqaqsaq. This story was more confused, with the location of the Janes' death now at Pond Inlet and Albert not sure if he was killed by a knife or a rifle. Otherwise, it confirmed the stories told to Munn.

Native Albert – Chesterfield Inlet, May 1921

During the winter of 1920–1921, I was up in the Melville Peninsula, and there met some natives belonging to the Igloolik tribe, who sometimes go to Pond's Inlet, on Baffin Land to trade. Two of these natives, named Mik-ko-to-ek and I-kok-shak told me that the white man who run [sic] a trading post at Pond's Inlet, had been killed by a native named Kai-o-ga-ke-uk, brother of Ok-ke-a-ok of Chesterfield district. This man Kai-o-ga-ke-uk lives around the trading post at Pond's Inlet. The killing was done during the winter of 1919–1920. The two natives Mik-ko-tu-ek and I-kok-shak were at Pond's Inlet at the time of the killing.

These natives did not tell me whether they actually witnessed the deed, but Mik-ko-te-uk told me that he kept the dogs away from the dead man's body whilst the man who killed him went and put his coat on.

These two natives told me that all the natives around Pond's Inlet were afraid of this white man, as he had repeatedly told them during the past two years, that he was going to kill all the natives dogs first, and then kill all the natives. As a result, they were very much afraid of him. The two natives who told me, said they, too, were afraid of him. They could not say whether he was crazy or not. These two natives did not say how Kai-o-ga-ke-uk killed the white man, whether by knife or rifle. This native is still up around the Pond's Inlet district. The body of the white man was buried by either Kai-o-ga-ke-uk or the other natives. My informants did not say which. This white man, according to my informants, had long since traded off nearly all his stock, had some food left for himself, but he had eaten the last of it shortly before he was killed. The buildings or belongings of the white man were not interfered with by the natives after he was killed. This trading post is right on the sea shore at Pond's Inlet according to my informants.[57]

Of interest in this version is the importance attached to the proper handling of the body, the fact that the *qallunaaq*'s belongings were left intact, and the threats that he had made about killing the dogs and the Inuit. The news that Nuqallaq had a brother in the Chesterfield area suggests that he was more worldly and had travelled more widely than assumed, although as son of a shaman from the Igloolik area, this likely was to be expected. Inspector Reames sent these two reports, written in May 1921, by special packet to Port Nelson to ensure that the information reached the RCMP commissioner "before the schooner leaves for Pond Inlet this summer." Unfortunately, the CGS *Arctic* did not sail that summer as anticipated, nor did Reames' reports reach the investigating officer who went north with a Hudson's Bay Company supply ship.[58]

Meanwhile Munn had closed the post at Sannirut in the spring of 1921 and spent most of his time at Igarjuaq, which he now called Pond Inlet. Alas, in packing Janes' personal effects to deliver to his widow, Munn

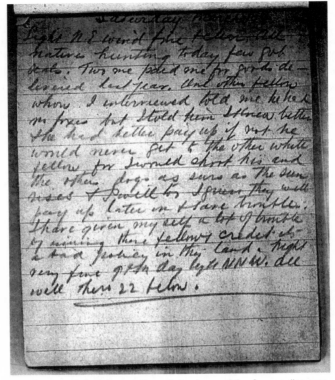

Last entry in Robert Janes' diary, Saturday, 14 March 1920: "as sure as the sun rises + I will too." NAC – RG 18/3280/1920-HQ-681-G-4 (1).

made a critical error when he included the trader's personal diary, an item of major importance to any police investigation or legal defence. He may even have thought he was protecting evidence by bringing it south and delivering it to the authorities. At the time of his departure, he was unaware that a Hudson's Bay Company supply ship was bound for Pond Inlet with an RCMP officer aboard. Hearing the news at his trading post in Cumberland Sound, he changed his plans. Instead of going to Newfoundland as intended, he headed straight to London where he had Janes' furs and ivory assessed by an independent appraiser. He then offered to pay the Janes family the sum of $9,500 for the furs and any goods and chattels remaining at his trading post. This was a generous offer, considering the condition of the furs, but it did not cover the money owed to Prowse. Nonetheless, the family gladly accepted.[59] Realizing the importance of Janes' diary, Munn forwarded it directly to the authorities in Ottawa, noting particularly the last entry. Alas, there is no reference in the police files that the diary or Munn's second report was ever sent back north.

5

Police Investigations

In the spring of 1921 the decision whether to investigate Janes' death depended upon government approval of the proposed expedition to Ellesmere Island. Even if there had been clear evidence of a criminal act, the logistics of launching an investigation in North Baffin without a base of operations were inconceivable. The only permanent "settlement" in the area that year was the AGES trading post on Eclipse Sound, with its annual supply ship sailing out of Britain. Considering the Conservative government's reluctance to finance law enforcement in a region inhabited by only a handful of non-natives, any hope of establishing police detachments in the Arctic Islands hinged upon the urgency, or perceived urgency, attached to the sovereignty issue.

Concerns about Arctic sovereignty had resurfaced in 1920, following Canada's request to the Danish government for assistance in restraining Greenland Inuit from killing musk-ox on Ellesmere Island. The reply received on 26 April 1920 included a letter from Knud Rasmussen, a young Dane in charge of Greenland's most northerly trading post, in which he declared that Ellesmere Island was a "No Man's Land" and that the only authority in the district was exercised through his station. The Danish government cautiously stated that they thought they could "subscribe to what Mr. Rasmussen says therein."[1] The Canadian government submitted a formal protest on 13 July 1920 and set up an ad hoc committee, the Advisory Technical Board, to study the question and report to the Department of the Interior.

The validity of British title was again questioned. Although commonly expressed as "new interpretations of international law," the issue was essentially the same as described by W.F. King in 1904–05. This time, however, it was given more force when Under-Secretary of State for External Affairs Sir Joseph Pope officially acknowledged the authority of "Oppenheim's Treatise on International Law." A report to the minister of the

Department of the Interior explained that the "new" interpretation did not emanate from the jurists but from Canada's own experts who had re-examined existing international law.[2] Oppenheim's treatise was clear: "If such period lapses without any attempt by the discovering State to turn its inchoate title into a real title of occupation, such inchoate title perishes and any other State can now acquire the territory by means of an effective occupation."[3] It was now feared that British discovery claims were insufficient to maintain title to portions of the uninhabited Arctic Islands. Particularly vulnerable were Ellesmere and the smaller islands to the west, where Norway's Otto Sverdrup and American Donald Macmillan were reported to have made a number of recent discoveries.[4]

The situation took on a greater sense of urgency in the fall of 1920 after Rasmussen announced plans for the Fifth Thule Expedition which was expected to follow a route from Greenland across Arctic Canada to Alaska. Although the stated objective was to conduct scientific studies, Canadian officials worried about a hidden agenda when they learned that the Danish government was funding the project. In the opinion of the Technical Advisory Board, Denmark was aware of the weakness of Canada's title and seemed to have "initiated steps with a view to extending its authority to Ellesmere Island."[5] Additional concerns arose when an American newspaper reported that Donald Macmillan had announced plans to search for uncharted lands west of Ellesmere with the object of claiming them for the United States of America. Another article stated that he intended to circle Baffin Island to map additional uncharted lands.[6] The board also learned that the latest *Century Atlas* published by a reputable American firm had highlighted the United States, Alaska, and Ellesmere Island in the same colour.[7]

The Technical Advisory Board prepared several reports clarifying the issues and proposed a number of actions that would accomplish "effective occupation." Various strategies were discussed, with consensus favouring the establishment of police detachments in the high Arctic to enable regular land patrols and enforcement of game laws. According to one proposal, the first two posts would be built on Ellesmere and Devon Islands, followed later by one at Winter Harbour on Melville Island. An annual government expedition would assist the police in setting up and supplying the new detachments, as well as providing other administrative services. Additional measures proposed in 1920 included the expansion of Hudson's Bay Company posts throughout the Archipelago and possibly the transfer of Inuit families from overcrowded areas in the south to uninhabited islands. All recommendations were designed to give visible evidence of "effective occupation."[8] Otherwise, it was feared that Britain's title to the Arctic Islands would lapse, or may have already lapsed, to become an "inchoate title."

Some measures initially recommended reflected a sense of panic, as evident in the proposal that Canada should send an advance party by "hydroplane" or by a dirigible from Britain. This suggestion was rejected outright by the minister of the Interior, but he did approve the idea of refitting the CGS *Arctic* and sending an expedition north the following summer to establish two RCMP posts in the eastern Arctic. On 1 December 1920 Dr John Davidson Craig, a member of the International Boundary Commission, was appointed to take charge of preparations. Although assigned to the office of the Commissioner of the Northwest Territories, Craig's innocuous title of "advisory engineer" reflected the secrecy attached to his position, similar to the equally ambiguous "Technical Advisory Board." His first step was to hire Captain Pickels of Mahone Bay, Nova Scotia, to sail the ship and supervise its refit. After nine years as a lightship anchored in the St Lawrence, the CGS *Arctic* was moved to the government dry dock and work began immediately.[9] As the ship had been virtually dismantled in 1911, the refit proved to be a major challenge and a costly one.

Preparations came to an abrupt halt in February, when Sir Ernest Shackleton approached the Canadian government about possible sponsorship for his exploration plans in the high Arctic. Although his proposal did not fit the needs of the police or the Department of the Interior, certain politicians were enamoured with the idea of a Canadian expedition led by the famous explorer. As a result the supplementary estimate required to finish work on the CGS *Arctic* was withheld as the question of command turned into a political issue. By mid-May there was still no final decision.[10] Meanwhile, the RCMP commissioner had added a third police post on Bylot Island to the plan, to facilitate investigation of the death of Robert Janes, and nine RCMP officers and constables were placed on alert for imminent departure.[11]

In the interim, Deputy Minister W.W. Cory of the Department of the Interior announced internal changes to deal with the growing population in the Mackenzie Valley and sovereignty issues arising from the oil discoveries at Norman Wells. Cory, who had been commissioner of the Northwest Territories since July 1919, appointed four members to the NWT Council to allow enactment of new legislation. The Northwest Territories and Yukon Branch was set up within the department to oversee all government activities in the North, including measures to protect Canadian sovereignty. As director, Oswald S. Finnie would have a major influence on all decisions related to the eastern Arctic, including the proposed government expedition.[12]

Discussion of the sovereignty question moved to a higher level in the spring of 1921, as the under-secretary of state for External Affairs, Canada's high commissioner to Britain, the minister of the Interior, and even

Prime Minister Meighen were brought into the discussion.[13] By May of
that year Winston Churchill as secretary of state for the Colonies was personally forwarding dispatches from "His Majesty's Minister in Copenhagen" to Canada's governor general.[14] Unexpectedly, the cabinet in mid-
May "declared against the expedition proceeding that year," apparently
anticipating a less costly diplomatic resolution.[15] Three weeks later the
governor general received a telegram from the British Colonial Office, stating that the Danish government had provided written assurances that the
Fifth Thule Expedition was strictly a scientific investigation and that "no
acquisition of territory whatsoever was contemplated."[16] The sovereignty
issue was put on the back burner, as were RCMP Commissioner Perry's
plans for his new Arctic police detachments.

When notified that the expedition had been cancelled, Perry drafted a
letter to the Privy Council Office to recommend that no further action be
taken on the Janes' case at that time.[17] He also wrote to the victim's father to
explain why it was impossible to send a police party to Baffin Island that
summer. Instead he would await a further report from Captain Munn, but
he promised that a formal inquiry would follow if there were "any evidence
of foul play."[18] Within days, Perry reversed his position, after learning that
the Hudson's Bay Company was planning to establish a trading post at
Pond Inlet that summer. Previously the company had only three posts on
Baffin Island, at Lake Harbour (1911), Cape Dorset (1913), and Frobisher
Bay (1914). This year they announced that they were adding three more, at
Pangnirtung, Amadjuak, and Pond Inlet.

Perry again wrote the Privy Council Office, this time requesting approval to send two officers to Pond Inlet on the HBC ship. Appealing to
concerns about sovereignty, he argued that as well as investigating the
alleged murder, the police would be conducting "administrative acts to
confirm authority and possession over that territory" and at the same
time monitoring the activities of Knud Rasmussen and Donald Macmillan. In his opinion, "this would be an economical way of having the
Janes murder investigated, and necessary action taken ... the only expense being their passage and board with the H. B. Company."[19] In the
end, however, only one police officer would be sent. Sergeant A.H. Joy,
who had accompanied Inspector Phillips for the inquests at the Belcher Islands the year before, was promoted to staff-sergeant and assigned to take
charge of the investigation.

Alfred Herbert Joy was born near Bedford in England in June 1887. He
left school at the age of twelve to work as a farm labourer, first in England and later on the Canadian Prairies. After he joined the North West
Mounted Police in 1909, his rise through the ranks was short of
meteoric. He was promoted to the rank of corporal in 1912, sergeant in

RCMP Commissioner A. Bowen Perry, 1900–1922. RCMP Collection.
NAC – PA 210276.

1916, staff-sergeant in 1921, and eventually to inspector in 1927. RCMP
historian Harwood Steele described him as "tall, broad-shouldered, and
strong." His "weather-beaten face was full of quiet determination, his
deep-set eyes were those of one who sees and travels far."[20] Others
referred to his "gift for making friends and commanding the respect" of
his fellow officers.[21] Inuit elders remembered "Sarjan" for his physical
strength and being a "good man."[22] In Canadian history books, he
would be lionized for his long and death-defying sled patrols in the high
Arctic.

Prior to Joy's departure Commissioner Perry apparently issued two sets
of instructions on the conduct of the inquiry. Those published in the 1922
RCMP annual report were of a general nature, directing Joy to "make a
thorough inquiry" into the alleged murder of Robert Janes and to "take
such steps as are required to bring the guilty parties to justice."[23] More

specific instructions were given in a letter from the commissioner, defining
the process and procedures:

I wish you to make a thorough investigation of this case and acting on the information you obtain, take any action which may appear advisable. It will be necessary
for you to first prove that a murder has actually taken place and to do this, in your
capacity as a Coroner, you will have to have the body exhumed and an examination
made of the same, in an endeavour to produce evidence showing the cause of
death; then if you can obtain enough men to form a Jury you will hold a Coroner's
inquest and should the evidence disclosed, at same warrant it, in your capacity as a
Justice of the Peace, you will arrange for the laying of the "Information and Complaint" against the alleged murderer. After issuing a Warrant to Apprehend, you
will have him arrested and a preliminary enquiry held by yourself, as a Justice of
the Peace, and should the evidence against the accused prove sufficient, you will of
course commit him for trial.[24]

To fulfil his obligations, Joy was given the authority to act as justice of the
peace (times two), postmaster, coroner, and customs officer. Along with
personal effects and copies to file of the evidence collected at headquarters, he took reference books on statutes, criminal law, and coroner's
procedures, as well as a copy of the Northwest Territories Act and its
amendments. He also took an ample supply of paper, ink, pens, and
a typewriter and ribbon.[25] Staff-Sergeant Joy was – in the true sense – a
one-man show.

The Hudson's Bay Company's new steamship *Baychimo* was reportedly
an impressive sight, representing a "grand image" to the Inuit and the
small trading companies who dared think they could compete. Aside
from the ship's captain, officers, and crew, most on board were "Bay men"
moving to their next posting. On this trip the notable exceptions were HBC
Superintendent Ralph Parsons and Staff-Sergeant Joy. There were actually
two Parsons aboard. Ralph's younger brother, Wilfred, would be in charge
of the new post at Pond Inlet, assisted by veteran trader Gaston Herodier
and an interpreter by the name of Jimmy Ford.[26]

About 150 miles from Pond Inlet the *Baychimo* ran into severe weather as
the captain searched in vain for the entrance to Eclipse Sound. When the
fog thickened, the ship anchored, and a scouting party was sent ashore in
hopes of establishing their location. Much to their surprise, they discovered
supplies piled on the banks and realized they had unknowingly entered
Albert Harbour. Ralph Parsons, with a party of ship's officers and Staff-
Sergeant Joy, landed at Igarjuaq to look for an Inuk to guide them into the
sound. He returned shortly with two boats full of natives eager to examine
the strange ship. Some were wearing seal clothing, others dirty, torn cloth
garments. Two wore British postal uniforms. After a meal of tea and corn-

Staff-Sergeant Alfred Herbert Joy of the Royal Canadian Mounted
Police, 1924. MacGregor Collection.

beef sandwiches, the Inuit took out their pipes, whereupon Parsons was
quick to offer a fresh supply of tobacco. Wilfred Caron, now employed by
AGES, joined the party on board and regaled the Bay men with stories of
"native treachery" and how if "not given square deals, they shoot to kill."

After downing a few drinks, Caron sat down with Joy to discuss the
Janes case. He told the police officer that Nuqallaq had moved to the
Igloolik area for the winter and had talked about eventually settling in the
vicinity of Repulse Bay. He also reported that Munn had taken Janes' furs
and belongings south to give to his family and that they contained a very
important journal that incriminated the dead man. In the first of what
would be a continual stream of memos to his "Officer Commanding,"[27] Joy
recorded his conversation with Caron and set out his strategy. He stated

that his first task after locating the body would be to track down Nuqallaq and arrest him, as if there were no question of his guilt. "If he does not return here before the beginning of February," Joy stated, "I shall make an effort to follow him and effect his arrest, providing I can get the necessary native assistance. I shall first recover Janes' body at Cape Crawford, and, as far as I can understand from Caron, it is hardly possible for me to get out there this fall by open water. This being the case, I shall have to leave this trip until February or later when the ice in Admiralty Inlet is set fast, and proceed with the arrest of Nookadlah [sic] on first available opportunity afterwards."

For an officer who had just stepped off the boat, these were ambitious plans. He had much to learn about high Arctic geography, as evident in his remark that it should be easy to locate the body at Cape Crauford, since there were "no other graves around the spot." Joy, however, learned quickly and set out on his mission with unusual determination and wisdom that would earn him the highest respect among his peers. His lengthy memos and crime reports left a clear map of his progress, his thoughts, and his frustrations.

The arrival of the lone police officer and the Hudson's Bay Company men was viewed much differently by the Inuit at Igarjuaq, as illustrated in a story that was passed down to the next generation:

Noah Piugaattuk – Igloolik, 16 January 1989

Those at Igarjuaq feared that some white people might take revenge ... While the Inuit were sleeping early in the morning, a ship dropped anchor out of sight of the community. They then took a boat and rowed in, making sure that they did not make any sound. As a matter of fact the oar locks were cushioned so as not to make any sound. No doubt they were trying to take [the Inuit] by surprise as they slept and they were well prepared. That was the time when there were anxious moments.

They were after the Inuit. My father-in-law Uirngut was an early riser. When he woke up in the morning ... early as usual, he did not have his wife with him so he went outdoors while everyone else slept. [It was] just as the daylight had started to show. He saw a boat just about to land. The only houses in this place were the trading post and the warehouse. The one that was occupied was furthest from the beach.

When [Uirngut] saw them, he saw that they were dressed differently with head gear. They were armed so he started to run towards the house of the one that he shared a wife with. They were still sleeping by then. He hurried over and got in after knocking on the door with much force. Quvviuginnaq [Caron] got into his underwear and opened the door quickly. He told him about the boat that by this time [was] on the beach close to the warehouse. They had checked the place and finding nothing, they had started for the house by the time he [Caron] got to the door. They were armed and ready. Quvviuginnaq yelled at them and the aggressors immediately stopped.

He then stomped on the floor and said some harsh words and making a motion with his arms at the same time. The aggressors stopped to listen. The aggressors stopped in their tracks and he invited them over. They started to walk up to the house and looked more relaxed. [Caron] had protected the Inuit from these aggressors. They had tried to surprise them. My father-in-law saved them all [by warning Caron].[28]

This portrayal of events may seem overly dramatic, but Inuit fear of the *qallunaat* was deep and difficult to put into words. For those living in North Baffin, it may have been even more intense because of the reported massacre by whalers thirty years earlier.

Once a site for the new trading post had been selected on the long beach between Igarjuaq and the Salmon River, everyone including the Inuit worked feverishly to unload the supplies. Construction of the buildings was made easy with the use of pre-assembled sections, but even then, the speed at which they were erected was phenomenal. Two hundred tons of cargo were unloaded and two houses completed, all in less than two days. At 6 p.m. on the first day of September, Gaston Herodier, Wilfred Parsons, and Staff-Sergeant Joy climbed into the company's motor boat and set off for their new home. After sending off two rockets and a "few shrill whistles" to announce its departure, the *Baychimo* headed out of the sound, bound for Pangnirtung.[29]

For the next twelve months Joy would be quartered at the HBC manager's house and totally dependent upon his cooperation for use of the company's interpreter, guides, dogs, and motor boat. Jimmy (Tooktosins) Ford, an Inuk of mixed blood from Labrador, would translate at the inquest and preliminary inquiry, as well as for numerous statutory declarations. On several occasions Joy had tried unsuccessfully to obtain the services of Takijualuk (Tom Coonoon), known to be the best interpreter in the area. Yet each time he was asked, Tom always sent word that he was too busy working. While it was understandable that he would be reluctant to assist anyone living with the competition, his long-time association with Nuqallaq was more likely behind his apparent unwillingness to help the police.

At first Joy had difficulty tracking down anyone who had witnessed Janes' death. In an interview with Qumangaapik (Koomanapik), he finally learned the names of those who had been present at the hunting camp and their possible whereabouts. With the exception of Uuttukuttuk and Ululijarnaat, they were all at Arctic Bay or Igloolik. Joy realized that the Inuit were avoiding him, but he was careful not pressure them for information.[30] In late September, he made an attempt to reach Cape Crauford in the HBC

Hudson's Bay Company post at Pond Inlet, 1922. The inquest into the death of Robert Janes was held in the manager's house on the right. W.H. Grant Collection. NAC – PA 185920.

motor launch, accompanied by Caron and several Inuit. When a sudden storm hit at Low Point on Navy Board Inlet, the engine failed and they began to drift aimlessly in the blinding snow. Fortunately, the boat drifted into Milne Inlet and the party made their way back by foot to the trading post.[31]

Another month passed before Joy finally met his first witness, Ululijarnaat, who was known to the police as Oorooreungnak, or Roori for short. Because of Roori's difficulty in understanding Jimmy Ford's dialect, Joy was forced to use an intermediary, thus preventing him from taking an official declaration. Roori's initial story was consistent with his later statements – with one major exception. The good-natured Inuk failed to mention that he had helped Nuqallaq by enticing Janes to step outside of his igloo so he could be shot.[32]

On his overland trip to locate Janes' body, Joy hired Ululijarnaat, Urulu, and Tuurngaq as dog drivers and guides. With three *qamutiit* and thirty-five dogs, they left Eclipse Sound in early December, long after the sun had disappeared from the horizon. It would take two weeks to reach Admiralty Inlet and another five days to locate the canvas-covered box set high on a ledge on the west bank. The body was already decomposing but still "fully dressed, the upper part in heavy red woollen underwear, which was covered by an ordinary cloth vest" and with caribou pants over the leggings. Deer-skin mitts still covered the hands. By observing the wounds, it was obvious to Joy that they were not self-inflicted or accidental and that Janes had been dressed in his vest and pants at the time of the shooting. The party transported the box over to the east side of the inlet, where it was cached to await their return journey. Then Joy with his three guides continued southward in search of witnesses.[33]

At Arctic Bay they found seven large sod huts that provided living quarters for forty-seven people. Joy was impressed by the cleanliness of the camp and apparent good health of the Inuit. Here he learned that Urulu, Ivalu, Jock, and his son Panikpak had made the wooden box for Janes' body and moved it from its original location to the west side of the inlet. Joy was told that this was a "Christian act." Three witnesses to the shooting and several others agreed to return with the police officer so that their statements could be translated by an interpreter and properly recorded. Their party now included seven *qamutiit* and a full complement of dogs – an impressive sight. Joy arrived back to Pond Inlet on 21 January, six weeks after his departure.[34]

Some stories about the trip do not appear in official police reports, such as how Ululijarnaat saved Joy's life from an attacking polar bear when the police officer's rifle jammed. Or how Joy, unaware of Roori's involvement in the crime, had insisted that Janes' body be lashed to the Inuk's *qamutiik* and could not understand why he frequently dismounted to complain that the dead man's spirit was trying to ride with him.[35] On their return the frozen body was stored in the HBC warehouse – laid out, as it were – in the motor launch.

As coroner, Joy first performed an autopsy to establish the cause of death, then asked the three resident fur traders, Wilfred Parsons, Gaston Herodier, and Wilfred Caron, to sit on a jury for the inquest. The proceedings were held in the HBC living quarters over a period of almost three weeks, from 23 January to 11 February to determine whether the deceased had met his death through natural causes, accident, or "from culpable conduct of others."[36] Eight Inuit were called to tell their stories. The first two, Tuurngaq and Urulu, had been with Joy when the body was located and were required to verify its identity Otherwise, those testifying were all at the camp at the time of the shooting.

In the following statements, it is important to consider where the "Inuit story" ended and the questioning began. Compared to Munn's informal session with the Inuit hunters, this hearing was far more solemn and professional – more like an inquisition. Towards the end of each witness's testimony, the coroner apparently asked whether they personally heard Janes make threats to kill their dogs. The operative word was "heard" as opposed to "were told."

Ululijarnaat's story was similar to his earlier statement, except that this time he explained how he had enticed Janes out of his igloo. He reportedly said that he did so at Nuqallaq's request but claimed that he did not know for what purpose, or so it appeared on the recorded testimony.[37] Since we know from other accounts that Ululijarnaat was a key figure in the planning of Janes' death, it is inconceivable that he would not know why Janes had to be brought out of the igloo before he could be shot. There was either a problem of translation here or possibly a little editorial licence by the

---

INQUEST INTO THE DEATH OF ROBERT JANES

23 JANUARY – 11 FEBRUARY 1922

POND INLET

CORONER – Staff-Sergeant A.H. Joy

JURY – Wilfred C. Parsons (Hudson's Bay Company Manager)
          Gaston Herodier   (Hudson's Bay Company, Assistant Manager)
          Wilfred Caron   (Manager/Agent for the AGES trading post)

INTERPRETER – Jimmy *Tooktosins* Ford

CALLED TO GIVE EVIDENCE:

23 January	– Toonga	(*Tuurngaq*)
23 January	– Ooroloo	(*Urulu*)
23 January	– Oorooreungnak	(*Ululijarnaat*)
30 January	– Munne	(*Maniq*)
30 January	– Kahinahl	(*Qaunaq*)
31 January	– Sinnikah	(*Siniqqaq*)
9 February	– Ootookito	(*Uuttukuttuk*)
10 February	– Kutchuk	(*Kassak*)

UNANIMOUS VERDICT

"... that Noo-kud-lah, alias Ki-wat-soo, Eskimo, did feloniously and of his malice aforethought kill and murder the said Robert Janes by shooting him through the body and head with a rifle, from which he instantly died.

And so do further say that Oo-roo-re-ung-nak, Eskimo, and Ah-tee-tah, Eskimo, did feloniously and of their malice aforethought aid and abet the said Noo-kud-lah alias Ki-wat-soo in committing the said felonious act."

(RG 18/3281/1920-HQ-681-G-4 (Supp A)

Participants at the inquest into the death of Robert Janes.

coroner, who was likely still thankful for the Inuk having saved his life on the trip home. Although Joy now realized the nature of Ululijarnaat's participation, he reported that he still thought it might be minor and let him return to his camp. The Inuk had been absent from his family for more than six weeks and feared that his wife and children would be short of food and seal oil.[38]

Maniq was the next to testify, stating that Janes had seemed friendly the first day, but soon began to demand furs for debts he claimed were owed to him. He went on to explain how the trader had taken foxes from Iqipiriaq, saying that "he had advanced him a boat the previous year for which he did not pay enough, and the foxes he had just taken would balance the account." Maniq claimed they were all frightened that Janes would kill them and that he was personally glad that the man was dead. His testimony clearly implicated Aatitaaq, whom he claimed had pushed Janes to the ground after the second shot had only wounded him. Maniq was one of six who gave Nuqallaq a fox skin for killing Janes.[39]

Qaunaq was up next and reiterated how everyone was afraid of Janes. He stated that he did not personally hear the trader threaten to kill the Inuit or their dogs, but had been told by others. This was an apparent contradiction to his statement made to Munn a year earlier, in which he claimed that he had heard Janes threaten to kill the Inuit if they did not give him their foxes. He also stated that he was happy Janes had been killed and that he too had given Nuqallaq a fox skin.[40] After his testimony Qaunaq left for Igloolik but fell ill at a place called Qurluqtuq (Koulooktoo). He died there two weeks later.[41]

Siniqqaq repeated a similar story about how Janes became "mad," how much they all feared him, and how relieved he had been when Janes was killed. The use of the word "mad" here and on other occasions is never defined as to whether it meant mad as in angry, or mad as insane. Like the other witnesses, Siniqqaq admitted that he had not heard Janes say that he would kill their dogs.[42]

Although the intent of this line of questioning was not yet clear, the reason so many did not "hear" Janes make the threats seemed obvious. As explained by several witnesses, when Janes was angry he spoke in English. Thus only Nuqallaq, Uuttukuttuk, and perhaps Miqutui would have actually "heard" him threaten to kill the dogs. Apparently Joy did not have sufficient evidence at this time to consider the possibility. With regards to the fox skins given to Nuqallaq, Joy would eventually realize that this was token appreciation. The sum total of the gifts – six fox skins and one bear – was hardly enough to suggest "material benefit" as a motive for killing Janes.

Janes' former guide seemed to offer substantial evidence that the fur trader might not have been of sound mind. Uuttukuttuk explained how they had only one dog team and little to feed them and about meeting Kaukuarjuk, who travelled with them for two days and slept in their igloo. Otherwise, they did not see a soul until they arrived at Cape Crauford. He also reiterated how on several occasions Janes had threatened to kill Inuit dogs. At the hunting camp, Uuttukuttuk was certain that Janes "was going to shoot the dogs because the natives would not sell him any dogs or foxes." The Inuk also recounted how Ululijarnaat had come into their igloo and asked Janes to go outside because there were Inuit who had some furs for him, and how, after the trader left, Ululijarnaat had told him "he ... is going to be killed now."[43]

Uuttukuttuk also described how he had searched Janes' pockets after the shooting and found only four keys and a "small bag containing two coins and a medal," noting that the pocket knife was missing because Nuqallaq had given it to Ululijarnaat. He went on to explain how he had helped Nuqallaq, Aatitaaq, and Ululijarnaat wrap the body in fur blankets, place it on a *qamutiik*, and take it to the mainland shore. With their help, he had brought the deceased's furs and belongings back to Eclipse Sound and handed them over to Munn's agent – except, he pointed out, for the tobacco and half the cartridges which Nuqallaq had shared with Aatitaaq and his brother Ijjangiaq. While much of his testimony was a narration of what had happened, he left no doubt about Janes' abusive character and the nature of his repeated threats:

Uuttukuttuk – Pond Inlet, 9 February 1922

Janes told me before we left his place for Arctic Bay, that he was going to borrow some dogs from the natives on Admiralty Inlet, and pay for them when the ship came up. If they would not let him have any, he would shoot their dogs ... Janes was unable to get anybody besides me to travel to Aivilik [Repulse Bay] with him. I did not want to go at first, but after he told me he was going to shoot the dogs, I agreed to go with him ...

When Janes told me at Cape Crawford he was going to shoot the Eskimo when they went to his place on Eclipse Sound, I told him that if he shot [at] the Eskimo first, they would shoot him. He replied "he did not care, he was getting old and he would be hungry if the ship did not come up for him."[44]

Yet the crime report summarizing the proceedings and statements at the inquest made no mention of Janes' repeated threats, only that Uuttukuttuk was "the only witness stating that he, personally, heard Janes say he would shoot the natives and their dogs when they went to his place on Eclipse Sound"(underlining was Joy's) but that he had not told anyone else about the threats until after the shooting.[45]

Kassak was the last to testify and seemed to present clear-cut evidence against Nuqallaq. Since he had been living in the same snow house as the suspect and his wife, his story carried a great deal of weight. Moreover, he claimed that when he talked to Janes, the trader did not get angry when told that he did not have any foxes to pay him.

Kassak – Pond Inlet, 10 February 1922

During the evening after the second day we went hunting, Noo-kud-lah told me he had better shoot Janes before he killed somebody. Noo-kud-lah told me he was afraid he would kill the people. When he told me this there was only myself, Noo-kud-lah and Noo-kud-lah's wife in the igloo. I did not tell anybody what Noo-ku-lah had told me about shooting Janes. I am sure of that. I did not hear any of the other Eskimo say, up to this time, that they were afraid of Janes ...

[On the third day] I did not hear anybody say that day that Janes was going to be killed that night ... somebody, I don't know who, sent for me to go to Noo-kud-lah's igloo, and when I got there Noo-kud-lah's wife was crying. She did not speak to me nor I to her. I thought her husband had made her cry. I had not been in the igloo long when I heard a gun shot. I did not go out. I did not think anything about it, any more than it might be somebody's rifle jammed. Not long after, I heard a second report. I did not go out then to see what was happening. I heard the people talking outside. Then Noo-kud-lah's wife said to me, "Perhaps Janes is killed now" ... It was then that I first learned definitely that Janes was going to be killed. I did not go out to see the body, because I was too much afraid. Noo-kud-lah came in soon after this and told us he had killed Janes, then left the igloo immediately. I became very much afraid after this because I thought the white men would come and kill us all.[46]

Kassak's statements clearly supported Joy's suspicions that Nuqallaq had manipulated the Inuit fears. As it happened, however, this witness's story would change considerably when he was asked later to give evidence in front of the accused.

The crime report summarizing the findings of the inquest indicated that Joy had discounted the repeated threats to kill the dogs and was more interested in the possibility that Nuqallaq had exaggerated or lied about what Janes said.[47] Yet there was no evidence that he was a liar and schemer or, aside from fur-trader gossip, that he had any reason to want Janes dead. On the other hand, if Joy could prove that Nuqallaq had lied to incite fear, then any suggestion that there was consensual agreement to kill Janes would be irrelevant. It should be noted that under Canadian law in 1922, a person was *not* "presumed innocent until proven guilty."[48] Thus, the burden was on Nuqallaq to prove that he was innocent. According to Newcombe's opinion concerning the Belcher Islands case, all that was required to assure a conviction was to show a motive of revenge or material benefit. At this point it was still too early to see where Joy was leading, but his reports suggest he may have had certain preconceived ideas, either from Munn's agents or perhaps Alfred Tremblay. One thing was certain: Joy's investigation would be thorough and well documented.

On 11 February 1922, the coroner's jury reportedly deliberated for twenty minutes, then returned with a unanimous verdict,

that Noo-kud-lah, alias Ki-wat-soo, Eskimo, did feloniously and of his malice aforethought kill and murder the said Robert Janes by shooting him through the body and head with a rifle, from which he instantly died. And so do further say that Oo-roo-re-ung-nak, Eskimo, and Ah-tee-tah, Eskimo, did feloniously and of their malice aforethought aid and abet the said Noo-kud-lah alias Ki-wat-soo in committing the said felonious act.[49]

At least that was the wording of the official statement which each juror dutifully signed.[50] How this might be translated into Inuktitut remains a mystery.

That same day Joy prepared warrants for the arrest of the three men. This time, however, the officer received no help from the Hudson's Bay Company in rounding up his suspects. Thus his earlier idea of "tracking down" Nuqallaq was no longer an option. An entry in the HBC journal sums up the traders' views rather succinctly: "Wish the thing was finished as we are absolutely sick of it."[51] Six weeks later, on a warm day in March, Janes' body was carried on a *qamutiik* to a site on the shore and finally laid to rest about a mile or so northwest of the trading post. Joy, Parsons, Herodier, the interpreter Jimmy Ford, and two Inuuk attended the "funeral."[52] Caron, who so disliked the man, was notably absent.

To everyone who visited the trading post, Joy let it be known that he wanted the three suspects to come to Pond Inlet so he could question them – which seemed a little misleading since he already had issued warrants for their arrest. In the interim he took additional statements from witnesses who arrived at the post.[53] Joy also summarized the information he had obtained from Caron over the winter, noting that his account seemed consistent with Inuit stories, particularly with regard to Janes' attack on Umik and raids on the government supply caches at Albert Harbour and Beechey Island.[54] When Naqitarvik (Nahkahdagbe) explained how much Janes had promised him for his furs, Joy suggested in his report that the amount owed the Inuk should be estimated and sent to the executors of his estate with a request for payment.[55]

In April, Takijualuk reported that a particularly infectious form of fatal dog disease had spread throughout North Baffin, suggesting that Nuqallaq might not have been able to travel to Pond Inlet as was his usual custom in the spring.[56] In hopes of facilitating matters, Joy sent Anguiliannuk (Angnoyleanoo) with food and dogs to Igloolik, along with a request for Nuqallaq to come to the Hudson's Bay Company post. Qamaniq, Nuqallaq's father-in-law, agreed to add three more dogs as further incentive.[57]

Almost three months had passed since the inquest, and none of the suspects had responded to Joy's call. While waiting, he went to Tulukkaat to take an inventory at Janes' former post. The main building, which doubled as living quarters and storehouse, was crudely built and in Joy's estimation contained nothing of any value. From the state of the equipment and interior, he concluded that "nothing but seal oil was used for fuel and light for

Grave of Robert S. Janes on the shores of Eclipse Sound, 1923. The inscription reads, "In the Memory of R S Janes of Newfoundland – Died at Cape Crawford, March 1920." NWT Archives M 79–006–0005.

some time." There were also two abandoned Inuit houses in poor repair and "useless to dismantle." As far as he was concerned, the buildings and contents were worthless.[58]

On 30 May, Ululijarnaat arrived at the HBC trading post with his family. To his astonishment, he was placed under "open arrest" and told not leave. Three days later, Ijjangiaq arrived and reported that his brother Aatitaaq was unlikely to come to the post. Appealing to an Inuk's sense of honour, Joy responded by sending him back with provisions for his brother's travel, including sixteen pounds of flour, fifteen pounds of biscuits, two pounds of sugar, one and a half pints of molasses, and a half-pound of tea. When Aatitaaq finally arrived in mid-June, he reported that he could not stay because he had left his family at Navy Board Inlet. Believing him to be a "trickster," Joy sent another Inuk to collect his family and belongings.[59]

On 3 July, Nuqallaq finally arrived with his wife, Ataguttiaq, and his son Kijuapik, about fifteen years of age.[60] He explained that he had been delayed because he came upon Anguiliannuk who had fallen ill at Qurluqtuq (Koolooktoo)* and nearly died. Although he knew his friend had been sent to summon him, he decided it was only proper to accompany the sick man back to Igloolik before returning to Pond Inlet. Joy delayed making an arrest while he again tried to get Takijualuk to act as the interpreter, this time

---

* Qurluqtuq was the same location where Qaunnaq had died only months earlier.

at Nuqallaq's request. Once again he was unsuccessful. A week later Joy finally executed the warrant for Nuqallaq's arrest. With the help of the Hudson's Bay Company interpreter, Joy tried to make him understand the seriousness of the charges laid against him, but he remained silent, refusing to comment.[61]

At Button Point, or Sannirut, as it was called in Inuktitut, Staff-Sergeant Joy as justice of the peace opened the preliminary hearings into the murder of Robert Janes on 10 July 1922. As before, Jimmy Ford would be the interpreter. Joy gave no reason for conducting the inquiry at the AGES post rather than at the HBC manager's house, but considering the journal comment at the time of the inquest, it is possible that Parsons simply refused to allow further use of his quarters for formal hearings and the like. Accessible only by water, the tiny post at Sannirut was relatively isolated and thus was unlikely to attract curious onlookers who might have come to trade at the HBC post.

The session lasted a little over four and a half days, but stretched over a ten day period as they tried to locate Uuttukuttuk, who was once again reluctant to testify. This time eight witnesses were questioned, as were the three accused. Eight additional "statutory declarations" were received "in absentia." Joy explained the procedure. The hearings would be conducted with only the accuseds and the testifying witness present while the evidence for the prosecution was presented, but when hearing the evidence for the defence, all the witnesses, both for prosecution and defence, would be present. According to Joy, this was done "to avoid the tendency of the Eskimo, through their deficient memory of details, to repeat what the former witness has said, and to get each witnes' [sic] own independent testimony."[62] Apart from the reference to "deficient memory of details" – which was highly unlikely – the move to treat the witnesses for the prosecution differently was only one of the many anomalies that would arise in the quest for Arctic justice.

Kassak, Ataguttaaluk, Siniqqaq, Ijjangiaq, Maniq, and Uuttukuttuk were all called upon to give evidence for the prosecution. Previously recorded statements by Kaukuarjuk, Nutarariaq, Ivalu, and Kunuk were also submitted at this time. Out of apparent concern for his brother, Ijjangiaq contradicted his earlier testimony that described how Aatitaaq had pushed Janes to the ground after he was wounded. Now he claimed that he had only seen him push the wounded trader "along" and away from Nuqallaq.[63] There were other inconsistencies that suggested that some of the Inuit testifying at the inquest might have tried to give answers to please the policeman but changed their stories when asked to testify in front of the accused.

The witnesses were each asked to give their name, their marital status, where they came from, how they came to be at the camp near Cape Crauford, and who else was there. Then they were asked to tell what had happened in the days leading up to Janes' death. At the end of each testimony,

AGES post at Button Point (Sannirut) on Bylot Island, site of the preliminary hearings into the alleged murder of Robert Janes. Main building is barely visible at centre left. W.H. Grant Collection. NAC – PA 212519.

a number of short sentences appear that seem to be responses to specific questions, such as in the final portion of Ijjangiaq's testimony:

Ijjangiaq – Sannirut, 11 July 1922

It was getting a little dark at the time. I could easily distinguish Noo-kud-lah, Oo-roo-re-ung-nak and Ahteetah, and Mikootooee and Janes, because I was standing right amongst them.

I gave Noo-kud-lah a piece of a bear skin for shooting Janes. I was glad to see Janes killed, that is why I gave Noo-kud-lah the bear skin.

I was scared of Janes, that is why I was glad to see him dead.

I said to Noo-kud-lah on one occasion that he had better kill Janes himself, because Janes had been mad with him lots of times. I do not remember what day it was.

I never heard anybody else say this to Noo-kud-lah.[64]

As at the inquest, all were asked whether they personally heard Janes threaten to kill the dogs or the people. Some said they heard about the threats from Nuqallaq, but others named Iqaqsaq, Aatitaaq, Kunuk, or their wives as the source of their information. Ijjangiaq claimed that it was Uuttukuttuk who told him "that Janes was going to shoot the people and take their dogs."[65] Several hunters stated that while Janes spoke a little Inuktitut, they found it hard to understand – an observation that appears nowhere in Joy's summary report of the hearings.

It appeared that the witnesses were also asked questions about when it had been decided that Janes should be killed, where the actual planning took place, and by whom. Everyone seemed to agree that the first discussion took place after the trader's angry outburst at finding Kunuk had no furs. There was less urgency when Janes quietened down, but they wanted to be certain that he did not have access to a gun or knives, lest he try to kill one of them while they were sleeping. Most agreed that the final decision to kill Janes occurred when the hunters met the two women out on the ice:

Ataguttaaluk – Sannirut, 10 July 1922

When we were part way between the hunting grounds and the village, on our way home, we met Koon-noon's wife and Noo-kud-lah's wife. They had run away from the village because they were scared of Janes. They said he had got mad again, but they did not say who with. There were quite a few Eskimo talking together when we met the two women. I remember Noo-kud-lah, myself, Munne and Nootah-gayook. Noo-kud-lah said then he would just as soon kill Janes, because he had been mad so many times with him. When Noo-kud-lah said this, somebody said never mind if you do kill him, I think we all said that ...

A little while after we returned to the village, I went and stood near the door of Kahlnahl's igloo, and as I was going there I saw Munne, Oo-roo-re-ung-nak and Noo-kud-lah standing there. Noo-kud-lah then said to me, "I am all ready to kill Janes now," and I replied "all right go ahead and kill him."[66]

At the end of his testimony, Nuqallaq asked Ataguttaaluk whether "on one occasion when Janes was mad at Cape Crawford, did you not say you could have shot Janes then if you had a gun?" He replied "Yes, I did say it."[67] Nuqallaq asked similar questions of other witnesses, showing that others had also been willing to kill Janes and that he was not alone in wanting him dead.

The same format was followed with each testimony, with the three prisoners asked at the conclusion if they wished to question the witness. With the exception of an occasional query from Aatitaaq, it was Nuqallaq who repeatedly asked for clarification on certain points. Sometimes he revealed an error or inconsistency in a witness's statement, but usually he was simply adding new information or clarification. In fact, his questions reflected a surprising degree of intelligence and insight for an Inuk with no formal education. This was particularly evident in his questioning of Kassak. Unlike the others, Kassak maintained that he was not afraid of Janes

PRELIMINARY INQUIRY
10 – 20 JULY 1922
AGAINST
NOO-KUD-LAH ALIAS KI-WAT-SOO
OO-ROO-RE-UNG-NAK AND AH-TEE-TAH
CHARGED WITH THE MURDER OF ROBERT JANES AT CAPE CRAUFORD
15 MARCH 1920
S/SGT A. H. JOY, JUSTICE OF THE PEACE, PRESIDING

WITNESSES FOR THE PROSECUTION
EACH WITNESS EXAMINED INDIVIDUALLY BEFORE THE ACCUSED

10 July	Kutchuk	(*Kassak*)	Pond Inlet
10 July	Ahtootahloo	(*Ataguttaaluk*)	Arctic Bay
10 July	Sinnikah	(*Siniqqaq*)	Arctic Bay
11 July	Edineyah	(*Ijjangiaq*)	Arctic Bay
11 July	Munne	(*Maniq*)	Arctic Bay
18 July	Ootookito	(*Uuttukuttuk*)	Pond Inlet

STATUTORY DECLARATIONS FOR THE PROSECUTION
(READ BEFORE THE ACCUSED)

18 July	Kowkwatsoo	(*Kaukuarjuk*)	Pond Inlet
18 July	Nootakgagayuk	(*Nutarariaq*)	Pond Inlet
18 July	Koonnoon	(*Kunuk*)	Arctic Bay
18 July	Ivahlung	(*Ivalu*)	Arctic Bay

STATEMENTS BY THE ACCUSED
WITH STATUTORY WARNING BUT WITHOUT EXAMINATION
(ALL WITNESSES PRESENT)

19 July	Nookudlah	(*Nuqallaq*)	Pond Inlet /Igloolik
19 July	Oorooreungnak	(*Ululijamaat*)	Pond Inlet
19 July	Ahteetah	(*Aatitaaq*)	Arctic Bay

STATUTORY DECLARATIONS FOR THE DEFENCE
(READ BEFORE THE ACCUSED)

19 July	Amooahlik	(*Amarualik*)	Arctic Bay
19 July	Penneloo	(*Paniluk*)	Pond Inlet
19 July	Kamanuk	(*Qamaniq*)	Pond Inlet
19 July	Munoo	(*Manu*)	Pond Inlet

WITNESSES FOR THE DEFENCE

20 July	Ahtooteuk	(*Ataguttiaq*) Pond Inlet
20 July	Wilfred Clement Caron	L'Islet, Quebec

Witnesses and depositions at the Preliminary Inquiry.

and that he had refused to take part in any discussion about him. Nuqal-laq's questions seemed to recast Kassak's disinterest into insensitivity.

Nuqallaq's Questions and Kassak's Answers – Sannirut, 10 July 1922

Q. Did you not know the dogs was [sic] going to be killed by Janes?
A. Yes.
Q. Were you not with us when we met the women on the ice?
A. Yes.
Q. Are you sure all the Eskimo at Cape Crawford were scared of Janes?
A. Yes.[68]

With the notable exception of Kassak, most Inuit said they were glad that Janes was dead, and several retold their story about giving Nuqallaq fox skins or other furs in appreciation.

After Kassak, Ataguttaaluk, Siniqqaq, Ijjangiaq, and Maniq had finished testifying, the court was adjourned for five days, until such time Uuttukut-tuk could be found. In the end, his testimony differed little from that given at the inquest, except for adding further evidence that Janes was irrational and making all sorts of threats after his argument with Kunuk:

Uuttukuttuk – Sannirut, 18 July 1922

[Janes] did not speak to me when I first went in but some time afterwards he said to me, "I was talking today to the fellows who have debt with me. I wanted some foxes from Koon-noon. I heard from Amooahlik some time ago that Koon-noon had a bag of foxes. If I cannot get foxes, I want dogs. I almost shot a dog today and a man afterwards, any man that had the most dogs. If I do not get foxes or dogs, I am going to shoot the men when they come to my place at Patricia River. I will get behind the barrels and shoot them when they are coming in." Janes did not tell me what man nor whose dogs he was going to shoot.

I told Janes then that if he was going to shoot the people I was afraid of him. He told me not to be frightened because he would not touch me, then he said if I got frightened and ran away from him, he would come down to Pond Inlet afterwards and shoot the people.[69]

Uuttukuttuk also stated that Nuqallaq had asked him to remain with Janes the day he was killed, out of concern that "if there were no men at home, he was afraid Janes might get a gun and shoot some of the women."[70]

During the cross-examination Nuqallaq brought out further points that emphasized Uuttukuttuuk's concern about Janes' behaviour and his will-ingness to take any measure to protect the families at Cape Crauford. As before, Nuqallaq's questions were worded in such a way that, directly or indirectly, they seemed to add important new information.

Nuqallaq's Questions and Uuttukuttuk's Answers – Sannirut, 18 July 1922

Q. When you came to my igloo and I told you to watch Janes and see that he didn't take anything with which to kill the people. Did you not say that if Janes took anything to kill the people you would kill him yourself?

A. Yes I did.

Q. Did you not say if you had known Kowkwatsoo was scared to come back to the camp to sleep, you would have killed Janes yourself?

A. Yes, I said it after Janes was dead.

Q. Did you not take out Janes' gun on purpose so that he couldn't get it if he got vexed?

A. Yes I did. I took out Janes' gun because I knew he was going to ask for foxes that day and he would look for his gun to frighted [sic] the people.

Q. Did Janes not get mad with you once on the journey to Cape Crawford?

A. Yes; he got a little mad once when the dogs took us ashore, and he told me that I didn't know the way and to beat the dogs with the whip.

Q. Did you not get mad with Mikootooee when he told Janes lies about the rough road to Igloolik?

A. Yes I did, after Janes was dead.

Q. Did I not tell you two days before Janes was killed that I was going to kill him?

A. I do not remember it.[71]

The last question made no sense, unless Nuqallaq was clever enough to insert a trick question. More likely it was a problem of translation. Given the line of questioning, it would seem more reasonable for Nuqallaq to ask, "When did I tell you I was going to kill Janes"? On Joy's own re-examination, Uuttukuttuk explained that Miqutui admitted on the second day he was at Cape Crauford "that he had told Janes the road to Aivillik was worse than it was. He told me the road was not too bad at all."[72]

Joy's summary of Uuttukuttuk's testimony seemed biased, particularly when he cited only short, selected references to support his contention that the threats made by the white fur trader were exaggerated and that Nuqallaq seemed to be the source of these of stories. While claiming that Uuttukuttuk "did not tell any of the Eskimo what Janes had told him about shooting the people until after he was dead,"[73] Joy ignored the fact that the Inuk had corrected himself, and said, "I do not remember telling any-body."[74] In fact, one could argue that Uuttukuttuk's story only confirmed that Nuqallaq had neither exaggerated nor lied about Janes' threats.

If Nuqallaq had thoughts of revenge, it was not part of his plans prior to
his arrival at Cape Crauford. In a statutory declaration submitted on behalf
of the prosecution, Nutarariaq (Nootakgagayuk), who had travelled with
Nuqallaq, described their journey to Admiralty Inlet:

Nutarariaq – Pond Inlet, 28 April 1922

In the spring of 1920 about March, I left Navy Board Inlet where I had been living
all winter, with Oo-roo-re-ung-nak, Kutchuk and Noo-kud-lah to go to Cape Crawford. We stopped at Adams Island [Tuujjuk] at the mouth of Navy Board [Inlet] for
about two weeks. While at Adams Island, Kowkwatsoo came to our camp and
gave us the news about Janes going to try and pass by way of Admiralty Inlet
south to Aivillik. He also told us that he had given Janes some molasses for which
Janes had thanked him very much, because he was short of provisions. After we
started for Cape Crawford from Adams Island, we travelled on Janes' track until
we reached Admiralty Inlet, then we went across the Inlet to Cape Crawford, and
Janes' track went straight down the Inlet towards Strathcona Sound. Arriving at
Cape Crawford, we found Janes there. He had arrived there the day before. When
Noo-kud-lah heard Janes was there, he said to me that Janes was mad with him
and that he would go to Janes' igloo and see if he was still mad with him, so that he
could watch out for himself, because he was afraid of Janes. Noo-kud-lah went to
Janes' igloo before he took off his kouletang and returned soon afterwards and told
me Janes was not mad with him now.[75]

Nutarariaq's reference to the tracks heading south were likely those made
by Uuttukuttuk when he was sent to look for Inuit camps on Strathcona
Sound. If Nuqallaq had intended to follow Janes in hopes of taking
revenge, then he would have headed south as well, rather than heading
north to visit the hunting camp on the ice.

The statutory declarations presented in absentia for the defence all spoke
of Janes' abusive actions, whether taking furs from Aatitaaq or chasing
Umik with a snow knife. But instead of showing that the death was a
matter of self-defence, these statements seemed to support the idea that
Nuqallaq and Aatitaaq might have just cause to seek revenge. On a few
issues there was no consensus, such as whether someone had told Ululijarnaat to lure Janes out of the snow house or if had been his own idea. Nuqallaq thought Aatitaaq had made the suggestion; Aatitaaq believed it was
Ululijarnaat's own idea; and Ululijarnaat could not remember.[76]

Various statements placed Miqutui at the centre of events and the discussion, yet he was one of the key witnesses that Joy had been unable to track
down. Several believed his lies about the trail had led to Janes' death. Both
Ijjangiaq and Aatitaaq also believed that it was Miqutui who had told

Nuqallaq to "shoot him again" when Janes was lying wounded on the ground.[77] One Inuk stated that if both Miqutui and Nuqallaq had not come to the camp, then Janes would not be dead. Otherwise, no one suggested that Nuqallaq had done anything wrong – no one, that is, except Staff-Sergeant Joy and the jurors at the inquest.

Nine days after the inquiry began, Joy finally called upon the accused. The charges against each prisoner were read aloud, then each was given a "statutory warning" that was likely even more incomprehensible when translated into Inuktitut:

Having heard the evidence, do you wish to say anything in answer to the charge? You are not obliged to say anything unless you desire to do so; but whatever you say will be taken down in writing, and may be given in evidence against you at your trial. You must clearly understand that you have nothing to hope from any promise of favour, and nothing to fear from any threat which may have been held out to induce you to make any admission or confession of guilt, but whatever you now say may be given in evidence against you upon your trial, notwithstanding such promise or threat.[78]

Joy admitted in his report that "although the form was complied with and the best explanation possible given them, I was convinced that it was beyond their comprehension."

Nuqallaq was the first to tell his story, which he did with refreshing candour not evident in the previous testimonies. Even the text of the translation suggests a self-confidence of someone who believed he had done no wrong. He was first asked to describe what had taken place in the spring of 1918 that had caused Janes to threaten to kill him if he came near his post.

Nuqallaq – Sannirut, 19 July 1922

When Janes was here [Eclipse Sound] two winters, I went deer hunting in the spring from Pond Inlet. I stopped at Janes' place one day. I was playing ball and Janes came out to me. I fixed up my komatik ready to leave and went to my own house and put on my clothes and Janes came in to see me. Janes told me to go from his place, I was not his sailor,* I belonged to Pond Inlet. He told me to hurry up and leave his place. He then asked me if I was afraid and I said "no." I went back to Pond Inlet again. Florence was at Janes' place at the time. Florence came back to Pond Inlet after I did.

* The word "sailor" was used to refer to someone employed by the whalers. In the 1920s it was used in the generic sense to refer to an employee.

Aatitaaq, Nuqallaq, and Ululijarnaat, under house arrest for the murder of Robert Janes. L.T. Burwash. NAC – PA 99050.

I heard from Wilfred Caron and Tom [Takijualuk] afterwards that Janes almost shot me at his place, but Florence stopped him. I did not believe this. I went up again a few days afterwards. I went in Ivahloo's house, and Janes' wife, Kud-loo, told me there that Janes did not want to see me at his place. Janes used to send for the people when they arrived and give them something to eat, but he did not send for me. I put a cartridge in my gun and put the gun in Ivahloo's porch. I thought if Janes is going to shoot me, I am going to try and shoot him at the same time. I waited for Janes to go to bed, because I thought he would shoot me as I was leaving the place. When I came back from deer hunting that same trip, I did not pass Janes' place.

I waited at Pond Inlet a few days, then I went deer hunting again with some men from Igloolik. The Igloolik men went in Janes' house, but I stayed out on the ice because I was scared of Janes. When I came back from this trip I passed Janes' place and gave the people some meat and came on to Pond Inlet. Later the same spring, I was at Button Point when Janes came there. I did not see him because I was hidden from him in Caron's house until Janes went away. I do not remember whether it was Tom or Caron at Button Point then. Afterwards I saw Janes again at Button Point the same spring and as soon as I got there Janes went right off. Janes never chased me from Button Point with a gun. I never tried to go where Janes was, after I heard from the other Eskimo that Janes did not want to see me.

I only told [Maniq], who was there from Arctic Bay, that I put a cartridge in my gun ready to shoot Janes if he tried to shoot me, and I told Oo-took-ito afterwards. Oo-took-ito asked me if I would shoot Janes if he came out without a gun, and I said "no," only if he comes out with a gun.[79]

Having explained his previous confrontation with Janes, Nuqallaq went on to describe the situation at Cape Crauford:

Nuqallaq – Sannirut, 19 July 1922 (continued)

If Janes didn't used to take a knife or a gun to the people before when he got vexed, I would not have shot him at Cape Crawford. As soon as I got to Cape Crawford two years ago this spring, I went to Janes' igloo to see if he was mad, and he was alright [sic] then. Janes told me then that he was not vexed with me because he was going away. Janes was alright until [Miqutui] came. After Janes said he was going to stay, he asked me to try and get some foxes from the Eskimo for him, the Eskimo what was at Cape Crawford. He also wanted me to go and get him some grub from Florence* at Button Point for the foxes I got from the people. I asked Koon-noon if he had any foxes and he told me "no." When I told Janes Koon-noon had no foxes, Janes told me I was telling lies, and then got mad with Koon-noon and all the people. Janes wanted foxes from the Eskimo that had debt from him, and foxes from the other people, and pay them later when his ship came up. When the Eskimo would not give Janes foxes, he said he was going to shoot the dogs. He told me he wasn't afraid, "never mind if the Eskimo shot him afterwards." He said "never mind if I have to shoot a man afterwards." Janes said Kowkwatsoo should know all about the foxes, and I called Kowkwatsoo to come out. Janes said to Kowkwatsoo when he came out, I suppose you have talked too much against me, that is the reason the Eskimo will not give me any foxes now. He said to Kowkwatsoo also that he supposed he would talk about it again when he got back to Pond Inlet so that the people on the ship would hear about him getting mad. Janes said again "never mind if I kill somebody, never mind if I kill some of the people, and afterwards most of the dogs," then he went off to his igloo in a hurry. I told the Eskimos there that Janes was going to shoot the people now, so you people better get your guns too. Ahteetah grabbed Janes by the arm and told Janes not to get vexed with him, and Janes said again "never mind if I shoot the people." Janes then went to his igloo and looked for his gun in the porch. I was standing there watching him, and he said to me "I wonder where my gun [has got] to." He then called me in his house and said to me "I wonder if Oo-took-ito got my gun, and I asked him why, and he said he was going to work on his gun. I said to him, "I thought you was going to shoot the people," and Janes said "I got a little vexed just now as I was going to shoot some dogs." I said to Janes, "you were talking about shooting the people just now, if you shoot the people somebody will shoot you." Janes got alright [sic] then, but he was shivering just the same. He got pleased then and got me and Edineyah something to eat.

---

* Nuqallaq's reference to the former agent, Florence, rather than to Diment who was in charge at the AGES station in 1920, suggests that Nuqallaq might not have traded there since the previous September.

Janes then said to me, "if you get to Pond Inlet before me, stop my wife, because she and her husband are going south. If you catch her and you do not stop her, I shall take the gun to you again."

He also said to me that when he got to Pond Inlet he would watch [Takijualuk] when he was sleeping, then shoot him because he was getting short of grub, then do the same with Florence.

I told Koon-noon, Epireyah and Mikootooee first, that I was going to kill Janes. I went round and told them I was going to kill him, and they all said it was alright [sic] and Mikootooee said "sure, go ahead and kill him, he has been vexed with you more than once and he took a gun to you." Ahteetah would not have been into it, it is not his fault, but when I was going to kill Janes I sent for him to help me. I told Ahteetah and Oo-roo-re-ung-nak in my own house and in Kahlnahl's house.[80]

Missing in this story, compared to earlier accounts, is Nuqallaq's statement that he had agreed to kill Janes, but not unless he got angry again. His attempt to absolve Aatitaaq of blame is also interesting. Based on the transcript, and assuming there was no editorializing during the typing, it appears that Nuqallaq was still taking a leadership role in protecting his people.

Joy's reaction to this long and very detailed explanation was surprising. In his summary report to his superiors – essentially the RCMP commissioner's office – he seemed to ignore the description of Janes' repeated threats at Cape Crauford and instead focused on Nuqallaq's attitude, stating that "the actions of Noo-kud-lah and later Ahteetah and Edineyah in following Janes into his igloo after his trouble with Koon-noon, and Noo-kud-lah's remarks to him while there, indicates aggression rather than fear." Joy went on to suggest that "the fact that Janes fed them in his igloo at this time points out that he had recovered from his anger as far as they were concerned."[81] Although it seems obvious that they would not have eaten with him if he were still angry, Nuqallaq's actions were more likely inspired by hopes of calming him down to prevent any possibility that he might carry out his threats.

After the accused gave their statements, four statutory declarations were read in absentia. Statements by Paniluk, Qamaniq, and Manu described Janes' attack on Umik with a snow knife, whereas Amarualik related how Janes had taken Aatitaaq's furs against his will. On the last morning Ataguttiaq and Wilfred Caron would finally give their testimony for the defence. Joy had relatively little to say about Ataguttiaq's statement, even though she declared that Miqutui, the leader from Igloolik, had told her husband to kill Janes.

Ataguttiaq – Sannirut, 20 July 1922

I think it was the second day after Janes got mad with Koon-noon. I went Koon-noon's igloo and saw ... Koon-noon's wife [Miquitui] putting on her kouletah [skin parka] to run away from Janes. She told me Janes was going to get mad again when the other fellows came back from seal hunting that night, and she was scared. I saw [her] going out on the ice and I followed her. I followed her because I was afraid of Janes because he was going to get vexed when the fellows came back.

[Koon-oon's wife] and I met the men on the ice returning to the village. My husband and Munne and Kutchuk and Mikootooee and Koon-noon were in the party. I told my husband I followed [her] because I was scared of Janes. My husband asked me, "why didn't I put on my kouletah?" and I said I was too afraid to get it. I heard Mikootooee from Igloolik ask my husband if he hadn't any pity for his wife when she ran away without her kouletah. Mikootooee said "Janes took a knife to your father and he took a gun to you, you had better shoot him" ...

I did not hear anybody else say to my husband that evening or any other time he had better shoot Janes. They didn't used to talk in my sight.

My husband told me once, after Janes got mad with Koon-noon, that he wished he could leave Cape Crawford, in the night, because he was scared of Janes after he got vexed, and if he was to leave during the night Janes might get mad again and shoot somebody, because he used to do the talking for Janes.[82]

None of this seemed of much interest to Joy, whose attention seemed focused on any evidence that supported a motive of revenge.

Wilfred Caron was the last to testify, stating that Janes was a disreputable character who held a deep grudge against Nuqallaq and repeatedly threatened to kill him. Submitted as evidence was a letter Janes had written to Caron, in which he threatened to kill Nuqallaq if he ever came near his post. He reiterated that the other traders had warned him that his abusive tactics towards the Inuit might prompt some form of retaliation, but Janes claimed he was not afraid of them.[83] Unfortunately, Caron's testimony only added support to the theory that Nuqallaq and Aatitaaq had ample reason to take revenge.

The inquiry officially ended on 20 July 1922, and the three accused were "committed for trial to the RCMP Guardroom at Pond Inlet." This statement was only window-dressing for the home audience. There was no prison or guardroom, only temporary dwellings for the prisoners and their families in the Hudson's Bay Company's storage sheds. As described in a subsequent RCMP annual report, they were under "open arrest," which meant "staying in the vicinity."[84] They were also allowed to keep their guns and ammunition so they could hunt for food.[85]

In his summary report on the preliminary hearings, Joy admitted that he had difficulty understanding the fear felt by the Inuit after witnessing Janes' dispute with Kunuk, saying "they were scared only in such a way that they were unable to describe." From his perspective, "it does not seem possible, with about twenty-one men in the camp, nearly all of them with a gun in his possession and Janes without one, there could have been much fear on the part of the Eskimo."[86] In spite of testimony to the contrary, Joy saw Janes as a terrorized and misunderstood victim. He stated that although "there was ample proof that Janes abused some of the Eskimo to a great extent, and that he was very indiscreet with his remarks about shooting them," he implied that they should have known it was a bluff because "he had never pointed a gun at any of them." Given the evidence presented at the hearings, Joy's overly sympathetic portrayal of the white trader was surprising:

At Cape Crawford he was an unappreciated guest, so to speak, in a camp of some twenty grown men, with some of them nursing old grievances against him; he had lost the authority he once held over them when he had a store full of trade goods at the back of him; they saw him destitute of provisions and equipment and apparently neglected by his people "outside," from the fact that a ship which he had predicted to arrive in each of three summers was never sent up for him, and at the first sign of anger his death was quickly and effectively planned in cold blood without giving him a chance to escape.[87]

If Joy had great difficulty understanding an Inuk's fears, he had no problem identifying with those of a *qallunaaq*. Moreover, the suggestion that Janes should have been allowed to escape was illogical. Janes had never been a prisoner. Nor did the Inuit ever take advantage of him. Quite the contrary, they appeared to make every effort to appease his anger in hopes that he would soon leave. If they had tried to force Janes to leave on his own without a gun, he would have surely died, as would any guide who agreed to accompany him. To give him back his gun would have put everyone at risk of being killed. Janes had become a serious liability, but he had brought it upon himself by threatening to kill their dogs. To an Inuk, dogs were critical to the ability to hunt and travel – hence essential for survival.

Staff-Sergeant Joy, however, seemed unaware of the importance the Inuit attached to their dogs. Yet Constable H.P. Lee, very much Joy's junior, would write the following after spending two years at the Craig Harbour detachment, from 1922 to 1924: "What estates and bank accounts are to civilized men, dogs are to the Eskimo hunters of the North. Without a dog-team the native is helpless; without dogs he cannot hunt, or travel, and, next to a rifle, they are his most valued possessions."[88] In the not too distant future, Joy would have time to reconsider his views during his many long-distance sled patrols. In the summer of 1922, however, he dismissed the importance of Janes' repeated threats to kill the Inuit dogs and possibly one of the hunters, regarding them as simply "indiscreet remarks."

Joy also seemed to ignore the fact that Janes had alienated the other white traders who might have been able to help him. He knew full well that he could not expect sympathy or assistance from that quarter. Thus with Miqutui's news that the route to Iglooik was impassable, Janes was desperate. Somehow, he had to get more furs to buy food and to pay for his way home. His comment to his guide, that he did not care if someone shot him, reflected the degree of his depression. In this state of mind, he was more likely to harm someone as he no longer cared about the consequences. Without access to Janes' diary, Joy had no proof of this. He only had the word of the Inuit – whom he chose not to believe.

Instead Joy focused his attention on Nuqallaq and his probable motives. In the report to RCMP headquarters summarizing his findings, he related how he was convinced that the Inuk had masterminded the entire plan:

It is evident that several of the Eskimo suggested to Noo-kud-lah that it was up to him to kill Janes, by pointing out the numerous injustices Janes had done him and his father previously, and, inspired by this and his personal dislike for Janes, he did not hesitate in committing the act. I have no doubt, too, that he and Ahteetah would be the only two men there with the courage enough to do it in cold blood.

Noo-kud-lah is undoubtedly a capable and fearless man, and by far the most intelligent of all the Eskimo in this district. This can be judged to a certain extent by the interest he took in the trial, in comparison with Oo-roo-re-ung-nak and Ahteetah, and by the questions he put to the witnesses on his own behalf. I can quite understand him being the master mind in the affair at Cape Crawford.[89]

The theory that Nuqallaq had somehow manipulated events to seek revenge has no basis in the evidence presented. Nothing in the written testimonies supports such a conclusion.

Two days after the hearings ended, Aatitaaq became very agitated and insisted on making a further statement. This time he tried to explain facts that he thought were important. Stating that a woman had urged him to shoot Janes for taking away his furs, he explained how he had gone to get Kunuk's gun with the intent to kill Janes but had put it away when someone had brought Janes some foxes and made him "happy" again. He then described a similar action and response when Janes was angry with him and had stolen his furs six months earlier, and how Janes "got better" after he brought him more flour from Beechey Island and a gift of two bearskins. Aatitaaq also tried to explain that he did not take any of Janes' belongings other than what was owed to him. He was obviously distressed, apparently confused as to what he had done so wrong to offend the police officer.[90] By

Joy's interpretation, however, the only significant point in this new statement was that "the suggestions regarding the killing of Janes were made
promiscuously at Cape Crawford," in reference to Aatitaaq's statement that
a woman had urged him to shoot Janes.[91] Perhaps ignorant of Inuit cultural
values, Joy seemed unaware that concern for their women and children
would have put extreme pressure on the hunters to protect them.

Meanwhile, the investigating officer was having frustrations of his own.
In a short memo to his superiors, he pointed out that one of the witnesses
at the preliminary trial had sufficiently implicated himself that he too
could be charged as an accomplice:

It will be seen by the evidence of Munne [Maniq] given at the preliminary trial ...
that he was sufficiently implicated in the murder of Janes to be charged as an
accomplice, but had this been done, there would have been no incriminating evidence against Ahteetah, who took a more direct interest in the affair from the start
under the influence, apparently, of Noo-kud-lah, and sufficient evidence to put
Munne [Maniq] on trial, so far as is known yet, could only be gotten by the statements of the accuseds themselves.

Munne made it his business to be present when the final plans were made to
effect Janes' death; he put a komatik in front of Noo-kud-lah to conceal him from
Janes' view, and then stood watch to let Noo-kud-lah know when Janes was
approaching.[92]

By his own admission Joy no longer had sufficient evidence to convict
Aatitaaq without Maniq's statement. If he were to introduce this as evidence, he would be under obligation to arrest Maniq as an accomplice. Yet
the accused men could only testify against each other if the court agreed to
try each one separately. After alerting justice officials to the problem, Joy
apparently left it to their discretion to resolve the issue.

Maniq's complicity must have come as a surprise, since his earlier statements gave no indication that he was directly involved. Joy's belated
awareness of the problem, several weeks after writing the report on the
hearings, suggests that he had not listened carefully to the simultaneous
translation. He was duly concerned about the changing statements and
notified headquarters accordingly: "It will be observed that there is a material difference in some of the statements made by the witnesses before
the accuseds at the Preliminary Inquiry ... and those made by the same
men in the form of Statutory Declarations previously, and it is possible
that there may be even a greater variation in the evidence of these people
when the case comes up for trial next year. For this reason, I will endeavour to
get every witness possible here for the trial"[93] (italics added).

Note that Joy uses the word "when" and not "if" in reference to the trial.
This memo, dated 10 August 1922, was written five days before the CGS

Arctic arrived at Bylot Island that summer. Until then Joy had no communication with his commanding officer – now Inspector C.E. Wilcox – who was on board the ship. His assumption that there would be a trial the following summer suggests that there may have been a tentative decision on the probability prior to his departure for Pond Inlet, providing that he could find Nuqallaq and take him into custody. If this were the case, then it would be important to show that the motive for the killing was one of revenge rather than fear, to assure a conviction. Perhaps Staff-Sergeant Joy was simply following orders.

While it is expected that a historian in the twenty-first century might view the case from a different perspective than someone living in the 1920s, the detailed minutiae in the evidence tended to obscure the underlying motives that sent Joy to Pond Inlet in the first place. Once the sovereignty issue was no longer critical, Commissioner Perry required another form of leverage to acquire government funding for his Arctic detachments. Otherwise, he had no means of enforcing Canadian laws, and thus no moral right to administer Canadian justice. A pending trial, however, would put pressure on the government to allow his plans for the new detachments to go forward. Although Perry had initially dismissed the importance of the Janes' case, certainly something in mid-June of 1921 had caused him to change his mind in a matter of days. Who or what remains a mystery.

After writing his report on the preliminary hearings, Joy seemed to shift his attention to his prisoners' state of mental and physical health. Both Aatitaaq and Nuqallaq, he observed, were "under severe mental strain" and looked unwell: "They have taken the investigation far more seriously than I ever anticipated, and the strain has had a marked effect." He related how he had granted them privileges to go narwhal hunting with the others at the floe edge, but that they had refused. The two seemed to have little communication with other Inuit; in fact "they seemed to have been ostracized by them." Ululijarnaat, on the other hand, appeared "entirely at ease," and was described as "a good-natured hard-working man, who prefers to be alone with his five children ... and is very much devoted to them." Joy continued:

All three prisoners are under open arrest and each living with his family. By allowing this it will be a source of consolation to them until other conveniences are arranged for and until their case is finally dispensed with ... Should these men be convicted, I would respectfully suggest that some temporary arrangement, at least, be made for their wives and families, otherwise they will be thrown in the hands of a none too well provided for community, and they seem to have a marked respect for their family connections as far as their wives and families are concerned, which conditions seem to exist throughout the district.[94]

While it was clear that Joy believed there would be a trial, he apparently was not certain the accused would be convicted. His plea for at least a temporary arrangement to provide for the families in the event that the men were removed from the community was strangely reminiscent of the report by Inspector Phillips following the inquest on the Belcher Islands. Phillips's argument, that the women and children would suffer unjustly if the hunters were removed from the community, was sufficient to cancel plans for the intended trial. One cannot help query Joy's motive in this report. Did he have second thoughts about those charged in the Janes case? Or was he suggesting that the welfare of everyone would be best served if the accused were sentenced to hard labour at the police post? At this point, however, it would be up to the judicial system to decide if the accused should be convicted and on what charge, or whether circumstances warranted clemency or discharge.

Joy had been given the unenviable task of enforcing the law in a region where the Inuit had received no formal legal instruction other than Bernier's attempts a decade earlier to explain about doing "what was right." On paper the region was claimed to be part of the Dominion of Canada. In practice it was essentially a lawless frontier, where authority depended upon physical might. Moreover, Robert Janes had been essentially a squatter on Inuit lands, and as a Newfoundlander he was not even a Canadian citizen.

Joy's accomplishments in a few short months were phenomenal, given the language barriers, lack of communication with the outside world, travel limitations, and time constraints. Aside from his authority as a police officer, he was required to act as detective, coroner, lawyer, judge, psychologist, and warden. As mandated by his superiors, he sat in judgment on three prisoners who had no legal experience and no independent counsel to advise them or protect their rights. Although his investigation was exceptionally thorough, Joy's attempt to maintain objectivity and ensure a fair hearing would have been unrealistic even in the best of circumstances. While there was no evidence that he had abused his authority, it would now be up to the Canadian judicial system to rectify any inequities made in the line of duty. Whether by choice, or circumstance, Staff-Sergeant Joy had conducted his last official murder investigation.

Quite apart from possible flaws in the investigative process or in the interpretation of the evidence, fate would intervene to make it even more difficult for Nuqallaq to gain a fair trial. While Joy was patiently waiting for his suspects to arrive at Pond Inlet for the preliminary hearings, an event occurred a thousand miles away near the mouth of the Coppermine River that would greatly alter attitudes toward Inuit violence. On 1 April 1922 at the Tree River detachment, an Inuk prisoner by the name of Alikomiak shot and killed an RCMP corporal as he lay sleeping and later a fur trader as he was approaching the post. Police officials were convinced that the previous leniency shown to Sinnisiak and Uluksuk was responsible for this flagrant disregard for Canadian law and order.

While this event did not affect Joy's investigation, it would clearly influence how his superiors would interpret his reports. For many years the police had argued the need for more murder cases to be brought to trial to show Inuit the consequences of breaking Canadian laws. Thus instead of the possibility that the case might be dropped, as in the Belcher Islands case, there was now a very real possibility of overreaction. As events unfolded, it appeared that Nuqallaq would be tried and punished not so much for what he did at Cape Crauford but for what Alikomiak had done at Tree River.

6

Awaiting Judgment

In spite of numerous setbacks, the Department of the Interior still hoped to send the CGS *Arctic* north the following summer. Then in October 1921 work on the ship came to an abrupt halt when Captain Pickels died suddenly of a massive heart attack. Another heated federal election and a change of government created further uncertainty about the future of the project. Yet officials in the Department of the Interior continued to support RCMP plans to build three police posts in the high Arctic and establish an annual supply expedition. In their view, adequate protection of sovereignty could not be achieved without the means to enforce law and justice throughout the Arctic, including the Archipelago. As before, the northerly, uninhabited islands were considered most vulnerable to potential threats from foreigners.

Compared to the Conservative government's preference for prestigious expeditions by famed explorers, the Liberals under Mackenzie King proved more disposed to the idea of a perfunctory police patrol and finally approved the required appropriation. If there had been any doubts in the spring of 1922, the murder of Corporal William Doak and trader Otto Binder at Tree River ended them once and for all. As expected, Dr John D. Craig was named commander of the expedition. Retaining his title of "Advisory Engineer," he still reported to the deputy minister of the Interior, although more frequently through O.S. Finnie as director of the Northwest Territories and Yukon Branch.[1]

Craig's choice of Captain Bernier to sail the CGS *Arctic* came as a surprise to a number of individuals. Other than the fact that he was held in high regard by the Liberal government, there had been another consideration. In February the Arctic Exchange and Publishing Limited (AEPL) had applied to the government for the sole right and responsibility for trade and administration throughout the Archipelago. Alfred Tremblay, who listed his profession on the corporation's charter as "explorer," was the president, with

John Davidson Craig, commander of the 1922 Arctic Expedition, on board
the CGS *Arctic*. John D. Craig Collection. NAC – PA 210045.

J.E. Bernier appearing as one of the other four shareholders. Reportedly, the
corporation had a capital of $500,000. In return for supplying any new
police detachments, Tremblay requested free use of the CGS *Arctic*, with the
intent to place Captain Bernier in command. With his book used as a means
of introduction, Tremblay actively lobbied the Quebec ministers of the new
Liberal government but found no support in the bureaucracy. Craig in particular strongly rejected the idea.[2] On 30 May 1922 Tremblay's ambitious
plans ended with finality when Captain Bernier was officially appointed to
sail the CGS *Arctic* for the Canadian government.

Compared to the government expeditions of the pre-war years, the times
and circumstances had changed dramatically. There would be no gala

Captain Joseph Elzéar Bernier (Kapitaikallak), aboard the CGS *Arctic*, 1922. Indian and Northern Affairs Collection. NAC – PA 118126.

send-off or press coverage when the ship departed from King's Wharf at Quebec City, only a few family members saying private farewells. For the next few years, what would become known as the annual Eastern Arctic Patrol was under strict orders to maintain secrecy until all the proposed police posts had been established in the Arctic Islands. Radio communications from the ship were to be brief and in code. All news releases were censored by officials of the Department of the Interior before distribution. These measures were considered essential because of "the importance of achieving certain results in connection with the maintenance of sovereignty in the north without attracting undue publicity."[3] There was a wireless aboard the ship, keyed with an old spark coil, but the range was limited. Long before the ship reached the Arctic Circle, the ship would lose all radio contact with Ottawa.[4]

The participants on the expedition also had changed in character compared to former years. Commander Craig would be assisted by the expedition's secretary, William Harold Grant. Other members of the government party were professionals with specific tasks, such as Squadron Leader Robert E. Logan, sent by the Canadian Air Board to locate sites for future landing strips; a surveyor crew to determine the locations of the

RCMP Inspector C.E. Wilcox and his men aboard the CGS *Arctic*, on their way to open the first police detachments on Baffin and Ellesmere Islands. W.H. Grant Collection. NAC – PA 176557.

new trading posts and police detachments; George Valiquette, a cinema-photographer to record the activities of the expedition; and medical officer Dr Leslie Livingstone to assess the health of the Inuit. RCMP Inspector C.E. Wilcox was in charge of nine officers and constables, who were to build and staff the new detachments planned for Pond Inlet, Dundas Harbour on Devon Island, and an undetermined location on southern Ellesmere Island. With the exception of Captain Bernier and some of his crew, this was a first-time experience for everyone.

Times had changed in other ways. After two years as a lightship in the St Lawrence River, the CGS *Arctic* had suffered severely from the weather and neglect. Although it had been repainted on the outside, the engines and fittings were in poor shape, requiring numerous stops for repairs during the voyage. The living quarters were cramped, crew and passengers suffering sleepless nights because of the stench rising from the bilges. Fifty years later Major Logan, now retired, claimed that he could still smell the "disinfectant, dead rats, dead fish and rotten vegetables."[5] The ship was a profound disappointment to Commander Craig, who wrote in his diary that "no boat but a Government boat would be allowed to sail in the condition the 'Arctic' was in." He recommended purchase of a new vessel with a superior image so that the Inuit might "recognize the authority of the government." As might be expected, his advice was ignored.[6] In truth, the formerly proud CGS *Arctic* was a dismal sight compared to the new steam-powered HBC supply ships.

Once the expedition was under full sail, morale on board improved considerably in an atmosphere steeped with anticipation of adventure and new horizons. The government party and police officers were as enthusiastic as tourists on a cruise ship. Many carried cameras to record images of their fellow travellers and passing icebergs. Commander Craig and his secretary kept diaries, as did RCMP Corporal Finley McInnes and many others. All knew that their mission was to protect Canada's tentative claims over the Arctic Islands, but that did not prevent them taking time to anchor to a large ice floe for a casual stroll or to shoot a polar bear who wandered close to the ship. With each new experience, everyone dug cameras out of duffle bags to record the occasion.[7]

There were serious moments as well, such as Captain Bernier's lecture to the policemen going north the first time. Concerned about their relations with the Inuit, he emphasized that they were Canadian citizens and as such should be treated fairly and justly. In particular, he warned that one must never promise an Inuk "anything that you do not intend to fulfil because a native has also a very high sense of honour and he will never deceive you wilfully." Bernier also talked about the importance of regular exercise and recreation to ensure a fit body and mind. For those who were not paying careful attention, he distributed copies of his address "for study at their leisure."[8]

There were also humorous moments, like the time Bernier brought out a case of wine to toast the crossing of the Arctic Circle, only to find that the cook and steward had been "into the sauce" and had filled the bottles with cold tea. He came to the rescue with a bottle of Jamaica rum from his personal stores and poured everyone a double portion.[9] Yet under the surface of the excitement and frivolities lay more sombre thoughts of what lay ahead. There had been no word from Staff-Sergeant Joy since the previous summer, and no one quite knew what to expect.

The ship reached Bylot Island in mid-August but was blocked by ice from entering Eclipse Sound. Wilfred Caron and five Inuit from the Sannirut post came out to meet them in an old whaling boat. They were waving and shouting, their excitement increasing when they recognized their old friend Kapitaikallak. The welcoming party must have raised a few smiles among those on board as well, as Caron was dressed like an Inuk in multicoloured sealskins and knee-high skin boots (*kamiik*), whereas the Inuit hunters looked more like *qallunaat* in their canvas coats and corduroy pants.[10] Bernier invited his nephew below for a meal, where they discussed ice conditions and other matters with Craig and Wilcox. Everyone was relieved to learn that Joy had been successful in his investigation

Captain Bernier with William H. Grant, secretary for the 1922 Arctic Expedition. W.H. Grant Collection. NAC – PA 209174.

and had arrested three Inuit on a charge of murder. Caron left shortly to find an Inuk guide, then set off with two policemen for Pond Inlet.[11]

As they waited for their return, Craig and a small party went ashore to examine the station at Sannirut. In the absence of a wharf, a whaleboat was used to transfer the passengers to a rock shelf situated below a twenty-foot embankment. Above was a small Inuit camp comprised of one canvas tent and two sealskin *tupiit*. Caron lived in a nearby wooden house covered with tar-paper but reportedly comfortable inside. Another building of similar construction was used for storing furs, whale skin, and blubber. Outside stood several large barrels and steel tanks full of whale oil. The Inuit women were dressed in sealskin boots and pants. The hoods of their parkas (*amauti*) were trimmed with green and red braid. In his diary the expedition's secretary noted that some of the women had faint "streaks" on their faces, but he was unsure whether these were faded tattoos or temporarily painted on.[12]

Two more days passed before Staff-Sergeant Joy finally appeared alongside with two *qamutiit*, accompanied by Caron, Corporal Jakeman, Constable Anstead, and a number of Inuit. It had taken them almost thirty hours by canoe and dogsled to reach the ship. After a round of warm greetings and handshakes, Joy handed over his reports and joined Inspector Wilcox and Commander Craig in serious discussion.[13] Although likely informed by his fellow officers, Joy would now learn the details of how Alikomiak had shot RCMP Corporal William Doak and Otto Binder while under house arrest – a tragedy that made Joy's accomplishments seem even more remarkable. The story of his investigations and of taking the three prisoners into custody without incident must have held his audience spellbound. Film footage shows him wearing a wool plaid shirt and knitted cap, his eyes sparkling and a grin stretching from ear to ear. In a re-enactment of his arrival scene for the camera, he is standing up in a canoe atop a *qamutiik* pulled by a team of dogs, as opposed to running alongside a sled that was pulling the canoe.[14] Joy had received a hero's welcome.

Much had happened since he had left Ottawa over a year ago. He would learn, for instance, that Commissioner Perry had retired and that he would now report directly to Inspector C.E. Wilcox, commanding officer of the "Ellesmere Sub-District." And now, because of the Doak and Binder murders, there was no longer any doubt that those responsible for the death of Robert Janes would be brought to trial. Under normal circumstances the Department of Justice would be required to approve a trial for a capital offence, but because of the unusual restrictions on communication and travel, some sort of contingency arrangement had been agreed upon with regard to approvals. Thus the final decision on the location and timing of the trial would be made over the next few days by Inspector Wilcox in consultation with Commander Craig, then cleared with Joy before the ship returned south.

Since the ice still blocked the entrance into Eclipse Sound, it was decided that Joy should return to Pond Inlet to watch over the prisoners while the ship proceeded northward to Ellesmere Island. Yet there were other problems they had not anticipated. An epidemic of what was termed "dog disease" had killed over a hundred that winter, severely limiting the number available for use at the new detachments. In addition, there was no skin clothing available for purchase as the two trading companies had bought up everything that year. Takijualuk reported that country food was also in limited supply, as everyone had been too busy working for AGES or the

Qattuuq, his wife, Ulaajuk, and their children at Sannirut, prior to boarding the CGS *Arctic* to work at the new RCMP detachment on Ellesmere Island. W.H. Grant Collection. NAC – PA 209523.

HBC to do much hunting. An even more serious problem arose when it was discovered that no one was willing to leave the area to work at the new detachments planned for Ellesmere and Devon Islands.[15]

After much persuasion, Qattuuq, who had been hired by Caron to replace Nuqallaq at the AGES post, finally agreed to accompany the police on the promise that it would only be for one year.[16] His wife, Ulaajuk, was reluctant to leave, having four young children aged between three months and eleven years. Then just minutes before the ship departed, they finally packed up their *tupiq* and boarded the CGS *Arctic* – or "*Aati*" as it was called in Inuktitut.[17] The young couple had earned the distinction of being the first Inuit hired by the RCMP north of Hudson Strait, but they would find the company of six policemen poor substitute for their friends and relatives. For Ulaajuk especially, it was a lonely and unpleasant experience.

Ice conditions once again altered their plans. Unable to enter Fram Fjord as planned, Commander Craig chose a protected site near Smith Island that would be later named Craig Harbour in his honour. Someone discovered old stone foundations of Inuit houses nearby which were thought to be over two hundred years old. Otherwise there was no sign of any human habitation. Over the next eight days everyone was occupied with unloading supplies and building the detachment. Aware that they were unlikely to see another living soul until the same time the following year, Inspector Wilcox, Corporal Jakeman, Constables Anstead, Fairman, Fielder, Lee, and

Must, along with the Qattuuq family, stood silently on shore as they watched the ship depart in late August, just after midnight.[18]

The original plan to have Inspector Wilcox supervise the new detachments from a central location on Devon Island seemed reasonable on paper. But once it was realized that there was no means of communication or easy travel between the three islands, coupled by the unexpected delays and an acute shortage of Inuit help, it was decided to postpone construction of the Devon Island post until another year.[19] On their return to Pond Inlet they passed by Munn's ship at Sannirut where he was pumping whale oil. There is no record of any discussion about Janes' murder between Munn and Joy, although some dialogue likely occurred. Unfortunately, once the preliminary hearings were held and the officer's report submitted to Inspector Wilcox, any information Munn might offer could not change the course of action now in play. Joy did inform the English trader that his company would have to buy a licence as well as pay customs and export duties. Previously unaware that such regulations existed, Munn willingly complied.

Still unable to reach the site of the HBC post, the ship anchored in Albert Harbour where they unloaded twenty-five tons of coal and took on 120 tons of stone for ballast. The Inuit did most of the work, for which they were reportedly paid with tea and sea biscuits, ten pounds of tobacco, one hundred rounds of ammunition, and several bunches of beads. Takijualuk was compensated for damage to his whale boat with an undetermined amount of tobacco.[20] Following in the tradition of the whalers, Bernier hosted a party on the deck of the ship with about 150 Inuit in attendance. According to the expedition's secretary, "the women were in native dress with beads worked in all over their deer-skin clothes although some had on sealskins. They were a jolly lot, some big, some small, fat and lean ... The women seem to have padded shoulders and partly padded ankles ... Lime juice was served to them as well as hard tacks, the music was started consisting of an accordion and a violin and they started to dance a sort of square dance and some other dance."[21] Afterwards everyone moved over to the *Albert*, where Munn acted as translator for Craig's talk on why the police had come to Pond Inlet.

The location of the RCMP post was the subject of considerable debate. Joy had selected a site near the Salmon River, but it was inaccessible that year because of ice conditions. As they considered other options, it was soon apparent that there were few choices. The best anchorages and building sites, Squadron Leader Logan pointed out, had been purchased by Bernier and were now owned by Munn. Other locations that might have been favourable for building purposes were bordered by such shallow water that supply ships would have to anchor a mile or more from the shore. In

Construction of the RCMP detachment at Craig Harbour, 1922. W.H. Grant Collection. NAC – PA 173051.

the end, the detachment would be located on the beach, just east of the Hudson's Bay Company.[22]

Before leaving, Munn arrived in his motor launch to get clearance papers for his fur and whale oil exports. Joy seized on the opportunity to borrow his boat and take Dr Livingstone to a sick man near the Salmon River. Originally the medical officer had planned to stay at Pond Inlet that winter, but plans changed when one of the surveying crew suffered a serious accident and required daily attention.[23] Otherwise, Pond Inlet would have been the first location on Baffin Island to have its own resident medical doctor. Munn offered the police temporary use of his buildings at both Sannirut and Igarjuaq and suggested that he was willing to sell the Bylot Island property for a dollar an acre.[24] He also reported hearing rumours that three Inuit had been murdered at the Sabellum Trading Post at Qivittuuq, near Home Bay. Reluctant to send inexperienced officers on patrol to investigate, Joy instead sent a memo south with Commander Craig, requesting construction of a new detachment at Pangnirtung the following year in order to facilitate a proper inquiry.[25]

No sooner had the *Albert* departed with Munn and Caron on board than the HBC *Bayeskimo* appeared in the sound. The next day both ships moved to the beach in front of the trading post, and the Inuit began unloading the supplies. The company's buildings, stretched out along the shore, consisted of the living quarters for the manager and his assistants, a combined store and warehouse, a number of storage sheds, and a powder house where guns and ammunition were kept. All were built of wood and, with the exception of the storage sheds, neatly painted white with green trim. The HBC flag flew from a tall pole between the storehouse and the manger's house. On either side were eight or ten tents, but unlike the canvas tents at Igarjuaq and sealskin *tupiit* at Sannirut, these were made of caribou skins. There was only one usable kayak (*qajaq*) at the post, although a number of uncovered frames were lying about. Fewer Inuit were reported to be living here compared to Igarjuaq, and for some reason they seemed to be much older.[26]

Work had just started on the detachment when bad weather and high winds sent everyone to the ship for shelter. Bernier insisted on leaving before the ice came in, leaving Joy with the three newcomers to complete the construction. The CGS *Arctic* safely exited by Pond Inlet and sailed across Baffin Bay to Godhavn, Greenland, where the government party was welcomed ashore. Commander Craig was particularly impressed with the neat buildings and the happy, well-dressed native population. In an appendix to his report that year, he praised the policies of the Danish government and urged the Canadian government to provide similar support for their Inuit, particularly with regard to health and educational services. Like those of Bernier and so many others before him, his pleas fell on deaf ears. Only O.S. Finnie took notice and promised to send someone to examine the situation and make a report. Craig also stressed the need for a new ship, or possibly a second one, to allow the government expeditions to fulfil even the most basic functions.[27] An attempt was made to search for another vessel, but when the first choice proved inadequate, no further action was taken.

Over the next year Joy would be a role model, teacher, and mentor for Corporal Finley McInnes (Uqarajuittuq), Constable H.P. Friel (Makkulaaq), and Constable William MacGregor (Umilik). The first task for all four was to complete the detachment building before winter set in. Without assistance from the ship's officers and crew, they had to rely on their own skills, and in this case creativity was born of need. When it was discovered, for instance, that all the putty had been left at Craig Harbour, they tried mixing a can of white lead with flour to hold the glass panes in their frames. Much to their surprise, it worked. When they tried to light the stove in the well-insulated building, they also learned that "airtight" was "airless," leading to a number of experiments with cross ventilation.

Once the construction was completed, they began opening their barrels of supplies. The government issue of winter clothing came as a complete surprise and was the subject of much amusement and derision. Although attractive to look at, the outfit was constructed of double layers of long-haired goatskin, making the ankle-length trousers too stiff to walk in. They became museum pieces that were never worn. Instead, the women at Pond Inlet came to the rescue and found enough caribou skins to sew each of the newcomers a parka and knee-length pants. Wearing only heavy trousers and a mackinaw shirt underneath, they found their new outfits and sealskin *kamiik* comfortably warm and dry even in the coldest weather.

Schoolhouse at Godhavn, Greenland. Mission schools were introduced in the mid-eighteenth century. By 1920 there was a school in virtually every community. Commander Craig urged adoption of similar policies for Canadian Inuit. W.H. Grant Collection. NAC – PA 209737.

Compared to the previous year, the policemen had considerable time on their hands as there were no crimes reported and thus no investigations. As opportunities presented themselves, they began to collect information about the area and its history. With Inuit help, they drew local maps to show the location of their camps, wildlife resources, sled trails, and caribou crossings. They also learned about Inuit culture and acquired some Inuktitut. Their education while on patrol encompassed some of the small but crucial details of Arctic life, such as how to keep hungry dogs out of one's snow house, the importance of stowing dog harnesses and leads on top of a snow house to prevent them from being eaten, the ability to predict a weather change, and the art of using a dog whip without wrapping it around one's head. Assistance was given to the sick, where and when possible. Fortunately, there were no major outbreaks of disease that winter, as both their medical supplies and knowledge were found to be inadequate.[28] In his free time Joy began investigating the ruins of ancient stone houses in search of artifacts belonging to the Tuniit (Dorset people). With the help of his men and the Inuit, his collection grew to more than seven hundred specimens, which were carefully catalogued and sent to the Victoria Memorial Museum in Ottawa.[29]

The "employed Natives," as they were called in police reports, proved invaluable. Kautaq looked after the dogs and supplied them with country food, while his wife, Aarjuaq, sewed clothes for the policemen, and what she could not make herself, she arranged for other women to fill their needs. She was also responsible for cleaning the detachment and washing their clothes. Payment was made to her husband, provided from the police stores in the form of food, clothing, or cooking utensils. There were no official reports on the prisoners that winter and apparently no problems, although Corporal McInnes did recall giving them tobacco now and then, as it was one item not included in their weekly rations.

Most RCMP officers complained privately that nothing in their training prepared them for the basic necessities of Arctic survival.[30] For the most part, it was a matter of learning by experience – and in some cases, the hard way. McInnes would recall one such encounter some fifty years later:

Joy wanted to go up to Milne Inlet to have a look at the coast there. He wanted some-one to go with him, and I said "Well, I'll go." By this time, we had detachment work all caught up, more or less, and so he said he would walk the beat and look for ptar-migan, if I would take the dog team. We had some rough ice and you had to go quite a distance to go around this ice. Well, I had never driven dogs, and to make matters worse, if an Eskimo borrows another Eskimo's dog team (unless he is an expert dog driver) he would have an awful time, because they wouldn't obey any commands.

Anyway, I started out. It wasn't too bad when the going was good, but when I got into this rough ice, they would just stop. I would get at the back of the sled, and I would push and yell at the dogs. And they would sit there and just look back at me. They were laughing at me all the time. Then, I would get mad and take a run at them, and got tangled up in the long traces. They wouldn't do anything for me. So, I had this big whip, oh it must have been 60 or 65 feet long. It had a short handle – just a hand grip – and I tried to use that. In the wind, it's impossible to use the whip even for a good driver, on account of the long lash. Well, I tried to use it anyway, and the lash went around my head and I had a pretty sore nose from it. But I sure was mad – I think the tears came sometimes.

Finally, I got out of the rough ice and got to where it was good going. I had to un-tangle the traces. There is a bridle on the sled and these traces have ivory toggles and you thread them onto the bridle. They used to braid regularly, with the back-ward and forward crossing of the dogs. So, you would have to take it off and use your fingers to unweave the braid. Well, I no sooner got it off the bridle, when the whole bunch of dogs just bolted. And I hung on. I don't know for how long or how far they dragged me on the ice, but I sure was mad enough not to let go. Anyway, I got them stopped by the time Joy was able to come out to where I was.[31]

It is said that the officers who thrived in the Arctic were a special breed unto themselves, possessing inordinate stamina, determination, and above all, a sense of humour. Those who had difficulty did not volunteer for a second tour of duty.

Aarjuaq, Pond Inlet, 1923. As the wife an "employed Native," she was responsible for sewing policemen's winter outfits as well as washing clothes and cleaning the detachment. McInnes Collection.

Even a veteran like Joy could find himself in trouble. McInnes related one instance when the two were out hunting near Janes' old trading post. It was high tide, and water had accumulated between the sea ice and the mainland. As they were heading toward the land with the dog team, Joy decided to follow some wolverine tracks:

He decided to wade through the tide water – it must have been 50 yards across – but it was shallow enough that he could wade it. He had on one of those light parkas, a cotton parka over a windbreaker. It was quite large and it hung below his knees. I didn't want him to go because I was leery about him getting wet, but he thought it wouldn't go over his boot tops. So he gradually put his foot over where the main ice was and it wasn't far down, and he thought he had hit bottom. Then he put his other foot down and all at once – he must have been standing on a little ice ledge – it broke. This ballooned the parka he had on. It had air in it and it just ballooned all around him. Now, it is kind of laughable, but it was serious at the time.[32]

McInnes managed to get him out of the water at the edge of the land-fast ice, then took the dogs and *qamutiik* back to where they were camped, while Joy ran along the shore – reportedly for miles – in an effort to get warm. Reaching their tent, he dried off and changed his clothes, but he would have to stop several times on the thirty-five mile journey back to the detachment to put on dry socks inside his sodden *kamiik*. Even the slightest risk of frostbite or hypothermia was taken seriously in the Arctic.

The three prisoners remained at Pond Inlet with their families, reportedly doing odd jobs around the detachment. They were free to hunt and fish wherever they wished, so long as they reported their destination and did not take their wives and children with them. On one occasion Joy and McInnes had been out hunting and returned to find a note on their tent saying, "Nookudlah to Bylot Island to hunt." Since there were no signs of tracks in the blowing snow, they quickly made their way back to the detachment, where they learned that Nuqallaq had asked Constable Friel if he could hunt on Bylot Island. He was told to take the note to Sarjan and ask permission. When the Inuk found their tent empty, he simply left the note and continued on. The police had no recourse but to wait, as the wind and fresh snow had obliterated any sign of footprints. In a few days Nuqallaq returned, seemingly unaware he had done anything wrong. Inadvertently – or deliberately – he had tested the system, and in the process had earned the officers' trust.[33]

Uuttukuttuk and Kassak were hired as dog drivers and guides to assist McInnes and MacGregor in collecting the witnesses for the trial from Arctic Bay and Igloolik. At first the Inuuk were reluctant to go as they feared the Iglulingmiut would be hostile. Nonetheless, they set off in late February, even though they knew the witnesses would have a long wait at Pond Inlet before the trial. Their main concern was the possible difficulty in locating them and in travelling once the snow began to melt. Nuqallaq was asked to accompany them, because he knew the exact location of their camps. An HBC party with interpreter Jimmy Ford joined them for part of the trip, as did Takijualuk, who was on his way to Igloolik to trade for Captain Munn. Not far from Qurluqtuq (Koulooktoo), the site where Quanaaq had died and Anguiliannuk had taken ill the previous year, Nuqallaq accidentally shot himself in the hand. Although the other Inuit suspected the wound was self-inflicted, McInnes thought it unlikely. Nevertheless, MacGregor

Constable H.P. Friel (Makkulaaq), in the caribou-skin outfit and sealskin mukluks made by the women of Pond Inlet. McInnes Collection.

escorted him to a nearby camp and made arrangements for his return to Pond Inlet. Siniqqaq, who had also been at the hunting camp at the time of Janes' death, was hired to replace him.[34]

Travel was difficult owing to the stormy weather, deep snow, and lack of dog food. Even with help from the fur traders, it took them thirty-three days to reach the camps of the Iglulingmiut. Contrary to their guides' fears, the police received an exceptionally warm welcome and were provided with generous quantities of food for their starving dogs. Eager for news, the people explained that they normally divided their trade evenly between Pond Inlet and Repulse Bay. The distance was greater to Repulse but travel easier. Nevertheless, they continued to visit Eclipse Sound because many had relatives there.

In spite of the scarcity of dogs, McInnes was impressed by the apparent prosperity and the abundance of food in the Igloolik camps. Yet he noted that many seemed to suffer from "defective eyesight," with three adults appearing to be totally blind and several others having lost the sight of one eye. His patrol report described the Iglulingmiut as divided into five different camps comprising thirty-five families in total, all within a radius of forty miles. The largest, with fourteen families, was located a few miles north of Igloolik Island where seals, walrus, and eider ducks were plentiful. With the caribou migration route only a short distance away, they usually had ample supplies of skins for clothing and extra to trade. This year, however, they barely had enough for their own use. The effects of the dog disease had been devastating and severely limited their ability to hunt. Those who once had fifteen to twenty dogs now had only one or two. A few had none at all. Otherwise, they reported having a good trapping season in spite of an overabundance of wolves and were delighted that the fur traders from Pond Inlet had arrived with supplies of ammunition, tobacco, and food.[35]

McInnes was fascinated by the intensity with which the Inuit in the area had embraced Christianity without supervision from Catholic or Anglican missionaries. When introduced by lay preachers, the new religion sometimes incorporated certain traditions of shamanism, resulting in syncretism, otherwise described as a "syncretic" form of religion. McInnes reported that some camps were "very enthusiastic over religion, which they follow in their own crude style, singing hymns and reading from their testament several times a day. The most attractive pastime, however, is trying to count the numbers of the pages and the hymns." To show that they were "Christianized," they attached a white flag of sorts to the end of a shovel which was tied to their *qamutiit*.

McInnes described how hymn singing had been incorporated into welcoming ceremonies: "While at the village they greet all arrivals by the grown population lining up on the most prominent place in front of their igloos, side by side. When the arrival is within hearing distance, they all join in singing a hymn. The arrival approaches the lineup within a few yards, then stops his komatik and remains standing until the hymn is finished. The singers then advance in single file and greet him with three shakes of the hand … The same formalities are gone through on the return of a resident of the village, even if he leaves only for a few hours."[36] McInnes also reported that at the first camp they visited they were expected to shake hands with the children and even the babies in the women's amauti. All the time, not a word was spoken, but once the formal handshaking ceremony had ended, the Inuit "started talking and laughing and told us how glad they were to see us." They said as well that they would be glad when the inquiry was over.

McInnes in his patrol report made no reference to the fact that Nuqallaq and Umik had been preaching the new religion at Igloolik. Nor, for that matter, did Joy in his reports. The exclusion seems deliberate, as this was fairly common knowledge and even described by Therkel Mathiassen in his published report on the Fifth Thule Expedition.[37] Given the protest sparked by the resident Anglican missionary during Sinnisiak and Uluk-suk's trial in 1917, Joy may have thought it wise to avoid any mention of Nuqallaq's subsequent conversion to Christianity.

The return trip to Pond Inlet followed a more direct overland route and took only eleven days compared to thirty-three on the outbound journey. This time the police were accompanied by most of the witnesses, except for Umik and Miqutui, who wanted to search for Ijjangiaq and his family, not heard from since November. Arriving at Pond Inlet on April 20, McInnes estimated he had covered over six hundred miles.[38] For him the long patrol had been a learning experience in more ways than one.

There was one day after we hit land again, that I was walking ahead of the dog drivers. I was quite a bit ahead and looked behind. They had stopped and there was a man quite a distance behind me. I didn't understand, so I gradually slowed my walk to see what this was all about. He got up pretty close, but without him noticing, I was sort of keeping an eye on him. Finally he got walking right behind me and then right beside me, and in a quiet voice he told me that I was going the wrong way. It was odd – he could have hollered something to me. I found out that he didn't holler or yell because he didn't want to lift his voice to a white person lest he might offend me.[39]

With a very few exceptions, most police in the 1920s recognized how dependent they were on their Inuit guides when on patrol. Not only was their assistance a necessity to lead the way and drive the dog teams but the Inuit also built the snow houses, lit the oil lamps, dried out the wet cloth-ing, repaired the runners on their *qamutiit,* and found sufficient country food to feed both the police and their dogs.

Aatitaaq's son Uujukuluk (Oyukulak), who was only a young boy at the time, recalled some of the events that year but did not seem to be aware that his father had been under arrest.

Uujukuluk – Arctic Bay, 1977

When winter came, and the sun had almost disappeared, another Qallunaat came to pick up the body, and we all travelled to Pond Inlet. By spring, I was used to the police, not the least bit frightened of them anymore, and thoroughly enjoying the whole thing. There were four policemen [by September]. That summer they built a

Typical Inuit winter camp in North Baffin, circa 1923. McInnes Collection.

house. Somebody went to fetch the people from Igloolik and Arctic Bay, and one by one, they were brought to this new house and questioned. When the people were questioned, I was told to leave – now that I was no longer afraid, I was always hanging around. I think [my father] started working for the [police]. We set off to meet some people, but when we heard that they had starved, we turned back. So we spent the summer at Pond Inlet.[40]

Among the people who had starved were Uujukuluk's aunt and uncle. After McInnes and MacGregor had left for Igloolik, Aatitaaq had approached Joy for permission to go in search of his brother Ijjangiaq who still had not been seen or heard from. Fearing he might be without dogs, he took along his son and a sizable dog team in hopes of bringing back the entire family.[41] To have granted the prisoner permission to leave with a full dog team only a few months before the trial reflected the extraordinary rapport that had developed between Joy and the accused.

Aatitaaq had still not returned when Umik arrived at the detachment with the grim news that Ijjangiaq, Panikpak, and Kudnoo, along with their wives and children, had apparently died of illness and starvation near the Sirmik Islands at the head of Admiralty Inlet. Kudnoo was discovered outside the igloo, along with three of the older children. Because he had more flesh on his body, it was thought he might have died from illness. The three women were found in a sitting position inside the snow house, frozen stiff, mere skeletons. There was no food or fuel to be seen, only a few dog bones. They appeared to have died sometime between the first week of February and the end of March, possibly around the time the police patrol had passed nearby. Although there was no sign of the other two men, it was thought that their bodies were likely buried somewhere under the snow. Aatitaaq had passed Umik on the trail and, on hearing the news, had continued on to search the full length of the Admiralty Inlet for his brother. He found nothing but a few pieces of clothing and some tracks.[42]

When Siniqqaq returned from the patrol to Igloolik, he reported that he had hunted with Ijjangiaq the previous summer but had left him in the fall. He met him again in November, along with Panikpak, Kudnoo, and their families. Although they were low on dogs, ammunition, and food, Siniqqaq had not been overly concerned and had left them cartridges, a gun, and some caribou meat before departing for Milne Inlet. In hindsight, he now believed that some sort of sickness must have occurred to prevent them from reaching Arctic Bay. The bodies of Ijjangiaq and Panikpah were found later, each in a small snow house only feet apart.[43]

McInnes took two more statements on the Janes case from witnesses brought back from Igloolik. Both Tupirnngaq and Iqipiriaq reiterated that everyone had thought Janes should be killed.[44]

Iqipiriaq – Pond Inlet, May 1923

During that day while I was out hunting I frequently heard the Eskimo, all of them, talking about Janes being mad, and several remarked that Janes better be dead ... Everybody there said they were scared of Janes because he might kill somebody anytime. I said Janes better be dead, and all the men at Cape Crawford said Janes had better be dead. It was common talk among all the Eskimo. Everybody was scared of Janes and nobody wanted to kill him.

Iqipiriaq also complained that "as soon as I had arrived at Cape Crawford ... Janes told me he wanted five foxes from me for the rifle [he had given me], but when he gave me the rifle, he had told me that he did not want any pay for it." He also admitted that after giving Janes the furs, he had warned Paumi that he wanted them back if Janes was killed. The willingness to hand over their furs after Janes' angry outburst appeared to be an attempt to appease the angry trader, or at least a way of securing their personal safety until such time as someone finally killed him. The "before and after" fears expressed by other Inuit also appeared in Tupirnngaq's statement, in which he explained that "I was glad at first that Janes had

RCMP detachment at Pond Inlet, painted and ready for inspection, summer of 1923. Officer on the right is Constable William MacGregor. MacGregor Collection.

been killed but after awhile I thought the white people might make trouble for the Eskimo and I became scared again."[45]

As agreed to the previous summer, Joy began moving the prisoners, witnesses, and their families over to Sannirut in the first week of August. The trip across Eclipse Sound was difficult, according to McInnes. The witnesses and their families had been sent ahead in small boats, with the police, prisoners, and food supplies following "in a small open boat that possibly carried about ten people." It was powered by an "old outboard motor called an iron horse" and moved along at roughly six knots [an hour]. Dense fog and floating ice made the trip a harrowing experience.[46] Although the exact date of their arrival is unknown, by 7 August Joy was recording further statements at Button Point (Sannirut), this time from Miqutui and from Paumi and his wife. Unlike in previous sessions, Takijualuk was the interpreter, a factor that may explain the different tone and substance of the remarks.

The statement by Paumi's wife confirmed how deeply the Inuit, especially the women, feared Janes. The men, however, still seemed reluctant to say anything that might implicate them personally.[47] The signed declaration by Miqutui, the camp leader from the Igloolik area, was particularly significant. He admitted saying in front of Nuqallaq after witnessing Janes' angry tirade that "if somebody wants to kill Janes, go ahead and shoot him" – even though he claimed that he was standing too far away to "understand what Janes was saying." Of greater interest to the police was his statement that he later warned that "there would be trouble" if they killed the trader. He also denied Ataguttiaq's claim that she had heard him tell her husband to go ahead and kill Janes.[48] Paumi, with whom Janes had lived while at the Inuit hunting camp, confirmed that the white trader had indeed announced that he was going to gather everyone together on the night of his death and that he intended "to put them more afraid" than the day before.[49]

While some of these statements supported portions of previous testimonies, there were inconsistencies, just as Joy predicted. Or perhaps, to phrase it in another way, some details were clearly inconsistent with Joy's original premise. Overall, they indicated that the belief that Janes posed a serious danger and should be killed was far more widespread than originally thought. As a consequence, the theory that Nuqallaq had somehow masterminded the whole affair to seek revenge seemed less likely. Whatever thoughts were in the investigating officer's mind at the time, he did not record them. Meanwhile, the police, their prisoners, the witnesses, and all their families waited patiently for the arrival of the CGS *Arctic*. And they would continue to wait as days moved into weeks. As food ran low, Inuit went hunting on Bylot Island and came back with snow geese, contravening the Migratory Birds Act.[50]

7

Trial by Jury

In the early twentieth century the pomp and ceremony attached to the administration of Canadian justice was a far cry from the show trials of medieval England. Yet vestiges of language and ritual remained in the criminal courts to remind prisoners and onlookers of the solemnity of the occasion and the seriousness of the accusations. The British tradition of long black gowns with stiff white collars worn by the court party continued, with the Union Jack still prominently displayed as a reminder of the heritage vested in the learned body of jurists administering criminal justice in Canada. Application of these rituals, language, and principles to a criminal court in the Arctic would be difficult. The nature of this particular case and conditions at Pond Inlet would make it doubly so.

Although Joy's report on the preliminary hearings had presented an ironclad case against Nuqallaq, his subsequent memos suggested there might be complications. Unknown to him at the time of writing, he was no longer reporting to Commissioner Perry. On 1 April 1922, Cortlandt Starnes had been appointed acting commissioner of the Royal Canadian Mounted Police, following Perry's retirement effective the same day that news of Corporal Doak's murder reached headquarters. Starnes had been on the force for over thirty years and was no stranger to the North, having served in the Yukon during the declining years of the gold rush, and before that replacing Superintendent Moodie at Fullerton Harbour.[1] In his new position he was determined to put an end to the violence among Canadian Inuit. There would be no disagreement on the need for a trial, but there were inherent problems related to customary procedures and approvals because of the inability of communicating with Pond Inlet until the following summer.

Upon receiving triplicate copies of the reports and testimonies, Acting Commissioner Starnes immediately forwarded a set each to the deputy ministers of the Departments of Justice and the Interior. In a covering letter to Justice, he officially recommended that a public trial be arranged at

RCMP Commissioner Cortlandt Starnes, 1923–1931. *RCMP Quarterly*,
October 1935.

Pond Inlet the following summer. Although Inspector Wilcox and Commander Craig had given Joy approval to proceed with preparations, only
the Department of Justice had the authority to sanction a trial.[2] Since three
Inuit were being held under house arrest pending trial, and there was no
way of communicating any change of plans until the government ship
arrived next summer, it was up to the commissioner to present an irrefut-
able argument in support of a trial. Starnes complied, stating that the case
must be considered in the context of the violence in the western Arctic
where Inuit murders were "becoming alarmingly prevalent," and noting
the rumoured murders at nearby Qivuttuuq (Kivitoo) as well. In his opinion the overall situation justified the need for strong and decisive action in
bringing the accused murderers of Robert Janes to trial. Thus, as a consequence of events occurring elsewhere in the Arctic, Nuqallaq and his accomplices were to stand trial for murder as a lesson to all Canadian Inuit.

Starnes also put forward a strong argument on the merits of the case,
claiming that this crime "was not committed in a heat of passion but was
deliberately planned and carried into effect." He then reiterated Joy's
views that "Janes appears to have been somewhat indiscreet in his manner
towards the Eskimos," but there was "no justification for Nookudlah to do

this white man to death."[3] This was the first hint in the written record that killing a "white man" might be viewed differently than killing an Inuk. At the time this was a generally accepted view among Canadians of European descent, and the distinction applied as well to North American Indians and blacks.

In terms of location, the commissioner argued that a court should be convened at Pond Inlet as it was more economical than bringing the accused and all the witnesses to a southern location. Moreover, he believed that it would "have a deterrent effect on the Eskimos ... In my opinion, some such steps appear to be necessary in order to impress upon the natives that their disregard for human life will not be tolerated."[4] Although budget considerations had influenced past decisions, Starnes now believed the situation was so alarming that cost was no longer a factor.

The Department of Justice concurred, with the result that two trials were ordered for the following summer, one at Herschel Island in the western Arctic, the other at Pond Inlet. To assist in educating Inuit on Canadian law and justice, the police had wanted a clear case of criminal intent that could be successfully prosecuted and a severe punishment exacted. Justice officials believed they now had two such cases. As an effective deterrence against future disregard for Canadian laws, both trials would be open to the public, with as many members of the community in attendance as could be accommodated. At Pond Inlet, however, the term "public" referred only to Inuit and would not include journalists or missionaries. As noted earlier, Joy made no reference to Nuqallaq's conversion to Christianity, which might have sparked interest if it were brought to the attention of the Anglican Church Mission Society. Similarly, no journalists would be allowed on the expedition. Instead the public would be informed through government reports and press releases and by way of a movie film taken by the cinema-photographer hired to accompany the expedition.

For the Department of the Interior a trial at Pond Inlet would serve two purposes. Although the stated objective was to show the Inuit "that Canadian laws must be respected,"[5] a court trial in the high Arctic presented a unique opportunity to show the world that Canada was fulfilling the legal obligations required to maintain sovereignty. Thus it was important that news of the trial reached the appropriate officials in Denmark, Norway, and the United States, in a way that did not alert anyone to the possibility that the Canadian government had concerns about its sovereignty over the Arctic Islands. For this reason the Department of the Interior believed that publicity must be tightly controlled until such time as the RCMP had completed construction of all the new Arctic detachments. Officials in the Department of Justice disagreed, arguing that the trial should be well publicized to show that the government was upholding the laws of the country. After several articles appeared in local newspapers prior to the court party's departure, the dispute was put before Prime Minister Mackenzie King, who sided with the minister of the Interior. Henceforth all press releases were to be submitted to his department for approval.[6] This policy would be extended to any article or book written by a passenger, government official, or crew member of the expedition. The censorship policy was enforced on through the Second World War and Cold War, although by then the sovereignty rationale had been replaced by the need for military secrecy.

The costs and responsibilities for the trial were shared by the Departments of Justice and the Interior. The RCMP commissioner was given the task of finding an interpreter. Munn, with a supporting letter from Captain Bernier, suggested the German-born American William Duval as a likely candidate.[7] Duval, then sixty-five, was fluent in Inuktitut and known to the Tununirmiut through his employment at the Igarjuaq whaling station twenty years earlier. In 1922 he had left the AGES post in Cumberland Sound to have major dental work done in the United States.[8] In terms of experience, his qualifications were excellent, and no one seemed concerned about his age when suggesting his name. From his standpoint, the government's offer was generous: a flat fee of $150, plus free passage for himself and a ton of trade goods to the destination of his choice. Since his wife and daughters were awaiting his return at the AGES post, this arrangement was particularly convenient to both himself and his employer, Captain Munn.[9]

That winter, however, Munn reluctantly sold the syndicate's entire holdings to the Hudson's Bay Company. His ship was getting old, and his friends advised him that they did not have the resources to compete with the superior ships and purchasing power of his new rival. In spite of his distaste for the aggressive tactics of the business-minded Superintendent Ralph Parsons, he had no choice. In March 1923 the AGES properties were sold for the sum of £28,000, plus the ivory on hand. In return the syndicate agreed not to conduct any future trade in Canada, and Munn personally was restricted from trading "furs or any other Arctic produce" north of 55° latitude, or east of 95° longitude.[10] Duval, meanwhile, had signed a contract to work for the new owners of the Usualuk post. In essence, the government was now paying to transport a future HBC employee and his trade goods back to his family and trading post.

As part of the agreement Parsons was expected to honour any shipping contracts pre-arranged by the syndicate. After the fact, Munn informed him that this had included bringing Janes' former Inuit wife and her husband back to Pond Inlet in time for the trial.[11] After some hesitation, the HBC superintendent consented to have the *Albert* sail directly from Peterhead to Cumberland Sound, pick up the two witnesses, and deliver them to Pond Inlet.[12] Superintendent Parsons also agreed to allow Munn one last trip on the *Albert* to bid farewell to the Inuit he had come to know so well. Neither commitment was fulfilled as promised. Two days before the departure of the CGS *Arctic*, Parsons telephoned to say that the ship was "stranded" on the coast of Scotland and her trip to Cumberland Sound would be cancelled. When notified of this change of plans, Commander Craig reported that the expedition would not have time to stop at Cumberland Sound on the way north. Although there seemed to be little else one could do at this point, the Department of Justice telegraphed the ship to advise the judicial party to proceed ahead as planned, notwithstanding the probable absence of two witnesses.[13] The change in plans also denied Munn the opportunity to observe the trial. Although he had accepted alternate passage on the HBC *Nascopie*, the supply ship was not scheduled to arrive at Pond Inlet until mid-September.[14]

The court party was appointed only a few weeks before the departure date. The choice of lawyer Louis-Alfred-Adhémar Rivet as the stipendiary magistrate appeared to be a patronage appointment for his years of service as a Liberal member of parliament for Hochelaga (1904–11). Descended from a venerable French family, Rivet had been admitted to the bar in 1895 and later would be named a judge of the circuit court for the district of Montreal.[15] At the time of his appointment, he had never been to the Arctic nor had any prior knowledge of the Inuit people or their customs.

According to newspaper reports, there was confusion about the appointment of legal counsel. Initially Commissioner Starnes had understood that François Biron, a lawyer from Montreal, would be acting for the Crown and had included this information in his instructions to Staff-Sergeant Joy.[16] A week later Starnes read in a Quebec newspaper that Adrien Falardeau had already been appointed to the position and that Leopold Tellier, a younger, less experienced lawyer would be counsel for the defence. Neither gentleman had any previous experience in the Arctic. Nor does it appear did Biron, who in the end joined the party as clerk of the court. Indicative of further confusion, or possibly just poor communications, a news item in the *Ottawa Citizen* reported that "two Eskimos," rather than three, would be tried for having "killed a mounted policeman," rather than a fur trader.[17]

After a flurry of last-minute activity, the expedition left Quebec City on 9 July 1923 without Captain Bernier, who was to board the ship a few days later at Father Point on the St Lawrence River. John Davidson Craig was once again commander of the expedition, but this time he was joined by his wife under rather unusual circumstances. Although there were no official arrangements to have her accompany her husband, Gertrude Craig boarded the ship at Quebec City, allegedly intending to get off at Father Point. She did not.[18] Her name is not on the passenger list, but she appears in various photographs taken over the course of the expedition, frequently wearing the same distinctive hat and fur-collared coat. Nor was she the only adventurous woman that summer. Apparently Judge Lucien Dubuc,

COUR D'ASSISES DANS LES REGIONS ARCTIQUES

AU PROCES DE TROIS ESQUIMAUX ACCUSES DE MEURTRE, A POND'S INLET, DANS L'EXTRÊME NORD: de gauche à droite, Me L.-A. RIVET, C.R., de Montréal, qui agira comme juge présidant le tribunal; Me LEOPOLD TELLIER, de Montréal, qui agira comme avocat des accusés; Me ADRIEN FALARDEAU, C.R., de Québec, qui agira comme avocat de la couronne.

L. A. RIVET TO HOLD TRIAL IN FAR NORTH

L. A. Rivet, ex-senator for Hochelaga, has been appointed stipendiary magistrate with judicial powers to try two Eskimos in the Arctic regions who some months ago killed a mounted policeman. He will sail with Captain Bernier by the Arctic on July 1st for Pond's Inlet, where the trial will take place. Mr. F. X. Biron, a Montreal lawyer, will act for the crown and Leopold Tellier, of the same city, for the defence.

Above: A Montreal French language paper (unidentified) announced that Adrien Falardeau, a lawyer from Quebec City, would act for the Crown and that "*trois Esquimaux*" would stand trial for the murder of Robert Janes. *Bottom:* The *Ottawa Citizen*, 20 June 1923, announced the trial involved *two* Eskimos accused of murder and that Mr F.X. Biron, a Montreal lawyer, would represent the Crown. Both papers announced that Mr Tellier, a young lawyer from Quebec City, would act as counsel for the defence. RG 18/3280/1920-HQ-681-G-4 (3).

in charge of the trial at Herschel Island, took along his wife, children, and their nanny.[19]

Within four hours of the ship's departure from Quebec City, an unexpected tragedy took the lives of the ship's third officer, Wilfred Caron, and Craig's secretary, Desmond O'Connell. Caron, who had expected to appear at the trial as a witness for the defence, reportedly slipped and fell overboard while attempting to free a foresail sheet. A lifebelt was thrown out immediately and a lifeboat lowered. O'Connell was in the rescue boat when he thought he saw Caron and jumped in the water to try and reach him. After hours of searching, neither body was found.[20] According to the wireless operator, an atmosphere of gloom enveloped the crew and passengers. Only moments before, O'Connell had been entertaining everyone with the banjo and a rendition of "Mr Gallagher and Mr Shean."[21] Caron as well had always been popular among his shipmates, who called him "Ti-loup," meaning, the little wolf.[22] It would be a week or more before the bodies were washed up on the shores of the St Lawrence.[23] Bernier learned the details of the tragedy when he boarded the ship at Father Point and was devastated.

Staff-Sergeant Joy would have no idea that three witnesses planned for the defence – Caron, Kalluk, and Inuutiq – were not arriving that summer. The absence of Caron, in particular, would be critical, as he was the only non-native who had could testify from firsthand observation as to Janes' mental state prior to March 1920 and his relationship with the Tununirmiut. As Nuqallaq's former employer, he was also a potential character witness. Wireless communication was still faulty aboard the ship and, as before, the cgs *Arctic* had no means of making contact with Pond Inlet. Nor did Joy have any way of notifying his superiors that another witness, Aatitaaq's brother, had died of starvation that winter.

In a memo to be delivered on the ship's arrival at Pond Inlet, Commissioner Starnes had instructed Joy to "provide subsistence and lodging" for the court party and "to make their stay as comfortable as possible." He also sent two square tents for use at the trial and directed Joy to have his men in full dress uniform "to give as much dignity as possible to the proceedings."[24] Where the four gentlemen and their interpreter might find "comfortable lodging" is somewhat of a mystery, especially as it had been agreed the previous summer to hold the trial at Sannirut on Bylot Island. Since everyone on board would know that Munn had sold all the property to the Hudson's Bay Company, they may have assumed – in error – that the Sannirut station had been abandoned or was no longer available for use, possibly forgetting that no one at Eclipse Sound would be aware of the ownership change until the arrival of the first ship.[25]

The availability of jurors had not been considered when the decision had been made to drop off the court party at Sannirut for the trial and pick them up after the ship returned from Ellesmere Island. A potential problem was resolved when Judge Rivet insisted on remaining with the ship for the entire voyage. Rumours among the ship's crew suggested that he had been upset with jokes about being attacked by "ferocious natives" if he sentenced an Inuk to death.[26] Commander Craig offered a different explanation for the change in plans: "We had intended going direct from Godhavn to Ponds Inlet so that the trial might be held while we were attending to our work farther north. Mr. Rivet, however, asked that we attend to our northern work first, partly so that he might be able to see more of the country, and partly so that the 'Arctic' might remain at Ponds Inlet during the trial, the ostensible reason for this being that a jury might be selected among the officers and crew of the ship."[27] Irrespective of the reasons, no one thought to inform Joy of the change in plans. Nor did the court party consider that others might be inconvenienced with the new arrangements. Instead, the excitement of a conducted tour of the Arctic seemed to have taken priority over the business at hand.

Although the official purpose of the trial was to show "the Eskimo that Canadian laws must be respected,"[28] the secondary agenda of reinforcing sovereignty was partially fulfilled when the CGS *Arctic* stopped at Godhavn. Here the ship's officers, government officials, and judicial party were wined and dined by Greenland dignitaries. An enterprising news correspondent wired the story of their visit to his newspaper in Copenhagen. As a result, five days before the *Arctic* was able to make radio contact with Canadian authorities,[29] the purpose of the trial – and inadvertently the general outcome – appeared in the *Berlingske Tidende* on 19 September 1923. The following is the substance of the article, as translated by the British attaché in Copenhagen, who sent it to the British Colonial Office, which then forwarded it to the governor-general of Canada:

The "Arctic" with Dr. J. Craig the head of the mission, a judge, two advocates, a recorder and an interpreter on board, arrived at Godhavn on July 30th where purchases of dogs and provisions were made. This comprehensive legal company was destined to demonstrate both to the white and Eskimo inhabitants how far the British arm of Justice could extend. Their destination was Ponds Inlet where they intended to pass sentence on two Eskimoes who had murdered a white man. The case is stated to have already cost the Canadian Government over a quarter of a million dollars.[30]

While the alleged cost seemed exaggerated, the reporter went on to describe the purpose of this and future expeditions, claiming that "neither scientific nor practical investigations form the objective of these visits, but first and foremost a demonstration of Canadian sovereignty over Artic [sic] America is intended."[31] The reference to passing "sentence on two Eskimoes" rather than three might have been a journalist's error or a problem in translation, but two similar mistakes, the earlier one in the *Ottawa Citizen* and this one based on information provided by the court party, seemed more than a coincidence. Yet even if justice officials had agreed with Joy's concerns and decided that the evidence against Aatitaaq was insufficient for a conviction, the inability to communicate and the lack of legal counsel meant his release would have to await formal acquittal at the trial.

During the party's visit to Greenland, the importance of cinematography was demonstrated by the showing of films taken the previous summer of the new police detachments at Pond Inlet and Ellesmere Island.

Members of the court party on board the CGS *Arctic*, July 1923. *Left to right:* François Biron (clerk of the court), Adrien Falardeau (Crown prosecutor), and Leo Tellier (defence counsel). Indian and Northern Affairs Collection. NAC – PA 102583.

Commander Craig reported that "the moving picture projector has been of inestimable value. The showing of our last year's pictures in Godhavn [Greenland] alone was well worth the outlay, and we also showed them to MacMillan and his men at Etah." Aside from the obvious promotional value in being able to show Danes and Americans visual evidence of the Canadian government's effective occupation of the Arctic Islands, Craig also described how the films were shown to Inuit audiences at Pond Inlet and Pangnirtung. These not only provided entertainment but indirectly showed the Inuit the extent of government activities elsewhere in the eastern Arctic.[32] The camera used in 1923 was supplied by Fox Movietone Films, apparently with the intent to produce an edited documentary for distribution to American movie theatres.[33]

After departing from Greenland, the CGS *Arctic* sailed directly to Craig Harbour where they found Inspector Wilcox and his six men in good health and the morale high. Qattuuq and Ulaajuk were less fortunate, having lost two children that winter to influenza. Not surprisingly, they insisted on being returned home.[34] Inspector Wilcox, who was in charge of the Pond Inlet detachment as commanding officer of the Ellesmere Sub-District, had not seen or heard from Staff-Sergeant Joy and his men for over a year – nor had anyone on the ship. Yet, no one seemed the least concerned about their well-being or the status of their prisoners.

George Valiquette, the cinema-photographer hired to film the 1923 Arctic Expedition, seen here shooting film at Godhavn, Greenland. Louise Wood Collection. NAC – PA 207809.

In anticipation of moving the Ellesmere Island post further north to the vicinity of Cape Sabine, the detachment at Craig Harbour was closed and everyone brought on board, including the dogs. En route they stopped at Etah in North Greenland to hire two families to replace Qattuuq and Ulaajuk. Ironically, they were from the same group that had initially caused the Canadian government protest to Denmark about their hunting on Ellesmere Island. Unable to reach Kane Basin because of ice, the ship returned to Craig Harbour and reopened the detachment. Only three policemen remained behind this time, along with the two Inuit families from Greenland.

Apparently without concern for those waiting at Button Point, the expedition first explored some of the fjords near Craig Harbour, then stopped at Dundas Harbour on 15 August to check out the site for another detachment.

Panikpak (Panigpa), one of the Greenlanders hired to work at the Craig Harbour detachment, with the expedition's medical officer, Dr Leslie Livingstone. Panikpak's grandfather migrated from North Baffin in the late nineteenth century. McInnes Collection.

Mrs J.D. Craig poses with Inspector C.E. Wilcox in remains of yacht *Mary* left at Beechey Island during the Franklin Search for use by shipwrecked sailors. Indian and Northern Affairs Collection. NAC – PA 186867.

From there they sailed through Lancaster Sound to Beechey Island, where everyone went ashore to examine the historical sites related to the doomed Franklin expedition. According to RCMP historian Harwood Steele, the visit was a highlight of the trip: "The opportunity was seized to visit nearby Beechey Island, Franklin's last winter quarters, and acknowledge Canada's debt to the old explorers. Every man [and woman] in the expedition able to do so went to the Franklin cenotaph, keystone of Canada's Arctic Dominion, and with all at attention, the Union Jack was slowly hoisted to the top of the flagpole above the cenotaph, and fluttered in the breeze amid complete silence for a minute. At the conclusion of the ceremony three hearty cheers and a tiger were given for His Majesty the King."[35]

At a leisurely pace, the CGS *Arctic* headed to Strathcona Sound, where the passengers disembarked to examine the site where Bernier had discovered iron pyrite twelve years earlier. From outward appearances the commander, his wife, Inspector Wilcox, and the judicial party were being escorted on a "grand tour" of the high Arctic.[36]

Finally at 9 a.m. on 21 August, the ship reached Pond Inlet by way of Navy Board Inlet, seemingly forgetting that Staff-Sergeant Joy and the Inuit were waiting on Bylot Island – by now, for over two weeks. Joy vented his frustration in the first paragraph of his report on the court proceedings:

As a result of an understanding between Captain Bernier and S/Sergt. Joy last year, the prisoners and witnesses were all being held at Button Point this spring for the arrival of the ship. The ship having arrived at Pond Inlet via Lancaster Sound and

CGS *Arctic* anchored off Pond Inlet during the murder trial, 25–31 August 1923. NWT Archives. N79–006–0001.

Navy Board Inlet, it was necessary to make a trip to Button Point to get the prisoners and witnesses. The "Arctic" arrived at Button Point on the evening of the 22nd inst., but owing to the heavy sea running at that time, the natives and their equipment could not be taken on board until the following evening. At 7pm on the 23rd the ship left Button Point and arrived here at 7am on the 24th. Final preparations for the trial were immediately made.[37]

Joy's annoyance was likely aggravated by the fact that he almost lost two men in the attempt to board the ship in the heavy waves. A canoe had tipped and two policemen had to swim some distance in the frigid waters to reach safety.[38] The trip back was bedlam, according to Craig, who wrote that the ship was now carrying "roughly 45 white people, 60 Eskimos, and about 80 dogs."[39]

Dr Leslie Livingstone, the expedition's medical officer, had refused jury duty "on ethical grounds," seeing his first duty to administer to the Inuit.[40] The ship's officers, however, had little choice in the matter. According to one account, they were all watching the Inuit dancing to accordion music on the ship's deck, when a "uniformed mountie" appeared and selectively handed out six blue slips of paper, summoning them to serve on the jury the next day.[41] All but one were francophone, which created the additional task of translating English and Inuktitut into French. According to the police report on the trial, it appears that the Crown prosecutor was assigned the task of translating the English translation into French for the jury.[42]

The murder trial officially opened at 10 a.m. on 25 August 1923, with the CGS *Arctic* anchored just offshore serving as living quarters for the judge

The court party, government officials, RCMP officers, and jurors heading to Pond Inlet for the murder trial, 25 August 1923. NAC – PA 207872.

and his party. Descriptions of the trial found in RCMP reports suggested an exciting display of pomp and ceremony, yet the movie film taken of the court party's arrival indicates otherwise. The weather was overcast, with rain or wet snow obscuring visibility for most of the day. The motor launch sent to pick up the party seemed to arrive out of a grey mist, somewhat akin to the landing of an advance party in an old spy film. The passengers with their long dark overcoats, black fedoras, and briefcases climbing out on a rickety dock and trudging up the path to the detachment created a sinister image. The film showed no crowds of Inuit observing their arrival. In fact, there were no Inuit in sight that morning. Perhaps it was too early, and they were still sleeping off the effects of their trip back from Sannirut and the dance on board the ship the night before.

The trial itself was conducted inside the police detachment, with the judicial party wearing long black gowns and stiff-collared white shirts.[43] The RCMP officers, resplendent in official red uniforms, included Inspector Wilcox as the officer commanding, Staff-Sergeant Joy as the newly appointed deputy sheriff, Corporal Jakeman as an orderly to the judge, and Constables Fairman and Fielder as official escorts for the prisoners. The interpreter, William Duval, appeared somewhat self-conscious in a dark suit, white shirt, and tie, whereas the jurors seemed proud to be wearing their officers' dress uniform. The Union Jack was displayed prominently behind the judge, who faced the Inuit sitting in rows on wooden chairs. The front row was reserved for the police in their scarlet tunics.[44] The jury sat on one side at the front of the room, whereas the prisoners, legal counsel, clerk of the court, and the interpreter sat on the other. The Inuit witnesses and spectators were described in a newspaper article as "stolid-faced" and "unkempt," wearing "heavy skin clothes." This may be a relatively accurate

Witnesses and observers, at the trial. *Left to right:* Siniqqaq, Piunngittuq, Iqipiriaq, Nutaraarjuk, and Javagiaq. Dewey Soper Collection. NAC–PA101 834.

description of the men, but photographs taken of the women at the time of the trial showed them dressed in summer apparel, some with handsome beading, and all with their hair neatly tied back or in braids. Nonetheless the atmosphere was oppressive, with as many Inuit as possible crowded into the sixteen by twenty-five foot main room of the detachment.[45]

The court convened at 10 a.m. on Saturday morning, 25 August 1923. The case of "His Majesty the King v. Noo-kud-lah and others" was called and the indictment read to the three accused. They were said to have responded with a plea of "not guilty," even though there was apparently no Inuktitut translation for the word guilty.[46] Six officers from the CGS *Arctic* were called as jurors and sworn in: Léon Lemieux (as foreman), Albert Theriault, William George Earl, Eugene Blouin, Luger Lemieux, and Alfred Levesque. In his opening remarks, translated into Inuktitut by William Duval, Judge Rivet explained the nature of Canadian laws and the judicial procedures that would ensure a fair trial. As reported by Commander Craig, Rivet "informed the natives of the purposes of the trial, assured them of justice and fair play, explained that the proceedings were exactly in accordance with the customs of civilization, and stated that had a white man killed an Eskimo the proceedings would have been exactly the same. The natives plainly exhibited curiosity and appeared much interested in the proceedings. The prisoners, however, did not seem to realize the gravity of the situation."[47] The judge's remarks would have been difficult to translate into Inuktitut as there was no such thing as a trial in North Baffin customary traditions. Moreover, the prisoners had told the truth, and so far they had not been severely punished or killed. To them the occasion was just more of the same, that is, more people asking more questions.

Although it was not expected that a trial held in the high Arctic during the 1920s would follow strict protocol, the judicial officers and police did attempt to replicate the dignity and pageantry of a southern supreme court. Yet there were many circumstances over which they had no control. The simultaneous translations, for instance, back and forth between English and Inuktitut with clarification in French for the jurors created noise and confusion. This, added to the inherent problems in interpretation and the cultural gap in comprehension, made the conduct of a fair trial a formidable challenge.[48] Progress was slow and tedious, made worse, according to Commander Craig, because an Inuk "when questioned is more likely to give the kind of answer that he thinks is expected than to analyze his own thoughts on the subject."[49]

Alex Stevenson, who when he worked for the Hudson's Bay Company at Pond Inlet had access to the draft transcript left at the detachment, gave a more insightful description of the proceedings: "Witnesses were interrogated through the interpreter and often a question was put six or seven times before the answer was obtained. In some cases, answers were merely the kind of replies that the witness believed were expected of him. Delays were occasioned when witnesses were allowed to stand down for recall after a session of unproductive questioning. The scarlet-coated police escort would lead one witness away and another would be called to the stand. 'We would have three witnesses on the stand so to speak at once' commented the Judge on a later occasion."[50] And so the trial proceeded with all the rituals and procedures, tedious as they must have seemed to the seated Inuit. Women and children might be excused if they wandered out to have the photographs taken by the official photographer.

Canadian trial procedures in the 1920s appear to have been less adversarial than current practices in North America. Crown prosecutors would consider it their ethical duty to make available all evidence for and against the accused to ensure that justice was fairly served. Thus, a prosecutor might call a witness favourable to the defence. Once questioned, the defence counsel had the right to "cross-examine" each witness on the evidence already presented. Should either counsel wish to ask this witness about another aspect of the case, that witness would have to be re-called. At final, the court would hear evidence already submitted at the preliminary hearings, supplemented by evidence subsequently gathered and disclosed to the defence. After the last witness had been called by the Crown, defence counsel would have the opportunity to recall witnesses for

Women and children posing for George Valiquette during the trial. Louise Wood Collection. NAC–207811.

purposes of giving evidence not already introduced by the Crown, or to call new witnesses to provide evidence in support of his clients. This process explains the order in which the witnesses were questioned and re-called at the Pond Inlet trial.[51]

A major difficulty in this case was the lack of time available for defence counsel to meet with the accused and adequately prepare for their defence. Given that the prisoners had arrived at Pond Inlet at 7 a.m. after a sleepless night on the deck of the ship, it seems hardly possible, with only one interpreter, that he had sufficient time to interview his three prisoners and prepare his case. Moreover, there is no record on file that he made any attempt to contact the accused prior to commencement of the trial. Mindful of the extenuating circumstances, the court proved to be exceptionally flexible in allowing evidence not previously introduced. On two occasions witnesses were called who had not previously made an official statement: William Duval and Miquitui, Kunuk's wife.

Following the preliminaries and the opening statement by the Crown, eight witnesses were called to testify for the prosecution that day.[52] The first to take the stand was Staff-Sergeant Joy, to explain how he had conducted his investigation. He was followed by Urulu, who had accompanied the

STIPENDIARY MAGISTRATE'S COURT OF THE NORTHWEST TERRITORIES
REX V. "NOOKUDLAH, OOROOEUNGNAK, AND AHTEETAH"
POND INLET, 25-30 AUGUST 1923

Stipendiary Magistrate Presiding   Hon. Louis-Alfred-Adéhmar Rivet
Orderly to the Judge   Constable B.C. Jakeman

Legal Counsel   Alan Falardeau, Prosecution
Leopold Tellier, Defence

Clerk of the Court   François X. Biron

Interpreter   Wilfred Duval

Deputy Sheriff   Staff-Sergeant Alfred Herbert Joy
Escorts for the Prisoners   Constables F.L. Fairman and C.G. Fielder

Jury   Léon Lemieux, Foreman
Eugene Blouin
William George Earl
Luger Lemieux
Alfred Levesque
Albert Theriault

Witnesses for the Prosecution (in order of appearance)	Witnesses for the Defence (in order of appearance)
Staff-Sergeant A.H. Joy	William Duval
Oo-orloo (*Urulu*)	Penneloo (*Paniluk*) on re-call
Kutchuk (*Kassak*)	Staff-Sergeant A.H. Joy on re-call
Ahtootahloo (*Ataguttaaluk*)	Kamanuk (*Qamaniq*)
Omee (*Umik*)	Munoo (*Manu*)
Munne (*Maniq*)	Oomee (*Umik*) on re-call
Sinnikah (*Siniqqaq*)	Ahtooteuk (*Ataguttiaq*)
Ootookito (*Uuttukuttuk*)	Mikootooee (*Miqutui*) *Kunuk's wife*
Deposition by Edineyah (*Ijjangiaq*),deceased	Staff-Sergeant A.H. Joy on re-call
Ootookito (*Uuttukuttuk*) on re-call	Ahteetah (*Aatitaaq*)
Kowkwatsoo (*Kaukuarjuk*)	Nookudlah (*Nuqallaq*)
Nootagagayook (*Nutarariaq*)	
Koonnoon (*Kunuk*)	
Ivahlung (*Ivalu*)	
Palmee (*Paumi*)	
Ekussah (*Iqaqsaq*)	
Mikootooee (*Miqutui*)	
Ekepireyah (*Iqipiriaq*)	
Penneloo (*Paniluk*)	

Participants at the murder trial, Pond Inlet, 1923.

police officer to retrieve Janes' body from the shores of Admiralty Inlet. Kassak and Ataguttaaluk were called next, to explain the events at the camp before Janes was killed. Then Umik was called. His statement, recorded after his arrival at Bylot Island that summer, had explained in detail why and how Janes had come after him with a knife at Tulukkaat.

Umik – Sannirut, 8 August 1923

I went to see Janes in his house, he then asked me about the tobacco I received for
the fox skin and deer skins, and when I told him he immediately began to swear at
me, and caught me by the chest and held his other hand as if he was going to punch
me. He then pushed me out the house, and as I was going through the door, Janes
picked up a knife and held it as if he was going to strike me. I did not move, I
thought he was only trying to scare me, but he afterwards struck at me with the
knife but I jumped away, and the knife just missed my side. I then ran away, and
Janes threw a piece of deer horn at me and a piece of whale bone, but neither of
them touched me. I was very scared and shaking all over. I went to my tent and got
my rifle ready, so that if Janes came after me, I was going to shoot him, but he
returned to the house and did not come out again.[53]

Ironically, had Umik shot Janes when he was being attacked, in all likelihood he would not have been convicted, as it would have been a clear case
of self-defence.

Cultural differences, which are apparent when comparing points of
Canadian law to accepted Inuit customs, were also evident in how the
questions asked of each witness were interpreted. While the Inuit were
trying to explain what happened with regard to what was important by
their traditions, that same evidence was measured according to Canadian
law. This was particularly noticeable when the Crown prosecutor tried to
show that the Inuit knew the difference between right and wrong. As explained later by Alex Stevenson,

In the examination of each witness, dialogue similar to the following took place
between Mr. Falardeau and the witness:
    "Did one Eskimo ever kill another Eskimo?"
    "Yes."
    "What happened to him?"
    "He ran away."
    "Why?"
    "He did not want to be killed."
    "Who would kill him?"
    "The dead man's relatives."[54]

What was missing was the chance to explain that if a dead person's relatives accepted the action as necessary, they would forgive the killer. In this
instance Nuqallaq had not run away, believing his action was warranted
and fully supported by others in the community. While it is true that he
later moved back to Igloolik, he did come forward on his own when he
mistook Peter Freuchen for a policeman, to explain what had happened.

As shown in Stevenson's example, what might "justify" an action in an Inuk's perception might "condemn" it under Canadian law. Thus while all the witnesses knew they would be asked questions, they had no way of knowing how their answers might be interpreted to the disadvantage of the prisoners.

Maniq and Siniqqaq followed next. Both had been present at the hunting camp when Janes arrived. Maniq had actually helped Nuqallaq hide behind a *qamutiik* and stood "on watch" to alert him when Janes was coming. Siniqqaq, however, was absent when Janes was killed, but he could tell the court how the white trader had taken Aatitaaq's furs away from him. Had each been asked if they had "heard" Janes say he would kill the Inuit or their dogs, they would likely have answered "no" as they had done before. The Crown prosecutor's calling upon Uuttukuttuk next suggests the intent to show that Janes' former guide had not told anyone else about the trader's threats to kill people and their dogs. Yet Uuttukattuk's answers were confusing, and he was visibly frightened. According to one source, he apparently ran off and hid, necessitating his recall at a later time.[55] Years later an elder would suggest that Uuttukuttuk might have been at least partly to blame for the trader's death because he had taken him to the hunting camp at Camp Crauford instead of directly to Igloolik as planned. The implication was that he was afraid of being alone with the trader.[56]

The previous statement by Ijjangiaq (by this time deceased) was then submitted, essentially absolving his brother Aatitaaq from any wrongdoing. The court, which had opened at 10 a.m., with two recesses for meals, finally adjourned at 10:15 p.m. on Saturday night and remained in recess until Monday morning. On Sunday the *qallunaat* reportedly slept and read, whereas the Inuit gathered for games, dancing, accordion music, and general merrymaking – creating suspicions among the court party that perhaps they were not taking the trial seriously.[57]

When the court reconvened at 10 a.m. sharp on Monday morning, the Crown prosecutor resumed his examination of the witnesses, calling upon Nutarariaq, Kunuk, Ivalu, and Paumi. All had been present at the camp at the time of the shooting. Paumi's statement to Joy that summer suggested that he was sorry to see Janes killed, even though he knew that the trader had intended to meet with the hunters that night and put more pressure on them to hand over their furs. He also explained how frightened he was of Janes, how he had offered to give him all his foxes without pay to keep him happy, and how later he became afraid again after his father told him that the *qallunaat* would find out and "make more trouble for the Eskimos."[58] Similar fears were expressed by others. Although most concurred with Iqipiriaq's claim that "all the men at Cape Crawford said Janes had better be dead," referring to the collective responsibility inherent in consensual

Inuit used the Sunday court recess as a time for games and general merrymaking. McInnes Collection.

agreement, from a legal perspective this could be interpreted as collective guilt.[59] Underlying all else was a profound fear of the *qallunaat* and the possibility that they might take revenge for Janes' death.

On Tuesday, Falardeau questioned further witnesses, this time Iqaqsaq, Miqutui, and Iqipiriaq. Although they had not testified at the inquest or preliminary hearings, their statements had been recorded at Button Point while waiting for the ship to arrive. As Joy predicted, more contradictions surfaced. Miqutui, for example, admitted that he had said that the white trader should be killed following the dispute over Kunuk's furs, but he also maintained that he later warned Nuqallaq that the "white people would make more trouble" if he killed Janes. Iqipiriaq, on the other hand, firmly refuted Kassak's earlier claim that he had not participated in any discussions about what action should be taken, and placed Kassak at the centre the afternoon before Janes was killed.[60]

The "many questions in succession" seemed to tire and confuse the Inuit, and the additional delays for translation into French and English prolonged the ordeal.[61] Years later, Ataguttiaq told her children that the judge became "very angry" when some Inuit gave contradictory answers. His exact words were not recorded, but when translated, alarmed the Inuit, who believed that they were all going to be killed. Captain Bernier was reported to have declared that "If you are going to kill them, I'll leave – and I'll leave without you."[62] Martha Akumalik, who was present at the trial as a young child, also remembered people talking about the contradictory stories that made the judge angry. In her version, "Kapitaikallak [Bernier] then said that he pitied the people, and he went to his ship, entered his cabin and didn't come out again. He didn't want to see his people suffer." She believed that the interpreter had caused the problem because he was speaking too quickly and that Nuqallaq had intervened and "saved the people":

Martha Akumalik – Pond Inlet, 18 March 1994

Qiugaarjuk [Nuqallaq] grabbed this interpreter and told him, "Look, look, you are giving out contradictory information and you're confusing the people. Wait until that person has finished speaking before you start interpreting what he had said." So the interpreter then started to wait until the person had finished talking before he started interpreting. That was when the people started to understand what was being said.[63]

An excellent interpreter in his time, Duval seemed in the film footage to look and act older than his years and may have had difficulty in translating the intent of the judge's statements. The challenge of providing continuous simultaneous translations over a period of five days would exhaust even the most accomplished interpreter. On the other hand, it is equally possible that the judge might have been intemperate in his frustration. Certainly in a later interview, Judge Rivet was reported to have said that if the Inuit had been *qallunaat*, "he would have held about twenty of the witnesses as accessories to the murder."[64]

After two and a half days of testimony for the prosecution, the defence counsel finally had the opportunity to call on his witnesses. In an unexpected move William Duval testified first, apparently at his own request. Author Kenn Harper, who has researched and written extensively on Duval, suggested that the interpreter felt "empathy for the Inuit who could not possibly understand the implications of the proceedings of which they were a part."[65] As a member of the court party, his appearance as a witness was yet another deviation from accepted procedures, but then, this was a most uncommon trial where anomalies seemed to be the norm rather than the exception. Even today, determinants governed by physical and human geography still demand flexibility in the administration of Arctic justice.

Paniluk, who had once worked for Janes, was recalled at this point, as was Staff-Sergeant Joy. For the record, counsel established the death of Wilfred Caron who had been expected to testify for the defence. Qamaniq and Manu then took the stand in that order, both of whom had worked for Janes. Umik was re-called, after which the court finally adjourned at 7:30 p.m., this time with only one recess for lunch. On Wednesday the

Court in recess. *Left to right:* Defence Counsel Tellier; Dr Livingstone and an unidentified RCMP officer; Mr Falardeau leaning against the wall talking to a government official; two unidentified police officers with William Duval; Mrs Craig, Inspector Wilcox, and an unnamed individual. Tredgold Collection. NAC – PA 187325.

weather suddenly changed, bringing warm air and sunny skies. In a session lasting for only three hours, Ataguttiaq and Miqutui (Kunuk's wife) were both questioned, with Joy once again recalled to the stand. The testimony by Miqutui must have been considered critical by the defence, as this was the first time she had been asked to make a statement. Significantly, she was also the only one who could confirm or refute Ataguttiaq's story about setting out to find the hunters so they could warn them of Janes' renewed threats. Previously, Joy had not attached much importance to Ataguttiaq's story, yet now the court heard evidence from both women. One cannot help wondering if the presence of Mrs Craig had some influence on the matter.

After Nuqallaq and Aatitaaq had testified, the session ended rather abruptly at 1 p.m., with an advisement that the lawyers' submissions would be heard the following morning. Ululijarnaat was never questioned. Other than the fact that crowded courtroom was likely hot and airless, an unforeseen event may have prompted the early recess.[66] According to one juror, a pod of narwhals was sighted from a window while court was in session, eliciting exuberant cries of "*Qilalugait!*" and followed by a mass exodus of Inuit hunters with rifles in hand. By the juror's account, the judicial party did not know what was happening and sought refuge under the tables.[67] If this was so, a subsequent report by British-born Inspector Wilcox that the trial had been "conducted throughout ... with all the decorum of a

Preparing for a re-enactment of the trial for the cinema-photographer, 29 August 1923. From the far right, jury foreman Léon Lemieux, Staff-Sergeant Joy, and Inspector Wilcox in the fur hat. NAC – PA 210046.

Supreme Court in civilization"[68] must have raised a few smiles among those present.

Given the unexpected break in the weather, George Valiquette set up his film camera in readiness for a photo session. He was immediately surrounded by curious women and children, who came to inspect his "magic box" with the name "Fox News" prominently displayed on the side. Unable to film the proceedings in the dimly lit courtroom, he arranged for the court party and jury to stage a re-enactment of the trial outside the detachment on the sunny west side, with a British flag draped over the window as a backdrop. A table and chairs were set up for the participants, with the judge and lawyers dressed in their black gowns and the jurors in dress uniforms. Scenes that survived the editing include the jury being sworn in, examination of Staff-Sergeant Joy, an elderly Inuk talking to William Duval, and apparently the jury foreman delivering his verdict – even though he had yet to do so. The accused were notably absent, as were the witnesses, although the latter may well have been off hunting narwhal.[69] Meanwhile Dr Livingstone took the opportunity to examine the three prisoners and issued certificates stating that he had "found no physical defects."[70]

When court reopened at 10 a.m. on Thursday morning, another weather change had brought a return of gloomy skies and snow flurries. Counsel delivered their submissions with Tellier, the lawyer for the defence, asking that "the life of the Eskimos, their ignorance of the laws of civilization, and the provocation given them by Janes be taken into consideration by the jury in arriving at their verdict."[71] He also argued that the evidence against Aatitaaq was weak and urged that he be acquitted.[72] Mr Falardeau for the prosecution was similarly sympathetic in his summation, stating that "in civilization, he would ask for a verdict of murder," but because of "the ignorance of the prisoners," he recommended that a conviction be entered for manslaughter. He also informed the jury "that they could, if they desired, recommend the accuseds to the clemency of the court." Compared to the beginning of the trial, when one juror had remarked that it "looked bad against Nukudlah," it was apparent that attitudes had shifted.[73] On the recommendation of both counsel, the hard line originally proposed by Commissioner Starnes was replaced by a more sensitive and reasonable approach. Before reviewing the material evidence for the jury, Judge Rivet praised the efforts of the lawyers, the interpreter, and in particular Staff-Sergeant Joy.[74]

The jurors took only twenty minutes before returning with a verdict. According to one member, this was quite understandable as they had discussed the case for an hour the night before.[75] Rightly or wrongly, it appears that they had more or less made up their minds prior to hearing the lawyers' summations and the judge's "charge to the jury." Reflecting a slightly different mindset than counsel, they found Nuqallaq "guilty of manslaughter" and ignored the opportunity to urge clemency. Ululijarnaat was also found guilty on the same charge, but in his case they did recommend leniency. Aatitaaq, on the other hand, was found "not guilty" for lack of evidence.

Without further deliberation Judge Rivet sentenced Nuqallaq to ten years in Stony Mountain Penitentiary. Ululijarnaat was given two years of hard labour in "close confinement" at Pond Inlet, and the charges against Aatitaaq were dropped. The judge again took the opportunity to impress upon the prisoners the "enormity of their crime," telling them that while their sentences were light, any recurrence would be dealt with far more severely.[76] Ten years in a southern penitentiary could hardly be considered a "light sentence," but anything less would make it difficult to justify the expense of the court party, let alone the cost of the new police detachments and the annual expedition to supply them.

The court was adjourned, and Nuqallaq was immediately led outside and taken aboard the CGS *Arctic* where he was handed over to Corporal Jakeman, who would be responsible for his custody. Official reports of what followed were written to impress the Canadian public and bore little resemblance to what really happened. Thus Inspector Wilcox would claim that "it is hardly possible that a native, with the prestige that Noo-kud-lah must have had with the other Eskimo at the time he killed Janes, could have been subjected to greater humiliation than to be led away directly under the eyes

Nuqallaq with short hair after the sentencing, 30 August 1923. McInnes Collection.

of not less than one hundred of his relatives and friends."⁷⁷ Photographs suggest a quite different story. Excluding the *qallunaat* onlookers and dogs, the Inuit who had gathered after the trial numbered fewer than forty, including men, women, and children. Moreover, Nuqallaq did not appear in the least humiliated and instead seemed to enjoy being the centre of attention as the judge and police lined up to have their photograph taken with the prisoner. If anything, he appeared proud and confident, with a smile that suggested serenity and inner strength. The inspector's comments might have been designed to justify the cost of the police investigation and trial, but in this case the pictures were "worth a thousand words."

Before the ship's departure the police were asked to gather everyone together to hear the judge explain "the objects of the trial and the reasons for the police coming into the north." With Duval again translating, Rivet emphasized that the RCMP were there "not only to protect the white man from the Eskimos, but also to see that justice was done to the Eskimos in all their dealings with the white man."⁷⁸ Others had slightly different

Posing for the cameras after the trial. *Left to right:* Constable Tredgold,
Nuqallaq, Constable Fairman, and Judge Louis A. Rivet. T.H. Tredgold
Collection. NAC – PA 187327.

interpretations. Inspector Wilcox, for example, described how the judge
had told the Inuit that "they could expect kindness and protection from
the Police if they behaved well, but if they committed any crime they
could expect to be punished."[79] RCMP historian Harwood Steele remarked
with unveiled sarcasm that this was the same "old explanation given
in '74 to the prairie Indians, transferred to the Arctic." Referring to reports
that the Inuit gave "three generous cheers for the judge," Steele concluded
his version of the "Janes Murder Case" with the paradoxical proclamation
that "Justice had come to the World's End."[80] Martha Akumalik, having
witnessed the incident as a child, described the "cheers" as just "a lot of
noise, because they were saved from being killed."[81]

The claim that Nuqallaq had no further communication with his people
after being led away was also untrue. According to Mr Earl, one of the
jurors, both Nuqallaq's wife and his father visited him aboard the ship and
brought gifts for those who would be looking after him. Ataguttiaq was
reported to have been upset and crying, but in Earl's opinion, "Nookudlah

Judge Rivet, far left, explaining the outcome of the trial and the advantages of Canadian citizenship to the Inuit. William Duval to his right was translating. NAC – PA 207904.

did not seem to mind in the least. He spoke a little English and asked for water," which was quickly brought to him. This was a seemingly minor incident, but one that his father and wife might interpret as meaning that he was well looked after and still very much in control.[82] Certainly his demeanour suggested that he may still have thought, as he earlier explained to Peter Freuchen, that "he would first go to the white man's land" before it was decided whether he would be punished.[83]

When the CGS *Arctic* departed that evening, another scene was staged for the Inuit, this time to dramatize the prisoner's removal from the community. Martha Akumalik recalled her last glimpse of Nuqallaq:

Martha Akumalik – Pond Inlet, 1994

I can still see it in my mind, that time. The ship had its sails all up. As it turned out, it was the ship's cabin, all painted white, and he was in front of the white cabin so he could be seen more clearly by his wife, Ataguttiaq, and she was crying and I thought, I guess she loves him dearly. I was full of thoughts then.[84]

As it happened, Nuqallaq experienced an unorthodox sendoff for a convicted man. He was joined on board ship by nine Inuit families with all their worldly belongings, as the ship carried them back to their camps along Navy Board Inlet, and for those from Arctic Bay and Igloolik, to Baillarge Inlet just north of Strathcona Sound.[85] At one point, according to Commander Craig, the ship was carrying "roughly 25 whites, 60 Eskimos, and 80 dogs."[86] One is not quite sure whether the frequent tabulation of human passengers and possessions was to show the need for a new ship or merely a reflection of Craig's own astonishment.

Nuqallaq on display as the ship leaves Eclipse Sound. NAC – PA
207907.

While the ship delivered its human cargo to the mouth of Admiralty Inlet,
Sergeant Joy was busy writing a summary report based on the handwritten
transcript of the trial recorded by the clerk of the court. For reasons unstated,
this draft transcript was not submitted to the Department of Justice but instead remained on file at the Pond Inlet detachment, along with notes written by one or more of the Francophone jurors. This might be explained by
the fact that once the charge had been reduced to manslaughter, it was no
longer considered a "capital" case that required a transcript be kept on file in
Ottawa. In the mid-1950s the handwritten draft was apparently ordered destroyed along with other records.[87] There is evidence that a copy of the draft
document may still survive, but since it is still a restricted document until officially released by the RCMP, it cannot ethically be cited in a publication.[88]

For those who had expected a death sentence, the outcome must have seemed anticlimatic. No one took notice of the subtle irony that the body of Robert Janes still remained buried in a shallow grave on the shore of Eclipse Sound, while a government ship carried his killer south. Nor was there any further thought given to the disposition of the victim's remains. Ten days later, almost as an afterthought, Joy provided an explanation for Aatitaaq's acquittal in a separate memo to his commanding officer, who would wait another year before receiving it.

I omitted to state that when prisoner Noo-kud-lah came [to] the stand he stated that Ahteetah took no part in the killing of Janes; that he went to Ahteetah to get his assistance, he gave the excuse that he was too young and did not want to have anything to do with it, although he went out [of] the igloo with Noo-kud-lah and Oo-roo-re-ung-nak, and remained with the party until Janes was dead. The evidence against Ahteetah was weak from the commencement, and although they saw Ahteetah with his hands on Janes, after he was hit by the first bullet, they were unable to say whether it was for the purpose of assisting Janes or preventing his escape, and these being the only witnesses against Ahteetah, there was not sufficient evidence to warrant a conviction.[89]

Although elders at Pond Inlet were still convinced that Aatitaaq was let go because he was the youngest of the accused and had a family with small children, a *qallunaaq* might have other explanations, such as the possibility that Joy or Nuqallaq – or perhaps both – had conscience pangs because of the death of Aatitaaq's brother. From a strictly legal perspective, it was evident that Joy did not have enough evidence to convict Aatitaaq unless the three accused were tried separately, as he had requested. For whatever reason, this option was rejected. In the summer of 1923 Arctic justice worked in mysterious ways.

The jury's failure to urge clemency on Nuqallaq's behalf may seem hardhearted based on our current knowledge of the case. Yet there were extenuating circumstances, over and above the judge's charge to the jury. At some point the jurors had learned that Nuqallaq's first wife had committed suicide, allegedly after being subjected to a beating.[90] While this information appears to have been acquired through gossip, it could not help but influence their opinion of the accused. Even today a number of Inuit still believe that this was the reason he was punished more severely than the others. While the source of such a story was undoubtedly Inuit, it was not surprising that the fur traders and police might discuss this among themselves to justify the outcome of the trial. Elder Noak Piugaatuk from Igloolik, now deceased, was convinced that Nuqallaq's abusive behaviour was the reason he had been singled out for harsh punishment, but he did not think the subject was formally discussed at the trial.

Noah Piugaatuk – Igloolik, 1989

So then they arrived and that is when the questioning started. Qiugaarjuk was known for his abusive behaviour toward his wife. He had a first wife, who got so tired of him that she took her own life. When the two were out hunting alone out on the land, it was said that when they returned they found that she had lost a lot of weight. Because he was the one who murdered the white man and in addition because he tended to abuse his wife was also put into consideration when he was arrested.

One must understand that there was very little else the Inuit could have done but to terminate the white person, but because he [Nuqallaq] was an abusive man towards his wife, that he was why he was arrested.

[Killing Janes] was the main reason for his arrest, but his conviction also put into consideration that he was an abusive man. They did not talk about his abusive behaviour at that time, but it was known that his wife had taken her own life because of him. And then when he remarried it was to someone that was too much younger than he was and there was a facial scar which was caused by him. She was about my age, slightly older than I am. Qiugaarjuk was taken away on account of that.[91]

Initially Ataguttiaq's father had been reluctant to allow her to marry Nuqallaq because of the stories, but in the end he believed that she was a strong-willed girl and would probably be "all right" with him. Ataguttiaq stated that she had wanted to marry Nuqallaq even though she was aware of his reputation.[92]

Rumours still abound about Nuqallaq's abusive tendency, but likely the most accurate account was told by Ataguttiaq herself to Father Guy Mary-Rousselière.

Ataguttiaq – Pond Inlet, 1974

I knew [Nuqallaq] – who was known as Qiugaarjuk – a long time ago when I was still a young girl. He and his first wife were middle-aged and I saw them often as a child. I was still a child when she killed herself with a gun shot at San-nirut, in the house of the whites uninhabited at that time. Nuqallaq was gone out on the ice, hunting seal. After the suicide her in-laws who lived at a distance were notified. But he was not told that his wife had killed herself until he came back.

I don't remember how long he remained widowed but one day he wanted to have me as his wife. He saw my parents about it, but they refused because his wife had killed herself and he was now quite old. We left there a short time later, but he followed us and finally I married him.[93]

Ataguttiaq on the right with her best friend, Ukpikjuujaq, 1923. NAC – PA 42118.

Accusations of wife abuse would not make Nuqallaq any more or any less guilty of Janes' death, but it could have had an influence on the jury's decision whether to recommend clemency for a prisoner with a history of violence.

Ululijarnaat's relatively light sentence raised few questions. His cheerful disposition and willingness to lend assistance made him popular among Inuit and *qallunaat* alike. He was also reputed to be an excellent hunter and a good provider for his family. A few Inuit still recall vague stories about his having saved the life of a police officer. As one might expect, his sentence of two years "hard labour" seemed almost farcical. Both he and Aatitaaq acted as guides and dog drivers for the police, and on at least one occasion went out on patrol together. Ululijarnaat was not paid for his work during the two years of his sentence, but he was given a gun and supplied weekly with ammunition and staple foods for his family. Nuqallaq would not be so fortunate.

When Captain Munn finally reached Pond Inlet aboard the HBC *Nascopie*, he was reportedly distraught to learn that the trial had ended and Nuqallaq had been taken away. At least that was the impression he gave to the Inuit who had once worked for him:

Isapee Qanguq – Igloolik (no date)

After the affair of Sakirmiaq [Janes] and the time Qiugaarjuk was taken away, another ship arrived to Mittimatalik. It was said that their boss [Munn] started to act irrationally at the white people who were there, including the police and the Company manager who was called Nujaqangittuq [Wilfrid Parsons]. He was upset and mad at these white people for allowing an Inuk to be taken away by the people that had made the judgement. He was in a hurry so he could catch up to "AATI" [CGS *Arctic*] so that he could get the Inuk back to his people. It was said that he was not afraid of anyone. So it is said that he did not catch up to the ship, so the Inuk was taken down south. This happened when the Inuit did not know the ways of the white people and he was really upset, that the Inuit had been treated the way they did with the Sakirmiaq affair. It was said that he was taking sides with the Inuit and said that the Inuit knew what they were doing and the killing was done to defend the Inuit. He had also said that as the Inuit did not know the ways of the white people and the fact that the Inuit population was very minimal, that they should be left alone.[94]

Of course Munn, or Kapitaikuluk, as he was called by the Inuit, could not have freed Nuqallaq even if he had managed to catch up with the ship. But true to his promise, he did try to gain the Inuk's early release from prison. In his autobiography Munn would refer to him as "My Friend Nukudlah, the Murderer."[95]

   While the official police reports attempted to portray the trial as an unqualified success, most *qallunaat* observers at the trial remained silent. Therkel Mathiassen of the Fifth Thule Expedition, who was engaged in archaeological studies on Eclipse Sound that summer, witnessed the proceedings first hand, yet made no public comment. Peter Freuchen, a fellow member of the expedition, was not present at the trial, but his references to the event in subsequent publications were derisive of Canadian justice. He described meeting Nuqallaq's father the summer after the trial, and told how Umik viewed his son's trip to the South as an "achievement" and had insisted that his success was a result of his conversion to Christianity. At other camps Freuchen discovered that Nuqallaq was considered a hero: "The fame of the murderer had reached the place ahead of us and was still a great sensation. He had been promised room and board for ten years in the great house of Canada. The house was kept warm in the winter, there would be women to sew clothes for him, and he would never have to go hunting for his food."[96] Scholars tend to treat Freuchen's stories with suspicion, but his cynical views of Canadian justice appeared

Gertrude Craig with Judge Rivet and Therkel Matthiassen of the
Fifth Thule Expedition, Pond Inlet, 1923. NAC – PA 210047.

in his book the *Vagrant Viking*, which was published throughout the western world. If Canadian officials hoped that the trial would show the world that they were effectively administrating its Arctic territory, this was not the sort publicity they had in mind.

Not everyone agreed with Freuchen. Morris Longstreth, author of *The Silent Force: Scenes from the Life of the Mounted Police in Canada* (1927), claimed to have had access to police records and to have interviewed a number of officers. He too was cynical, but for different reasons: "The long-drawn tale makes it clear that Nookudlah had killed a white man. It is true, of course, that this white man invaded his land, brought strange customs, ignored the native cardinal principal of good nature, provoked natives, terrified them with threats to kill them and their dogs. But a white man had been killed and must be avenged. It is the natives' misfortune if they had not heard of the custom called the law. Nookudlah must be punished. Otherwise, white traders might not feel safe to trade jack knives for foxes. The immoral ethic of conquest has been pleased to clothe itself in legal terms. It is a sign that as brigands, we at least grow politer."[97]

Under the sarcasm lies an uncomfortable element of truth. The trial was not driven by any idealistic quest for justice but motivated by a dual purpose: on the one hand, to teach the Inuit a lesson to ensure *qallunaat* could live among them without fear, and on the other, to make a statement to the world that Canada was effectively administrating its Arctic lands. Some have argued that the trial represented an important first step in colonizing the Inuit people. Yet Canada would be a reluctant colonizer, inspired not by a desire to acquire Inuit lands or subjugate the inhabitants but by the necessity to protect the legacy of British polar explorers.

The 1923 murder trial at Pond Inlet was not a particularly proud moment in the annuals of Canadian legal history, but it might have been worse. At some point in the proceedings, common sense prevailed when it was acknowledged that the Inuit of North Baffin were ignorant of Canadian laws. As a result Nuqallaq would not be sentenced to death for killing Robert Janes. Perhaps suppression of the trial transcript was understandable under the circumstances, but human frailties notwithstanding, the bending of truth and unwarranted censorship is not as easily forgiven – or forgotten. As it happened, the worst was yet to come.

8

To Prison and Return

After returning the witnesses and their families to the vicinity of their camps on Navy Board Sound and Admiralty Inlet, the CGS *Arctic* stopped briefly at Pond Inlet to pick up the government party and Joy's report on the trial, then proceeded south to Cumberland Sound. Upon arrival at Pangnirtung on 11 September, the ship's crew and police immediately set to building the detachment not far from the HBC post. Major L.T. Burwash, a former Yukon gold commissioner, would remain at Pangnirtung that winter to study the needs of the Inuit and make recommendations to the government. Inspector Wilcox was appointed officer in charge of the new police post, assisted by Corporal McInnes and Constables MacGregor and Fielder. The primary objective for establishing the new detachment was to facilitate investigation of multiple murders reported to have taken place at Qivittuuq, a small trading post on the Baffin coast north of Cumberland Sound.

Since the detachment had been first alerted to the violence, more information had been collected from Inuit arriving at Pond Inlet from the south. Staff-Sergeant Joy was told that the post manager, an Inuk, had assumed the role of a lay preacher. Suffering from bouts of insanity, he became obsessed with the idea that he was the son of God and ordered the death of two Inuuk. In the end he was killed by a blood relative just as he was about to bludgeon another member of the group. Commander Craig attached little importance to the incident, adding "justifiable homicide" and his initials in the margin of Joy's second report. It was forwarded to O.S. Finnie for comment, who replied that it was obviously a "case of insanity" and presumed "no further action will be taken in the matter." Instead he suggested that the Inuk who killed the insane man should be commended for acting "in the defence of the other members of the tribe."[1] Still, the murders had been reported, requiring police to investigate. Moreover, a full and detailed report would help justify the cost of the new detachment.

There was no mention of whether Nuqallaq was allowed to go ashore at Pangnirtung, but he did participate in another picture-taking session. The weather had been so warm during the trip that no one had reason to use the skin clothing supplied by the government. A number donned the outfits to have their pictures taken for posterity, with Mrs Craig's white fox outfit confirming that her voyage had been planned well in advance. A photograph taken of her standing beside the prisoner indicated that he was taller and more robust than he looked standing beside the judge and his police escorts. Everyone, it appeared, wanted to have a picture taken with the prisoner. Someone even took a photograph of four police officers in uniform sitting on the ship's rail with cameras held to their faces, reportedly photographing the prisoner. Some albums suggested the expedition had acquired a surrealism unrelated to its purpose, more like a cruise-ship tour of the Arctic, with Nuqallaq as the star attraction on the final leg of the voyage.

Compared to the hype and rhetoric in Inspector Wilcox's account of the trial, Commander Craig's preliminary report written to O.S. Finnie as the ship sailed home seemed flat and lifeless. He stated that the sentences imposed "were generally approved of as being just and satisfactory," perhaps implying that not everyone was in agreement. His own sympathy for the prisoner was evident in the request that special instructions be forwarded to the penitentiary concerning Nuqallaq's care, "particularly as to the temperature of his cell, his clothing, and food, and tobacco."[2] Craig's intentions were well placed, but it is doubtful he would have had much influence once the prisoner was placed in the warden's care.

The official press release on the expedition deliberately downplayed the trial, perhaps hoping to avoid the negative press that had accompanied the earlier trial of Uluksuk and Sinnisiak, and more recently, the Herschel Island trials. Judge Dubuc, who had presided over Alikomiak's trial, was singularly unsuccessful in avoiding public condemnation for having sentenced him to death by hanging for the murders of Corporal Doak and Otto Binder. Bishop Lucas had attended the trial and voiced his outrage to the western press, claiming that prisoner was only a lad in his late teens and should not be hung. He also argued that the outbreak of Inuit violence only started after Binder had taken an Inuit woman as his wife. The case attracted even more attention when it was discovered that the court party had brought a hangman with them on the ship and that a grave had been dug for the accused prior to sentencing.[3] The story was picked up by the Toronto newspapers, and several petitions were circulated to request a stay of execution.[4]

With the attention focused elsewhere, the cgs *Arctic* managed to slip into her berth at Quebec City with minimal press coverage. Once radio contact had been established, a coded telegram was sent to Ottawa giving the ship's location in the Strait of Belle Isle, with an estimated time of arrival deliberately leaked to the press. Meanwhile, a secretary was flown to meet the ship at Father Point and assist Commander Craig in preparing an official press release, with delivery to the daily newspapers timed to arrive well after the ship had docked and the prisoner was on his way to Winnipeg.

The news release was accurate except for "errors of omission" and an overly positive report on the status of Inuit health. Otherwise, the censorship rule was in force, requiring anyone on the trip wishing to write a story for publication to first submit it to the department for approval. The radio operator, it appears, circumvented the rules by simply handing over his diary notes to a reporter from the *Toronto Star Weekly*. The subsequent article was long, detailed, and accompanied by many photographs, an equivalent of the newspaper's earlier coverage of the Herschel Island trials. Even then, the Pond Inlet trial failed to raise any protest – likely because Nuqallaq had not been sentenced to hang on the gallows.

Most daily newspapers tended to repeat the press release almost word for word, thus giving intended emphasis to the scientific nature of the expedition and various "good news" items, with only a few sentences on the trial. The conclusion of the article in the *Toronto Globe*, however, was a prime example of inaccurate journalism and imperious nonsense: "Two death sentences were imposed, one for killing a policeman and one for killing another Eskimo. The Eskimos were much impressed by the proceedings, and the Judge addressed a mass meeting after the trial ... and read them a lesson on the advantages of British citizenship."[5] Obviously there was no photograph of the "mass meeting," which would have shown less than forty Inuit in attendance, at the most. The *Montreal Star*, however, took top prize for creative journalism when it reported that Pond Inlet was located "a little north of Labrador," and that a new detachment at Cape Sabine was needed to "check the incursion of Icelanders, who have been crossing over to Ellesmere and running foul of the Eskimos in an effort to bag musk oxen."[6]

The *Quebec Telegraph* was at least more accurate when it described how "the trial was said to have spread fear among the Eskimoes and much is expected as a result."[7] This newspaper also managed to have a reporter at Father Point when the CGS *Arctic* stopped to pick up a secretary to assist Commander Craig, and again at King's Wharf in Quebec City when the prisoner was led off the ship. The headlines were designed to attract the reader's attention: "Dramatic Account of Eskimo Murder Trial," and "White Man's Law of 'an Eye for an Eye' Listened to With Awe and Wonder by the Natives." The police officers accompanying the prisoner were asked what he thought might happen to him, and they quoted Nuqallaq as stating that "I know where I am going, to the white man's prison with strong wooden bars; and I am going there on a sleigh without dogs."

Describing the convicted murderer as "a very picturesque individual," the reporter added further details: "The prisoner did not seem the least bit perturbed at the thought of having to spend the next ten years at Stony Mountain Penitentiary in Manitoba; in fact, he grinned quite delightedly when the moving picture man proceeded to take a 'close-up.' He was dressed in a blue cloth suit with brass buttons, a green woollen cap, a khaki shirt and beaver boots, which, as explained by the police, was a bit different to his customary attire in the north country, where nothing but the skins of animals are worn by the natives."[8] Unfortunately, this particular film footage does not appear to have survived. The reporter was also clever to spot Mrs Craig disembarking with her husband.

Both Judge Rivet and Commander Craig agreed to be interviewed the following morning. Craig wanted to talk about the scientific aspects of his work and the government's future plans for the Arctic, but the reporter was relentless for news of the trial: "Mr. Craig was asked if the prisoner, being used to a wild free life in the open, would stand the strain of his incarceration or languish while mourning for his far-off home, and after a pause, the speaker stated that, although the prisoner was very hardy and healthy, he had heard the question raised and the consensus of opinion was to the effect that the Eskimo would never live behind stone walls, 'but' he said 'the authorities will, no doubt, look into this phase of the affair and a close watch will be kept on him.'"[9] For Craig to have said anything further would be admitting that Nuqallaq's ten years at Stony Mountain Penitentiary might well be a death sentence by another name.

By comparison, Judge Rivet seemed delighted to talk about the case, noting that he had extreme difficulty in understanding the evidence "on account of the Eskimo names." Under the circumstances, he explained that "he could not very well pass the sentence of death upon them because they were ignorant to a certain extent of the law." What was more disconcerting was the reporter's description of the "facts of the case" as described by the judge: "There had been trouble brewing between Janes, the trapper, and the three natives ... for a considerable length of time, and during the course of the evidence, it was learned that the trapper had threatened to steal the furs of the natives in retaliation for an alleged grievance. The three Eskimos, it was claimed, distrusted Janes and as there was also a question of jealousy existing regarding the wives of the natives, they decided to do away with him at the first favourable opportunity. And that is what happened, as we already know."[10] One can only hope that the reporter, not the judge, had misunderstood the so-called "facts." Unfortunately, this was the story that the English-speaking citizens of Quebec City would read in their evening newspaper.

A further example of the disparity between the "official word" and the "real world" can be found in Judge Rivet's final message to the Inuit at

Pond Inlet, as described to the same reporter: "Magistrate Rivet, in passing judgment, impressed upon the natives who were sitting around, the gravity of the offence and the manner in which it is punished in the white man's country ... He then proceeded to tell the natives, through the interpreter, the sort of punishment inflicted on a murderer in civilized parts of the world, and stressed the point that if a white man were to kill an Eskimo, the killer would certainly die on the scaffold."[11]

An incident occurring only weeks before the judge left for Pond Inlet questions this assumption. A new book by Donald Macmillan was brought to Commissioner Starnes' attention because of its description of a homicide that had taken place on Axel Heiberg Island in Canadian territory. According to the American explorer, a member of his crew shot and killed "Peeawahto," the Greenlandic guide who had accompanied the now famous Robert Peary on his polar expeditions. The only provocation was that the Inuk had refused to obey orders. After consulting Sir Joseph Pope, then under-secretary of state for External Affairs, Starnes decided that no action would be taken because the victim was a Danish subject, the murderer was now an officer in the United States Navy, and the incident had happened "a long time ago."[12] One hopes the decision would be different today if a foreign naval officer had shot and killed a Canadian Inuk because he refused to obey orders.

Likely Judge Rivet felt he had no other choice but to sentence Nuqallaq to ten years in prison for manslaughter. A great deal of expense had gone into building the police detachments and sending the court party north, which would be difficult to justify if the accused had received no more than two years "hard labour" at the police detachment. A light sentence would also have been embarrassing on the international front, after the court party had informed Greenland officials of the purpose of their mission and the exorbitant cost involved. As it turned out, the more serious mistake was not considering in advance the location of his incarceration. Stony Mountain Penitentiary was well known for its high incidence of tuberculosis, but when O.S. Finnie questioned why Nuqallaq had been sent to the Manitoba prison and not to a closer facility in the east, Judge Rivet replied that he had no choice. According to the Northwest Territories Act, section 54, residents were to serve all sentences of two years or more at a penitentiary in the Northwest Territories or Manitoba. At that time there was no penitentiary in the Northwest Territories and only one in Manitoba: Stony Mountain.[13] The outdated provision had never been amended, and efforts to do so at this time could not help Nuqallaq. Once he was inside the penitentiary, the warden assumed sole responsibility for his care.

Stony Mountain Penitentiary, located approximately twenty-five kilometres. north of Winnipeg, was built in 1875 to handle Indian offenders and new immigrants. Among its more famous inmates were Poundmaker and

Stony Mountain Penitentiary, twenty-five miles north of Winnipeg, circa 1930. Alfred Longman, Duncan Collection (3), Provincial Archives of Manitoba.

Big Bear, accused of treason in the Northwest Rebellion of 1885, popularly referred to as the Riel Rebellion. Both were released early and died shortly after of lung disease with symptoms similar to tuberculosis. Following a royal commission set up in 1897 to look into charges against certain guards and officers at the prison, reforms were reportedly enacted and major renovations to the facilities completed prior to Nuqallaq's arrival.[14]

Generally, however, prison rules at Stony Mountain were based on the "Auburn System," which demanded silence and isolation to avoid possible riots, along with hard work, rigid discipline, and minimal time for meals served in one's cell.[15] General W.S. Hughes, brother of Lt. Gen. Sir Sam Hughes of the Canadian Expeditionary Force, was appointed superintendent of penitentiaries in 1918. He had promised to enact a number of reforms, but only a few were actually implemented by 1923, notably the disappearance of the "stone pile,"and better medical services. Work facilities varied with different prisons, but most included machine, carpentry, printing, and paint shops, and a farm. A school and library had been added to the Stony Mountain program, which also allowed regular prayer meetings and Sunday chapel services. The objective was to reform and acculturate the new immigrants and Indians who still made up a vast majority of the inmates. This meant optimum exposure to the English language and the British work ethic.[16] Since retraining was not allowed to conflict with the "hard labour" imposed by the sentences, all "religious and secular studies were confined to noon hours, evenings, and Sundays."[17]

In 1923 regulation cells were approximately five feet wide, nine feet long, and ten feet high, all lined back to back on long corridors. Flogging was prohibited without special approval from the Department of Justice, but punishments might include a diet of bread and water, confinement to one's cell, or shackling to the cell gate. All inmates were required to have their hair cut short once a month and to shower or bath weekly.[18] The food was reportedly better at Stony Mountain than other penitentiaries, with breakfast consisting of milk, toast, porridge and sugar; a noon dinner of meat or fish, with bread, vegetables and tea; and supper consisting of three items from a list which included pancakes, rice pudding, bread, soup, and cocoa. There was also a full-time doctor on staff. The farm and school were considered superior to those at other facilities. Apparently unique to Stony Mountain was the practice of calling inmates by a number rather than a name. Nuqallaq's number was 2668, and he was assigned to work on engines in the machine shop.[19]

A number of stories about Nuqallaq's prison life survived in elders' memories. One frightening incident was said to have occurred on the night of his arrival.

Noah Piugaattuk – Igloolik, 16 January 1989

[When he first arrived] he was taken to a place of an Angajuqqaaq [boss, or a leader] to spend a night. His house was situated where there was nothing else, and because they were invited to stay, they were to sleep in this house … Because he did not think about it, he got undressed and went to sleep. As it turned out, he was not being very wise. The man who owned the house slept upstairs. They were situated in a place where they could see all around them. As he slept, something loud blared. The police who was his escort knew about the situation as he had gone to bed all dressed. As the sound blared, [Nuqallaq] got dressed and his escort came up to get him. As he hurried to get dressed, he saw a lot of white people that he had never seen before, a lot of them, all dressed. His escort was trying to help him to get dressed, and he was shaking from fear. He watched all these people, he noticed that one of them said something. There was something peculiar about these people. They appeared to have snouts. They were all men. Again something started to blare again and at once they left. The owner of the house did not want anything done in the house. When they went outside, they saw nothing. He never understood that part, that was an experience that really concerned him all the time he spent down south.[20]

Piugaattuk thought the incident had been staged to intimidate the new prisoner, and he was correct. Although one might have assumed that this was a routine fire drill, his reference to "snouts" suggests the men were wearing gas masks which were commonly used as part of prison riot gear. This exercise may well have been employed on the arrival of every new prisoner, as a warning of what to expect should one try to escape. Because Nuqallaq could not understand the man who "said something," the experience would be all the more terrifying. It was intended to intimidate the Inuk, and it succeeded.

That winter Captain Munn made a concerted effort to obtain Nuqallaq's early release from prison. By an act of Parliament in 1899, a first offender could obtain a "ticket of leave" or early release providing he was "a deserving inmate" and sentenced to a term of imprisonment of more than two years. He must also complete the remaining portion of his sentence under supervision in the community. Criteria for consideration included the prisoner's age, the nature of his crime, and "other circumstances," which could only be brought to the attention of the minister of Justice by a formal recommendation from the penitentiary's warden.[21] Munn allegedly visited Nuqallaq in prison, then returned to Ottawa and reported in person to W.W. Cory as deputy minister of the Interior and to RCMP Commissioner Starnes.

At Starnes' request, Munn reiterated his concerns in a letter, which he had copied and forwarded to both men. He described the condition in which he had found the prisoner and urged that they consider shortening his sentence. He thought that Nuqallaq seemed "much thinner" and appeared to be suffering from the heat as he was sweating profusely and had trouble sleeping.

He told me he feels the heat of his cell at night greatly, and sleeps badly. He added that at night he "cried in his sleep till it woke him" and that "he would soon be dead." That he understands he is being punished is evident from his question to me why "he was punished and not the other natives also" who were concerned in the murder. I explained this to him. He nodded and said "it is no matter now, soon I shall be dead." He has lost "the will to live." In my opinion, he is most unlikely to survive a second year in jail and when he realizes the ship has gone up north, he will give up any desire to live. I respectfully suggest that if he dies in jail, the moral value of his punishment to his tribe will be lost. I am no sentimentalist, and I have publicly advocated the hanging of the Western Arctic murderers. In Na-kud-lah's case, – the instructed verdict being manslaughter – I think Justice would be better served by sending him back on a Ticket of Leave, or as a prisoner in the Arctic to work for the Police, in order that he may tell his tribe what a Penitentiary is like from a native point of view. Na-kud-lah cried as I talked to him, and he is obviously much shaken and weak, for I knew him as a strong, very undemonstrative, and very fearless fellow.[22]

Also at Starnes' request, Munn forwarded a copy of his letter to the deputy minister of Justice. His visit appeared to give Nuqallaq some hope, for on 25 February 1924, he wrote a letter "To the Eskimos," to be sent to Pond Inlet. According to the translation, Nuqallaq had written that he was "suffering from the confinement" and "longing to return to his people."[23]

In the interim both Starnes and Cory also wrote to the deputy minister of Justice, requesting more information about the prisoner's condition and inquiring into the possibility of an early release. When Warden Meighen received copies of the letters, he protested that his prisoner was in fine health and had gained ten pounds, suggesting that either Munn had been misled or perhaps he had not visited the prison.[24] After a further inquiry from the Department of Justice, the warden attached a note from the prison doctor stating that a recent sputum test had proved negative. Another report, this time from the chaplain, described how Nuqallaq read his Bible daily and spoke of wanting to become a missionary when he returned home. Based on this new information, the warden saw no reason to consider an early release.[25]

Meanwhile the debate over Alikomiak's death sentence continued in the newspapers, until it was announced that the prisoner had been hanged at Herschel Island on 1 February 1924. The media had showed no interest in Nuqallaq's incarceration and the only support for his early release came from Munn, and those who had been indirectly responsible for his imprisonment – RCMP Commissioner Starnes and the director of the Northwest Territories and Yukon Branch, O.S. Finnie.

When Staff-Sergeant Joy returned home in the fall of 1924, he had brought a packet of letters from Ataguttiaq to be delivered to her husband. To ensure that they reached the prisoner and were not set aside to await an interpreter, Starnes sent them directly to the superintendent of penitentiaries, with a note to say that they were of a "personal nature"and required no translation. Hughes graciously acknowledged receipt of the packet, but did not indicate how or when they would be forwarded.[26]

In the fall of 1924 Starnes again wrote the superintendent to request an update on Nuqallaq's state of health. This time the prison doctor warned that, while he still had a negative sputum test, he had not "done too well" over the summer and perhaps it might be advisable to release him before the next summer.[27] Warden Meighen agreed and advised Superintendent Hughes that it would be unwise to detain Nuqallaq for another season: "I think if he was returned back, he will not be any the worse, for, in many ways, he has much improved, morally and intellectually by his incarceration. He has learned some English and will learn more. He has been supplied with a Bible in the Eskimo language, and my Chaplain thinks that he will go back as a missionary among his own people, knowing many habits and customs of civilisation that he was unaware of before."[28] Starnes and O.S. Finnie were in full agreement. Quite unexpectedly, however, Inspector Wilcox voiced his disapproval, arguing that an early release should be "on medical grounds only." In his view releasing Nuqallaq early would destroy Inuit respect for the police and Canadian laws that had resulted from the trial.[29] Starnes agreed to wait for more information before making a final decision.

Nuqallaq's time in prison was not spent in luxury as his friends had assumed. One story that impressed the male elders in both Igloolik and Pond Inlet was the account of a fight that was reportedly staged at Stony

Mountain Penitentiary. All forms of competition had been forbidden at that time,[30] but it appears that the popular fighting matches may have continued unofficially. Two versions of the fight are recorded here, each providing a somewhat different perspective on the purpose and outcome.

Noah Piugaattuk – Igloolik, 16 January 1978

[Nuqallaq] was the only one that was taken south. While he was down there, he endured things that scared him. It is said that he was fought by three men that were the relatives of the late Sakirmiaq. Qiugaarjuk was tall and heavily built and could use his strength. It is said that when he fought, he always had a policeman with him. A woman told him about these people that were planning to fight him, so then he was not taken by surprise …

He was asked to go to another place with another person. When he entered, he found that the room was bare and it was a large room. He saw three white people standing up and they appeared to be leaning right in front of him. When he got there, the smallest of the three went for him. Then the two got into a fight.

[The others] just watched the fight. The two were engaged in a fight for sometime. He still had reserve in him and he had no difficulty matching his weight because this man was not strong. Soon the white man started to sweat. He could throw him down if he wanted to, but he was trying to match him. Soon the white man got tired and was sweating so he stepped aside. Then the third one went for him. When he started to fight him, he discovered that he was stronger than the former. They were engaged in a fight and soon he too started to sweat, they would fall down and get up, he too started to sweat but soon they stopped fighting.

When he stopped fighting and got up, the biggest of the three went for him. As it turned out they had started off with the weakest and the strongest was to fight the last. When the two started to fight he discovered that he was the strongest of the three so he and this man were now really engaged in a fight. He was now sweating very hard. After they had fallen and he was getting up, he would wipe the sweat from his eyes. He almost got defeated when they finally stopped fighting. Had he been slightly weaker there is no doubt he would have been defeated. That was the only time that he got engaged in this kind of thing.[31]

This version of the fight attempted to explain the incident in the context of Inuit culture, in which a fighting match was seen as a competition between hunters to test their strength and endurance. Even the rationale for the fight was interpreted as the perceived right of a victim's family to avenge Janes' death. Otherwise the details are too precise and the situation appropriate to prison life in the 1920s to suggest that Nuqallaq was not telling the truth.

Another elder, this time from Pond Inlet, described the fight more succinctly, but from a slightly different perspective – no different than two

qallunaat historians describing the same event, each from their own perspective with regard to its importance and both of them accurate.

Ningiuk Killiktee – Pond Inlet, 1994

They were going to fight, I think they chose the strongest one. [Nuqallaq] beat him
and put him on the ground. They were going to do something to him, if he didn't
put him on the ground. Before they started fighting, Qiugaarjuk [Nuqallaq] said a
prayer. When they started fighting, he put the *qallunaaq* on the ground. When he
fought a stronger person the next time – when they started fighting again, he said
that he beat the *qallunaaq* again and they shook hands and he walked away. And
then the other *qallunaat* started clapping their hands. That's what happened. If they
had beaten him – I don't know. They were probably going to do something to
him.[32]

For Killiktee, a devout Christian, it was important to include Nuqallaq's
prayers in his version of the story. Considering the chaplain's report, there
is nothing to suggest that this part of the story was not equally true. Contrary to the views of sceptics, Nuqallaq's conversion to Christianity was
very real in his mind, even if originally inspired by a lay preacher rather
than a missionary. It could not, however, protect him from tuberculosis.

In the spring of 1925 Commissioner Starnes sent one of his men to the
penitentiary to check on Nuqallaq before he made an official request for his
early release. Unexpectedly, Inspector Mead was refused entry on the
grounds that others had come to the prison, spoken to the prisoner in Inuktitut, and then made improper reports. Even though the officer had letters
of authorization from Starnes and O.S. Finnie, he was told that the proper
channel of inquiry was through the deputy minister of Justice.[33] Unknown
to Mead, Nuqallaq had been sent to the infirmary weeks earlier.

Two days later the warden received a report from the penitentiary's surgeon saying that Nuqallaq had been admitted to the prison hospital suffering from influenza, a common complaint among the prisoners that winter.
The patient's recovery was slow, however, and he had a fever every afternoon. He was also reported to be suffering from a persistent cough and a
dramatic weight loss, dropping from 165 pounds to 146. This time his sputum tests came back from the provincial laboratory showing positive for
the presence of tubercule bacilli. The doctor's recommendation was clear
and firm:

Judging by the way the disease has taken hold of the patient, I am of opinion that
he will continue to fail very rapidly if still confined in the Penitentiary. Were he
living in the open air night and day, he would have a better chance of recovery.

[signed] J.J. McFadden, Surgeon.[34]

Starnes did not receive a copy of the letter until 16 April, at which time he immediately contacted the appropriate officials to reconfirm his support for Nuqallaq's release on a ticket of leave.[35] Based on the surgeon's recommendation, it appeared that the best chance for recovery was to return to the Arctic, where the air was cool and free from contaminants.

Efforts to get him removed to a hospital were delayed while they waited for official word of his release from the penitentiary. Finally on 28 April 1925 Starnes was informed that the governor-general had granted Nuqallaq his Ticket-of-Leave for good behaviour, acknowledging the letters that had been received from both Munn and Starnes. Under the terms of his release the police were to make arrangements for his return home and ensure that the former prisoner reported "from time to time if necessary" to the officer in charge at Pond Inlet. As a final note, the communique stated that "Noo-kud-Lah to be allowed his liberty under License only so long as he is of good behaviour."[36]

Concern then centred on the state of Nuqallaq's health. Although it may have been in the back of everyone's mind, Dr Livingstone was the only one on record to voice concern that Nuqallaq might spread the disease to others unless he was given immediate medical attention.[37] Starnes agreed. Telegrams and memos were sent to various authorities requesting transfer of the patient to an appropriate hospital. Finally on 8 May 1925, after further bureaucratic confusion regarding approvals and procedures, Nuqallaq was admitted to Dynevor Hospital, also known as the Selkirk Indian Hospital. Inspector Dann promised the commissioner that he would look in on the former prisoner whenever he was in the vicinity.[38] It was believed that once the disease was in remission, it would stay in remission when he returned to the Arctic.

Tuberculosis, commonly referred to at that time as consumption, was an infectious disease caused by the bacillus *mycobacterium tuberculosis*. The disease took many forms but was generally characterized by the growth of tubercules or nodules filled with pus. When the lungs were affected, there would be coughing and expectorate, sometimes streaked with blood. In an acute stage the abscesses would burst and spread the infection to other tissues. When in remission, the tubercules would calcify. The bacteria were carried in droplets of moisture, passing between humans by coughing and contact with sputum. Although the disease most commonly affected the lungs, it could also attack the intestines, bones and joints, lymphatic glands, brain lining, and skin. If the bacteria spread to the blood stream, it would cause a general septicaemia. Children and babies seemed more vulnerable to infections of the lymphatic tissue, bones, and intestines.[39]

Patricia Grygier, in her study on tuberculosis and the Canadian Inuit, described the disease at the turn of the century as usually associated with poverty and related "to poor diet, crowded living quarters and unsanitary

Dynevor (Indian) Hospital near Selkirk, Manitoba, circa 1920, where Nuqallaq was taken for treatment of tuberculosis after his release from Stony Mountain Penitentiary, 8 May 1925. Rupert's Land Collection 152, Provincial Archives of Manitoba.

conditions." As there was no known cure until the discovery of antibiotics, those affected were treated like lepers – looked down upon and avoided, for fear of becoming infected. Treatment in a sanitarium normally extended over a number of years and included exposure to fresh air and sunlight, cold baths, plenty of fresh fruit, and rest. With proper care, it was possible for the disease to go into remission for years, possibly a lifetime. What was not understood at that time was the effect the sunless Arctic winter would have on the disease. Although sensitive to sun, the bacteria were totally resistant to the cold, making Inuit particularly susceptible to the disease during the sunless winter months.[40]

On the first leg of his homeward journey Nuqallaq travelled by train to Ottawa, where he was given a room at RCMP headquarters in Rockcliffe, reportedly to keep him "quiet for health reasons and free from the curiosity or intrusion by the Press." Constable Timbury, who accompanied him from Manitoba, listed his effects, which included $3.15, one Ticket-of-Leave, and a ring with five stones (presumably a gift for Ataguttiaq).[41] The Inuktitut Bible given to him in prison was not listed, but it apparently returned with him to Pond Inlet.[42] For a moment it seemed there might be a complication when Dr Livingstone reported that the Danish consulate had expressed concern about the CGS *Arctic* docking at Greenland if they had a patient with tuberculosis on board. He advised that a doctor's certificate and a negative sputum test would be necessary to gain approval to land.[43] The next day an Ottawa doctor examined Nuqallaq and found no signs of

Captain Bernier and Nuqallaq on board the CGS *Arctic*, 1925. Richard Finnie Collection.
NAC – PA 100441.

"active tuberculosis," either clinically or in the sputum test, although he observed that the patient had a "low-grade, dry bronchitis, associated with cough."[44]

When Nuqallaq arrived at King's Wharf in Quebec City, he was all smiles when posing for the cameras, but it was a gentle and humble smile. He was grateful for his early release which, he believed, had come about because of talks with the prison chaplain.[45] Captain Bernier was on hand to welcome him aboard the ship, but J.D. Craig had been retired as commander after an accident at Father Point a year earlier in which he suffered a nasty concussion requiring hospitalization. There were a number of new faces, and some old. The commander of the expedition in 1925 was George Mackenzie. Also on board were Richard Finnie, son of O.S. Finnie; Mackenzie's secretary, RCMP historian Harwood Steele, son of the famed Sir Samuel Steele of the North West Mounted Police; Dr Livingstone as medical officer; RCMP Inspector Wilcox; and Staff-Sergeant Joy. Many years later Finnie would write about Nuqallaq's return trip home, noting with irony that "Staff Sergeant Joy, who had arrested him, was now his protector."[46]

Nuqallaq discovered that special arrangements had been made for him aboard ship. To prevent any possibility of spreading the disease to the other passengers, the doctor ordered him to remain on deck, with sleeping quarters provided in one of the whale boats lashed to the deck and covered by a sheet of canvas to protect him from rain and snow. All of his meals were to be delivered to his "private quarters" by a steward. Not everyone was in

Nuqallaq in his whale-boat sleeping quarters aboard the CGS *Arctic*, July 1925.
Richard Finnie Collection. NAC – PA 202074.

sympathy with the released prisoner, as Dr Livingstone later discovered. Apparently one of the stewards had taken great delight in telling the Inuk that he would never live to see Pond Inlet.[47]

Everything seemed to go wrong after the ship left King's Wharf, including a collision with a moored vessel and several engine breakdowns. Once they passed the Labrador shore, foul weather hit with a vengeance, according to young Finnie who had signed on as an assistant radio-operator:

The ship pitched and rolled. Everything that was not securely tied down went adrift. The deck was continuously awash. Rolling reached a point of no return. The ship would tremble with agonizing uncertainty at the end of a roll before sluggishly righting herself. Whether they were seasick or not, all hands became nerve wracked and fatigued from the effort of clinging to whatever supports they could find to avoid injury. The ship leaked more and more, her timbers strained and her seams loosened with too many encounters with ice and storms.[48]

Nuqallaq remained confined to the upper deck and his whale boat. He kept no diary and shared his thoughts with no one.

At first the doctor reported that Nuqallaq seemed to be improving. Then on 6 August, while the ship was caught in pack ice in Davis Strait, his condition suddenly worsened. Symptoms included severe pain in his chest, high fever, and bloody expectorant. The doctor strapped his side, confined him to "his quarters," and put him on a liquid diet. Others provided him

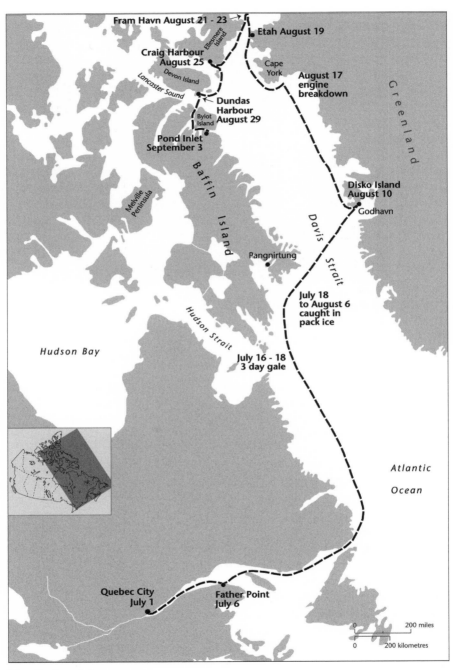

Fram Havn August 21 - 23

Etah August 19

Craig Harbour
August 25

Ellesmere Island

Devon Island

Cape
York

August 17
engine
breakdown

Greenland

Lancaster Sound

Dundas
Harbour
August 29

Bylot
Island

Pond Inlet
September 3

Baffin Island

Melville
Peninsula

Disko Island
August 10

Godhavn

Pangnirtung

Davis Strait

July 18
to August 6
caught in
pack ice

Hudson Strait

July 16 - 18
3 day gale

Hudson Bay

Atlantic

Ocean

Quebec City
July 1

Father Point
July 6

0   200 miles

0   200 kilometres

Nuqallaq's route home, 1925.

with extra clothing and a second layer of canvas to cover the whale boat. In spite of these measures, his appetite continued to decline until he was eating only milk, eggs, and – according to Dr Livingstone – whisky.[49] Inspector Wilcox's report on 24 August did not offer much hope that he would reach Pond Inlet alive.

Weeks passed as the ship made its rounds. In spite of having an active case of TB aboard, the ship did dock at Godhavn, but only the doctor was allowed to disembark as the community was reported to be suffering from an outbreak of whooping cough. This did not prevent Commander Mackenzie from inviting members of the Greenland parliament on board for a movie show and refreshments.[50] As days grew into weeks, Livingstone reported that Nuqallaq had convinced himself that "Pond Inlet would be full of ice which would prevent the ship from reaching there and [that] he will die before he arrives home."[51]

Finally on 3 September 1925 the CGS *Arctic* anchored in Eclipse Sound with Nuqallaq barely alive. His reunion with Ataguttiaq was photographed by Richard Finnie, while Harwood Steele as the RCMP's official historian recorded the occasion. With improved radio equipment on board the ship, he was also able to send a cablegram for Commissioner Starnes and O.S. Finnie, transmitted through Godhavn Station in Greenland to Bergen, Norway, via Iceland, and thence to Ottawa. The text read as follows:

CONSO PRESS. SEPTEMBER 3RD

NOOKUDLAH after exile two years reunited pretty wife Ahtoteuk undoubtedly village Belle (stop) and native friends (stop) when Arctic anchored Ponds Inlet today (stop) soon as stepped ashore small crowd gathered witness connubial meeting (stop) couple rubbed noses in each others arms (stop) man has been glad to get back (stop) Ahtoteuk laughing (stop) smoking cigarette seemed enjoy limelight (stop) couple quickly retired to tent provided where Ahtoteuk lit native lamp began cooking meal (stop) seal meat (stop) welcome Nookudlah received from friends not as warm as expected (stop) Royal Mounted Police appreciative (stop) camera clicked Nookudlah (stop) nattily dressed white mans suit (stop) sophisticated manner contrasted strangely (stop) Ahtoteuk in white kooletah or hooded pullover (stop) seal skin boots trousers and clashed with long haired seal skin clad men surrounding him (stop) Nookudlah little say beyond glad be home and anxious sit down good square meal (stop) this partly to awe Eskimos (stop) naturally regard one who has seen so much (stop) but more to knowledge his disfavour among whites and still always immunity under strict supervision (stop) though Natives realize he has been treated leniently in being brought home so soon (stop) police anticipate no decrease respect for law that account[52]

There was no doubt about the effectiveness of the punishment once the Inuit witnessed the return of Nuqallaq as a frail ghost of his former self.

Ataguttiaq and Nuqallaq reunited, 3 September 1925. Richard Finnie Collection.
NAC – PA 202073.

Had he not returned, some might continue to believe that he was living in
luxury somewhere in the white man's world. Yet in the reports and memos
of both Starnes and Finnie, there is no evidence that their efforts to bring
about his early return were based on anything but genuine concern for his
welfare. Viewed from the present, their actions seemed inspired by compassion, but were possibly also an attempt to make amends for something
that should not have happened – without acknowledging responsibility.

   In anticipation of his arrival at Pond Inlet, the police had provided
Nuqallaq and his wife with a tent and tried to make his living quarters
as comfortable as possible.[53] They also provided rations to last for three
months. Dr Livingstone, however, feared death was inevitable and was
concerned that Nuqallaq might pass the disease to others. Yet he wrote that
he was unable to offer any means to prevent it, other than supplying the
sick man with sputum cups and giving instructions as to their disposal.
Even then, he noted that when he had examined his patient just before leaving, his own hand was smeared with sputum from the bedding. As alcohol

seemed to be the only medicine Nuqallaq could tolerate, the good doctor left a quart of rum at the detachment for his use. There seemed little else anyone could do. Livingstone's report reflected the angst of a conscience plagued with guilt and no means of resolution.[54]

The cinema-photographer was totally insensitive to the situation and immediately set up his movie camera to direct a re-enactment of the prisoner's return home. Nuqallaq was asked to walk towards the house where Ataguttiaq was alleged to be staying and wait for a friend to knock on the door. The subtitle read, "Mr. Nookudlah Returns Home After Many Moons in the Strange Land of the White Man," without reference to his having been imprisoned for manslaughter. The prolonged scene of their rubbing noses was unnatural, akin to an invasion of privacy, but the scene of the two walking hand in hand over the tundra into the midnight sun was a heartbreaker for anyone knowing what lay ahead. An edited version that includes these scenes is still available for purchase from Fox News Film Archives in New York.[55]

By late October Corporal McInnes reported that Nuqallaq seemed to be recovering and had been seen hunting seals on the ice. In November he left Pond Inlet to go with his wife and others to Arctic Sound, some fifty miles from the detachment.[56] One of the elders remembered the story about an accident which seemed to have had a disastrous effect on Nuqallaq's health and mental state:

Martha Akumalik – Pond Inlet, 1994

Nuqallaq and Kipumii had been out hunting for seal, when Kipumii fell into the water. Unable to reach him, Nookudlah tried to shout for help, but his lungs were so bad that he could not make himself heard. Fortunately, others reached Kipumii just as he was sinking and he was saved.[57]

The incident was said to have had a demoralizing effect on a man who had once been respected among his peers for his strength and courage. Curiously, it appears that no one told the Inuit – not even Nuqallaq's wife – that he had contracted tuberculosis. When he began spitting up blood, everyone thought his lungs had burst because they had "worked him too hard" at the penitentiary.[58] The police visited Nuqallaq in mid-November, and reported finding him "confined to his igloo owing to his weak state of health, due probably to the effects of his trip."[59]

A few weeks later Ataguttiaq arrived at the detachment to say that her husband had fallen into a coma and died on 5 December 1925. The wording of the draft report cited above was changed after his death. The final version described "living in a damp cold igloo" as the cause of his poor

Nuqallaq resting as friends watch over him, 1925. Note the tin can used as sputum cup. McInnes Collection.

health.[60] The police provided the widow with food rations, and she left to live with the families who had provided support for the couple during the past few months.

Although Nuqallaq would never become the missionary he had dreamed of while in prison, he died among his own people and with Ataguttiaq, whose memory was probably the only thing that kept him alive on his voyage home. His body was buried at Iqaluit in Tay Sound. Ataguttiaq's son reported having visited the grave site and found that "it was carefully marked by a rock border."[61]

Ironically, it was the truthfulness of Nuqallaq's own statements that led to his conviction under the Canadian justice system. One wonders if he ever thought about "what honour lies in truth," as he lay ill and racked with pain. Or why the *qallunaat* god had not been powerful enough to protect the son of a shaman. "Death by tuberculosis" was said to be a frequent occurrence at Stony Mountain Penitentiary. In that sense Nuqallaq was only one example of a much larger problem. To dwell on the travesties of history is futile, but to learn from past gives purpose to the living. Canadian officials had much to learn.

9

Aftermath

With Nuqallaq now absent from the scene, one would have hoped that the Inuit could bring closure to this unfortunate episode. Not so. The continued presence of the police and, to a lesser extent, the Hudson's Bay Company would serve as a constant reminder of the settlement's origins. Although government intervention in their lives would have been unavoidable in any circumstances, the death of Robert Janes had accelerated the pace of change, threatening their cultural traditions and individual freedom.

Some changes were beneficial, such as the economic advantages derived from trade with the Hudson's Bay Company. More winter camps appeared on the shores of Eclipse Sound, several days journey to the trading post but at a respectful distance from the police detachment. There would also be spiritual changes in their lives as Christianity gained widespread acceptance with the arrival of both Roman Catholic and Anglican missionaries. Yet infectious diseases became increasingly prevalent, sometimes wiping out entire families. There was also the constant fear that police might come and take someone away who had inadvertently broken the white man's law. Concerns about sovereignty and violence had diminished greatly by 1939, but there was no going back. The past could not be erased. Quite unintentionally, Sakirmiaviniq had indelibly changed the lives of Inuit in North Baffin.

The most immediate consequence of the trial came about as a result of the disruption in hunting practices and the onset of disease for families who had spent the summer on Eclipse Sound. Staff-Sergeant Joy acknowledged the problems when he reported that "the necessity of keeping so many Eskimos here for the arrival of the ship prevented several families from making their annual summer deer hunt. As a result, skins for clothing were scarce, and the movements of some families were materially handicapped."[1] He did not, however, tell the whole story. In spite of arrangements made to

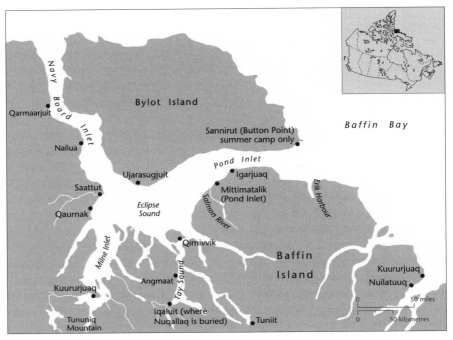

Eclipse Sound, circa 1930.

transport families to the mouth of Admiralty Inlet after the trial, a number faced hunger in varying degrees, having been unable to cache sufficient food for the winter. The intense contact with *qallunaat* had also resulted in disease, with the elderly and children particularly susceptible. A chain reaction set in when illness affected the ability of the people to hunt, in turn leading to malnourishment and, in extreme cases, starvation.

In early March 1924 Staff-Sergeant Joy, accompanied by Constable Friel, Ululijarnaat, and Qattuuq, set out for Arctic Bay and Igloolik. At Admiralty Inlet they discovered that most camps were short of meat and seal oil, and had been for most of the winter. Without adequate food, the dogs were in wretched shape, making travel difficult.[2] There is no record of what assistance the police provided, but apparently it was not enough. Peter Freuchen of the Fifth Thule Expedition visited the Pond Inlet detachment in Joy's absence and on heading north, discovered a camp that had been without food for six days near Low Point on Navy Board Inlet. He sent word back to the detachment for help, but by the time Qattuuq had returned from Admiralty Inlet and set out with supplies, he found only one family who reportedly had been ill and were waiting for the return of the rest of their party with food.[3] The police appeared to make light of Freuchen's concern.

Captain Bernier reported that a "flu epidemic" at Pond Inlet had taken the lives of thirteen people that spring. One of them was Qattuuq.[4] Ululijarnaat had also been sick but had recovered. The police were asked to investigate whether there was something different in his diet that had increased his resistance.[5] Relatively little was known at that time about the susceptibility of indigenous peoples to infectious diseases, and even less about means of prevention.

In his books *Arctic Adventure* and *Viking Vagabond*, Peter Freuchen described a tragic episode of disease and starvation that had occurred later that spring. After a short visit at Pond Inlet in 1924, Freuchen and his party of Greenland Inuit headed back to Admiralty Inlet to hunt. Freuchen claimed they came upon a group of Inuit, more than half of whom had died of starvation as a result of a severe storm. The survivors were said to be suffering from an acute illness marked by the eruption of large boils. Freuchen also implied that there was evidence of cannibalism and that he left his Greenland guides behind to look after the sick while he travelled overland with a young orphan to get help. The official report submitted to the Expedition tells a much different story.

Following the untimely death, in 1933, of Knud Rasmussen, the leader of the Fifth Thule Expedition, Therkel Mathiassen was asked to write the introductory volume based on the reports each member had submitted to the Expedition Committee. Freuchen's report tells how his party lost their tents in a storm and found shelter at an Inuit camp on Admiralty Inlet. Apparently it was one of his own Greenland guides who had suffered from large boils and could not continue on. As a result, Freuchen left all his men at the Inuit camp and was guided by an Inuk hunter by the name of Mala. to Pond Inlet, where he made contact with the Danish ship and redirected it to Admiralty Inlet to collect his party.[6] At no point did he witness starvation, cannibalism, or disease among the Canadian Inuit. Instead, it seems he used a composite of previous starvation stories, then further embellished them to create a personalized episode. Significantly, his first book describing the false starvation incident was published after Rasmussen's death. That he dared to republish the story eight years after Mathiassen's official report suggests a blatant disregard for the veracity of the Expedition.

Freuchen's books about his Arctic adventures were popular, and his criticisms about the deplorable state of the Canadian Inuit were read far and wide, in several languages. He singled out Pond Inlet for unusually severe criticism, in particular the living conditions of "the wealthier Eskimos" who were described as living in "filthy huts made of wood" full of refuse and rotten food. In his opinion, a new way of life was useless without proper education.[7] Freuchen's criticism was appropriate in light of conditions in Greenland, and the irony implicit. To show Denmark that Canada was effectively administering the Arctic Islands, the government had publicly

Wooden homes made out of packing cases were used by Inuit employed by the Hudson's Bay Company at Pond Inlet, circa 1927. Rev. A.L. Fleming Collection. NWT Archives N79-050-0331.

flaunted its willingness to spend a quarter of a million dollars on a court trial, yet appeared incapable of looking after the basic needs of Canada's most northerly citizens.

The flu epidemic in the spring of 1924 was only a harbinger of more difficult times ahead. Less than a year after Nuqallaq's return home, the police reported numerous "unidentified" infectious diseases. When the Inuit arrived from Igloolik and Arctic Bay in the spring of 1926, many were thought to be suffering from influenza. Not long after they had departed, the detachment received an urgent request for assistance. Near the entrance to Milne Inlet, Corporal McInnes found two separate camps where the occupants were suffering from high temperatures and their bodies covered with sores. Some of the children were reported to have "huge swellings on their necks which would come to a head and burst," after which they seemed to get better. Others suffered from "lung trouble," marked by sore chests, high temperatures, and coughs that produced "large quantities of pus." Detailed descriptions were sent to Ottawa in hopes that medical staff might help with a diagnosis.[8] Another report described finding Piunngittuq, Alfred Tremblay's former guide, at a camp on the west side of Emerson Island, suffering from pain in his chest that was described as "probably from inflammation of the lungs." He died within days. Others at the camp had been sick and recovered; a woman and a child had died the day before; a few were still sick. Some complained of pain in the chest and limbs.[9]

That same spring a report described a similar situation at Sannirut, where men, women, and children were reported to be suffering from "the prevailing disorder of lung trouble." Other reports referred to the "prevailing lung disease," but only one ventured a diagnosis. When the police patrol reached the Hudson's Bay Company outpost at Clyde River, they were informed that an"epidemic of pneumonia" had made its appearance in April. This time, however, Inspector Wilcox was unequivocal when he stated that "the prevailing lung disease *tuberculosis* had caused the deaths of four adults as against two births" (italics added). Although this was the first and only reference to tuberculosis, it was apparent from Wilcox's urgent plea for help that he considered the situation a crisis. He warned that "unless medical assistance is given these people at once, inside 10 years the native population of North Baffin will be wiped out."[10] Since the Inuit at the trial were found free of any disease and none had been reported by Dr Livingstone in the summer of 1925, there seems little doubt that Nuqallaq had infected those Inuit who had gathered at Pond Inlet to meet the CGS *Arctic*.

Wilcox's calls for medical help went unheeded. Instead, the first community in the eastern Arctic to have a resident doctor would be Pangnirtung in 1926. When the Anglican Church opened the doors of its first mission hospital on Baffin Island five years later, once again it was at Pangnirtung. In the summer of 1929 two Anglican ministers and two Roman Catholic priests arrived to Pond Inlet to establish their missions, but still there was no resident doctor.

Not everyone associated with Nuqallaq appears to have acquired tuberculosis. Ataguttiaq, for instance, did not appear to suffer from any debilitating form of the disease, nor did her parents, nor Kipumii, Nuqallaq's hunting partner. Since they had all been in good health at the time of his return, they may have been able to build up immunity as sometimes happened with families of a consumptive child. The travesty lay in the lack of knowledge about the disease. The medical profession was not aware, for example, that the bacteria thrived in the cold and dark, making the sunless Arctic months particularly conducive to a rapid spread of the disease. Nuqallaq had passed away on 5 December, shortly after the sun disappeared below the horizon. But those he had inadvertently infected that fall would be vulnerable to rapid escalation of the disease during the dark period, especially those who were already in a weakened state of health or those who were short of food, as well as children and the elderly. Sudden exertion, such as a long sled trip from Igloolik to Pond Inlet, might have an adverse effect. Certainly, the cramped living quarters, deemed unsanitary by southern standards, created fertile ground for the disease. Only with the return of the sum and resumption of outdoor living would the bacteria begin to lose its virulence. For some, it was too late.

The attempts to get Nuqallaq released were well intentioned, his supporters believing that it was his best chance for survival. There was a popular consensus that country air was beneficial to the sufferer as opposed to a polluted urban environment, but no one on the voyage north could have anticipated the stormy weather which appeared to have caused the disease to become active again. However, this does not explain why – if he was too infectious to sleep below deck with the rest of the *qallunaat* – Nuqallaq was allowed to return to home to live in the close confines of damp tents and igloos. The conspiracy of silence continued when the ship reached Pond Inlet, for apparently no one told Nuqallaq or any of his family that his illness was infectious and could be passed on to others, if they were not careful.[11] The Inuit knew that Nuqallaq was dying, but they thought it was because his lungs had been damaged by working too hard in prison – a convenient explanation that would add to an Inuk's fear of the white man's justice.

If there was an error in letting Nuqallaq return home, it was made far worse by denying immediate medical attention once an outbreak of the disease had been identified by the police. This apparent insensitivity may be related to a change in jurisdiction. Prior to 1925 the responsibility for the Inuit had been unofficially assigned to the Northwest Territories Council and influenced in good measure by the liberal-minded O.S. Finnie. By an amendment to the Indian Act in 1924, that responsibility was transferred to the Department of Indian Affairs under the direction of the Superintendent-General Duncan Campbell Scott, well known for his insensitivities in dealing with the Canadian Indians.[12] His first action was to challenge the costs of welfare rations submitted by the police at Pangnirtung and Pond Inlet and to demand a strict accounting for every distribution. It was unlikely that he would consider additional costs of providing medical services at Pond Inlet. Instead, the presence of tuberculosis in North Baffin remained a well-kept secret from the Canadian public.

Understandably, no one wanted to be blamed for the spread of tuberculosis as a result of releasing an infected prisoner. And certainly, no one wanted to be criticized for allowing him to be sent to Stony Mountain Penitentiary in the first place. From the perspective of a politician or bureaucrat, it must have seemed better to let "sleeping dogs lie" – and be swept under the carpet. The only problem was that this "sleeping dog" was sick and would infect others, until the carpet was too small to hide everyone. By then, however, it would be someone else's problem. While it is true that medical knowledge was insufficient to offer a cure for infected Inuit, early study of the disease in Arctic communities might have saved the lives of countless others.

The next chapter in this saga reflects the degree to which government officials were determined to keep that secret. After spending the winter in

Pangnirtung, Dr Livingstone set out by dogsled for Pond Inlet in the spring of 1927, partly to assess the health of the Inuit in the region. He carried medical and surgical supplies with him, but had a difficult time and barely made it to Pond Inlet alive. Significantly, there is no report on file in the department concerning tuberculosis. Nor is there any mention of the disease by Dr Frederick Banting, who joined the eastern Arctic Patrol as an interested passenger that summer.[13] Banting, who later became famous for his discovery of insulin, made front-page headlines in the *Toronto Daily Star* for his attack on the Hudson's Bay Company for unfairly exploiting the Inuit and on the Canadian government for not doing more for them in the way of health services and education.[14] Curiously, there was no mention of tuberculosis.

Livingstone spent a second winter at Pangnirtung before being replaced in 1929 by a young doctor from McGill University, Hugh A. Stuart, who had just completed his internship at the Royal Victoria Hospital in Montreal. By now the responsibility for Inuit Affairs had been transferred back to the NWT Council, and thus once again it would be O.S. Finnie who issued the instructions on the care of the Inuit to Dr Stuart. He was to do all he could "for their food and welfare" but to keep patrol expenses "low as possible." In addition to his medical responsibilities, he was told that the department "was interested in the prevalence or scarcity of game and fish, the climate and other conditions" so they could "keep the Minister informed, and, if desirable, supply the press with reliable information for public consumption."[15] The directive implied that a report on the state of Inuit health was not for "public consumption." During this period Stuart would also oversee construction of the Anglican mission hospital at Pangnirtung, although it would not be ready for patients until 1931.

Likely briefed by Livingstone, Stuart decided to attempt a similar sled patrol to Pond Inlet and experienced equal difficulty. Inspired by his adventure, the twenty-five year old doctor wrote an article for *Maclean's* magazine. Unaware that it required prior approval by the department, he sent the manuscript south with the supply ship. Editor Napier Moore was delighted with the article and contacted the Department of the Interior to ask where they might send a cheque for Dr Stuart. Finnie responded immediately, invoking censorship rules instituted in 1922, to say that the article could not be published without approval by his department. Moore protested, but sent the article over for review. In the end, it was published with only one change. Apparently it was not appropriate for the public to read that the purpose of Dr Stuart's trip "was to investigate the prevalence of tuberculosis among the Eskimos of the east coast of Baffin Island." Instead, the article that appeared in *Maclean's* on 15 March 1931 would state that the trip was "one of my regular medical patrols for the Department of the Interior to investigate the health of the Eskimos."[16]

Finnie, who was on the record for advocating measures to improve Inuit
health, cannot be held solely responsible for the censorship. Civil servants
follow the dictates of their political masters. After the defeat of the Liberals
in the 1930 summer election, he was now reporting to a Conservative government that had even less sympathy for the plight of the Inuit. Shortly,
Finnie's entire department was dissolved and he was let go. With the economic ills of the Depression dictating political action, any concerns about
the spread of tuberculosis among the Inuit likely fell on deaf ears.

After completing his two-year assignment at Pangnirtung, Dr Stuart went
to work at the Mayo Clinic in Boston. When he wrote to request passage
on the eastern Arctic Patrol the following summer, he was informed that
they would welcome his services but that he would not be paid. When he
applied again two years later, he was refused outright.[17]

By now, tuberculosis had spread beyond North Baffin. According to medical historian Walter Vanest, Uluksuk,* one of the two Inuit convicted of
manslaughter in the deaths of Fathers Rouvière and Le Roux, had been diagnosed at the Anglican hospital in Aklavik as having an incurable form of
tuberculosis. Uluksuk was discharged and sent home on the supply ship to
Coppermine, where he shortly died – but not before touching off another
epidemic of "galloping consumption" that quickly spread throughout the
region.[18] If the consequences of Nuqallaq's return home had been given the
attention it deserved in 1926, perhaps this second tragedy might have been
averted. In this case, censorship cannot be blamed on necessity or even on
ignorance. Whether influenced by callous indifference or simply fear of
public criticism, government inaction caused untold suffering and deaths
among the Inuit population.

Tuberculosis spread rapidly but unevenly throughout the eastern Arctic.
In 1934 Dr J.A. Bildfell reported from the Pangnirtung mission hospital that
tuberculosis "so eclipses every other disease condition that it might be said
that there prevails but one disease among them."[19] Pressures to build a TB
sanatorium at Pangnirtung mounted, but Dr Livingstone rejected the idea
when appearing before the NWT Council, claiming that the Inuit had "lived
for long periods with a more or less dormant pulmonary tuberculosis."[20]
He had no medical proof to back up this assertion, but his words were
enough to convince the council that they could ignore the problem. Thus,
while there was periodic pressure to "do something" about tuberculosis,
the public was not informed of the epidemic. In the end, unfavourable reports by American military officers stationed in the Arctic during the
Second World War finally forced the government to take action.

Meanwhile, the two concerns that had prompted the decision to investigate
Janes' death – Arctic sovereignty and Inuit violence – had long since disap-

---

* Vanest spells his name Uloqsaq.

peared as priority issues in the eastern Arctic. The sovereignty question in particular would be resolved without issue. The police post established at Port Burwell in 1920 was now considered adequate to guard the entrance to Hudson Strait. The Craig Harbour detachment, while ineffective in stopping the Greenlanders from hunting on Ellesmere Island, initially met the criteria for "effective occupation" of Ellesmere Island.

In 1924, the year following the trial, a detachment was built on Devon Island, ostensibly to guard the entrance to Lancaster Sound. Those present at the flag-raising ceremony named it the Bernier Detachment and placed a sign to that effect over the front door. Ottawa officials expressed displeasure and immediately renamed it Dundas Harbour. Thus, without specifying the location, the "Bernier Detachment" still appears in police records as a separate post in operation for only three months.[21] The Inuit had their own name for the new post – Tallurutit, meaning "tattoos on the chin" because of the distinctive stripes on the nearby cliffs. Owing to the difficulty in getting Canadian Inuit to move to otherwise uninhabited islands, the police again hired Greenland Inuit to work at the newest detachment.

Aware that the Greenlanders continued to hunt in the vicinity of Buchanan Bay on Ellesmere Island, the police established another new post in 1926, this time on the Bache Peninsula midway along the eastern coast. The Craig Harbour detachment was closed, only to reopen in 1933 after supply difficulties forced closure of the Bache post. The permanence of the Eastern Arctic Patrol was now assured as government expeditions were needed annually to supply the detachments, but the CGS *Arctic* was no longer large enough for the task. The 1925 voyage that carried Nuqallaq home would be its last. That fall the government sold the ship for the paltry sum of $9,000 to the Hudson's Bay Company, which immediately ordered it dismantled. Adding insult to injury, the hull was towed away and left to rot on a sandbar not far from Captain Bernier's home in Levis, Quebec. For the next six years the government chartered a steamship, the SS *Beothic,* to conduct the annual patrol.

The police continued to hire Inuit from Etah, North Greenland, to work at the Ellesmere detachments.[22] Having hunted there most of their lives, they knew the best routes for sled travel and the location of wildlife. One of the first to work for the police at Craig Harbour was Panikpak, the grandson of Qillaq, leader of the Qidtlarssuaq migration that had crossed from Baffin Island to Greenland in the mid-nineteenth century.[23] The police were well aware of the historical links, perhaps the reason why they took no overt action nor submitted official reports when Greenlanders were discovered on the island.[24] The main attraction was the abundance of polar bears which were used to make the distinctive white fur pants that were part of the traditional clothing.

Staff-Sergeant Joy was put in charge of the Bache detachment when it first opened, with the mandate to conduct patrols to the uncharted islands

Unidentified police officers standing in front of the new RCMP post at Dundas Harbour, Devon Island, August 1924. Note the "Bernier Detachment" sign over the door. NAC – PA 202076.

west of Ellesmere. Greenlanders were hired to assist at this isolated post, and Nukappianguaq (Nookapinguak) from Etah, an exceptional hunter and guide, accompanied Joy on some of the longest, most arduous patrols in the RCMP's history. Ironically, the very same Greenlanders who had initially aroused concerns with their hunting of polar bears on Ellesmere Island were now assisting the police in protecting Canada's sovereignty.

Thus, the sovereignty issue would be resolved with minimal expense relative to the original estimate. The creation of the Arctic Islands Game Preserve in 1926 provided an excuse, at least on paper, for the RCMP to conduct extensive patrols throughout the uninhabited islands to ensure that wildlife regulations were adhered to. These expeditions by dog sled, sometimes referred to as the "sovereignty patrols," were well publicized at home and abroad to show the world that Canada was effectively enforcing the laws of the country. That same year new regulations were passed requiring foreign scientists and explorers to obtain permits for their research in the Canadian Arctic. Although the American explorer Donald Macmillan still refused to seek permission, others willingly complied, indicating "tacit recognition" of Canadian title to the lands. These measures, sometimes referred to as "paper sovereignty," ended any thought of expending large sums on economic development and settlement of the islands.[25] Increasing evidence of tacit recognition also ended any immediate hope of the government providing education and health services for the Canadian Inuit.

Diplomatic negotiations also played a role in eliminating a potential threat to Arctic sovereignty. In 1925 the Northern Advisory Board was established to study and advise the government on Arctic sovereignty issues. The board's report on a possible Norwegian claim resulting from Otto Sverdrup's discoveries once again raised doubts about the legality of British title. The police patrols throughout the uninhabited regions were a partial solution, but the strategy now was to resolve any outstanding questions through diplomatic negotiation. At the request of a special sub-committee, Under-Secretary of State for External Affairs O.D. Skelton was given a free hand to deal with the Norwegian government, thus removing responsibility for international negotiations from the Department of the Interior. In 1930 Canada successfully negotiated a payment of $67,000 to Otto Sverdrup in return for Norway's agreement to drop any claims to the area. At this point it was believed that Canada's title to the Arctic Islands was secure.[26] Although it was the responsibility of the RCMP to ensure it remained so, the possibility of any further threats seemed negligible.

Inuit violence, the publicized justification for the police investigation and murder trial, also became a matter of diminishing concern in the eastern Arctic. Nonetheless, the RCMP took the responsibility for maintaining law and order seriously, even if their task was now primarily to educate the Inuit on Canadian laws as a means of preventing criminal acts. After the trial Staff-Sergeant Joy had remained at Pond Inlet for another year in the event there was general unrest or further violence. There was none.

Meanwhile at Pangnirtung the police investigation into the Qivittuuq murders was deferred until spring to take advantage of optimum travel conditions. Finally in March 1924 Corporal McInnes, Constable MacGregor, and two Inuit guides set out for the small trading post on the east coast of Baffin Island, just south of Home Bay. The post had been operated by the Sabellum Company of London, but was supplied very irregularly. Around 1911 Niaquttiaq was placed in charge of the operation. Unlike those at the trading posts on Eclipse Sound, the Inuit here were in poor health and often struggling to survive in an area of relatively poor food resources.

With the mission at Blacklead Island now closed, Niaquttiaq assumed the role of a lay preacher and began teaching a syncretic form of religion that combined various rituals of Christianity with those of shamanism. Over the winter of 1921–22, it was evident that he was suffering from increasing mental instability. He now claimed that he was "filled with the spirit of God" and inspired many bouts of religious frenzy. After ordering two Inuuk killed without cause, he was finally shot by his cousin Killaapik, just as he was about to bludgeon a woman to death.[27] In tears, Killaapik turned

Qivuttuuq Murder Investigation Patrol, Spring 1924. This photo appears to have been taken at Padlei on their return home. MacGregor Collection.

and offered his rifle to the dead man's widow and asked her to kill him. She refused.[28]

The Inuit believed that Killaapik had no other choice and were surprised that the police had bothered to investigate something they believed was their own affair. Even today, elders believe that Niaquttiaq was insane and the situation dealt with in a manner consistent with Inuit traditions.

Timothy Kadloo – Pond Inlet, 1994

I heard from my older brother ... [past] Clyde River there was someone who had rabies, Niaquttiaq. My uncle Killaapik killed that person when I was a boy. I heard he was the only one that was capable, even though he was his cousin.[29]

Corporal McInnes recommended that no one be prosecuted and instead urged regular visits to the community to monitor the situation and provide guidance if necessary. The strategy to prevent violence through education and surveillance was a stark contrast to the objective of instilling fear of punishment at the Janes murder trial. As a consequence, the Inuit in the vicinity of Cumberland Sound were reported to have been far more willing to seek help from the police than those residing in North Baffin.[30]

In his report McInnes was critical of the missionaries for having distributed the syllabic Bibles without providing ongoing instruction and supervision.[31] At Blacklead Island Reverend Peck had acquired a loyal following, many of whom travelled to outlying camps as lay preachers. With the distribution of the Inuktitut Bibles, the ability of the Inuit to read and write syllabics grew at a phenomenal rate, even though they did not understand the meaning of the passages. The mission had closed prior to the outbreak of the Great War and there were no trained clerics in the region until 1928, when an Anglican mission was opened at Pangnirtung. Similar incidents of syncretic movements with accompanying religious hysteria had been reported earlier in southern Baffin and would surface again in the Ungava region (1927) and on the Belcher Islands (1941). The police blamed the absence of missionaries for these incidents, whereas church officials believed shamanism was the cause. In Niaquttiaq's case, his own mental instability was believed to have been the major contributor to the hysteria.[32]

At the time of the police investigation, the trading post at Qivittuuq consisted of four small shacks and a somewhat larger one-roomed house occupied by the widow of the deceased trader. Nearby was a graveyard where Scottish whalers used to bury their dead. The ten families still living at the site were in poor health. One woman was blind and others were reported to have poor eyesight. The police officer suspected syphilis might be the cause, a disease that might also explain Niaquttiaq's "delusions of grandeur." To the north, Paniluk's camp at Tikkakat near Cape Henry Kater had five families, including one elderly woman who was also blind.[33] Neither location offered the plentiful food resources found around Eclipse Sound and Igloolik.

The new Hudson's Bay Company post at Clyde River had the potential of bringing more economic stability to the area. Established in 1923 as an outpost of the Pond Inlet operation, it lay roughly equidistant between Pond Inlet and Quivituuq, at a former anchorage site of the rock-nose whalers. Although named after the great river in Scotland, Clyde River was somewhat of a misnomer as there was no major river leading into the long inlet. Fifteen Inuit families were reported in the vicinity.[34] In total the population between Qivittuuq and Pond Inlet was relatively small, but likely proportionate to the availability of the area's wildlife resources. Not surprisingly, police reports indicated that these camps were more prone to food shortages and infectious diseases compared to their neighbours on Eclipse Sound.

In 1927 the RCMP were called to investigate the death of another white fur trader, Hector Pitchforth, an Englishman who had been hired to replace Niaquttiaq as manager of the Qivituuq trading post. Although he died of natural causes, his story should be considered in juxtaposition to the circumstances encountered by Robert Janes. By nature a loner and possibly unnerved by the murders that had preceded his arrival, Pitchforth decided to move from Qivittuuq and set up a post further north near Cape Henry Kater. For reasons unknown, he sent his assistant home.[35] When RCMP officers McInnes and MacGregor first met the Englishman on the trail, they found him to be a strange man, seemingly naive, disorganized, and incapable of managing a trading post.[36] He was visited in the spring of 1925 by the HBC traders from Clyde River and in 1926 by the police patrol from Pond Inlet. On the latter occasion, he refused an offer to take him out after his ship had failed to appear the previous summer. By then he was quite deaf and suffering from residual snow-blindness. Unknown to him, the Sabellum Company had sold their ship, and in spite of promises to his brother to make alternative arrangements to bring him home, none had been made. When last seen alive, the trader was also thought to be suffering from scurvy and an injured leg.

Upon receiving reports that there had been no signs of activity around the post that winter, Constable Murray set out from Pond Inlet to investigate. Forcing the crude locks on three sets of doors leading into the main room, he found Pitchforth sitting bolt upright in his bed with a gun at his side, frozen stiff, having apparently died of natural causes. The room was littered with dirty clothing and dishes, a number of rifles and shotguns, and bags of fox pelts lying on his bed. The trader had kept a diary in which he wrote that he had become increasingly fearful that the Inuit intended to harm him and had refused to let them enter the house. The last entry date in his diary was Christmas 1926.[37] In addition to the Qivituuq murders, the story of Janes' death likely fed his paranoia. The Inuit had their own version of what had happened.

Elisapee Kanangnaq Ahlooloo – Arctic Bay, 1974

At that time there was a *qallunaaq* who had a store beyond Clyde River. There had been other *qallunaat* with him before, but they had gone and he began to lose his mind with loneliness. He began to imagine that the Inuit wanted to shoot him and started to build a fort of rocks around his house. The Inuit had no intention of killing him; he was going mad.

When he was building his fort, he slipped on a rock, fell, and hurt his head. Afterwards, he started shooting at the Inuit, who ran away. He died out there and the only reason the police knew what happened, and did not blame the Inuit, was that he had recorded everything in his diary. His body was taken to Pond Inlet and the police came to see whether anything had been stolen from his house. When the police determined that nothing had been stolen, they divided up his goods – including guns and provisions – among the people.[38]

There is no police record of having disposed of Pitchforth's goods, perhaps for good reason. It is unlikely their commanding officer in Ottawa would have understood.

At Pond Inlet, the police reportedly placed Pitchforth's body in one of the storage sheds, still frozen in a sitting position but now upright in a boat. According to Inuit stories, some used to wave and say "Hello, Hector," as

Fur trader Hector Pitchforth at Cape Henry Kater, summer 1924. He died of starvation in late December 1926. NAC – PA 201197.

they passed by. Only an Inuk can explain that they did not mean to be irreverent.[39] When summer arrived and the body thawed, Pitchforth was finally laid out to rest in a shallow grave alongside Robert Janes – two *qallunaat* traders whose ships failed to come. Both became irrational as consequence but died under very different circumstances.

The Hudson's Bay Company men would have few concerns of being stranded without supplies, but Janes's death would affect their operations in other ways. Prior to 1921 they had conducted their business in the eastern Arctic without fear of police intervention. In northern Quebec, for instance, the managers had assumed the role of sole authority in their respective regions, to the point that most Inuit believed that the HBC and not the "government" held supreme power over the land. Suddenly their actions were under close surveillance at both Pond Inlet and Pangnirtung, and they would protest vigorously at any attempt by the police to interfere.

Tensions were rarely exhibited openly at either settlement, but reports by the post managers and detachment police to their superiors would result in polite but open confrontation at the senior level.

The first instance occurred when Staff-Sergeant Joy returned to Ottawa in the fall of 1924, with a copy of a five-year contract that the HBC manager had Inuit hunters "sign" in return for an annual payment of twenty dollars. With the mark of an x on a piece of paper printed in English, an Inuk unwittingly agreed not to engage in any employment or transaction with other individuals. Under the terms of the contract, the company could prevent Inuit from trading at their store if they failed to comply. If they refused to sign, they were told that they would not be favoured in any trading negotiation.[40] Inspector Wilcox added his own comments to Joy's report, claiming that it was "the popularity of the police" that had made the Inuit vulnerable to "much under-handed treatment at the hands of the traders."[41] This was a perceptual blind spot on his part, since most Inuit in North Baffin believed that the traders were their friends, whereas they feared and mistrusted the police.

In the spring of 1925 a police study of trading practices throughout the Arctic showed that the Hudson's Bay Company had been grossly underpaying the Inuit for their furs while asking more for store goods compared to prices offered to white trappers. Described as "alleged extortionate methods," the report showed how one Inuk received $100 worth of trade goods for furs that had a market value of $9,600.[42] HBC Superintendent Parsons responded with distain, attributing tensions between the police and the traders to the "unfortunate selection of the police personnel sent north, many of whom abused their authority."[43] While the practice of committing the Inuit to contractual arrangements was suspended, no action was taken on the alleged exploitation.

Detachment police were reluctant to interfere at the local level with trading practices and instead reported any irregularities to their commanding officer. If deemed important, the report would be passed along to the RCMP commissioner, who in turn forwarded it to Governor Sale of the Hudson's Bay Company. Normally, a full year passed before the company completed its own investigation and made a formal response to the police. By that time the officer initiating the complaint would have been reassigned elsewhere, making follow-up difficult if not impossible.

Sometimes the best interests of the Inuit were ignored by government officials. Such was the case when the Northwest Territories Council put a halt to the company's expansion plans by banning any new trading posts in the proposed Arctic Islands Game Preserve. Aware of the implications, the HBC intensified its expansion program in advance of the legislation and opened two new posts in the summer of 1926, at Arctic Bay and at Fort Leopold on Somerset Island. When it was realized that the posts had

```
                    C O P Y


       ROYAL C.NADIAN MOUNTED POLICE.

                         Register No........

       HUDSON'S BAY COMPANY

       HIRING CONTRACT.
   Capacity.              Hunter.
```

I, Oo-took-oo-too,

of Ponds Inlet, Baffinland,   do hereby agree on this

11th day of August, 1924, to faithfully serve the Hudson's

Bay Company in the capacity of hunter and in such other

capacity as the said Company shall appoint for the term of

Five years, to be computed from the 11th day of August, 1924.

I do also hereby agree not to engage in any other employment

whatsoever, than that of the said Company for the said term

of Five years and to deliver my entire hunt of furs to the

said Company for the said time of five years.

In compensation for the above mentioned services the Hudson's

Bay Company agrees to pay me twenty $20.00 dollars per annum

and also pay me for my aforementioned annual hunt turned over

to them at the prices allowed Eskimo hunters by the said

Company. In witness whereof these Presents have been

executed at Pond Inlet, Baffinland, on this eleventh day of

August, 1924.   his   Oo-took-oo-too X His
Witness Akoomalikmark   (Name of Employee) For the H.B.C. mark W.C.Parr
      "   Toopingmathis.

A copy of "Oo-took-oo-too's" contract with the Hudson's Bay Company. NAC,
RG 18/3307/HQ-1090-G-2.

been built without permits, the NWT Council rejected the applications and
ordered them closed.[44] The Iglulingmiut and Tununirusirmiut thus lost
the advantage of a nearby source of trade goods. The traders blamed the
closure on the government, with the result that the detachment police
bore much of the Inuit resentment over the closure.

Also in 1926, the Hudson's Bay Company found itself defending the
manager at Lake Harbour for his participation in the shooting death of an

Inuk who was allegedly insane. This occurred after company employees and a number of Inuit set out by *qamutiit* in search of the man, who had reportedly gone berserk and killed members of his own family. Once they located the lone igloo where he had been hiding, they surrounded it and fired their rifles in unison to avoid any individual being blamed for his death. RCMP Corporal J.W.G. Wight travelled from Pangnirtung to investigate the rumours and reported that HBC employees had not only participated in the western-style vigilante execution but had purposefully avoided reporting the incident to the police. In his view the traders had taken the law into their own hands on the assumption they had full authority to do so.[45] To put an end to this perceived abuse of power, a detachment was established at Lake Harbour in 1927, thus completing a line of RCMP posts that stretched from Port Burwell at the mouth of Hudson Strait to the Bache Peninsula on Ellesmere Island.

Viewed retrospectively, the investigation of Janes' death had caused a domino effect in terms of *qallunaat* intervention in Inuit lives. Had there been no police post at Pond Inlet, it is highly unlikely that the Qivituuq murders would have been reported, and thus there would have been no need to build a detachment at Pangnirtung. Similarly, if there had been no police at Pangnirtung, it was unlikely that the shooting near Lake Harbour would have come to their attention. Within seven years of Janes' death, the RCMP finally had sufficient bases to enforce law and order throughout the eastern Arctic. With increased protection against the possibility of violence, it was inevitable that the Hudson's Bay Company would expand trading operations throughout the Baffin region to take advantage of untapped fur resources. Missionaries soon followed. Sometimes referred to as the "triumvirate rule" by the HBC, the RCMP, and the churches, the first phase in colonial occupation of Baffin Island was complete.

Throughout this period, fear of the police at Pond Inlet continued in spite of an all-out effort by detachment police to improve relations. Their work was made even more difficult in 1925 after responsibility for the Inuit was transferred to the Department of Indian Affairs, headed by Duncan Campbell Scott. Not only were their urgent requests for medical aid ignored, but police requisitions for "destitute rations" were challenged as being too generous. The RCMP were required to account for every item distributed to the Inuit from their store and submit their lists to the department for approval. Still dissatisfied with the cost, Scott recommended that distribution of all welfare should be handled through the Hudson's Bay Company.[46]

Police frustration with directives from Indian Affairs peaked with the issue of a poster to be displayed prominently at each trading post and

Hudson's Bay Company manager's house with fox furs hanging to dry, Pond Inlet, circa 1932. Courtesy of former RCMP Constable Robert Christy.

detachment in the eastern Arctic. The wording implied that the powers belonging to the Department of Justice had been transferred to the local police, giving them unrestricted powers to kill a murderer. Once again the intent to instil "fear" as a deterrent worked against police efforts in the field. As one officer complained, "the message made it impossible to establish a trusting relationship" with the Inuit.[47] As result of criticism, the poster was withdrawn from circulation four years later, coinciding with the transfer of responsibility for the Inuit back to the Northwest Territories Council.

Confronted with reports of a youth having shot and killed his father without provocation, Pond Inlet police were faced with the dilemma of how to carry out the "King's command." Although there is no file on the case in RCMP records, several elders vividly recalled the event.* Even if they had wished to, the family could not hide the incident from the police as the deceased was to begin work at the detachment in a matter of weeks. When a constable arrived on the scene, the wife thought he had come to kill her stepson.[48] While it seems inconceivable that a law officer would consider shooting anyone in cold blood, the poster had clearly stated that "If a man kills a man, the King sends his servants, the police, to take and

---

* Although the story was recounted in detail by one elder and confirmed by others, it must be treated as hearsay in the absence of RCMP files on the case. As a result, the names of those involved are protected under the Privacy Act and cannot be published. My decision to include the story is based on its importance in showing how the poster was interpreted by the Inuit and the strategy apparently adopted by the police to resolve the problem.

KNOW YE

The King of the Land commands you, saying:

"THOU SHALT DO NO MURDER"

Why does he speak thus?

Long ago our God made the world, and He owns the world.

The people also He made, and He owns them.

The King of the land is commanded by God to protect the people well.

The white people and Indians and Eskimos have him for their ruler. He is their ruler, therefore he commands, saying:

"THOU SHALT DO NO MURDER"

But if a man kills a man, the King sends his servants, the police, to take and kill the murderer.

But ye do not kill the murderer, nor cause him to be killed. This only the King's servants, the police, ought to do

But when a man commits murder, at once tell the King's servants, the police, and they will take and bind the murderer and the ruler will judge him.

Thus our God commands us so that you are to follow the King's command

DUNCAN C. SCOTT,

In Charge of Indian Affairs, Ottawa, Canada

Poster issued by the Department of Indian Affairs in 1925 and distributed to RCMP detachments and trading posts throughout the Canadian Arctic. Fleming, *Dwellers in Arctic Night*, 1928.

kill the murderer." There was no reason why the woman would believe otherwise. Even then, she explained the policeman's visit in terms an Inuk could understand – that the officer had wanted to avenge the father's death because he had been hired to work for RCMP. As it happened, the wife, along with her young baby and stepson, were brought back to the detachment to await the arrival of her older brother, who agreed to look after them. One elder thought the youth was not punished because he "was too young." Another thought his step-uncle had "saved" him from being killed. Significantly, no one credited the RCMP for sparing the young man's life.

The detachment police had been faced with a quandary: they had no jail, and the government ship was not due to arrive for months. With the shooting of Corporal Doak still fresh in memory, it was likely considered too dangerous to let an alleged murderer roam around the detachment under "house arrest." Corporal Hugh McBeth, the officer-in-charge, appears to have adopted an Inuit solution. With first-time offenders, it was generally the responsibility of a camp leader to take the person aside and counsel the individual. If he was not repentant and refused to change his ways, then harsher measures would be discussed and applied, if there was community consent. In this case, the police would have been faced with a more serious dilemma if there was evidence that the lad truly constituted a serious threat to others.

By Michele Therrien's interpretation, the Inuktitut term for customary law is *piqujaq*, translated literally to mean "what is asked by an authorized person to be done."[49] Although they were never written down, everyone understood the rules and the options available to resolve the matter.

Emile Imaruittuq – Igloolik, 1998

Before the court system came into our lives and before the RCMP, we always had rules in our camps. Misbehaviour has always been a part of life, and when there was misbehaviour, the community elders would get together and deal with that individual. The only way to deal with such people was to talk to them face to face … [On the other hand] murder is a serious offence. Once a person has committed murder, that person becomes a threat to the community for the rest of his life … In the past, they dealt with a murderer with extreme caution at all times, because they knew it was always possible he would re-offend.[50]

In the case of the boy who shot his father, the failure of the police to follow the "rules" outlined in the poster created untold confusion. Perhaps if for no other reason than he had somehow escaped "death at the King's command," some elders believed the boy was a shaman with power to cause the deaths of others.[51]

Two other cases of suspicious deaths occurred in the region, this time at the Dundas Harbour detachment. Both deceased were police officers – one in June 1926 and the other in September 1927 – each reportedly a result of an accidental discharge of their rifles.[52] There were no witnesses to either incident and there are no reports on file of any official investigation. The following summer, however, Joy, now promoted to the rank of inspector, was sent to take charge of the post. At the same time, the Greenlanders who had been employed at the detachment were summarily sent home and replaced by two Inuit families from Pond Inlet, including none other than

Ataguttiaq and Kipumii, at Dundas Harbour circa 1928. Shortly after
Nuqallaq's death, Ataguttiaq married her late husband's hunting partner.
They worked for the RCMP at both Pond Inlet and Dundas Harbour.
L.T. Burwash, photographer. NAC – PA 100084.

Nuqallaq's widow, Ataguttiaq, now married to her late husband's hunting
partner, Kipumii.

Because it seemed an unlikely coincidence that two police officers could
have accidentally shot themselves a year apart at the same detachment,

rumours and speculation spread throughout the Inuit community. Ataguttiaq's son, only a young child at the time but now an elder at Pond Inlet, described the situation and his own suspicions:

Sam Arnakallak – Pond Inlet, 27 September 1994

At Tallurutiit [Dundas Harbour], they used to have Greenlanders. When we moved there, we were the first Canadian Inuit. They sent the Greenlanders out on a ship. After they left, there were two graves. We went there in 1928 and there were two RCMP graves, and I used to hear that they shot themselves. The first one shot himself and later on, the other one shot himself ... I think myself that they were shot because of jealousies. I think they were shot by Greenlandic husbands. I think they were just saying that they just shot themselves. I suspected this because they wanted to exhume them. They wanted to know where they shot themselves and where the bullet entered and left the bodies.[53]

Arnakallak admits that he was the only one who thought the two policemen might have been shot by Greenlanders, but if his suspicions were correct, it would explain the absence of any official report. For obvious political reasons on both the domestic and international scene, it would have been unwise to open the case to further investigation if there was even a remote possibility that a jealous Inuk, particularly a native of Greenland, had killed a police officer. Instead, the record shows that there were no further suspected murders in the vicinity of North Baffin through to the Second World War.

In a perfect world it might have been wise to allow Inuit to regulate their own social behaviour until it was necessary to adapt to changes evolving in their own culture. The dilemma in the "real world" was how to match the political demands that Canadian laws be enforced for sovereignty reasons with the realities of Inuit life in the high Arctic. Recognizing that the police had the same objective as the Inuit – to keep peace and stability in the community – it should not be surprising that they might see advantage in adopting some aspects of Inuit customs. Such flexibility could only be achieved at the detachment level and only if the region remained isolated from the vision of southern officials. Policy interventions from Ottawa, as in the case of the poster "Thou shall do no murder," were unwelcome obstacles.

Frustration at the detachments might have been resolved in 1929, when responsibility for the Inuit was transferred back to the Northwest Territories Council. Any effect of the change, however, was too fleeting to be measured. The return of the Conservative government and the budget cuts driven by the Depression resulted in virtually every agency responsible for activities in the North being cut back to the bone. The Eastern Arctic Patrol would no longer have its own ship but would rent space on the HBC supply ship *Nascopie*. The Hudson's Bay Company, having suffered temporary discomfiture by policies of the Finnie administration, was now back in the driver's seat with unchallenged monopoly control of the Arctic fur trade.

The Liberals' return to power in 1935 saw only a moderate rearrangement of titles and reporting functions. Finnie's former department was now a mere bureau run by a skeleton staff, reporting through the Lands, Parks and Forests Branch to the Department of Mines and Resources. The decision-making power for Canada's North rested in its deputy minister, who was now commissioner of the NWT Council. Aside from the hospital at Pangnirtung, health care for the Inuit of Baffin Island did not exist. Year after year the government reported that Inuit were in excellent health, in spite of insider reports to the contrary. Censorship of the written word was still carefully managed, but in the absence of serious sovereignty threats, propaganda took on a more subtle approach. In addition to the use of films and photography, artists A.Y. Jackson and Lawren Harris were invited to join the Eastern Arctic Patrol to paint the landscape into the portrait of Canada's northern identity.[54]

The underlying objective for the government was to gain "maximum benefit at minimal cost." The case before the Supreme Court in 1939 regarding the status of the Canadian Inuit had nothing to do with any desire to plan for their future – quite the contrary. The sole purpose was to decide who would save money by having the other side declared responsible for Inuit welfare costs. The province of Quebec won when it was decreed that Inuit were like Indians and thus should be considered wards of the federal government. Since the decision was never legislated, the Inuit remained, as before, Canadian citizens without rights. Until 1951 they were classified by the Canadian Electoral Act as ineligible to vote, alongside the insane and inmates of prisons.

The jurisdictional changes and budget cuts seemed to have little discernible effect on the daily routine at the detachment. The arrival of two Roman Catholic priests and two Anglican ministers in 1929 meant that the police were no longer required to make "house calls" to the sick and dying. In terms of popularity, the Hudson's Bay Company now had competition. Although the HBC post brought economic stability to Inuit lives, Christianity offered freedom from the fears and taboos of shamanism. Unlike the earlier trading posts and whaling station, this time the tiny settlement at Pond Inlet would be permanent and would continue to expand, as did the consequences of an increasing non-native population and government intervention.

As noted at the beginning of this chapter, memories of the trial and its outcome would have a much longer-term effect on the community than antici-

Pond Inlet (Mittimatalik), circa 1935. The RCMP detachment is on the left, the Hudson's Bay Company on the right. The Roman Catholic and Anglican missions were located further to the right, beyond the camera's range. RCMP Historical Division, Ottawa, Ref. No. 2339.

pated, largely driven by misguided perceptions. Part of the mistrust lay in confusion over the questions asked by the police and the regular sled patrols. Initially the Inuit did not understand the importance of keeping records about wildlife resources, successes in trapping, the availability of country food, births, deaths, and Inuit health. Thus the questions asked of them each year were troubling and viewed with suspicion. Elders' recollections of the police dispensing rations and blankets to the needy are vague and for the most part long forgotten.[55]

Police work at Pond Inlet was made somewhat easier after 1932 with the acquisition of a motorized trap boat named the *Lady Laurier*. Yet the spring sled patrols continued west as far as Igloolik and south to Home Bay. At one time or another even the most seasoned officer found himself totally dependent upon the very people he had been hired to protect. A *polisialuk's* lack of skills frequently evoked derision and criticism, although never to his face. Often the police were compared to children who had to be looked after and taught what to do. Memories were particularly vivid among those who had grown up at the Pond Inlet detachment and observed their parents at work. In later life, a number were hired as special constables.

Ningiuk Killiktee – Pond Inlet, 1994

When you [we] went by dog team in a snowstorm, we used to have to treat them like kids so nothing would happen to them. They tended to get cold and we didn't want them to freeze. We'd tell them what to do. We used to treat them like little children. Some of them would just sit there when they got cold. After they were here awhile, it was all right. When they found later [how to do things], it wouldn't be like that. It was hard that time in the wind. You didn't want anything to happen to them and you didn't want them to get lost. We would care very much for them because you were the only ones out there with them. Once we got home, we wouldn't care about them anymore. There were some you could work very well with and some who didn't do anything at all.[56]

Timothy Kadloo – Pond Inlet, 1994

The RCMP told us that they weren't exactly sure what to do, that they would need help. Like children, they would watch you before they actually knew what to do. But once they found out what to do, they would start helping out. They would end up helping a lot after that. They were a bit clumsy because they were *qallunaat* – because they were not used to this kind of activity. That's what we had to do, we had to help each other. We'd learn different things from them. They would help us sometimes.[57]

Sam Arnakallak – Pond Inlet, 1994

They were just like kids. When they were having tea outside and they weren't able to grasp the cup with their hands, the cup would be held for them exactly like children, because they were from a warm climate. All the foxes they caught would be prepared for them, but I never knew any of them who were really grumpy.[58]

The Inuit would have to dry their mitts and *kamiiks*. Once they stopped for the night, the [guides] would have to hurry and build an igloo as if they had small children. Once they put them in, they'd have to light the stove to get them warm. Then they [the guides] would have to stay outside to feed the dogs.[59]

Inuit couples were hired to work at the detachment. The men were expected to obtain country food, look after the dogs and their harnesses, and perform a number of menial tasks. Their wives were expected to clean the house, wash the dishes and clothes worn by the police, and sew all their skin clothing. Yet the women had no official status and their names did not appear on the police roster. Some men were hired temporarily to guide patrols or help with the spring cleanup. The term "employed natives" was used to designate a permanent male employee. After 1936 they were given the official title of "Special Constable" after a year's probation. Yet for many years, they were still paid only $15 a month. Most elders thought this was adequate because "things at the store didn't cost very much" and provisions such as accommodation, ammunition, and staple foods were free.[60] For patrol work an Inuk received an extra dollar a day, and more if the police required the use of his dogs. Relatively speaking, an RCMP con-

Inuk building a snow house on patrol with the RCMP. McInnes Collection.

stable received four times as much – $2 a day for the first three years. Initially, Inuit were "paid in kind" with goods available at the RCMP store;[61] no cash changed hands. As part of budget cuts in 1932, however, the police stores at the detachments were closed and replaced with special accounts set up at the Hudson's Bay Company, raising questions in some minds as to who held the ultimate authority.

Although complaints were rarely expressed to the *qallunaat*, there seemed to be lingering resentment among the Inuit over the tasks they were expected to perform when employed by the police. Some daily chores were viewed as drudgery, particularly if the police were quite capable of performing the tasks themselves.

Ningiuk Killiktee – Pond Inlet, 1994

When we first started working for the RCMP, we would fetch ice, because they needed water. Also, we would bring coal for their stove to their coal box. When the stove was full of ashes, we would have to dump them. We would haul out the garbage. If the stove went off during the night, we would light it in the morning. [The RCMP] didn't try to do it. They wanted us to do it. We had to do what they said. When they started using oil, we didn't have to do it any more.[62]

Timothy Kadloo – Pond Inlet, 1994

When I was going to work for the RCMP, there were dogs tied up here in Pond Inlet. They told me to come at the time they were going to clean up. They told me to clean up around the dogs, the faeces. I came here because of dog faeces and garbage. That's what happened to me.[63]

Sam Arnakallak – Pond Inlet, 1994

The men would have to work every day to put coals in the stoves and take the ashes out and go fetch ice for the water. They had to do that a lot of times during the day, but here were the good-looking men [RCMP] doing nothing, just sitting around.[64]

Letia Kyak – Pond Inlet, 1994

Clothes always had to be made for them, because they travelled by dog team for long distances. And they went to Ikiirasaq, Clyde River, Igloolik, and Arctic Bay. We would make [outfits] for them before they left. In the springtime, the Inuit would help clean up the land and do the painting to make the place look good. That's what they used to do.[65]

Joanasie Arreak – Pond Inlet, 1994

When I was a child, [the RCMP] wore everything made from caribou skins, like everyone else. Their clothing was made by the wives of those who were working for them. Every Saturday, they would give out provisions to the families of those working for them, probably enough to last a week.[66]

Sam Arnakallak – Pond Inlet, 1994

The women would wash clothes with their hands, sitting on the floor with a washboard and a basin. They would also wring them with their hands. In summer, I remember them with a small boat in which they carried the RCMP's clothes to the creek where they had places to build fires. They would heat up the water there, wash the clothes, and rinse them in the creek. Then they would take them back to the post and hang them to dry. There is still soot today where they used to build the fires beside the rocks.[67]

They may not have been listed on the official employee roster, but the wives of the special constables worked hard for their food and supplies. One officer thought that the women who cleaned up after dinner were paid with leftovers from the meals, noting that maple syrup was always a favourite.[68] Sometimes the police bought the women duffle cloth, underwear, cooking utensils, combs, or beads for their personal use.[69]

Corporal Hugh McBeth, known to the Inuit as Papigatualuk, earned high honours on all accounts. He was said to drop everything when an Inuk came in and would chat in Inuktitut for an hour or so.[70] McBeth spent a total of five years at Pond Inlet, on three different occasions, from 1928 to 1930, then 1931 to 1933, and again from 1943 to 1944. He also had the dis-

Young Kyak with Corporal Hugh McBeth (Papigatualuk) on the left, and Constable James Wishart (Tuksuk) on the right, Pond Inlet, circa 1932. Photo by Robert Christy.

tinction of teaching young Lazeroosie Kyak to read and write, then later hiring him as a special constable.[71] Kyak was the first of several Inuit who had grown up at the detachment during their formative years and became part of a second generation working for the RCMP. Having learned the ways of the *qallunaat* early in their lives, they seemed better able to mediate the cultural differences between Inuit and the police.

The RCMP who wrote autobiographical accounts of their years in the Arctic were generous in their praise of the Inuit, but such opinions rarely found their way into official reports. One exception was a memo by Corporal McInnes to RCMP Commissioner J.H. MacBrien. "It is impossible for a white man to think, and reason as an Eskimo," McInnes wrote. "They are not mentally deficient, but better developed mentally, than what is generally known, in all matter pertaining to their simplicity of life, honesty, generosity, and provision for the young and old. The Eskimo's [sic] have their faults, but in comparison with ours, it is possible they have a better philosophy than the white race."[72]

McInnes expressed more personal thoughts in his notebook. One in particular was insightful concerning relationships between Inuit and police – and why "fear" may have been used as a conscious strategy in that relationship:

At the back of the Eskimo mind, although seldom expressed, is a feeling of his superiority over the white man, and a belief we can show them nothing in connection with their country and animals which they do not know. There is also a latent fear of us, deadened by contact, reduced by fair treatment, and almost turned into contempt by over familiarity, but always in existence.

They have a strong opinion that we should not interfere too much in their affairs, and we should not, unless necessary. I have the opinion that reasoning with the native is almost impossible, some will go far [to] oblige you, but in vital matters I think it will be found that we will in the future have to rely on that fear of us, of which I have spoken.[73]

Cultural differences ran deep, but the use of fear to force compliance, even as a last resort, may explain some of the lingering resentment and mistrust. As Bernier and others had learned from firsthand experience, most Inuit believed they had superior knowledge of the Arctic, and it was exceedingly difficult to force them to do something they did not believe was right.

The use of fear as a tool of control would not be without cost. The tendency of an Inuk to acquiesce, then remain resentful, worked against the development of trust. In discussion with his sister, Arnakallak related how the police tended to order the Inuit around in the early years:

Sam Arnakallak – Pond Inlet, 1994

I think they were just like the RCMP today, but Inuit at that time would just say yes. I think they used to say "yes" too easily. I don't think that they thought there was anything wrong with saying "yes."[74]

Our parents were a lot more patient than people today. Today, if a little thing is done to us, we end up telling people this and that, and try to get them charged and arrested, but the Inuit in earlier times just sat there and took it. I don't think our mother did that, though. One thing I really noticed about our mother was that she would give the police harsh words every now and then.[75]

Anthropologists have explained that it was part of Inuit culture to defer to strangers or to those they feared – a practice known as *ilira*. Thus in spite of certain loyalties that developed between some policemen and their Inuit assistants, cross-cultural differences inevitably led to misunderstandings.

It would take decades before the Inuit of North Baffin fully understood the rationale behind police actions. The reverse was equally true.

Fear played a major part throughout this story – first, the intense fear that Janes would kill the Inuit or their dogs, then, the fear that they would be punished by the *qallunaat* to avenge his murder. Fear also was evident in the government's reaction to the fur trader's death – the fear that to "do nothing" would show Canada was unable to administer the Arctic Islands. And there was the fear that any sign of leniency might encourage another Inuk to kill an angry policeman or trader. Fear of Inuit violence was further complicated by a lack of understanding and respect for Inuit cultural traditions. Allegedly, there was also the judge's fear that the Inuit might kill him if he pronounced a death sentence, and there was genuine fear among the Inuit gathered at the trial that the judge might order that they all be killed to avenge Janes' death. In the Hector Pitchforth's case, he was so frightened after the Qivittuuq murders that he locked himself in his trading post and died of cold and starvation.

For the Inuit of North Baffin the outbreaks of disease and episodes of starvation seemed to worsen after the police investigation, particularly after the trial. If, as some believed, evil spirits were at play, they were certainly not appeased by the trial's outcome. The unexpected deaths of Nuqallaq's father and uncle prior to his return home only confirmed such suspicions. Some Inuit believed the incidents of starvation and other unexplained deaths were caused by competition among the shamans.[76] As we know now, fear of the unknown was the root force that gave a shaman the power to enforce taboos and rituals. We are all affected in varying degrees by fear of the unknown, but an Inuk by virtue of his cultural beliefs and traditions was particularly susceptible.

Of the many stories describing the intense fear at the time of the murder trial, one stands out over all others. In a story from Hugh Brody's *The Other Side of Eden*, an Inuk explains how fear of the police had affected him as a child, partially because his parents had used the police as a kind of "bogeyman to scare children into being good":

Qanguk – Pond Inlet, 1974

When the police arrived for the trial, they put on their red tunics and trousers with stripes. They had long knives swinging at their sides. We saw those knives. One of the policemen in these clothes came to visit our house. In he came – the *polisialuk*. I saw the sword. I thought for sure that some threat was about to be carried out. I had done something wrong. Something I had done had been found out. My parents' warnings were in my mind. This large man had come for me.

The *polisialuk* has brought his huge knife. He is going to cut my head off. I thought I was going to be beheaded! I ran behind a chair crying, trying to hide. But

I was to be more frightened. I was terrified: the *polisialuk* reached behind the chair, he wanted to pick me up. This was it! He took me in his hands. I was going to be beheaded. I screamed and cried in terror. The policeman had to hand me to my mother. At first I could not tell her what I was afraid of, I did not have the words in my head ...

Ah yes, we were so scared of white people. They seemed to us to be dangerous. They intimidated us.[77]

Qanguk's ability to express his childhood emotions so vividly a half-century later reflects the tenacity of the fear that gripped the minds of those witnessing the trial. As yesterday's children became today's elders, that fear of the police was passed down to their children and grandchildren, acquiring layers of reinforcement from incidents unrelated to its origins. Intervention by the special constables helped moderate the fears over time, but in the interim the police at Pond Inlet would be forced to adopt a more sensitive approach to law enforcement than envisioned by authorities in Ottawa.

In the absence of any further reports of violence in North Baffin, southern officials assumed that the trial had achieved its objectives and that the Inuit now "respected" Canadian law. In reality, it was not respect for the law that had ended the violence, but fear of the law.

10

Arctic Justice Revisited

To most southern Canadians the 1923 murder trial at Pond Inlet was of fleeting interest and soon forgotten. For the *qallunaat* directly involved, whether government officials, members of the court party, or the police, the incident was best ignored – or failing that, at least presented in the best possible light. As a result, confusion and seeming contradictions arise when written reports are compared with Inuit oral histories. For the most part, government accounts are governed by "need to know" criteria, whereas Inuit versions tend to personalize local events with added rationalizations in an attempt to make sense of it all. Neither version examines the underlying motives behind the police investigations and the trial.

Critics of government policies have used terms like "colonial subjugation" or "conquest without bloodshed" to describe the introduction of law and order to the eastern Arctic.[1] In this case, however, the circumstances differ from the usual pattern of imperial expansion and colonial governance. There was no urgency on the part of Canadian officials to settle the Arctic, no imminent need to take control of Inuit lands for economic development. Certainly there were no thoughts of "civilizing" the indigenous people through education or taking responsibility for their welfare. At best the process might be characterized as "reluctant colonialism," driven more by the need to protect a legacy than any prospect of national gain. Historian William R. Morrison suggests that this phase of "symbolic sovereignty" was characterized by a "proto-administrative state, in which many of the formalities of government were performed but most of the modern functions of government were neglected."[2] In this context, law enforcement and administration of justice were merely tools used to protect the discovery claims of the British Admiralty.

The gift of the Arctic Islands to the fledgling Dominion of Canada did not come without strings. The caveat in accepting the legacy, as noted earlier, was the promise that "the Dominion Government and Legislature were prepared to assume the responsibility of exercising such surveillance over it as may be required to prevent the occurrence of lawless acts or other abuses."[3] Thus with a stroke of the pen Britain was assured that the honour of her polar explorers would be protected by Canada in perpetuity, without further effort by the admiralty or cost to the treasury. Canadian statesmen might have had second thoughts had they considered why Britain had made no effort to colonize the Arctic Islands or to take responsibility for the welfare of the inhabitants, as the Danes had done for over a century in Greenland. Now Canada was faced with the cost of protecting Britain's honour and with it the associated obligation to civilize the Inuit. Britain's "gift" had thus become an unexpected financial burden on Canadian taxpayers and not one easily justified in the public forum.

Initially it was thought that unilateral declarations and "planting the flag" in remote areas of the archipelago might be adequate to assure British claims. When these measures proved insufficient, the RCMP presence was intended to provide visible evidence that Canada was maintaining law and order, in a manner similar to its role in settling the West and later the Yukon. But neither experience had prepared the Mounted Police for the remote isolation of the Arctic, where the dog-sled rather than the horse was the primary mode of transportation and igloos were superior to tents.

Once Staff-Sergeant Joy had succeeded in "getting his man," it did not seem important that Inuit had never received any formal instruction on Canadian law. After the suspects were arraigned and held over for trial, it would be the responsibility of the justice system to determine their fate. In the end, one Inuk was sentenced to ten years of hard labour in a southern prison on a reduced charge of manslaughter, not so much for what happened on the night of 15 March 1920 near Cape Crauford but because an Inuk over a thousand miles away had killed a police officer and fur trader without provocation. Under the rubric of "justice," Nuqallaq's punishment was designed to serve as a lesson to other Inuit of what would happen if they murdered a white man. Now the fur traders and police could go about their business without fearing for their lives. Moreover, the trial showed the world that Canada was successfully enforcing its laws throughout the Arctic Islands. Whether or not the trial was intended "to serve justice" is less clear.

Fortunately the Crown prosecutor prevented a serious miscarriage of justice by recommending that the murder charge be reduced to manslaughter. And so, in the words of Harwood Steele, official historian for the RCMP, "Justice had come to World's End."[4] At least, it was portrayed thus in government reports. Traditionally Canadians looked upon the rituals, procedures, and infrastructures of the British judicial system as a guarantee that justice would be served. At Pond Inlet in late August 1923 it was tested – and found wanting.

The Inuit elders of North Baffin had different views on what happened and why. They were ignorant of how Arctic sovereignty and violence in the western Arctic had affected their lives, and even if they had been told, they would not have understood. For those only peripherally involved, memories of the events were permeated with assumptions and rationalizations as they tried to create order out confusion and inconsistency. Some tried to explain why Nuqallaq was punished and not the others – he had a bad reputation; he used to tell lies; he was known to have beaten his first wife; his father was a shaman; and so on. Yet none of these allegations, even if true, explained why Nuqallaq was convicted of manslaughter.

The values of western society were beyond Inuit comprehension. Thus no one spoke of the more obvious reasons why Nuqallaq was punished: the fact that Canadian laws and justice were very different from their own, that they were being forced to accept a new authority or perish; and that Nuqallaq's punishment was meant as lesson to other Inuit so that they would never again be tempted to kill a *qallunaaq*. Similarly, no one seemed to notice that the trial had effectively pitted the word of one Inuk against that of another. Perhaps ramifications such as these were not easily expressed, if indeed they were understood.

None of the elders suggested that Nuqallaq had been wrong to kill the irrational fur trader. In fact the consensus was clearly that he had no other choice. Aatitaaq's own son, who had been present at the trial as a child, seemed to scorn the white man's court of law.

Uujukuluk – Arctic Bay, circa 1975

The people sat in rows and argued. All the men in the front row – and there were a lot – were wearing red tunics. There were three men on trial, including my father. One was taken away by ship, but the other two who were equally involved were left behind.[5]

Others made similar observations, but no one blamed individuals for what had happened – not Staff-Sergeant Joy, Judge Rivet, the lawyers, or the jury, all collectively described as "the people who came to ask questions." (Perhaps in my presence the elders were being polite, as I too had "come to ask questions.")

For those who were directly involved, the murder trial left an indelible impression: the days of tedious questioning, fears that everyone would be killed, men dressed up in long black gowns, policemen in red jackets with shiny brass buttons and pants with yellow stripes, and the man with the magic box who made pictures of everyone so they could watch themselves on a white sheet the following year. The Inuit smiled bravely for the cameras, but the fear that these "people who came to ask questions" might kill them was never far from the surface.

For Nuqallaq, his recollections of the trial would be clouded by his experience in prison, then by illness, guarded hope, and despair, until finally they were obliterated with death. For the people he left behind, the memories would be painful and made more so by insensitive rumours and gossip among the fur traders. Ataguttiaq's daughter related how someone had read parts of the trial transcript to her mother and left her to understand that the police thought her actions had somehow caused Nuqallaq to kill Robert Janes. Others kept saying things that she knew were not true. She was deeply hurt and refused to talk to anyone about the event, except for her immediate family.[6]

Then in 1974 she was persuaded by the kindly resident Catholic priest, Father Guy Mary-Rousselière, to tell her story on tape so that a record of what had happened would be preserved for future generations. She consented.[7] There is a long sigh as the tape starts to roll, and Anna Ataguttiaq begins the story that she kept to herself for so many years. The account is concise, believable, and consistent with the majority of other witnesses.

Ataguttiaq – Pond Inlet, 1974

After he became my husband, in the spring – early spring – after spending summer and winter, we left for Arctic Bay. When we were camped at Tuujjuk [Adams Island] – Kassak without his wife, Ululijarnaat and his wife, Nutarariaq and his wife, Kaujak, and also Enooya and his wife, Aapitaq. We were camped at Tuujjuk and men were catching walrus and polar bear.

We heard that Uuttukuttuk and Sakirmiaviniq had left Tulukkaat and were on their way to Arctic Bay, we did not see them because they were travelling further up the coast and we were at Tuujjuk. They went on their way and we did not pay any attention to them.

After it was daylight most of the time, we found out we were going to visit Arctic Bay. They were enjoying themselves catching polar bears and walrus. We would follow the coastline. Then, when they wanted to hunt polar bears we would go to the loose ice, and we would go back to land fast ice and camp for the night. They were enjoying themselves. Then we came across a camp on the ice at Kangiq [Cape Crauford]. I didn't know who they all were. There were a lot of people.

Uuttukuttuk and the qallunaaq were still there, staying with Paumi and his wife. There were other people there too, I am not sure who. We were just camping for the night and were going to carry on the next day.

The qallunaaq was visiting around with my husband, trying to get him to interpret for him, when a group arrived from their camps. There were the Kunuk family,

Miqutui and his family, the Aatitaaqs and the Ijjangiaqs. He was looking for fox furs and was visiting around with my husband trying to make him interpret. Once he got his fox furs, he wanted to travel to Igloolik through to Repulse Bay and to the south. He was planning to sell the furs along the way and trade for food from the *qallunaat* and make his way home down south. That's what he wanted to do.

There was a pair of sealskin pants and an old *qulittaq* filled with seagull skins and assorted items. He thought they were fox furs and accused them of lying and told the people that he had seen fox furs packed in a bag as they arrived. There was another *qallunaaq* at Igarjuaq called Quvviunginnaq [Caron]. He thought they were planning to sell the furs to him ... He would ask them "Do you have any furs? – No, I do not have any." It was then that, accusing them of lying, he started to get angry. They say that he started threatening to shoot them. Uuttukuttuk ended up hiding his rifle. As with us, we were just there for the night and were leaving again. He demanded my husband to stay and be his interpreter and forbid him to depart. So we stayed.

All of the men went hunting, but Uuttukuttuk and the *qallunaaq* stayed alone in the camp. I had a small igloo unfinished inside. Kasssak remained in our igloo. Miqutui came over and told us she wanted to follow the hunters. Uuttukuttuk had said that the *qallunaaq* would be extremely angry at the men when they came back. He said that he would challenge them if they refused again. Since he said that, she told us she was scared and wanted to walk to the hunters. She put on her *quliktaq* and decided to walk until she met the hunters. I did not have a *quliktaq* but I lost no time in following her, in my caribou *atigi*. I went with her because I was scared too.

As we were travelling, we ran into the hunting party. Miqutuit told them that Sakirmiaviniq was going to challenge them when they arrived and told them that she was here because she was afraid. And we started going home. We entered our home [shared with Nuqallaq's aunt Kaujgak and husband Kassak]. Someone came in and said that the *qallunaaq* was coming over to visit him ... after his meal. Some men came over. There was Ululijarnaat, Aatitaaq, and his younger brother. Those men came in and Kassak left to visit somewhere, I don't know where. They were talking about taking him when he came over, because he was a danger. They said he wanted to shoot the Inuit since they would not give him fox fur. I was frightened and I wanted to run away to a friend's igloo.

He told me "no" because he might catch on. Then they left and I was left all alone in the igloo. I stood up on the bed, thinking that I would make a hole in the wall and go to somebody else's home. I was pacing around and crying because I was so scared. Then I heard the gun shots. As I continued pacing, someone came in and said, "That's that. He is dead."[8]

Next year, since my husband had been told to return to Pond Inlet in the spring, we retraced our route there. We found a trader and a Mounted Policeman. We went to the RCMP post where my husband was arrested. We spent another summer there. My husband left by boat the next summer.

When he came back, two years later, he was dying. His lungs were ruined. He died shortly before Christmas. Soon after I married Kipumii … And since then I have lived in my land.[9]

And so Ataguttiaq tried one last time to let people know and understand what happened at the camp near Cape Crauford. It was over fifty years since Janes had been killed, yet with the exception of a few added details, her account did not vary substantively from the statement she gave to Staff-Sergeant Joy at the preliminary hearings. Her story deserves to be remembered and accepted as truth. Father Mary kept his promise, and it was not until after Ataguttiaq died that he published her story in the diocese newsletter, *Eskimo.*

A by-product of Nuqallaq's sentence was the introduction of tuberculosis throughout North Baffin. Even if the disease had been present before his return, which by all reports appeared unlikely, the Inuit on hand to welcome him home were doubly exposed. The decision to send Nuqallaq back to Pond Inlet was misguided, but with no malicious intent. On the other hand, the subsequent refusal to heed the detachment's pleas for medical help was unconscionable, and the attempts to suppress public knowledge about the spread of the disease reprehensible. The Department of Indian Affairs continued to publish laudatory reports about the health of the Inuit, constituting, in the words of Diamond Jenness, nothing more than a "cloak of pious and deceptive phrases."[10]

At this juncture one might pause and consider whether anything positive came out of the trial, or did Nuqallaq die in vain. True, aside from the aforementioned incidents of the young Inuk who killed his father, there were no other episodes of criminal violence in North Baffin for several decades, or at least none that were brought to the attention of the police. Had the Inuit learned the lesson intended? Possibly, but in the western Arctic, where Alikomiak and another Inuk were hung for murder, criminal violence continued for a number of years. Perhaps, then, the absence in North Baffin stemmed from an inherent lack of violent behaviour in their culture, and thus the lesson was unnecessary. Other mitigating factors might include the degree and nature of previous contact with the white man, and the subtle cultural differences that had evolved as a result of that contact. In the end, however, much depended upon the leadership and sensitivity of the officer-in-charge of each detachment, and his ability to circumvent the potentially harmful policies of the Department of Indian Affairs.

Elsewhere on the island there were reported cases of violence stemming from mental disturbances. In Cumberland Sound and more southerly locations, the term "insanity" was frequently used to describe personality changes in an individual who suddenly became morose or abusive. In one instance an Inuk killed his wife, then committed suicide.[11] The police were also called to mediate a number of domestic disputes claimed to be caused by insanity, and for the most part they were able to resolve the problem with counselling, in a manner similar to traditional Inuit practices. In 1932, for example, the police reported a case in which an abusive man was captured by fellow Inuit and brought to the trading post at Cape Dorset. He was then transferred to the police detachment at Lake Harbour, where he received a lecture and was returned home.[12]

Only as a last resort did police keep an individual at the detachment to monitor his or her behaviour.[13] Severe cases of schizophrenia or mental retardation, on the other hand, required protection from those who out of fear might try to kill the Inuk exhibiting aberrant behaviour. In this event, the afflicted individual would be kept under surveillance to await diagnosis by the medical officer on the eastern Arctic Patrol. If it was deemed necessary, the "insane" were transported south for treatment.[14] This prompted one Inuk to experience "a miraculous recovery" upon learning of the ship's imminent arrival.[15]

After many years without criminal violence, a second murder trial took place on Baffin Island in 1938, to try an Inuk by the name of Katcho who left his wife to live with another woman, then proceeded to kill her children. When this was reported to the police, they brought the hunter and his original wife back to the detachment where he was held under "house arrest" until the arrival of the government ship. Unlike the murder investigation at Pond Inlet, the police now had radio communication and were able to arrange for a judicial party the following summer. The commander of the Eastern Arctic Patrol, Major D.L. McKeand, was appointed the stipendiary magistrate; J.W. McLean of Winnipeg would act as the Crown prosecutor, with Fleet G. Whitaker of The Pas, Manitoba, representing the accused. The jury included Patrick Baird, a geologist from Berwickshire, Scotland; R.A. Perkins, a postal officer from Windsor, Ontario; D.A. Nichols, a physiographer from Ottawa; and three fur traders, W.J.G. Ford, J.R. Ford, and J.C. Cormack.

Following the precedent established at Pond Inlet, the trial was held in the main room of the detachment, but this time with only curious passengers from the *Nascopie* and a handful of non-native residents of Pangnirtung in attendance. The only Inuit inside the courtroom were the accused, his wife, and his father. By his own admission Katcho thought that he must have killed the children but claimed that he did not remember what had happened. In his words, "I didn't have my right senses at the time." His father testified that his son had a bad fall when he was a child and never recovered. Three medical doctors examined the accused: Dr Thomas Melling, medical officer on board the *Nascopie*; and passengers Dr R.L. Sutton of Kansas City, and Dr Donald Forward of Ashtabula, Ohio. They all agreed that he was insane. The jury deliberated for seven minutes and essentially confirmed the medical diagnosis. As a result Katcho was taken south for treatment and never heard from again.[16] Yet even in this instance there was lingering confusion about the purpose of his departure, with one elder at Pangnirtung still convinced that he had been taken away because he was a murderer and perhaps killed, since he had never returned home.[17] The problems of alleged insanity such as occurred at Pangnirtung and other areas to the south did not seem as prevalent in North Baffin. This may be related to the fact that the remoteness of the Tununirusirmiut and Igluling-miut camps allowed Inuit to handle such problems in a traditional manner, undetected by the police.

The problem of administering British-style justice to people with differing cultural values did not go unnoticed, prompting considerations of possibly modifying the application of the criminal code for the Inuit. When R.A. Marriot was assigned to write the history of the Eastern Arctic Patrol in 1939, he had the opportunity to witness firsthand the jury trial at Pangnirtung. He explained the conundrum in his report:

The matter of dispensing white man's justice to natives is a knotty problem, and one to which governments with any native minority are giving serious consideration. To call an Eskimo a "primitive" is a harsh term. As a race, the Eskimos are a peace-loving people, remarkably intelligent, and with a high sense of honour. Crime, as we know it in the outside world, seems to be practically unknown … Imprisonment or even deportation, used in both cases as a deterrent punishment, was not highly successful. The prisoner, instead of becoming a social outcast, for the time being was more the object of envy of the other Eskimos, who had to fend for themselves. The old Eskimo custom of ridding a camp of a dangerous man, either a murderer or a lunatic, found quite a lot of favour in the eyes of the white man living in the country. Naturally, under the present code, this practice is impossible and has been stamped out, and it is only when very rare cases, such as that of Katcho occurs, that the problem presents itself. It is one which is likely to require a lot of consideration before it is finally settled.[18]

In 1945 there was further discussion with T.L. Cory, legal advisor to the Bureau of the Northwest Territories and Yukon, who suggested that "the only way to punish an Eskimo is to humiliate him; to make him 'lose face' in the eyes of his community," and offered the suggestion of public flogging.[19]

In April 1966, Judge J.H. Sissons would preside over his last murder trial in the Northwest Territories. The case involved two Inuuk, charged with the murder of an Inuit woman who had been behaving irrationally and deemed a threat to the community. The execution was carried out with the consent of the community and at the direction of its leaders. As described in Dorothy Eber's *Images of Justice*, the case of *Regina v. Shooyook and Aiyoot* was tried before a jury which included two Inuuk and for the first time in the NWT, a woman juror. The verdict was debated at length by the jurors, with requests to the judge for further interpretation of the law. In the end, one Inuk was acquitted, and Shooyook was found guilty of manslaughter, accompanied by a strong appeal for clemency. Mr Justice Sissons responded by handing down a two-year suspended sentence to Shooyook.[20] Others suggested that banishment from the region would be more effective.[21]

As Eber points out, the verdict was considered a "high water" point in the administration of Inuit justice, for the jury's recognition that social and cultural factors might take precedence over the letter of the law. Of significant note, the defence counsel who made the eloquent plea for a verdict of "not guilty" was William G. Morrow, the man who would be shortly appointed as Judge Sisson's successor as chief justice of the Supreme Court of the Northwest Territories. Yet as testimony to the inability to resolve the inherent problems arising from disparate social and cultural values, the debate over judicial reform is still ongoing, while the rate of criminal violence in Nunavut is now the highest per capita in all of Canada.[22]

Although fear was the underlying catalyst in the actions of those involved in the death of Robert Janes, the "time in history" was a major factor in determining the outcome of the trial. Had Janes been killed ten years earlier, his death would likely have been ignored by the government or perhaps even understood. Ten years later, there might not have been a police detachment at Pond Inlet, but the Inuit would likely have heard about the hangings in the western Arctic and refrained from shooting a *qallunaaq*. In this sense, Nuqallaq was an Inuk, acting according to Inuit traditions – but at the wrong place at the wrong time.

One lasting impression in the minds of Inuit residing in North Baffin was of the confusion over the equality – or inequality – of Arctic justice. Clearly, if an Inuk were to kill a *qallunaaq* without provocation, one could expect the punishment to be death by hanging. If an Inuk killed another Inuk without provocation, as in the case of the boy who shot his father, it appeared that he or she might escape punishment altogether. The poster declaring "Thou shalt do no murder" said one thing, but the police failed to follow through. Inconsistency bred fear of the unknown. In time, deference and compliance too easily evolved into disrespect, and in a few instances, defiance.

The story that began with the death of Robert Janes did not end with the trial and the death of Nuqallaq but continued on through the complex adaptations of the social-contact relationships between Canadian law enforcement officers and the Inuit of North Baffin. Some relationships would be influenced positively by a shared experience. At Pond Inlet a quasi-symbiotic relationship was emerging, with the officers dependent on Inuit knowledge and the Inuit wanting the material benefits and perhaps even the prestige of working for the *qallunaat*. This could only be accomplished through cooperation, mutual respect, and sharing – all the ingredients for collective survival in the harsh Arctic environment. These relationships remained tenuous, however, as a result of both sides believing in their own superiority.

Of the many stories about the death of Robert Janes and the trial at Pond Inlet, some bear little resemblance to reality, but in the mind of each individual they are real. Perhaps with the distortions cleared and the uncertainties better defined, the people of Mittimatalik can look with pride on the origins of their community, knowing that Nuqallaq was defending himself, his family, and his friends from the threats of a man who had lost his sense of reason, and that he was doing so according to age-old traditions of the Inuit people.

Out of this microcosm of cultural conflict arising from "understanding differently," there are many lessons for humanity. The ultimate one learned on the frozen ice of Admiralty Inlet was that coercion and dishonesty are inconsistent with survival. Metaphorically, Nuqallaq was protecting more than his companions that night near Cape Crauford – he was protecting Inuit culture and a way of life.

Epilogue

The Second World War and ensuing Cold War brought renewed concerns about sovereignty as a result of the visible dominance of American soldiers and civilians at wartime defence installations or weather stations and air bases throughout the Arctic. This time, however, the newcomers alerted Canadian government and the world to the urgent needs of the Inuit people. In the 1950s a cadre of well-meaning Northern Affairs agents arrived in the tiny Arctic communities with new ideas on how to solve "the Eskimo problem." Not all were helpful, and some that seemed to provide benefits in the short term sometimes created new problems in the longer term.

Following World War II the widespread incidence of tuberculosis finally prompted the Canadian government to take action. In 1947 an X-ray program was initiated in conjunction with the Eastern Arctic Patrol, but suffered a setback after the *Nascopie* sank on a rock shoal offshore from Cape Dorset. The program was fully restored in 1950 with the launching of a new government ship, the *C.D. Howe*, which carried a team of medical experts and a portable X-ray unit to each community in the region. For the Inuit, who did not understand why they developed severe coughs and sometimes died, the cure seemed worse than the disease. With only hours of notice, Inuit of all ages were removed from the community and taken south for treatment in hospitals and sanatoriums. Sometimes they died without anyone notifying their families. In the mid-1950s, it was reported that one-third of all Inuit were infected with active or inactive forms of the disease. Another report in 1956 claimed that one out of every six Inuit was in a sanatorium somewhere in southern Canada.[1] In time the program brought the disease under control, but not without major disruption in Inuit lives.

Greenlanders continued to hunt polar bears on Ellesmere Island long after the end of the war. Even in the 1950s, when the sovereignty issue resurfaced

because of u.s. military activities, the police at Craig Harbour were still
reluctant to stop them. According to Ningiuk Killiktee, "Even when the
RCMP heard about them, they didn't mind because their superiors were not
there to see them."² Eventually wisdom prevailed and the contraventions of
the Arctic Game Preserve regulations were finally resolved in the 1960s by
issuing the Greenlanders hunting permits.

Progress also brought unexpected hardships. Beginning in 1949, the
payment of family allowances as credit at the trading posts had helped
alleviate the dramatic reduction in fur prices, but it also encouraged Inuit
families to congregate nearby, thus increasing the competition for wildlife
resources of the area. Dog disease and the establishment of day schools
accelerated the movement of Inuit off the land, greatly expanding the
small settlements which were ill-equipped to provide adequate accommodation. Vaccination against rabies and distemper was introduced as
needed at various settlements, but by the 1970s the snowmobile had all
but replaced the former dependency on dogs for travel in winter. In 1951
the Inuit were granted the right to vote, but in North Baffin there were no
elections for over a decade.

During the 1950s and '60s, removal of children to residential schools
created a generation of Inuit proficient in English, but led to language barriers that alienated them from their parents and elders. In some cases,
abuse at the schools would cause enormous problems in personal lives.
Add the availability of alcohol and later drugs, and it was inevitable that
crime and violence would increase. At Pond Inlet the problem was partially overcome when the first federal school was built in the 1960s, with
dorms for those whose parents still lived in outlying camps. The road to
"civilization" and modernity was full of rocks and pot-holes.

Meanwhile the *qallunaat* who figured so prominently in the events
surrounding the trial at Pond Inlet seemed to have faded into relative
obscurity. One exception was Staff-Sergeant Joy who, after earning fame
for his long, death-defying "sovereignty" patrols on Ellesmere Island and
points west, was promoted to the rank of inspector with prospects for a
promising career. Then in 1932 unexpected tragedy struck. Sometime during the pre-dawn hours of the day he was to be married, the consummate
RCMP officer, seemingly invincible, apparently suffered a massive stroke at
the age of forty-three and died alone in his Montreal hotel room.³

Other members of the force who were "bitten with Arctic fever" would
spend much of their careers at northern posts, but only a very few returned to a detachment for a second assignment, Corporals McBeth and
McInnes being the notable exceptions.⁴ In 1931 Cortlandt Starnes retired
from the force after forty-five years of long and dedicated service, eight of
them as commissioner.⁵ He was replaced by Major General Sir James
Howden MacBrien, a qualified pilot who inaugurated random inspections
by air in a small bi-plane.⁶ Times had indeed changed.

The stipendiary magistrate, the Hon. L.A. Rivet, returned to his law practice for several years until he was appointed a circuit court judge for the district of Montreal.[7] Apparently neither he nor the other members of the court party ever returned to Baffin Island. Government officials involved at the time of the investigation and/or the trial also faded from public view. After suffering a concussion at Father Point in July 1924, J.D. Craig was replaced for the remainder of the voyage of the Eastern Arctic Patrol by F.E. Henderson, a surveyor with the Dominion Lands Branch. Craig never returned to the Arctic but resumed his former position with the International Boundary Commission. Following the sale of the CGS *Arctic* to the Hudson's Bay Company in fall of 1925, Captain Bernier spent the next two years in command of a tugboat, until the government finally gave him an annual pension of $2,400. He died in December 1932 at the age of eighty-two. Shortly after, the ship's hull, which had been left to rot on a sandbar near Bernier's home at Levis, Quebec, is said to have mysteriously disappeared – perhaps in a storm, but no one knows for sure. Today all that remains of the CGS *Arctic* are hundreds of photographs and the ship's bell located in the Bernier Museum in L'Islet.[8] In 1931 O.S. Finnie, who as director of the Northwest Territories and Yukon Branch of the Department of the Interior, had tried in vain to increase government expenditure on the Inuit, was let go because of government budget cuts during the Depression. With him went his staff of scientists and experts, including Major L.T. Burwash and Dr Leslie Livingstone.[9]

Following Nuqallaq's release Henry Toke Munn turned his energy to lobbying the Canadian government to end the Hudson's Bay Company monopoly on the Arctic fur trade – without success. In 1926 he published his first book, *Tales of the Eskimo,* in which he described how a vein of gold was lost to the world when covered by a moving glacier. His autobiography, appearing in 1932, appealed to a much wider audience of armchair explorers. Munn never returned to the Arctic after his last visit in 1923 but divided his time for the next ten years between Canada and England. Plagued with arthritis, he eventually moved to the Seychelle Islands in the Indian Ocean, where he died in 1952.[10]

A few Inuit who had appeared as witnesses at the trial were known to have died in the episodes of disease and starvation in the years following the trial. The key participants, Ululijarnaat, Aatitaaq, and Ataguttiaq, all survived. Most believed that Ululijarnaat had never been really punished, although one elder suggested that perhaps his sentence was more like "community service." Several told the story about how he proved to the police that he was "capable" by going to Bylot Island in his kayak and returning with a stone to show that he had been there.[11] Others reported that he was never subjected to "hard labour" and seemed to enjoy his time "working" for the police.[12] Constable Robert Christy recalled that when he first arrived at Pond Inlet in 1932, he had thought Ululijarnaat was still a prisoner, because he was always hanging around the post asking if there was anything he could do.[13] As a result of an accident just before Christmas 1935, his foot became gangrenous, but he managed to cut off the affected parts and sew up the stub with caribou sinew before coming to the detachment for help.[14] Other stories describe how he would stuff his *kamik* with a piece of wood so he could walk. He reportedly died a few years later. Ululijarnaat is still fondly remembered by today's elders as a strong yet lovable Inuk – a great hunter and fine family man – who "worked for a time" at the RCMP detachment.

Aatitaaq, who was absolved of any responsibility and released, seemed to harbour resentment towards the *qallunaat*. He voluntarily stayed on at the detachment until Ululijarnaat was free to go and on at least one occasion joined him on a police patrol. Then he left Pond Inlet with his sons and began moving to various camps where there were "no Qallunaat and no houses." For a while he lived among the Nattilingmiut but returned when his boys began looking for wives.[15] According to a tale told by Ray Price in *The Howling Arctic*, Aatitaaq returned to Arctic Bay in 1938 and apparently terrified the new bride of Alan Scott, the HBC manager. After Scott took firm action, the Inuk and his sons seemed to settle down and proved to be excellent trappers. Later, however, after Mrs Scott had given birth to a daughter, Aatitaaq reportedly arrived at the post with a pile of furs and demanded the baby in return. When he was told him that there were not enough furs in the entire Arctic to buy the baby girl, Aatitaaq reportedly became very angry and "took a long time to get over it."[16]

By comparison, Anna Ataguttiaq lived a long and apparently happy life with her second husband, Kipumii. They worked for the RCMP for seven years, four of them at Dundas Harbour with her parents, Mukpainnuk and Qamaniq. In addition to her first born, Samuel Arnakallak, Ataguttiaq had four more children, three daughters, one of whom died at the age of two and another son.[17] She lived most of her life in or around Mittamitalak, had many grandchildren and great-grandchildren, and was described by Father Mary-Rousselière as the "dean of Pond Inlet women." She died in 1987.[18] Her third child, Elisapee Ootoova, is now recognized as a respected elder of the community, as is her only son, who previously worked as a special constable at both Pond Inlet and Grise Fiord.

For decades Pond Inlet remained relatively isolated and accessible only by boat or chartered air flight. Yet on two separate occasions the tiny hamlet received unexpected attention. First there was the two-dollar bill that showed Joseph Idlout's family in a hunting scene on the shores of Eclipse Sound. This was followed with a film of his life at Pond Inlet, "Land of the Long Day" (1951). Then in 1970 Lazeroosie Kyak, who had grown up at the Pond Inlet detachment and was later hired as a special constable, was doubly honoured when he became the first Inuk and the

Anna Ataguttiaq, seated on right, with some of her children, grandchildren, and great-grandchildren, spring 1984. Participants in the oral history project included her son Sam Arnakallak, standing on the stairs, and her daughter Elisapee Ootoova, in front, third from the left. Courtesy of Philippa Ootoowak (granddaughter-in-law).

first member of the Royal Canadian Mounted Police to receive the Order of Canada for his service to his country.

Budget considerations continued to limit the administration of justice in the Arctic, although this was somewhat alleviated in 1955 when the Department of Justice appointed and paid the salary of the Hon. Jack Sissons, the first full-time judge for the Northwest Territories. During his tenure he adopted a previously unheard of degree of flexibility in sentencing,[19] a practice continued by his successor, the Hon. William G. Morrow. Apparently after a visit to Stony Mountain Penitentiary, Morrow claimed that he "could not willingly sentence" any Inuk to such a place. Thus he frequently adjusted sentences to avoid incarceration in the South, particularly for Inuit from the high Arctic.[20] Significantly, it was in 1969 – more than forty-five years after the murder trial at Pond Inlet – that Judge Morrow presided at the trial of the last known "execution by consensual agreement."[21]

Occasionally there were periodic discussions about changing the criminal code to adapt to Inuit culture and conditions in the Arctic, including an earnest plea by justice official R.A. Olmstead following the 1941 murder trial on the Belcher Islands. For many years there was talk, but no action. In the 1990s, however, several projects were initiated on behalf of first offenders, including a special Elders' Sentencing Council at Pond Inlet and a Community Council at Lake Harbour. If appropriate, a youth might be asked to spend several months out on the land under the supervision of an elder instead of being incarcerated at the Baffin Island Correctional Centre in Iqaluit. Both councils, at last count, were reported to be effective in reducing the number of re-offenders. Under the new Nunavut government, which has assumed authority for both the criminal and civil justice, a commission has been set up to develop new guidelines that recognize traditional Inuit values.

At present the situation is grim. In stark contrast to the minimal incidence in the 1920s, the present crime rate on Baffin Island is estimated to be six times the national average, much of it related to alcohol and drug abuse.[22] On 1 March 2001 the residents of Nunavut were shocked to learn that an Inuk in Cape Dorset had shot and killed a police officer who had been called to settle a domestic dispute.

Efforts in fighting infectious diseases have been more successful, resulting in the virtual elimination of active tuberculosis and reduction of others through vaccination programs. Medical problems are now dealt with quickly and efficiently at the local nursing stations, where the staff have direct telecommunication links to medical expertise and, if necessary, emergency evacuation to the Iqaluit hospital. For specialized treatment, patients are brought south to centres in Montreal, Winnipeg, or Ottawa. Alas, the costs of such services are escalating and are currently under review. At present, the greatest danger to Inuit health stems from the increasing pollution of the air, the water, and the country food chain, over which they have little or no control.

The same magical lure of the Arctic that once attracted polar explorers and in 1923 prompted Mrs Dubuc and Mrs Craig to accompany their husbands to the trials at Herschel Island and Pond Inlet respectively continues to captivate thousands of tourists each summer. Judge Morrow's son was likewise impressed when he joined his father on his last circuit: "No matter where we flew in the Arctic, it always seemed surreal – we were not of this earth, but existed on a higher level of consciousness. We were above and beyond the dullness of the world left behind and I began to understand the romance of the circuit. How could one not feel like an explorer?"[23] With regular scheduled flights, the Arctic is now more accessible to visitors. No longer can Inuit problems be kept from public scrutiny. While such changes are beneficial, the ability to sustain ecotourism without adverse effects on the land and its people is the subject of ongoing study and debate.

The Nunavut Land Claims Agreement and the creation of Nunavut Territory marked the beginning of a new era that gave Inuit control over their resources and government. If advances in aviation technology were responsible for the rapid changes in the postwar years, the present generation is benefiting from computer and wireless technologies that allow full access to knowledge of the outside world without ever leaving home. Health services, education, business, wildlife conservation, and even government derive immeasurable benefits. For elders who were born in a tent or igloo, the changes they have witnessed in their lifetime are phenomenal.

Today Pond Inlet has a population of roughly twelve hundred men, women, and children, about 94 per cent of them Inuit. No alcohol may be purchased in the community, and visitors who wish to bring their own must first obtain a permit at the hamlet office. The first high school was named in honour of Takijualuk, out of respect for his skill as a translator. Today the hamlet has an up-to-date public school and a new high school, with equipment and facilities comparable to the best in southern Canada. There is also an indoor mall with a large Co-op store and a Northern Store on the other side of town, a nursing station and medivac service, a hockey rink and an airport with regular scheduled flights, a combined hamlet office and firehall, federal and territorial government buildings, a modern library and a visitors' centre, Roman Catholic and Anglican churches, a hotel with a dining room, a bed and breakfast, a single taxi, several outfitters, and a RCMP detachment. In spite of the increasing evidence of modernity, the Tununirmiut guardedly preserve their traditions, including their language, country foods, social values, and love of their children. Symbolic of growing respect for their heritage, the community is gradually reverting back to the use of the original Inuktitut name – Mittimatalik.

Near Iqaluit on Tay Sound, Nuqallaq rests in peace in the land he knew and loved. His spirit lives on – in every court case, in every effort to preserve Inuit culture, and in the hearts of anyone who has lost a loved one to tuberculosis. Meanwhile, the bodies of the two abandoned fur traders lie in shallow graves just west of Pond Inlet, still waiting for someone to take them home.

Graves of Robert S. Janes (*left*) and Hector Pitchforth, Pond Inlet 1991. Shelagh Grant.

Appendices

APPENDIX ONE

Notes on Research and Inuit Oral History

As noted in the preface, this study began with the arrival of large corrugated cardboard box containing diaries, notebooks, audio tapes, Inuit drawings, and photographs belonging to RCMP Corporal Finley McInnes. My realization that there was much more to be learned about the early police activities and social contact relationships with the Inuit of Baffin Island led to archival research and study of secondary sources. The absence of an Inuit perspective was glaring. As a result, I applied for, and received, a three-year Social Sciences and Humanities Research Council grant that allowed me to begin oral history interviews at Pond Inlet the following summer and at Pangnirtung in 1995.

The oral history component of this study required prior approval by the Pangnirtung Hamlet Council and similar consent through the ongoing Parks Canada Oral History Project at Pond Inlet before research licences were issued by the Nunavut Arctic Science Institute. All interviews were voluntary, and the elders were selected according to their knowledge of the subject and the stories they wished to tell. Not surprisingly, several who indicated a wish to talk about the RCMP at Pond Inlet during the 1920s and 1930s were the sons of Inuit families employed at the detachment. The interviews were conducted in Inuktitut, videotaped with audio back-up, then transcribed and finally translated into English, all by resident professionals living in the community. Videotaping the interview was considered important because of an Inuk's tendency to use body language in story telling. A phrase in Inuktitut, for example, might have two different meanings depending on whether accompanied by a nod or shaking of the head. Follow-up discussions took place in 1996, 1998, and 2000 to clarify and review stories selected for inclusion in the two manuscripts.

A picture may be worth a thousand words, but McInnes's collection of over five hundred photographs provoked more questions than answers, as only a few were identified by name, date, or location. This liability turned into an asset when the photos became a valuable tool in prompting elders' memories of the past. They in turn identified many individuals who would otherwise have remained nameless. In appreciation, an album of the Pond Inlet photographs was donated to the Rebecca

Idlout Library on behalf of McInnes's granddaughter, Andrea McInnes Williams. Additional photos were obtained from several private collections, as well as from the National Archives of Canada, the Manitoba Provincial Archives, the Northwest Territories Archives in Yellowknife, and the McManus Gallery in Dundee, Scotland. Video copies of movie clips taken at the time of the trial and on Nuqallaq's return home were obtained from the National Film Board.

Additional research included an intensive study of government records and private collections deposited in the National Archives of Canada and in the Northwest Territories Archives in Yellowknife. A wide variety of secondary sources was also examined, ranging from scholarly dissertations to more anecdotal popular histories. After several informal discussions, a interview was taped with former RCMP Constable Robert Christy who had been posted to the Pond Inlet detachment in the early 1930s.

Initially I had intended to incorporate my findings and the elders' stories into social histories of Pond Inlet and Pangnirtung, with particular focus on their formative years – the 1920s and 1930s. After several drafts, however, it was evident that the story of Robert Janes, his death, and the murder trial would dominate the Pond Inlet story. On the advice of my editor, I decided to publish *Arctic Justice* first, with a summary of this episode included in a more comprehensive history of North Baffin. This change of direction required additional research into judicial policies and legal precedents elsewhere in the Arctic. Since the crime had occurred on the frozen ice of Admiralty Inlet and involved Inuit from the vicinity of Arctic Bay and Igloolik, it was important to include elders' stories from these communities. Fortunately, there were previously recorded interviews from both settlements, included here alongside those obtained at Pond Inlet. Now a full decade after my discovery of the Janes grave marker on the beach near Salmon Creek, my curiosity is satisfied and the first manuscript is now complete.

OFFICIAL TRIAL TRANSCRIPTS

With the assistance of archivists at the repositories in Ottawa and Yellowknife, I carried out an extensive search for further documents. In consultation with the Department of Justice, it was finally conceded that no "official" transcripts for this trial had been filed in the public record. The consensus view was that once the charge against Nuqallaq had been reduced to manslaughter, it was no longer considered a capital case requiring submission of a trial transcript to the department.

However, in discussion with Bob Pilot, a former RCMP officer stationed at Pond Inlet in the 1950s, I learned that the Francophone jurors' "jot notes" and a handwritten draft transcript of the trial, allegedly signed by Clerk of the Court F.X. Biron, were left at the detachment, along with the testimonies of several witnesses. In the late 1950s, according to Pilot (now mayor of Pembroke), instructions from RCMP headquarters were sent out to each detachment in the eastern Arctic, requiring that all such papers and records be destroyed. Despite this directive, some kind of draft transcript is still in circulation, part of which I have seen. It appears authentic but it is clearly a preliminary draft as the pages I was shown contained several obvious errors. For example, the police were identified as the Royal Northwest Mounted Police, rather than the Royal Canadian Mounted Police, and the court was referred to as the Supreme Court of the Northwest Territories rather than the correct designation as a Stipendiary Magistrate's Court of the Northwest Territories. Bob Pilot agreed that someone at the detachment might have turned over some of the material to Father Guy Mary-Rousselière, who had been collecting stories about the community's history since he first arrived at the Sacred Heart Mission. Tragically, the priest died in a horrible fire that swept through the small chapel just weeks before my first research visit to Pond Inlet. If indeed, the transcript of the trial had been given to Father Mary, then it is still possible that it may have survived the fire. Otherwise, the source of this preliminary draft is a mystery.

Its presence at the Pond Inlet police detachment, would, however, explain the source of Alex Stevenson's information for his article appearing in *The Beaver* in 1973, a decade before police files on the case were opened to the public. Stevenson had been employed at the Hudson's Bay Company post at Pond Inlet in the late 1930s and likely read the file at his leisure. This would explain his knowledge about obscure aspects of the trial, but not his error in reporting that Nuqallaq had died in prison. Although he was careful not to quote from a "restricted" document, his interpretation of the trial proceedings was nonetheless significant.[1] Otherwise, I based the story of the trial proceedings on Staff-Sergeant Joy's summary report, the appendix in the RCMP *Annual Report for the Year Ending September 30, 1923*, and the prior testimony of the Inuit who were questioned before the judge and jury. While the draft transcript would have been interesting to read, in the end it proved redundant to this study.

INUIT ORAL HISTORY

Inuit oral history is a relatively new research tool for historians, in spite of its common use by anthropologists. By tradition and reputation, an elder's story is likely to be accurate – within the extent of his or her knowledge. As such, an interview is considered an "original" source, but it cannot be classified as a "primary" source unless the information is based on firsthand experience. For this reason, Inuit oral history should be interpreted in the same manner as a personal document.[2] There were other considerations. Unlike a *unikkaaqtuaq*, a story passed down through many generations, the information I was seeking was more recent, referred to in Inuktitut as *unikkaaq*. As a consequence, each story was carefully evaluated to determine the origin of the information, how it was acquired, when, where, and why. At Pond Inlet I was fortunate to have two interviews taped with Martha Akumalik, who had been present at the trial as a young girl, and others with the son and a daughter of Anna Ataguttiaq, Nuqallaq's widow. I also had access to the tape of an interview with Ataguttiaq in 1974, recorded by Father Mary-Rousselière. The information in each of the above tapes was consistent with the others and with the testimony by Ataguttiaq recorded at the preliminary hearings by Staff-Sergeant Joy. Hence they provided a data base upon which all other interviews and earlier recorded statements were compared.

With the exception of firsthand observations, some stories seemed to have acquired layers of opinion and rationalization through the passage of time, understandably since an Inuit elder is essentially a historian speaking for his own people. On the other hand, some elders were clearly more informed on this subject than others, depending upon his or her source of information. A few stories seemed to be enhanced by rationalizations to explain *qallunaat* behaviour. Follow-up discussions revealed that some stories may have been influenced by information learned from fur traders or the police. As an example, one elder thought that the reason Janes had been abandoned by the other traders was because he was a German and Canada was at war with his country. When told that Janes was of English origin and had lived in Newfoundland, he stated that he had only repeated what he had been told.[3] Such factual discrepancies do not diminish the value of Inuit oral history as a research tool – quite the contrary. Sometimes these histories may be even more valuable in identifying the differing perceptions as sources of misunderstandings.

Similarly, factual data, particularly those related to time and place, often required verification with other verbal accounts or written sources, primarily because Inuit descriptions were not always consistent with *qallunaat* terminology. In most cases, it was a matter of "understanding things differently" and obtaining confirmation to ensure that I fully understood their meaning. The degree of knowledge an elder might possess on any particular subject is also an important consideration in evaluating an interview. Elders' status is not based solely on age but on the respect held by a community for their knowledge and wisdom. If there is any doubt, a group discussion will reveal who might possess the most information on a specific topic. These qualifications aside, an interview with an Inuit elder can provide a multidimensional kaleidoscope of emotion, opinion, and insight – all invaluable in understanding a culture other than one's own.

An equally important consideration when embarking upon an oral history project is the choice of the interviewer, transcriber, and translator. Ideally all should be from the community to ensure optimum rapport with the elders and full comprehension of the local dialect. The question of whether a southern researcher should be fluent in Inuktitut is debatable. Certainly it would be helpful but not necessarily critical if the researcher were supported by a reliable team in the community. There is a strong consensus that it is unwise for southern *qallunaat* to conduct their own interviews because of elders' frequent use of words and phrases no longer in use – *inummarittut*, the "language of the older people."[4] Since the value of an elder's story is ultimately dependent upon the skills of the transcriber and translator, prudent selection of the support team is critical to the success of an Inuit oral history project.

In recent years there have been a number of oral history projects in Nunavut, some of which are accessible to researchers. Interviews conducted at Pangnirtung and Arctic Bay in the 1970s have both resulted in publications. As well, translations of the extensive interviews conducted by the Igloolik Inullariit Society are readily available to scholars at the Igloolik Research Centre. One recent endeavour is an on-going program of taping and translating elders' stories under the direction of Susan Sammons at Nunavut Arctic College in Iqaluit, in cooperation with anthropologists François Trudel, Frédéric Laugrand, Jarich Oosten, and William Rasing. The most recent publication, *Representing Tuurngait*, in the Memory and History in Nunavut series, is exemplary, and the authors should be commended for their efforts.[5] Still, there is much to be done in terms of integrating individual stories into regional histories that reflect the distinctive cultural traditions of each community. In terms of historical scholarship the accurate translation of a taped interview is essentially only the beginning.

Cross-cultural research demands a fair degree of creativity and innovation to en-sure a balance of perspectives. Many difficulties were anticipated, such as sorting fact from opinion in elders' stories, linking these accounts to events recorded else-where, correlating them in the proper time sequence, and placing all within the framework of the traditional values of two very disparate cultures. Elders who par-ticipated in the Pond Inlet project were gathered together several years later and asked as a group if they could help me with certain aspects of their stories, emphasiz-ing that they were the teachers and I was the student. With simultaneous translation, I was able to find a clear consensus on possible contradictions. In several instances, the "inconsistency" was a consequence of my own "understanding differently."

Some problems were not anticipated, such the multiple spellings of Inuit names in government reports and the fact that an Inuk might have two Inuktitut names and an English one as well. Because the Roman orthography for Inuktitut is pho-netically based, the spelling of an Inuk's name seemed to vary in police reports according to the recorder's pronunciation, especially if enhanced by a Scottish, Irish, or French-Canadian accent. At times I was unsure whether we were talking about one individual or three. For advice I relied upon the project coordinator, Lynn Cousins, as well as Martha Kyak and Elisapee Ootoova who assisted in proof-reading the translation of my research notes into Inuktitut.

Careful consideration was given to the question of integrating the Inuit stories with information gathered from secondary and archival sources, the latter obvi-ously written by southerners for a southern audience. To ensure that these inter-pretations and my own did not distort the Inuit perspective, I have set quotations from the elders' stories apart by identifying the name, date, and location of the in-terview. This same method has been used when citing Inuit statements recorded for the preliminary hearings and the trial. While I have treated these testimonies as Inuit oral history, I exercised special caution to determine the possibility of bias in-troduced at the time they were recorded. Each statement had been first written in longhand by Staff-Sergeant Joy, then typed with carbon copies – single-spaced on legal-size paper – then allegedly signed by the Inuk with an X after the text had been reviewed by the witness. Most were three or more pages in length, with an Inuk's penchant for detail leaving little to the imagination.

Realizing the potential for error or misunderstanding in the translation, I evaluated each testimony in terms of firsthand knowledge and consistency with the statements by other witnesses, and where possible, compared each to the story by the same individual told a year earlier to Captain Henry Toke Munn. Most discrepancies could be explained by the degree of individual involvement and fear of the police. Certainly, some Inuit were more intimidated than others and had no difficulty in expressing their fears.

The elders, by comparison, even though most at some point in their lives had been hired as special constables, admitted that at one time or another they had feared the police. This was clearly no longer the case. Yet in spite of the consensus that Nuqallaq had no choice but to kill Robert Janes, no one was willing to blame anyone. It was as if they were fully cognizant of the importance in weighing the time in history and attitudes that prevailed – in both cultures. One should never question the wisdom of a respected Inuit elder.

APPENDIX TWO

Inuit Names for People and Places

Current spelling in North Baffin dialect is followed (in parentheses) by the version found in government records circa 1920. Inuit relationships were derived from the witnesses' testimonies and thus are dependent upon the accuracy of the translation. The spelling commonly used in the North Baffin region may differ from usage in more southerly communities.

INUIT

Aaluluuq (Ahlooloo) – Nuqallaq's nephew, a young boy at the time of Janes' death; did not witness Janes' death but later recalled a subsequent conversation between Nuqallaq and his father concerning the incident.

Aarjuaq and husband, Kautaq – hired to work at the Pond Inlet police detachment from 1922 to 1926.

Aatitaaq (Ahteetah) – accused as an accomplice for helping to plan and assisting in the shooting death of Robert Janes; gave evidence at the preliminary hearings and the trial; held under house arrest for a year; acquitted at the trial for lack of evidence.

Akumalik (Akko-mo-lee) – lay preacher who came to Pond Inlet in 1920 from Cumberland Sound by way of Clyde River; responsible for converting Nuqallaq and Umik to Christianity.

(Alikomiak) – shot and killed RCMP Corporal William Doak and fur trader Otto Binder at the Tree River detachment in the western Arctic, April 1922.

Amarualik (Amooahlik) – not present at the hunting camp at the time of Janes' death; described to Staff-Sergeant Joy how Janes had earlier taken Aatitaaq's furs against his will and how Janes had removed government supplies from the cache at Beechey Island; was not present at the trial.

Anguiliannuk (Angnoyleanoo) – Nuqallaq's friend who was sent to Igloolik by Staff-Sergeant Joy in the spring of 1922, with instructions to bring the suspect back to Pond Inlet; became ill along the way and was found by Nuqallaq, who returned with him to Igloolik, thus delaying his arrival at Pond Inlet.

Ataguttaaluk (Ahtootahloo) – present the hunting camp at the time of Janes' death; reportedly a brother or brother-in-law of Maniq and Iqaqsaq, thus a son or step-son of Miqutui, a camp leader of the Iglulingmiut; gave evidence at the preliminary hearings and the trial.

Ataguttaaluk – survived starvation by eating her husband and children after they had died; was rescued and later married Ittuksaarjuat; the two became known as as the King and Queen of Igloolik.

Ataguttak (Attagosoak) – first hired by the police at Pond Inlet to guide patrols, 1925–27; employed full time at Pond Inlet 1930–32, then at Dundas Harbour and Craig Harbour; hired as a special constable at Craig Harbour in 1935.

Ataguttiaq (Ahtooteuk and later Atagutsiaq) – Nuqallaq's second wife and present at the hunting camp at the time of Janes' death; remained with husband at Pond Inlet while he was under house arrest; gave evidence at the preliminary hearings and the trial; looked after him when he returned home from prison until his death; married his hunting partner; gave birth to a son and four daughters; eventually became a respected elder in Pond Inlet with many grandchildren and great-grandchildren; passed away in 1987.

Ijjangiaq (Edineyah) – brother of Aatitaaq and present when the shooting was planned; witnessed Janes' death; provided a signed statement and gave evidence at the preliminary hearings; died of starvation in the winter prior to the trial.

Inuguk (Enoogoo) – brother of the woman whose husband was killed by his son (her stepson); prevented the arrest of the youth by promising that he would look after him.

Inuujaq (Inooya) – worked for Captain Munn at Sannirut, 1914–19.

Inuutiq (Innoto or Innuteuk) – worked at Janes' trading post; husband of Kalluk who was reported to be Janes' "Inuit wife."

Iqaqsaq (Ekussah) – reportedly a son or stepson of Miqutui; present at the hunting camp when Janes was killed; first gave evidence in a statement after he was brought from Igloolik in the spring 1923; gave evidence at the trial.

Iqipiriaq (Ekepireyah) – witnessed the killing of Janes; gave a statutory declaration in the summer of 1923; later gave evidence at the trial.

Ivalaaq (Ewahlah) – helped Jock and his son build a wooden box for Janes' remains and re-buried him in a rock crevice so animals would not disturb the body.

Ivalu (Ivahlung) – Kunuk's adopted son; present at the hunting camp when Janes was killed; his signed statement was read at the preliminary hearings; gave evidence at the trial.

Kalluk (Kudloo) – referred to as Janes' "Inuit wife" while living at his trading post at the mouth of the Patricia River; did not accompany him to Cape Crauford; reportedly gave birth to his child within days of his departure.

Kassak (Kutchuk) – lived in the same igloo with Nuqallaq and Ataguttiaq at the hunting camp near Cape Crauford; claimed not to have taken part in planning Janes' death; the only Inuk at the camp who claimed he was not afraid of Janes; testified at the inquest, the preliminary hearings, and the trial; worked as a guide for the Pond Inlet police 1923–24.

Kaugjak (Kaujak) – Kassak's aunt.

Kaukuarjuk (Kowkwatsoo) – an older Inuk; sometimes acted as a trader for Captain Munn; met Janes on the trail to Admiralty Inlet and spent two nights with him; left and joined Nuqallaq's party en route to Arctic Bay; was accused by Janes of turning the Inuit at Cape Crauford against him; fearing for his life, he slept out on the ice with Siniqqaq the night Janes was killed; provided a statutory declaration and gave evidence at the trial.

Killaapik (Kidlapik) – shot and killed his cousin Niaquttiaq at Qivittuuq in 1922, after Niaquttiaq had ordered the murders of two Inuuk and was about to kill another; the case was investigated, but no charges were laid.

Kipumii (Kipomee) – Nuqallaq's hunting partner after his return from prison; married Nuqallaq's widow, Ataguttiaq; both worked for the police at Pond Inlet, 1926–28; and later at Dundas Harbour, 1928–32.

Kunuk (Koonnoon) – an older Inuk from Arctic Bay (apparently not the same individual as Tom Coonoon, the interpreter known as Takijualuk); at the hunting camp near Cape Crauford; aroused Janes' anger when it was discovered he had no fox furs; provided a statutory declaration; gave evidence at the trial.

Kyak, Lazaroosie – born in 1919, son of Panikpak and Wilfred Caron; grew up at the police detachment where his mother and stepfather Uirngut were employed in the late 1920s and through the 1930s; married Letia in 1936; hired as a special constable at Pond Inlet, 1943–52, then at Craig Harbour and Grise Fiord, 1952–60; in 1970 became the first Inuk and first member of the RCMP to receive the Order of Canada; retired the following year; died suddenly in 1976.

Mala – Inuk hunter who guided Peter Freuchen from Admiralty Inlet to Pond Inlet in the spring of 1924 after his Greenlander party took ill and were forced to remain behind; later hired by the RCMP at Pond Inlet, 1930–34, at Craig Harbour, 1934–35, and as special constable at Craig Harbour, 1935–38.

Maniq (Munne) – present at Cape Crauford when Janes was killed; brother or stepbrother of Ataguttaaluk and Iqaqsaq; son or stepson of Miqutui; gave evidence at the inquest, preliminary hearings, and the trial.

Manu (Munnoo) – not present at the hunting camp at the time of Janes' death, but provided a statuatory declaration used at the preliminary hearings concerning Janes' earlier attack on Umik.

Miqutui (Mikootooee) – camp leader from Igloolik; worked as a guide for Captain Bernier during his early government expeditions 1905–11; the last to arrive at the camp near Cape Crauford; informed Janes (incorrectly) that the route was impassable to Igloolik; witnessed Janes' angry outburst at Kunuk; was not interviewed by Staff-Sergeant Joy until the summer of 1923; provided a signed statement and gave evidence at the trial.

Miqutui (Mikootooee) – wife of Kunuk (Koonnoon); ran out on the ice to warn the hunters that Janes was going to pressure them again; was called as a witness at the trial without having given a previous statement.

Naqitarvik (Nahkahdagbe) – not present at the time of Janes' death; told Staff-Sergeant Joy how he had helped Janes transport supplies from the government cache at Beechey Island and that he was owed a great deal of money for furs he had given the trader.

Niaquttiaq (Neahkuteuk) – operated the trading post at Qivittuuq for the Sabellum Company; suffered from bouts of insanity and believed he was the son of God; inspired sessions of religious frenzy; responsible for the deaths of two Inuuk; shot and killed by his cousin in 1922.

Nukappianguaq (Nuqapinguak) – Staff-Sergeant Joy's loyal and trusted guide from Etah, Greenland; worked with Joy at Craig Harbour, 1925–26 and Bache Peninsula, 1926–28; arrived at Dundas Harbour in 1931 to learn of Joy's untimely death; sent home to Greenland on orders by Canadian authorities; hired again at Craig Harbour in 1938.

Nuqallaq (Nukudlah or Nookudlah) – also known to the Inuit as Qiugaarjuk; son of the shaman Umik; accused of murder in the shooting death of Robert Janes; gave testimony at the preliminary hearings and the trial; convicted on a lesser charge of manslaughter; sentenced to ten years hard labour at Stony Mountain Penitentiary where he contracted tuberculosis; released after serving less than two years of his sentence; died shortly after his return to Pond Inlet.

Nutaraarjuk (Nootowadsoo) – reported to have been at the hunting camp at the time of Janes' death, but not heard from again.

Nutarariaq (Nootakgagayook) – travelled to Cape Crauford with Nuqallaq and party; provided a signed statement which was read at the preliminary hearings; gave evidence at the trial.

(Ouangwak) – arrested for murder of two Inuuk brothers near Baker Lake, 1920; escaped from prison at the Chesterfield detachment, 1921; apparently died of exposure.

Panikpak (Panigpak) – from Etah, Greenland; employed along with his wife at the Craig Harbour detachment, 1923–25.

Paniluk (Peneloo) – not present at the hunting camp at the time of Janes' death; described Janes' attack on Umik in a signed statement read at the preliminary hearings; brought news to Pond Inlet concerning the murders at Qivittuuq; gave evidence at the trial.

Paumi (Palmee) and his wife (Ootoogek) – provided shelter in their snow house for Robert Janes and his driver at the hunting camp near Cape Crauford; both provided signed statements to Staff-Sergeant Joy in the summer of 1923; only Paumi gave evidence at the trial.

Piunngittuq (Pewicktoo) – worked as a guide for Captain Bernier in the winter of 1910–11 and for Alfred Tremblay 1912–13.

Qamaniq (Kamanuk) – father of Ataguttiaq and father-in-law of Nuqallaq; not present at the time of Janes' death; described Jane's attack on Umik in a signed statement; gave evidence at the trial; was hired along with his wife Makpainnuk to work at the Pond Inlet detachment 1924–28 and at Dundas Harbour 1928–31.

Qattuuq (Kachoo or Kuchoo) and his wife Ulaajuk (Ulayuh) – first Inuit couple from Baffin Island hired by the RCMP; worked at Craig Harbour for one year

1922–23; Qattuuq continued to lead patrols for the police on his return to Pond Inlet; died in a flu epidemic in the late spring of 1924.

Qaunnaq (Kahlnahl) – witness to Janes' death; gave evidence at the inquest that implicated Aatitaaq; died suddenly of a mysterious illness two weeks later.

Qaunnaq (Kownang) – wife of the trader Niaquttiaq who had inspired bouts of religious frenzy at Qivittuuq; operated the trading post for several years after her husband's death.

Qillaq – leader of the Qidtlarssuaq migration from North Baffin Island to Greenland circa 1858–70; his grandson Panikpak was hired in 1923 to work for the RCMP at Craig Harbour.

Qumangaapik (Koomanapik) – employed at Pond Inlet as a special constable, 1935–40.

Sanguja (Sangoya) – worked for Captain Bernier in 1906–7; assisted Munn after his ship sank in 1912; later joined him on short trips, circa 1914–15.

Siniqqaq (Sinnikah) – at the hunting camp near Cape Crauford; slept out on the ice with Kaukuarjuk on the night Janes was killed; gave evidence at the inquest, preliminary hearings, and trial.

(Sinnisiak) – one of the two Inuuk arrested for the murder of two Oblate priests in the central Arctic; convicted of murder in the death of Father Le Roux but sentence commuted to manslaughter; served term of two years hard labour at Fort Resolution police detachment.

Saittuq (Shitoo or Sitoo) – Ululijarnaat's teen-age son; at the hunting camp at the time of Janes' death, along with his mother and another sibling.

Takijualuk (Tom Coonoo, Coonoon or Koonoo) – known for his exceptional skills as an interpreter; worked for Captain Bernier and later for the Arctic Gold Exploration Syndicate; refused to translate for the police until just before the trial.

Tooktosins or Tuusiniq (Jimmy Ford) – an Inuk of mixed blood from Newfoundland; employed by the Hudson's Bay Company at Pond Inlet, 1921–23; translated all but a couple of Inuit testimonies for Staff-Sergeant Joy.

(Tukautauk) – young Inuk on the Belcher Islands who had killed another Inuk, as directed by the elders; absolved of responsibility at an inquest held on the islands in 1920.

Tupirnngaq (Toopingin) – witness to Janes' death; brought from Igloolik in the spring of 1923 at which time he provided a signed statement about the events leading to Janes' death; believed everyone was afraid of Janes and thought he should be killed; was not asked to give testimony at the trial.

Tuurngaq (Toonga) – not at the hunting camp at the time of Janes' death; accompanied Staff-Sergeant Joy when he discovered Janes' body on the shores of Admiralty Inlet; called upon at the inquest to identify the body.

Uirnngut (Oingut), and his wife Panikpak – Lazeroosie Kyak's stepfather and mother; worked at the Pond Inlet detachment, 1928–34.

(Uluksak) – one of two Inuuk charged in the murder of two Oblate priests near Bloody Falls on the Coppermine River, 1912; death sentence commuted to manslaughter; with Sinnisiak served a term of two years hard labour at Fort Resolution police detachment; diagnosed as having tuberculosis at Aklavik hospital, 1932; returned to Coppermine to die, setting off tuberculosis epidemic in the region.

Ululijarnaat, sometimes spelled Ululijarnaaq (Oorooreungnak or Roori) – accused as an accomplice in the shooting of Janes for having enticed the trader out of his igloo so he could be shot; gave evidence at the inquest and preliminary hearings, but not at the trial; sentenced to two years hard labour at the Pond Inlet RCMP detachment.

Umik (Omik or Ooming) – Nuqallaq's father; not present at the time of Janes' death; a shaman who was converted to Christianity following the death of Janes; testified at the trial; later became a lay preacher to the Iglulingmiut, assisted by his son.

Urulu (Ooroloo) – not present at the hunting camp at the time of Janes' death; with Staff-Sergeant Joy when he discovered Janes' body; called upon at the inquest to identify the body; gave similar evidence at the trial.

Uujukuluk (Oyukuluk) – Aatitaaq's son, a young boy at the time of the trial; later as an elder he recalled details and his impressions of the trial.

Uuttukuttuk (Ootookito) – Janes' driver and guide for his aborted attempt to reach Igloolik and Repulse Bay; a reluctant witness who was questioned at the inquest, preliminary hearings, and trial.

INUIT NAMES FOR QALLUNAAT RESIDING AT POND INLET

Qallunaat were most often given Inuit names based on distinctive attributes, although occasionally their Inuit names were similar to their Euro-Canadian names.

Anginiqsaq (Reverend Harold Duncan) – named for being "the taller one" of the two Anglican missionaries who arrived at Pond Inlet in 1929.

Ataataalook (Gaston Herodier) – "the grandfather" in reference to his age; a veteran Hudson's Bay Company trader who helped establish the trading post at Pond Inlet in 1921. The high flat-topped mountain near Albert Harbour on Eclipse Sound was named Mount Herodier in his honour.

Ataatakkusaaq (Father Étienne Bazin) – one of two Catholic priests who arrived in 1929 to set up the Sacred Heart Mission at Pond Inlet; later began a mission at Igloolik.

Aullaq (Hector Pitchforth) – "going away soon" in reference to his frequent remarks that he was leaving shortly; an English trader for the Sabellum Company, hired to replace the deceased Niaquttiaq at Qivittuuq; moved to a site near Cape Henry Kater; died alone of natural causes in late December 1926, after he had locked himself in his cabin for fear that the Inuit would harm him.

Iggalik (Father Prime Girard) – "the one with glasses," he arrived in Pond Inlet in 1929 with Father Bazin.

Kapitaikallak (Captain Joseph Elzéar) – in reference to being "the short, stout captain" of the CGS *Arctic*. From 1906 to 1911 commanded three government expeditions to North Baffin waters, spending the first winter in Eclipse Sound and the last in Arctic Bay; from 1912 to 1919 he owned and operated a trading post at Igarjuaq in Albert Harbour, then resumed his position as captain of the CGS *Arctic* from 1922 to 1925, although this time he was not in overall command.

Kapitaikuluk (Captain Henry Toke Munn) – the "kind" captain; earned the rank of captain in the British cavalry; part owner of the Arctic Gold Exploration Syndicate which operated trading stations at Sannirut on Bylot Island from 1914 to 1922; at Igarjuaq, 1919–22; at Usualuk in Cumberland Sound 1917–22; spent two winters at Sannirut, 1914–15 and 1920–21; lobbied government officials for Nuqallaq's early release from prison, and later for the end of the Hudson's Bay Company's monopoly of the Arctic fur trade.

Maagii (Constable S. H. Margettes) – stationed at Pond Inlet from 1927 to 1929.

Makkulaaq (Constable H.P. Friel) – the "small one" of the four RCMP officers stationed at Pond Inlet, 1922–24.

Mikinniqsaq (Reverend John Turner) – "the smaller one" of the two Anglican ministers who arrived at Pond Inlet in 1929; moved later to Moffat Inlet where he remained until 1947, when he accidently shot himself and died shortly after being airlifted out to Winnipeg.

Nataqquq (Constable Robert Christy) – "double-jointed"; Christy was stationed at Pond Inlet from 1932 to 1934.

Nujaqangittuq (Wilfred Parsons) – the "bald one"; first manager of the Hudson's Bay Company trading post at Pond Inlet from 1921 to 1923; younger brother of Ralph Parsons, HBC superintendent of the eastern Arctic, 1918–30.

Papikattualuk (Corporal Hugh McBeth) – "someone who walks with his toes pointing outward" or knock-kneed; stationed at Pond Inlet in 1928–30, in 1931–33, and again during the war; respected by the Inuit for his exceptional fluency in Inuktitut.

Quvviunginnaq (Wilfred Caron) – "watery eyes"; Captain Bernier's nephew and had accompanied him on several earlier expeditions; periodically left in charge of his uncle's trading station at Igarjuaq; worked for Captain Munn at the Sannirut post from 1920–22; fell overboard and drowned en route to Pond Inlet, 1923.

Sakirmiaq (Robert S. Janes) – "second mate" in reference to his rank on the 1910–11 government expedition; returned to Pond Inlet to look for gold in 1912; returned in 1916 to set up a trading post; shot and killed at a hunting camp near Cape Crauford; known as Sakirmiaviniq, "no longer second mate," after his death.

Sivutiksaq (William Duval) – "harpooner"; a veteran whaler, worked for the Dundee Whaling Company at Igarjuaq from 1904–7; later for Captain Munn at Usualuk in Cumberland Sound; hired by the government in 1923 to act as translator for the murder trial at Pond Inlet.

Sarjan (Staff-Sergeant Albert Herbert Joy) – stationed at Pond Inlet 1922–24; sole officer responsible for the investigation into the death of Janes; also stationed at the Bache Peninsula post on Ellesmere Island, 1925–27, and at Dundas Harbour, 1928–29; promoted to inspector in 1927; famous for his long, arduous sled patrols in the high Arctic; died of a sudden stroke in 1932 on the day he was to be married.

Taamali (Alfred Tremblay) – former crew member of the 1910–11 government ex-
    pedition; joined Captain Bernier's private venture in 1912 and collected rock
    samples in northwestern Baffin in a continuing search for gold; author of *Cruise
    of the Minnie Maud* in which he was critical of Nuqallaq's behaviour.
Umilik (Constable William MacGregor) – referring to his moustache; stationed at
    Pond Inlet, 1922–23; at Pangnirtung, 1923–24; investigated the Qivittuuq mur-
    ders with Corporal McInnes.
Uqarajuittuq (Corporal Finley McInnes) – "a person who does not speak much";
    later called Nikpaqti because of his invention of an automatic harpoon gun for
    catching seals; stationed at Pond Inlet in 1922–23 and again from 1924–26; also at
    Pangnirtung in 1923–24, where he was in charge of the investigation into the
    Qivittuuq murders; returned to Pangnirtung 1932–34, at which time he was
    called Kuuruluk, "the cook."

INUIT CULTURAL GROUPS

Adkudnermiut – Inuit living along the eastern coast of Baffin Island, north of Cum-
    berland Sound and south of Cape Bowen.
Aivilingmiut – Inuit living in the vicinity of Repulse Bay
Iglulingmiut – generally refers to those Inuit living in the vicinity of Igloolik Island,
    including adjacent camps on Baffin Island.
Nattilingmiut – Inuit living in the vicinity of what is now known as Gjoa Havn and
    Pelly Bay.
Tuniit – "the ancient people," usually in reference to Inuit of the Dorset or Pre-
    Dorset cultures who arrived in the eastern Arctic several thousand years ago.
Tunijjuat – name used by Inuit for the early Thule people, who arrived in North
    Baffin only eight or nine hundred years ago, to distinguish them from their more
    recent ancestors and those belonging to earlier cultures (Tuniit).
Tununirmiut – Inuit residing in the vicinity of Eclipse Sound, literally those living
    "in the shade of the big mountain," referring to the Tuniq mountain range near
    the head of Milne Inlet.
Tununirusirmiut – Inuit who lived "in the shade of the lesser mountains," referring
    to the mountains around Arctic Bay.
Uqqurmiut – Inuit living in the Cumberland Sound region.

INUIT PLACE NAMES

Aggu (Agu) – an Inuit winter camp on the Baffin coast, just north of Fury and Hecla
    Strait.
Aivilik – name once used to describe the general area around Repulse Bay.
Ammaarjuaq (Amadjuak) – now abandoned, the site of a Hudson's Bay Company
    post in the early 1920s on the southern coast of Baffin Island, located approxi-
    mately mid-way between Kinngait (Cape Dorset) and Kimmirut (Lake Harbour).

Aukarnirjuaq – "where the sea never freezes"; an Iglulingmiut winter camp on the Baffin coast near the eastern outlet of Fury and Hecla Strait;

Igarjuaq – "the big fireplace" because it resembled a large *qulliq* or stone lamp when the fog lifted out of the valley like smoke; name of the whaling station and later the trading post located at the foot of Mount Herodier, near Albert Harbour. In Eclipse Sound; established by the Dundee Whaling Company in 1904; purchased by Captain Bernier in spring of 1910, by the Arctic Gold Exploration Syndicate in the winter of 1918–19, and by the Hudson's Bay Company in the winter of 1922–23.

Iglulik (Igloolik) – "the place where there are igloos or houses"; a relatively isolated island at the head of Foxe Basin, between Baffin Island and the Melville Peninsula; popular site for Inuit camps for thousands of years because of the abundance of wildlife resources; first visited by Europeans in 1822; hunters travelled to both Repulse Bay and Pond Inlet to trade with the whalers and, later, with the Hudson's Bay Company; first non-native to settle in the region was Father Bazin in 1931, followed in 1937 by the Hudson's Bay Company.

Igluligaarjuk (Chesterfield Inlet) – "a place with few houses"; first visited by British explorers in the late eighteenth century; by whalers in the mid-nineteenth century; site of the first Roman Catholic mission in the eastern Arctic (1911), also that same year, a Hudson's Bay Company trading post; in 1914, the North West Mounted Police moved their detachment from Fullerton Harbour to Chesterfield Inlet.

Ikpiarjuk (Arctic Bay) – "a pocket" as it is surrounded by mountains on three sides; located on Adams Sound off Admiralty Inlet; named by Captain William Adams Sr in 1872 after his whaling ship the *Arctic I*; site of Captain Bernier's winter quarters during the government expedition of 1910–11; site of a Hudson's Bay Company post in 1926–27, later reopened in 1936.

Iqaluit (in Tay Sound) – "the place where there are Arctic char." Many areas have sites bearing this name, but the one on Tay Sound south of Eclipse Sound is the location of Nuqallaq's final resting place.

Iqalungnit – site of the hunting camp where Nuqallaq died in late November 1925.

Kangiq (Cape Crauford) – a high point of land or promontory; English name given by Captain Edmund Parry after a British lord; sometimes spelled Cape Crawford (incorrectly); located at the tip of the Brodeur Peninsula in northwest Baffin Island.

Kangiqtualuk (Cumberland Sound) – this large body of water is surrounded by high mountains; occupied by Inuit for several thousands of years; first European to arrive was Scottish whaling captain William Penny Jr in 1837; location of a number of permanent whaling stations established by Americans and Scots, including Kekerten and Blacklead Island.

Kangiqtugaapik (Clyde River) – "nice little inlet near a high point of land"; located south of Pond Inlet; first *qallunaat* to visit were a British expedition led by Captain Edmund Parry in 1821 and several whaling ships; became a favourite watering place for whalers in the nineteenth century; first permanent settlement in 1924 with the establishment of a Hudson's Bay Company outpost.

Kimmirut (Lake Harbour) – "heel," referring to the shape of a rocky outcrop protruding into the bay; area inhabited by Inuit for thousands of years; first contact with the white man through trade with Hudson's Bay Company supply ships heading for Fort Churchill in the 1600s, later with American and Scottish whalers in the mid-nineteenth century; first permanent settlement began in 1909 with the arrival of Anglican missionaries, followed two years later by the Hudson's Bay Company, and in 1927 by the Royal Canadian Mounted Police.

Kinngait (Cape Dorset) – "high mountains"; site of Inuit camps dating back more than 3,500 years; located on the west side of Baffin Island's southern coast; visited by whalers in the mid-nineteenth century; site of a Hudson's Bay Company post in 1913.

Kivalliq – often referred to as the central Arctic; now an administrative district of Nunavut, comprising the communities on the western shores of Hudson Bay, stretching from Arviat to Hall Beach, and inland to Baker Lake.

Mittimatalik (Pond Inlet) – believed by some Inuit to be the "place where Mittima died," a site on the southeastern shore of Eclipse Sound occupied intermittently by Inuit for thousands of years. The Danish explorer Peter Freuchen believed Mittimatalik meant "where the gulls land," referring to the sand bar that was once offshore. Origin of the name is still in dispute. In 1818 Captain John Ross named the eastern gap between Baffin Island and Bylot Island "Pond's Bay," later shortened to Pond Inlet and used by the Hudson's Bay Company as the name for its trading post at Mittimatalik.

Nallua, sometimes Nadlua (near Low Point) – "where the caribou crossed" to Bylot Island; site of an Inuit campsite mid-way along the west side of Navy Board Inlet.

Naujaat (Repulse Bay) – "small gulls" in reference to the nesting place for seagulls; located on the southern shore of the isthmus between the central mainland and the Melville Peninsula; a mid-point of trade between Inuit from the south, those living near Pelly Bay, and those from Igloolik; frequented by whaling ships 1860–1910; first white permanent settlement in 1919 with the establishment of a Hudson's Bay Company post.

Panniqtuuq (Pangnirtung) – "the place of the bull caribou"; traditionally a hunting place for the Inuit of Cumberland Sound; first permanent white settlement began with a Hudson's Bay Company trading post in 1924.

Qikiqtarjuaq, (Broughton Island) – the "big island"; location of Inuit camps dating back thousands of years; now a government-created settlement, first as a DEW line site in 1955, then as a community for Inuit relocated from Padloping Island and Qivittuuq.

Qilalukkat (Salmon River) – running into Eclipse Sound west of Pond Inlet; where Janes claimed he had found traces of gold; Janes' grave lies on the beach just east of Salmon Creek, a tributary lying about two km east of the main river.

Qivittuuq (Kivitoo, Kevetuk, or Yakkie Harbour) – a popular watering site for whalers and gathering place for Inuit wishing to trade; site of a fur trading post owned by the Sabellum Company of England (1911–25) where incidents of religious fanaticism resulted in three Inuit murders in 1922; the post was eventually abandoned.

Qurluqtuq (Koolooktoo) – "where the water falls" in reference to the waterfalls on the Robertson River near the head of Milne Inlet off Eclipse Sound; the place where Qaunaq died suddenly of a mysterious illness after giving evidence at the inquest into the death of Janes; also where Nuqallaq accidently shot himself in the hand in 1923. Also the Inuktitut word for the Coppermine settlement because of its proximity to Bloody Falls on the Coppermine River.

Sannirut (Button Point) – "on the side" to describe the peninsula jutting out in the water; located on the southeastern corner of Bylot Island; popular location for spring hunting camps; site of the Arctic Gold Exploration Syndicate's trading post from 1914–22; important Dorset archaeological site.

Sirmik – group of islands near the head of Admiralty Inlet; near where Aatitaaq's brother Ijjangiaq and his family died of starvation after giving evidence at the preliminary hearings; also the general area of a mass starvation reported in 1924 by Peter Freuchen.

Tallurutit (Dundas Harbour) – "tattoo marks on the chin," similar to the unusual markings on the adjacent cliffs; site of a police post established in 1924 in Crocker Bay on Devon Island, closed in 1933; site used for two years as a Hudson's Bay Company outpost camp, 1934–36; police detachment re-opened temporarily after the Second World War; now abandoned.

Tikkakat (Tookeekan) – near Cape Henry Kater; close to the trading post operated by Hector Pitchforth until his death.

Titiralik (Canada Point) – "where there is writing" in reference to the name of Bernier's ship and date carved into a rock; on Bylot Island, mid-way along Navy Board Inlet; where Janes discovered coal and the remnants of large tree stumps.

Tuujjuk (Adams Island) – located on Lancaster Sound at the entrance to Navy Board Inlet.

Tulukkaat – "the ravens"; site of Janes' trading post at the mouth of the Patricia River on Eclipse Sound.

Tuluriaq (Toolooriaq or Low Point) – a point of land mid-way along the west side of Navy Board Inlet.

Tununiq – "in the shade of the big mountain," referring to the Tuniq mountain range near the head of Milne Inlet; usually refers to the area around Eclipse Sound.

Tununirusiq – "in the shade of the lesser mountains," generally referring to the less mountainous terrain around Arctic Bay on the east side of Admiralty Inlet.

Usualuk (Osho-Arlo Harbour) – "the place where there are clams"; site of the Arctic Gold Exploration Syndicate's trading post on Cumberland Sound, managed by William Duval.

APPENDIX THREE

Inuit Glossary

aarnguaq amulet.

aglu seal breathing hole.

aiviq walrus.

amauti parka with large hood for carrying babies.

angajuqqaaq boss or leader.

angakkuq (plural, *angakkuit*) shaman.

aqiggiq ptarmigan.

aqittungajuq someone who does not have much sense.

arvik bowhead whale.

iglu house made of snow blocks.

iglurjuaviniq old house made of stone.

igluvigaq unoccupied snow house.

ijuqtuq to laugh at or make fun of someone to correct their behaviour.

ilamanaqtuq to become a threat.

iliqqusiq a customary practice.

ilira a deferential or subservient reaction to intimidation by a stranger or unusual circumstance.

iliranaqtuq to be intimidating.

ilirasuktuq to be intimidated.

inuaqsiniq to murder someone.

inuaqtaujuq one who is killed by someone.

inuarniq a murder.

inuksuk (singular, plural, *inuksuit*) structure made of stones, often in the likeness of a man; having many functions, such as a beacon for travellers, a marker for a sacred spot, or the location of a trail when hunting caribou inland.

inuktitut the Inuit language.

inummarittut language of the older people.

inutuqaq Inuit elders (singular, *innatuqaq*).

inuunniuti the power of an *angakkuq* to kill.

iqaluit arctic char.

isuma   the capacity for reason (loss of *isuma* would be diminished capacity, as in an uncontrolled outburst of anger).

isumataq   camp leader (North Baffin).

iviutit   a song to embarrass someone.

kamiik   pair of sealskin boots.

kanngusuktuq   one who is shy.

kannguttituq   to be embarrassed.

maktaq or makta   skin of a bowhead whale, beluga or narwhal.

maligaq (plural, *maligaqat*)   something that is usually followed, like a custom.

maligaralaaq   a small *maligaq*.

nanuq   polar bear.

nattiq (North Baffin dialect), *natsiq* (South Baffin dialect)   seal.

niqpaqtii   rifle redesigned to aim down a seal hole (unique to Pond Inlet area).

niuvittit   the Hudson's Bay Company.

piqujaq   which is asked by an authorized person to be done; customary law.

qaggiq   festivities or celebrations.

qaggiq   large snow house for gatherings and feasts.

qajaq (plural, *qajait*)   a one-person hunting boat or kayak(s).

qallunaaq (plural, *qallunaat*)   initially the Inuktitut name for Europeans, but now generally refers to any white person.

qallunaatitut   the language spoken by the white man, usually refers to English.

qamutiik (plural, *qamutiit*)   large dog sled.

qarmaq   sod house.

qilalugaq (singular) a narwhal; *qilalugait*, a pod of narwhals.

qilauti   traditional Inuit drum.

qulittaq   outer parka of thick caribou hair (as opposed *to qaliruaq*, an inner parka with thin fur worn next to the skin).

qulliq   seal oil lamp.

Sanna (also known as *Sedna*)   the spirit woman who lived in the sea.

siqqitiq   the act of eating certain food forbidden by the shamans to signify one's conversion to Christianity (learned from lay preachers, not missionaries).

sivulaq   harpoon.

taqaugaq   quick to anger.

tirigusiit   something that was forbidden, or should not be done.

tuktu (North Baffin dialect), *tuttu* (South Baffin dialect), *tuktuit* (plural)   caribou.

tupiq (plural, *tupiit*)   skin tent.

tuurngait   spirits who help the shamans.

ugjuk   large bearded seal.

ulu   a crescent shaped woman's knife.

umiaq   large boat made of skins to transport women and children.

umiarjuaq   a big ship.

unikkaaq   story of recent origins.

unikkaaqtuaq   story passed down from generation to generation, like a legend.

Notes

PROLOGUE

1 Details of the crime scene were compiled from the coroner's report and various Inuit testimonies presented at the preliminary hearings. See National Archives of Canada, RG 18, vol. 3280, file 1920-HQ-681-G-4 (2).
2 Low, *Report on the Dominion Government Expedition to Hudson Bay and the Arctic Islands*, 165.
3 RG 18, vol. 3668, file 567–69 (1), Patrol Report to Clyde River, 9 June 1926, page 3. There was a number of reports of "lung disease" at the camps that winter and next spring, some of them serious and requiring police assistance. Only one report referred to the deaths of four Inuit from the "prevailing lung disease, tuberculosis," but it could not have been more direct. At the time of the trial the medical officer reported that he had examined approximately thirty Inuit at Pond Inlet and found them to be free of disease. Nor were there any reports of "lung disease" the following year.

CHAPTER ONE

1 Brody, *The Other Side of Eden*, 119.
2 Stager and Swain, *Canada North*, 90.
3 Ibid., 88–93.
4 As noted by Mathiassen in 1923. See Therkel Mathiassen, *Archaeology of the Central Eskimos*, 136.
5 Stager and Swain, *Canada North*, 95–8.
6 For more detailed descriptions, see McGhee, *Ancient People of the Arctic* and *Canadian Arctic Prehistory*; Mary-Rousselière, "Factors Affecting Human Occupation of the Land in the Pond Inlet Region from Prehistorical to Contemporary Times," and "Iglulik," in David Damas, ed., *Handbook of North American Indians*, and in the same volume, McGhee, "Thule Prehistory of Canada," and Maureau Maxwell, "Pre-Dorset and Dorset Prehistory of Canada."

7 A new study underway in the summer of 2001, under the supervision of Robert McGhee of the Canadian Museum of Civilization and Douglas Stenton, chief archaeologist with the Nunavut government, will be using new techniques to carbon date previously collected artifacts of both cultures to determine whether the dates overlap. Father Guy Mary-Rousselière, an amateur archaeologist who collected Inuit stories and studied artifacts from camps around Eclipse Sound, was convinced that they did.

8 Mathiassen (1927), 221. His comments were based on thousands of artifacts collected from the Eclipse Sound and Igloolik areas and compared to those collected at Repulse Bay and further south.

9 Mary-Rousselière, "Eskimo Toponymy of Pond Inlet."

10 Mary-Rousselière, "Iglulik," 442.

11 Personal communication, Douglas Stenton, 28 February 2001.

12 Information about the seasonal cycles in Inuit lives was derived from stories told by the elders at Pond Inlet, notably Timothy Kadloo, Ningiuk Killiktee, and Letia Kyak. Anthropologist Richard Condon also described these cycles in *Inuit Behaviour and Seasonal Change*.

13 Stager and Swain, *Canada North*, 90.

14 Letia Kyak and others affirm that as children they had been told that Mittima's grave was in the vicinity of a large rock on the beach. This story appears in an article by Father Guy Mary-Rousselière, "Mittima's Grave." Others accept the explanation by Danish explorer Peter Freuchen that Mittimatalik meant "where the bird lights," possibly referring to a sandbar that at one time extended some distance from the shore. See Freuchen, *Arctic Adventure*, 460.

15 Sutherland, "Strands of Culture Contact." Additional findings suggest the Norsemen may have travelled more widely than first suspected.

16 Cooke and Holland, *The Exploration of Northern Canada, 500 to 1920*, 22–4, 28.

17 Ibid., 138 and 142; also Parry, *Journal of a Voyage for the Discovery of a North-West Passage from the Atlantic to the Pacific*, 275–88.

18 Ross, "Whaling, Inuit, and the Arctic Islands," 239.

19 A.P. Low, *Report on the Dominion Government Expedition*, 164.

20 Ross, *Arctic Whalers, Icy Seas*, 49. See also Low, *Report on the Dominion Government Expedition*, 267–71.

21 This tradition continued with the government expeditions led by Captain Bernier on the CGS *Arctic* as seen in the National Film Board's silent movie outtakes of the CGS *Arctic* on the Eastern Arctic Patrol from 1922 to 1925. Also, *The Arctic Patrol*, Canadian Government Motion Picture Bureau, 1929, ISN 61875.

22 Goldring, "Inuit Economic Responses."

23 Ross, "Whaling, Inuit, and the Arctic Islands," 242–6; also Low, *Report on the Dominion Government Expedition*, 271–2.

24 Mary-Rousselière, *Qidtlarssuaq*, 141, and appendix 6, story by Inuguk, and appendix 7, story by Qanguq.

25 Goldring, "Inuit Economic Responses," 264–6.

26 Ross, ed., *An Arctic Whaling Diary*, 14–22.

27 Tremblay, *Cruise of the Minnie Maud*, 236.

28 Mary-Rousselière, *Qidtlarssuaq*, 144–6.

29 Backhouse, *A Legal History of Racism in Canada, 1900–1950*, 27–8. Although there was a debate in 1924 on whether Inuit should be brought under the Indian Act, it was rejected. Their status was again under debate in the 1930s, this time with regard to whether responsibility for welfare payments lay with federal or provincial governments. In April 1939 a decision of the Supreme Court of Canada established that the Inuit were Indians within the meaning of "aboriginal" in Section 91(24) of the British North America Act, and should be considered wards of the federal government. This decision was never supported by legislation with the result that the official status of the Inuit as full-fledged Canadian citizens remained intact.

30 Diubaldo, *The Government of Canada and the Inuit, 1900–1967*, 45.

31 Brody, *The Other Side of Eden*, 43–4; Stevenson, *Inuit, Whalers, and Cultural Persistence*, 117–20.

32 Brody, *The Other Side of Eden*, 43.

33 Cowan, ed., *We Don't Live in Snow Houses Now*, 25. "Ahlooloo" recalls how his father admonished his nephew for having killed the white trader Robert Janes, saying "You should not have killed a *qallunaaq*. Now you are going to see another one."

34 According to Noah Piuggttuk's explanation, the Inuit living at the Igarjuaq whaling station near Pond Inlet feared that "some white people might take revenge" for the death of a white fur trader (Interview IE-041, 16 January 1989, courtesy the Igloolik Inullariit Society, Igloolik Research Centre). In the Inuit statements taken for the preliminary trial, others also feared revenge.

35 Wakeham, *Report of the Expedition to Hudson Bay and Cumberland Gulf*, 44.

36 Low, *Report on the Dominion Government Expedition*, 182.

37 NAC, RG 18, vol. 3284, file 1920 HQ-1034-C-1, report from Port Harrison, 12 October 1921; RG 18, vol. 3313, file 1925 HQ-118-C-2. Governor C. Sale of the Hudson's Bay Company to W.S. Edwards, deputy minister of Justice, 12 October 1926; See also Hudson's Bay Archives, signed statement by the post manager, S.J. Stewart, dated 13 May 1927, at Port Harrison.

38 A Moravian, John Warmow, had accompanied the whaling ship captained by William Penny Junior that wintered over in 1857–58. See Ross, *This Distant and Unsurveyed Country*.

39 Trott, "The Rapture and the Rupture," 212.

40 Harper, "Writing in Inuktitut," 6–7.

41 Ibid. Therkel Mathiassen of the Danish Fifth Thule Expedition was surprised to find that most Inuit near Igloolik could both read and write in syllabics.

42 Pitseolak and Eber, *People from Our Side*, 40–4, 68–9; see also Grant, "Religious Fanaticism at Leaf Bay, Ungava," 163–5.

43 We know by his own report that Bernier had delivered Bibles in 1911 to the mission at Blacklead Island on instructions from Reverend Peck. See Canada,

Department of Marine and Fisheries, *Report on the Dominion Government Expedition to the Northern Waters and Arctic Archipelago*, 80. According to Stéphane Cloutier, who has been compiling a collection of photographs and documents related to the life of Captain Bernier, one of his men also distributed some of Peck's Bibles to the Iglulingmiut in the winter of 1910–11.

44 Many sources explain Inuit spirituality and shamanism. A more sophisticated analysis is found in Brody's *The Other Side of Eden*, 229–49; for description based on Inuit oral history, see Laugrand et al., *Memory and History in Nunavut*.

45 Low, *Report on the Dominionn Government Expedition*, 162–74. His knowledge was reportedly derived from the narratives of polar explorers and an ethnographic study of Cumberland Sound by Franz Boas.

46 Ibid., 165.

47 Nungak, "Fundamental Values, Norms and Concepts of Justice," 86. The concept that Inuit customary law was based on the objective of keeping peace in the community was recognized by anthropologists in the 1930s. See Birket-Smith, *The Eskimos*, 164.

48 Rasing, *"Too Many People,"* 116–32; Nungak, "Fundamental Values," 86–104; Finkler, *Inuit and the Administration of Justice in the Northwest Territories*; Graburn, "Eskimo Law in Light of Self- and Group-Interest"; Patenaude, "Whose Law? Whose Justice?" Of the many sources on this general topic, only a few are recent and pertinent to Baffin Island. Most studies on traditional laws of indigenous peoples are either outdated or relate only to the North American Indian or to Inuit from other regions of the Arctic.

49 Ryan, *Doing Things the Right Way*, 101.

50 Brody, *Living Arctic*, 126–7.

51 Possibly the first anthropologist, or at least one of the first, to recognize the subtle differences in Inuit customary laws according to subgroups within the culture was Leopold J. Pospisil. See his *Anthropology of Law*, 106–97, 124–5.

52 Hallendy et al., "The Last Known Traditional Inuit Trial on Southwest Baffin Island in the Canadian Arctic," 7.

53 Tremblay, *Cruise of the Minnie Maud*, 121; see also Oosten, Laugrand, and Rasing, eds., *Perspectives on Traditional Law*.

54 Morrison, *Showing the Flag*, 148.

55 Brody, *The Other Side of Eden*, 46–7.

56 Stevenson, *Inuit, Whalers, and Cultural Persistance*, 54–8; Boas, *The Central Eskimo*, 174. Boas believed that "blood feuds" were more in prevalent Canada's eastern and central Arctic. In a more recent study of the Cumberland Sound area, Marc Stevenson argues that these feuds declined with greater exposure to the *qallunaat*.

57 Emile Imaruittuq in Oosten et al., *Perspectives on Traditional Law*, 160–1.

58 Ibid., 164–71.

59 Matthiasson, *Living on the Land*, 31; citing Mutch, "Whaling in Ponds Bay," 485.

60 Mary-Rousselière, *Qitdlarssuaq*, 30–40. This book tells of a group led by Qillaq who were thought to have arrived in Eclipse Sound in the mid-nineteenth

century, retreating from possible attackers who might wish to avenge Qillaq for a murder in the Cumberland Sound area. Qillaq and his group were known to have attacked others at Eclipse Sound before heading off towards Admiralty Inlet and the Igloolik area.

61 Tremblay, *Cruiise of the Minnie Maud*, 30–1; see also Mary-Rousselière, "Igarjuaq."

62 Mary-Rousselière, "Igarjuaq." Also see Harper, "William Duval (1858–1931)," in Davis, ed., *Lobsticks and Stone Cairns*, 263–4.

63 Matthiasson, *Living on the Land*, 32, citing Mutch, "Whaling in Ponds Bay," 488.

64 Wachowich, *Saqiyuq*, 19 and 71.

65 Harper, "Writing in Inuktitut," 7.

CHAPTER TWO

1 MG 30 B57 (J.D. Craig Papers), vol. 1, file "Dispatches 1874–1923," correspondence from the Foreign Office to the Colonial Office, with regards to a request on 28 March 1874, from Mr Mintzer, a former member of the United States Navy Engineer Corps, and related memos. Copies of these documents were provided to John Davidson Craig who, as a member of the International Boundaries Survey and assigned to the office of the Northwest Territories Council in 1920, was given the task of examining all the historical documents related to British claims and transfer of the Arctic Islands.

2 Ibid., despatch from Lord Carnarvon to Lord Dufferin, governor-general of Canada, 30 April 1874.

3 Quoted in Smith, *Territorial Sovereignty in the Canadian North*, 5.

4 MG 30 B57, vol. 1, file "Dispatches 1874–1923," dispatch from Lord Dufferin to Lord Carnarvon, 4 November 1874.

5 Ibid., as described in a clipping from *New York Times*, 27 October 1876.

6 Ibid, memo from the Chief Hydrographer to the Colonial Office, 23 January 1879.

7 Morrison, "Canadian Sovereignty and the Inuit of the Central and Eastern Arctic," 246.

8 Zaslow, "Administering the Arctic Islands, 1880–1940, 62.

9 Millward, *Southern Baffin Island*, 15, 22, 26–32.

10 Wakeham, *Report of the Expedition to Hudson Bay and Cumberland Gulf*, 24.

11 Government of the Northwest Territories, *Kekerten Historic Park*, 23.

12 Morrison, *Showing the Flag*, 88–9. NWMP Comptroller White believed that no detachment should be built if it could not be serviced by a police boat.

13 Steele, *Policing the Arctic*, chapters 12–18.

14 Low, *Report on the Dominion Government Expedition*, xvii and 10.

15 Fetherstonhaugh, *The Royal Canadian Mounted Police*, 133–4.

16 Low, *Report on the Dominion Government Expedition*, 20–34.

17 Ross, *An Arctic Whaling Diary*, 37–8, chapters 2 and 3, and appendix K; also Morrison, *Under the Flag*, 86.

18 Morrison, *Showing the Flag*, 89–101.

19 Ross, *Arctic Whaling Diary*, 75, n16. Also cited in Morrison, *Showing the Flag*, 154.

20 Ross, *Arctic Whaling Diary*, 76.

21 Ibid., 146, n. 1.

22 Low, *Report on the Dominion Government Expedition*, 57–9; also 134–5 for comparison figures.

23 Ibid., 41–70.

24 Bernier, *Master Mariner and Arctic Explorer*, 283–304.

25 Ibid., 305–6; also Bernier, *Report on the Dominion Government Expedition to the Arctic Islands and Hudson Strait*, 8; Dorion-Robitaille, *Captain J.E. Bernier's Contribution to Canadian Sovereignty in the Arctic*, 36; and Mackinnon, "Canada's Eastern Arctic Patrol, 1922–68," 93–101.

26 Bernier, *Master Mariner and Arctic Explorer*, 305.

27 Ross, *Arctic Whaling Diary*, 147.

28 Price, "The North," 366–8; also Morrison, *Showing the Flag*, 7–8.

29 Jenness, *Eskimo Administration II*, 18–28. Jenness devotes an entire chapter to this period, titled "Wards of the Police, 1903–1921." With an annual budget of $5,000, there was actually very little the NWT commissioner could do.

30 RG 85, vol. 786, file 5997c. Correspondence between Reverend Peck and the Department of Indian Affairs from 1909–1912 shows that the department randomly paid between $100 and $200 a year for food to be distributed among destitute Inuit in Cumberland Sound. Other amounts, although meagre, were distributed upon request to the Hudson's Bay Company.

31 Fetherstonhaugh, *The Royal Canadian Mounted Police*, 135–170, 320. The enrolment declined dramatically during the Great War, prompting a major recruitment initiative in December 1918.

32 RG 18, vol. 2160, "northern patrols." See 1914 applicants' letters, a list of seventy-five potential candidates, and the final recommendations by Superintendent Cortlandt Starnes of "D" Division, 26 May 1914.

33 Morrison, *Showing the Flag*, 7–9, 109.

34 This left the police with the responsibility of enforcing laws, but by special agreement with the western provinces, serious criminal cases would be tried in their provincial Supreme Courts.

35 Price, "Remote Justice," 367–8.

36 Grant, *Sovereignty or Security?*, 13–14.

37 King, *Report upon the Title of Canada to the Islands North of the Mainland of Canada, 1905*, 6–8. Copy found in the J.D. Craig papers, MG 30 B 57, vol. 1, file "Reports and Memoranda 1905–1923."

38 Grant, *Sovereignty or Security*, 9–11.

39 MG 30 B57, vol. 1, file "Correspondence." Instructions from Deputy Minister Gourdeau to Bernier, 23 June 1906, 3.

40 Bernier, *Master Mariner and Arctic Explorer*, 306–14; quote, 312. It should be noted that this strategy appeared in his autobiography written over thirty years later and not in his published report.

41 Bernier, *Report on the Dominion Government Expedition*, 5. See letter of instructions. A justice of the peace did not have the authority to try a person for an
   indictable offence unless specifically granted "the powers of two," essentially
   the authority of two justices of the peace. See Graham Price, "Remote Justice:
   The Stipendiary Magistrates Court of the Northwest Territories" (LL master's
   thesis, University of Manitoba, 1986): 28–9.

42 As quoted from a letter by F. Gourdeau to Captain Bernier, 24 July 1906, in
   Dorion-Robitaille, 79.

43 Ibid.

44 Bernier, *Report on the Domion Government Expedition*, 11–26.

45 Ibid., 39, 45.

46 Ibid., 33–4.

47 Ibid., 34.

48 Ibid., 42–5.

49 Canadian Senate, *Debates*, 20 February 1907, 266–74.

50 Grant, *Sovereignty or Security?*, 11–12.

51 Bernier, *Report on the Dominion Government Expedition*, 316–17.

52 McClintock, *The Voyage of the "Fox,"* 13.

53 Ross, *Arctic Whalers*, 173.

54 "Obituary Notices," *Dundee Year Book, 1890* (Dundee, Scotland: 1891).

55 Dorion-Robitaille, *Captain J.E. Bernier's Contribution*, 93 and 96; the deed was
   dated 16 May 1910; see also Mary-Rousselière, "Igarjuaq."

56 MacEachern, "Edward Macdonald's Arctic Diary," 31, at entry for Tuesday, July
   5. Full transcript of the diary is available in the National Archives, MG 30 B 139
   (microfilm reel M 5506).

57 Department of Marine and Fisheries, *Report on the Dominion Government Expedition*, 13–15, 137. Unlike Bernier's previous expedition reports, this was one compiled by department staff from his log books and various reports by his officers.

58 MacEachern, "Edward MacDonald's Arctic Diary," 33.

59 Stéphane Cloutier of Iqaluit, who is currently working on the Bernier Collection
   of documents and photographs, reported that Lavoie's original notes make
   reference to having distributed syllabic Bibles near Aggu in October 1910. See
   Archives Nationale du Québec, P188/Fonds J.E. Bernier. Although there were
   no reports of lay preachers in the area at that time, Cloutier found other documents suggesting that at least one Inuk by the name of "Amarualik" could write
   in syllabics, and that a few Inuit at Igloolik may have originally come from
   Cumberland Sound. Also see Kenn Harper, "Writing in Inuktitut: An Historical
   Perspective," 7.

60 *Report ... of the D.G.S. "Arctic" in 1910*: 72.

61 Ibid., 137, 140, 155.

62 *Report ... of the D.G.S. "Arctic" in 1910*: 105; also Macdonald's diary entries
   throughout the winter; MacEachern, 35–9.

63 *Report ... 1910*, 145–57.

64 MacEachern, "Edward MacDonald's Arctic Diary," 40.

65 Titus Uyarasuk, interview IE-110, 22 February 1990, courtesy the Igloolik
   Inullariit Society, Igloolik Research Centre, Igloolik, Nunavut.

66 Ibid., 34–5; also personal communication with Alan MacEachern, 21 June
   2001.

67 *Report ... 1910*: 60, 76–7. Also National Archives Photographic Division, Bernier
   Album for 1910–1911. On the back of the photograph of Inuit pulling Janes'
   qamutik, Bernier wrote that his popularity was due to his generosity in supplying them with tea and biscuits.

68 *Report ... 1910*, 52, 77, 137–47.

69 Bernier, *Master Mariner*, 368.

70 MacEachern, "Edward MacDonald's Arctic Diary," 40.

71 MG 30 B 57, vol. 1, file "Correspondence," instructions to Vilhjalmur Stefansson
   from Deputy Minister G.J. Desbarats of the Department of Naval Service,
   29 May 1913.

72 Diubaldo, *Stefansson and the Canadian Arctic Expedition*.

73 RG 18, vol. 2160, file 25–28. See Crime Reports and Correspondence, 1914
   through to 1917.

74 Morrison, *Under the Flag*, 99–100.

75 Ibid., 100–3.

76 Graham Price, "Remote Justice," 165. The Department of Justice relied on Section 586 of the Criminal Code to invoke the concurrent criminal jurisdiction
   which allowed the case to be tried by the Supreme Court of Alberta.

77 For the full story see Moyles, *British Law and Arctic Men*. The reports of the
   investigation may be found in RG 18, vol. 2162, files 25–28, 30–1. Also see
   Diubaldo, *The Government of Canada and the Inuit, 1900–1967*, 22.

78 RG18, vol. 2162, file 30–1, Crime Report by Inspector F.H. French, 20 June
   1917, 17.

79 Graham Price, "Remote Justice," 217, citing the RCMP *Annual Report for the Year
   Ending 1928*, 38.

80 Morrison, *Under the Flag* (1984), 104.

81 Price, "Remote Justice," 217–20. A six-member jury, compared to the usual
   twelve prescribed under Canadian law, was acceptable in the Northwest Territories, based on the belief that it would be difficult to procure more than half
   a dozen qualified individuals in remote northern communities. See Finkler,
   Inuit and the Administration of Criminal Justice in the Northwest Territories,
   16–17, citing the Hon. Judge William G. Morrow, Royal Bank of Canada v
   Scott and the Commissioner of the Northwest Territories, *Western Weekly
   Reports* (4), 498.

82 Price, "Remote Justice," 217–20.

83 RG 18, vol. 3281, file 1920-HQ-681-G-3. Crime report 15 February 1921; memo
   from the acting Assistant Deputy of the Department of Indian Affairs to RCMP
   Commissioner A.B. Perry, 24 August 1921. Many "crime reports" tell of

violence, but not all were committed to trial. See RG 18, vols. 3293, 3294, 3281, 3276, 3297 for files on such cases.

84 Steele, *Policing the Arctic*, 222; RCMP *Annual Report for the Year Ending September 30, 1921,* 36.

85 RG 18, vol. 3276, file 1918-HQ-681-G-1. W.C. Rackin from HBC Great Whale River Post to J. Thomson, Fur Trade Commissioner, 18 April 1919.

86 Ibid., Thomson, to A.A. Mclean, RNWMP Comptroller, 19 May 1919; Acting RNWMP Comptroller L. Du Plessis to Thomson, 31 May 1919.

87 Ibid., Lanctôt to Newcombe, 11 July 1919, as explained in letter from RCMP Comptroller A.A. McLean to Commissioner A.B. Perry, 25 July 1919; Perry to McLean, 19 September 1919.

88 Ibid., "Crime Report re Alleged Murder of Ketaushuk," 29 September 1920.

89 Ibid., coroner's report, 23 September 1920, with Sgt. A.H. Joy, J.W. Phillips, Samuel Stewart Sainsbury, Bruce MacKendrick and David Louttit signing as witnesses.

90 RG 18, vol. 3277, file 1919-HQ-681-G-2. "Crime Report re Alleged Murder of Kookyauk," 1 October 1920; also Steele, 206–7.

91 RG 18, vol. 3277, file 1919-HQ-681-G-2, 23 September 1920, coroner's report on the murder of Kookyauk.

92 Steele, *Policing the Arctic*, 208.

93 RG 18, vol. 3277, file 1919-HQ-681-G-2. Report by Insp. Phillips, 29 October 1920.

94 Ibid., two letters from Rev. Walton to the RCMP commissioner, one dated 15 April 1921, the other undated.

95 Ibid., E.L. Newcombe to RCMP Comm. Perry, 29 October 1920.

96 Ibid., memo by Phillips, 8 June 1921.

97 RG 18, vol. 3313, file 1925-HQ-1180-C-2. Deputy Minister of Justice W. Stuart Edwards to Charles Lanctôt, Deputy Attorney General of Quebec, 15 January 1926. A copy of the report by Newcombe, 9 June 1921, was attached.

98 RG 18, vol. 3277, file 1919-HQ-681-G-2, Deputy Minister Newcombe to Commissioner Perry, 9 June 1921.

99 Ibid.

100 Based on the strategy adopted for the preliminary hearings into Robert Janes' alleged murder, it appeared that Joy, as Inspector Phillips' former assistant in the summer of 1920, had either read the judicial opinion carefully, was apprised of its implications by his superiors, or had considered its application to the Le Beaux decision – perhaps all of the above. Otherwise it seems too coincidental that the focus of Joy's investigation in 1922 would be to establish a clear motive of revenge.

101 RG 18, vol. 3281, file 1920-HQ-681-G-2, "Albert Le Beaux." This file contains the reports of the police investigations, a copy of the trial transcript, and related correspondence.

102 Ibid., report by RCMP Inspector G.F. Fletcher, 11 November 1921.

103 Morrison (1986), 250. Morrison also refers to Moyles, 8.

CHAPTER THREE

1 Dorion-Robitaille, *Captain J.E. Bernier's Contribution*, 92; Munn, *Prairie Trails and Arctic Bi-ways*, 178–84; Tremblay, *Cruise of the Minnie Maud*, xi.

2 Reader, "Preface," in Tremblay, *Cruise of the Minnie Maud*, ix. One should interpret the word "prospectors" loosely. Tremblay was a member of the ship's crew on the government expedition the year before.

3 Tremblay, *Cruise of the Minnie Maud*, ix–xiii, and 1–2; Dorion-Robitaille, *Captain J.E. Bernier's Contribution*, 92–106.

4 Noah Piugaattuk, interview IE-141, 16 January 1989, Igloolik Inullariit Society, Igloolik Research Centre, Nunavut.

5 Information supplied by Stéphane Cloutier, January 2001, based on interviews with Inuit elders, conducted for his research on Captain Bernier and Wilfred Caron.

6 Unless otherwise noted, the story of Munn's search for gold is based on chapter 9 of his autobiography, *Prairie Trails and Arctic By-ways*, 157–84.

7 Tremblay, *Cruise of the Minnie Maud*, 48.

8 Dorion-Robitaille, *Captain J.E. Bernier's Contribution*, see contract, 95. A detailed description of the property, which had been bought from Bernier by Munn, then sold to the Hudson's Bay Company, was provided by Philip Goldring of Parks Canada, who obtained the information from the Scott Polar Institute, MS 987/1/1–5.

9 Tremblay, *Cruise of the Minnie Maud*, 107–90.

10 Noah Piugaattuk, interview IE-181, 6 February 1991, Igloolik Inullariit Society, Igloolik Research Centre, Nunavut.

11 Tremblay, *Cruise of the Minnie Maud*, 105. Descriptions of Inuit and their camps are scattered throughout the book.

12 Ibid., 222–3.

13 Ibid., 175–98.

14 Ibid., 199.

15 Ibid., 199–214.

16 Bernier, *Master Mariner and Arctic Explorer*, 380. Bernier makes this statement in the context of Janes' death.

17 Igloolik elder Noah Piugaattuk claimed that Nuqallaq had accompanied Tremblay and Piunngatittuq only because it was dangerous to travel with only one dog team (Noah Piugaattuk, interview IE-181). This was not quite accurate since Coggan and the elderly Ootootia were also with Piunngatittuq. Nuqallaq had a full complement of twelve dogs, whereas Coggan had only nine and Ootootia seven (Tremblay, 217).

18 Tremblay, *Cruise of the Minnie Maud*, 223.

19 Ibid., 218.

20 Ibid., 220–35.

21 Ibid., 223–4.

22 Ibid., 236.

23 Oosten, Laugrand, and Rasing, eds. *Perspectives on Traditional Law*, 233.

24 Tremblay, *Cruise of the Minnie Maud*, 64. In his government report (1912) Bernier refers to an Inuk living in this area as Nassa, and another source refers to Massan. These may be the same individual as Tremblay's "Tom Lassa."

25 Ibid., 243.

26 Ibid., 139

27 Ibid., 112–19, 139.

28 Several elders at Pond Inlet compared the police while on patrol to children, because everything had to be done for them. See Oral History interviews, Ningiuk Killiktee, 18 May 1994; Sam Arnakallak, 28 April 1994; and Timothy Kadloo, 18 August 1994.

29 Tremblay, preface by A.B. Reader. We do not know how much Reader might have added or modified out of deference to the author when he translated and compiled Tremblay's notes for the book.

30 Caron may also have been at the post with his uncle in the winter of 1916–17. See Munn, *Prairie Trails and Arctic By-ways*, 230.

31 Information provided by Philip Goldring, obtained from Scott Polar Research Institute, MS 987/1/1–5. Files describe the objectives of the Arctic Gold Exploration Syndicate and the sale of its assets in 1923.

32 Unless otherwise stated or in reference to quotations, Munn's experiences at Pond Inlet are derived from chapters 9 to 11 of his autobiography, *Prairie Trails and Arctic By-ways*.

33 Ibid., 185–206.

34 Ibid., chapter 10.

35 Bernier, *Master Mariner*, 380.

36 Munn, *Prairie Trails and Arctic By-ways*, 207.

37 Ibid.; see also Bernier, *Master Mariner*, 371.

38 Dorion-Robitaille, *Captain J.E. Bernier's Contribution*, 97–105. See also Finnie, "Joseph-Elzéar Bernier," 13–15.

39 Munn, *Prairie Trails and Arctic By-ways*, 209–24. In a later testimony to the RCMP, Caron implied that he provided food to Florence to help him through the third winter.

40 RG 42, vol. 463, file 84–2–1 (2 and 3), Robert Janes to Hon. Sir Robert Borden, 15 April 1916, writing from Glovertown, Newfoundland. Janes thanked Borden for all his help in the past, without disclosing the specific nature of that help. The letter was forwarded to the Department of Marine and Fisheries, but there is no evidence of a reply.

41 Pieced together from a number of sources, including Munn, *Prairie Trails and Arctic By-ways*; see also reports by his former shipmates after Janes' death, RG 18, vol. 3280, file 1920-HQ-681-G-4 (1), letters from Arthur English and Emil Lavoie.

42 RG 18, vol. 3281, file 1920-HQ-681-G-4 (2). See report by Staff-Sergeant Joy concerning information received from Wilfred Caron, 13 April 1922.

43 Ibid.

44 Janes apparently had talked to his former shipmates about his plans to return to Pond Inlet to prospect for gold. Since Alfred Tremblay was also on the 1920 government expedition, he may have contacted him when trying to raise money for his venture. If so, Janes may have learned about Tremblay's "problems" with Nuqallaq, perhaps explaining his attitude toward the Inuk.

45 RG 18, vol. 3280, file 1920-HQ-681-G-4 (1), sworn testimony by James Florence of Peterhead, 3 November 1920; also statement by George Diment, 26 October 1920. According to their testimonies Nuqallaq was a good hunter, a recent widower, and said to be interested in having Kalluk as his wife.

46 RG 18, vol. 3280, file 1920-HQ-681-G-4 (2), report by S/Sgt Joy, 13 April 1922.

47 Ibid. (3), Sergeant Douglas from the Chesterfield detachment to Inspector Albert Reames, 17 May 1921.

48 Noah Piugaattuk, interview IE-041, 16 January 1989, Igloolik Inullariit Society, Igloolik Research Centre, Nunavut. Piugaattuk seems uncertain as to which agent was fighting with Janes, but by process of deduction it was the winter following the summer that no ships came, and that the same agent had a fight with him on board the *Albert* in the summer of 1919. Thus, the AGES agent in question must have been James Florence, and the fight must have taken place around February 1919.

49 Munn, *Prairie Trails and Arctic By-ways*, 225. Information provided by Philip Goldring showed that Munn had acquired the mineral rights to ten acres of land on the north side of Strathcona Sound. Although it was stated that there were no buildings on the site, Bernier took photographs in 1923 of a dilapidated building with a sign clearly identifying it to be the property of the Arctic Gold Exploration Syndicate.

50 Ibid., 225.

51 Noah Piugaattuk, interview IE-041, 16 January 1989, Igloolik Inullariit Society, Igloolik Research Centre, Nunavut.

52 RG 18, vol. 3281, file 1920-HQ-681-G-4 (4), sale agreement dated 15 December 1921, between Janes's father and Captain Munn, states that Munn paid the estate $9,500 for all the furs and ivory, plus the buildings and equipment. Sale was concluded by S.J. Foote, barrister, St John's, Newfoundland. See also the attached valuations for the furs and ivory.

53 RG 18, vol. 3280, file 1920-HQ-681-G-4 (1), copy of letter from Captain John Murray to Mrs Janes, dated 16 November 1919.

54 Munn, *Prairie Trails and Arctic By-ways*, 230–1.

55 RG 18, vol. 3280, file 1920-HQ-681-G-4 (2), statements taken by S/Sgt Joy from Amooahlik, 26 May 1922, and Nahkahdagbe, 7 June 1922.

56 Ibid., report by S/Sgt Joy concerning conversations with Wilfred Caron, 13 April 1922.

57 Ibid, statements by "Munoo," 11 May 1922, and "Kamanuk," 28 April 1922.

58 Noah Piugaattuk, interview IE-041, 16 January 1989, Igloolik Inullariit Society, Igloolik Research Centre, Nunavut.

59 RG 18, vol. 3280, file 1920-HQ-681-G-4 (2), statements by "Sinnikah," 24 June 1922, and "Amooahlik," 26 May 1922.

60 Ibid., (1), Janes' diary, entry at 14 March 1920.

61 Ibid., (2), report by S/Sgt Joy about information learned from Wilfred Caron, 13 April 1922; also Janes' diary and signed statement by George Diment in RG 18, vol. 3280, file 1920-HQ-681-G-4 (1).

CHAPTER FOUR

1 This section is based primarily on the statements of witnesses, first made to Henry Toke Munn, then later to the S/Sgt Joy. Some references which were inconsistent with the majority opinion were eliminated as unverifiable. With the exception of quotations and specific details, general references may be found in RG 18, vol. 3280, file 1920-HQ-681-G-4 parts 1–3, and vol. 3281, file 1920-HQ-681-G-4 part 4 and Supplements A and B.

2 RG 18, vol. 3280, file 1920-HQ-681-G-4 (2), "Effects of the Late Robert Janes at Patricia River and Pond Inlet" by A.H. Joy, 18 May 1922.

3 RG 18, vol. 3280, file 1920-HQ-681-G-4 (1), signed statement under oath by George W. Diment, 26 October 1920.

4 RG 18, vol. 3281, file 1920-HQ-681-G-4 (supp. A), statement by "Oo-took-ito" (Uuttukuttuk) given at the inquest (9 February 1922), 3.

5 Ibid.

6 Ibid. See also "Ootookito's" statement to Munn in RG 18, vol. 3280, file 1920-HQ-681-G-4 (1).

7 Ibid. Janes' diary entry for 4 March also stated: "Saw no sign of Nu – or natives," suggesting that his driver may have mentioned that Nuqallaq and his friends were in the vicinity. Also refer to the statement by Nookudlah at the preliminary hearings, 19 July 1922, in RG 18, vol. 3281, file 1920-HQ-681-G-4 (supp. B).

8 RG 18, vol. 3820, file 1920-HQ-681-G-4 (1), diary entry for Monday 9 March.

9 Ibid., diary entry for 10 March.

10 RG 18, vol. 3821, file 1920-HQ-681-G-4 (supp. A). The names here are from the list provided by Uuttukuttuk at the inquest. The spelling is based on current usage and will be used throughout unless citing an original document.

11 RG 18, vol. 3281, file 1920-HQ-681-G-4 (supp. A). See testimony by "Oo-took-ito" at the inquest; and (supp. B) the testimony by "Nookudlah" at the preliminary hearing; also RG 18, vol. 3280, file 1920-HQ-681-G-4 (3), statement by "Oo-took-ito" as reported by Captain Munn to RCMP Commissioner A. Bowen Perry, 15 October 1921.

12 RG 18, vol. 3280, file 1920-HQ-681-G-4 (3), Janes' diary. Contrary to reports by various Inuit, Janes recorded that three Inuit families arrived on 11 March and five on 13 March, suggesting he may not have been thinking clearly.

13 RG 18, vol. 3281, file 1920-HQ-681-G-4 (supp. C), testimony by "Mikootooee,"
   7 August 1923.

14 Although a number of Inuit maintained that his advice was not accurate, no one
   explained specifically why the elder might wish to discourage Janes from going
   to Igloolik.

15 RG 18, vol. 3280, file 1920-HQ-681-G-4 (1), Janes' diary; see entries 11–13 March
   and quote from 13 March.

16 RG 18, vol. 3281, file 1920-HQ-681-G-4 (supp. A), testimony by "Oo-took-ito" at
   the coroner's inquest, 9 February 1922.

17 Ibid. (supp. B), "Nookudlah's" statement at the preliminary hearings.

18 Ibid.

19 RG 18, vol. 3280, file 1920-HQ-681-G-4 (4), statement by "Mikootooee," 7 August
   1923.

20 RG 18, vol. 3281, file 1920-HQ-681-G-4 (supp. B), statement by "Nookudlah" at
   the preliminary hearings, 19 July 1922. Nuqallaq refers to "the other trader"
   as Florence rather than Diment, suggesting that he may not have visited
   Sannirut after Florence had been replaced. In his diary Janes refers only to the
   "other trader."

21 Ibid., statement by "Edineyah," 29 May 1922.

22 Ibid. (supp. A), statement by "Ootookito," 9 February 1922.

23 RG 18, vol. 3280, file 1920-HQ-681-G-4 (1), last page of Janes' diary, "Record of
   Expedition to Hudson's Bay by Robert S. Janes Commencing Feby 24th 1920."

24 RG 18, vol. 3281, file 1920-HQ-681-G-4 (supp. A). See "Ootookito's" testimony at
   the inquest, 9 February 1922.

25 Ibid. (supp. B), Ataguttiaq's statement at the preliminary trial.

26 RG 18, vol. 3280, file 1920-HQ-681-G-4 (4), testimony of "Ekepireyah," 15 May 1923.

27 Ibid., testimony by "Ekussah," 15 May 1923.

28 RG 18, vol. 3281, file 1920 HQ-681-G-4 (supp. B), statement by Nookudlah at the
   preliminary hearings, 19 July 1923.

29 Ibid. (supp. A). Quoted from "Ootookito's" testimony for the coroner's
   inquest.

30 "Oyukuluk's" story in We Don't Live in Snow Houses Now, 31.

31 RG 18, vol. 3281, file 1920-HQ-681-G-4 (supp. A), testimony by "Ootookito."

32 RG 18, vol. 3280, file 1920-HQ-681-G-4 (1), statement by George Diment,
   26 October 1920.

33 Story by Ahlooloo, in We Don't Live in Snow Houses Now, 25.

34 Peter Freuchen, Arctic Adventure, 437. Freuchen had also been told that the Inuit
   had built a large coffin in order "to placate his soul."

35 Wilfred Caron had agreed to work for Captain Munn after the sale of Bernier's
   property to AGES. See Munn, Prairie Trails and Arctic By-ways, 245.

36 RG 18, vol. 3280, file 1920-HQ-681-G-4 (1), report by H.T. Munn, handwritten and
   dated 1 September 1920, and a copy typed by Lorne McDougall, lawyer for
   the Arctic Gold Exploration Syndicate, who forwarded the letter to the RCMP

commissioner, along with the signed declarations by George Diment and James Florence. A covering letter was dated 17 November 1920.

37 Ibid.

38 Ibid.

39 Claude Minotto, "Le frontière arctique du Canada: Les expéditions de Joseph-Elzéar Bernier 1895–1925."

40 RG 18, vol. 3280, file 1920–681-G-4 (1). In the same file, see the statements by Diment (26 October 1920), Florence (3 November 1920), Caron (6 September 1920); also a letter from Munn to the RCMP, 16 December 1921.

41 Ibid., statement by James Florence, 3 November 1920.

42 Ibid., Commissioner Perry to E.L. Newcombe, deputy minister of justice, 24 November 1920, with attachments including "C.I.B. Memorandum" of the same date.

43 Ibid. Typewritten copy of news clipping (without date or name of the paper) was sent in a letter by J.T.E. Lavoie, addressed to "the Director" of the RCMP, 23 November 1920.

44 Ibid., correspondence, J.T.E. Lavoie to A. Cawdron, director of criminal investigations, 23 and 27 November, and 13 December 1920; Arthur English to Lavoie, 18 November, 4 and 5 December, 1920; J. Bernier to J.T.E. Lavoie, 29 November 1920; from Ambrose Janes, 11 March 1922. Also see part 3 of the same file, Ambrose Janes to RCMP commissioner, 21 May 1923.

45 RG 18, vol. 3280, file 1920–681-G-4 (1), Arthur English to Lavoie, 18 November and two letters dated 5 December 1920.

46 RG 18, vol. 3280, file 1920-HQ-681-G-4 (3), covering letter marked "Confidential" to RCMP Commissioner A. Bowen Perry from Henry Toke Munn, no date, but received at RCMP Headquarters on 15 October 1921. Attached report was titled "Enquiry into the Murder of R. Janes of Newfoundland, By Nu-kud-lah, Esquimaux." The statements by the witnesses and Munn's remarks came from this report.

47 Munn (1932), 245.

48 This assumption was not truly accurate. The Inuit from Igloolik travelled widely, and many worked for the whalers in Hudson Bay, and since 1916, they traded regularly at the Hudson's Bay Company post at Repulse Bay.

49 Munn, *Prairie Trails and Arctic By-ways*, 254–5.

50 Ibid., 249, 252–3.

51 Attagutsiak [sic] and Guy Mary-Rousselière, OMI, "Eye-witness Account of Robert Janes's murder," 8–9.

52 NAC, RG 18, vol. 3280, file 1920-HQ-681-G-4 (3), Freuchen to RCMP Inspector Frere at Chesterfield Inlet, 21 July 1923.

53 Ibid.

54 Ibid.

55 Ibid.

56 Ibid., Sergeant Douglas to Inspector A.E. Reames, 17 May 1921.

57 Ibid., statement of Native "Albert," witnessed by Inspector A.E. Reames, 5 May 1921.

58 Ibid., covering letter by Reames to the RCMP commissioner, 17 May 1921.

59 Ibid., the inventory of furs, ivory, and chattels, and covering document, to S.J. Foote, barrister, St. John's Newfoundland, 15 December 1921.

CHAPTER FIVE

1 RG 85, vol. 583, file 571, pt 1. See the report by the Advisory Technical Board for the minister of the Interior, 25 September 1920, 2.

2 Ibid., 3.

3 Ibid., report, "Arctic Islands – Sovereignty," with excerpts from Oppenheim's Treatise quoted at length on page 7.

4 MG 30 E 169 (J.B. Harkin Papers), vol. 1, file "Arctic Islands." See also reports titled "Arctic Islands – Sovereignty," 25 November 1920, and "Ellesmere Island," n.d., and correspondence related to Harkin's work for the Advisory Technical Board as the commissioner of the Dominion Parks Branch of the Department of the Interior.

5 Ibid., "Arctic Islands – Sovereignty," 11.

6 MG 30 B 57 (J.D. Craig Papers), vol. 1, file "Correspondence." News clippings were included in correspondence from W.W. Cory, deputy minister of the Interior, to Sir Joseph Pope, under-secretary of state for External Affairs, 14 January 1920.

7 Ibid., memo from W.S. Edwards, assistant deputy minister of Justice, to J.D. Craig, 10 January 1921.

8 RG 85, vol. 583, file 571, pts. 1, 2, and 3. See related reports and correspondence. For specific proposals, see in pt. 3, "Confidential Memorandum," 11 February 1922, and memo from J.D. Craig to Harkin, 2 February 1922.

9 RG 85, vol. 583, file 571, pt 3, memorandum by Minister of the Interior James Lougheed, 15 June 1921.

10 Ibid. See also MG 30 B 57, vol. 1, file "Memos and Reports, 1907–1923." See as well report by H.R. Holmden, assistant archivist, and report by L.C. Christie titled "Exploration and Occupation of the Arctic Islands," 28 October 1920. Further discussion appears in file "Correspondence 1907–1923." For previous communications with the Colonial Office, see file "Despatches, 1919–1921." Handwritten copies of most dispatches appear in RG 15, vol. 1, files "Arctic Islands," and "Arctic Sovereignty."

11 McInnes Collection, audiotape, "My First Trip to the Arctic," recorded in 1979 by former RCMP Corporal Finley McInnes.

12 RG 85, vol. 347, file 100, "Application for Reclassification of the Northwest Territories and Yukon Branch." See also *Annual Report of the Department of the Interior* (Ottawa, 31 March 1922), appendix A.

13 MG 30 B 57, vol. 1, file "Correspondence" – for example, Deputy Minister of the Interior to Under-Secretary of State for External Affairs, 14 January 1921; Prime Minister Meighen to Minister of the Interior Sir James Lougheed, 15 January 1921; High Commissioner W.L. Griffith to W.W. Cory, 28 April 1921.

14 RG 85, vol. 583, file 571, pt 3. As an example, see Secretary of State for the Colonies, Winston S. Churchill to the Governor General of Canada, Duke of Devonshire, 10 May 1921.

15 Ibid., memo by Minister of the Interior James Lougheed, dated 15 June 1921. The appropriation had been turned down on 18 May 1921.

16 J.D. Craig Papers, MG 30 B 57, vol. 1, file "Correspondence," telegram from the Secretary of State for the Colonies to the Governor General of Canada, 9 June 1921.

17 RG 18, vol. 3280, file 1920-HQ-681-G-4 (1), RCMP Commissioner to the President of the Privy Council, "Re: Murder of Robert Janes by Noo-Kud-Lah, Esquimo [sic] of Baffin's Land," n.d., but likely 13 June. The lack of a date or reference to a "copy" suggests this was a draft letter.

18 Ibid., Commissioner Perry to Ambrose Janes, 13 June 1921.

19 Ibid., Commissioner Perry to the President of the Privy Council, 24 June 1921.

20 Steele, *Policing the Arctic*, 226.

21 Harrington, "A.H. Joy (1887–1932)," in Davis, ed., *Lobsticks and Stone Cairns*, 223–5.

22 Stories by Noah Piugaattuk of Igloolik and Sam Arnakallak of Pond Inlet are two examples.

23 As cited in the *RCMP Annual Report, 1921*, 21.

24 RG 18, vol. 3280, file 1920-HQ-681-G-4 (1), RCMP Commissioner A.B. Perry to Staff-Sergeant Joy, 6 July 1921.

25 Ibid.; also reported on the audiotape, "First Trip to the Arctic," McInnes Collection.

26 Leo T. Jackman Papers, MG 30 B 34, vol. 1, file "Diary," entries for August 1– September 2, 1921. Unless otherwise noted, the details of the ship's arrival and construction of the post are derived from this source. For background on Ralph Parsons and family, see Parsons and Janes, *The King of Baffin Land*.

27 At the time of his departure, Joy received instructions directly from Commissioner Perry. Should plans to build permanent detachments on Ellesmere and North Baffin go forward, he would likely report to an area inspector or superintendent, as yet unnamed.

28 Noah Piugaattuk, interview IE-041, 16 January 1989, Igloolik Inullariit Society, Igloolik Research Centre.

29 MG 30 B 34, vol. 1, file "Diary," entries for 30 August – 3 September.

30 RG 18, vol. 3280, file 1920-HQ-681-G-4 (2), crime report, 19 September 1921.

31 Corporal Finley McInnes relates the story told to him by S/Sgt Joy, audiotape (1977) "First Trip to the Arctic," McInnes Collection.

32 RG 18, vol. 3280, file 1920-HQ-681-G-4 (2), crime report, 28 October 1921.

33 Ibid., crime report, 24 January 1922.

34 RG 18, vol. 3668, file 567–69 (pt. 1), patrol report by A.H. Joy, Pond Inlet to Cape
    Crawford and Arctic Bay, 25 January 1922.

35 Story told by S/Sgt Joy to Corporal Finley McInnes, audiotape (1979),
    "Pre-Janes Trial," McInnes Collection.

36 RG 18, vol. 3281, file 1920-HQ-681-G-4 (Supp. A). See the oaths and documenta-
    tion required for the proceedings, including "Oath of the Coroner before
    Issuing His Precept for Summoning the Jury," dated 23 January 1922, signed by
    S/Sgt Joy and witnessed by Gaston Herodier and W.C. Parsons; also RG 18
    vol. 3280, file 1920-HQ-681-G-4 (2) for crime report, 24 January 1922, in which he
    describes his examination of the body at Pond Inlet, 23 January 1922.

37 RG 18, vol. 3281, file 1920-HQ-681-G-4 (Supp. A), statement by "Oorooreung-
    nak," 23 January 1922. This was later contradicted by Janes' former guide.

38 RG 18, vol. 3280, file 1920-HQ-681-G-4 (1), crime report, 12 February 1922.

39 McInnes Collection, copy of "Information of Witness" signed by Parsons,
    "Munne," and Joy, 30 January 1922. This copy was not signed by an interpreter.

40 RG 18, vol. 3821, file 1920-HQ-681-G-4 (Supp. A), statement by "Kahlnahl,"
    30 January 1922.

41 RG 18, vol. 3280, file 1920-HQ-681-G-4 (2), crime report, dated 12 March 1922.

42 RG 18, vol. 3821, file 1920-HQ-681-G-4 (Supp. A), statement by "Sinnikah,"
    31 January 1922.

43 Ibid., statement by "Ootookito," 9 February 1922. It is noteworthy that the story
    he told Munn after his return from walrus hunting, i.e., about Janes saying,
    "If I had had a rifle today, I would have shot a Native,"was repeated almost
    word for word at the inquest, except that the last phrase was changed to
    "I would have shot a dog." This raises a number of questions, such which
    version was accurate? Or had Uuttukuttuk changed his story? And if so, why?

44 Ibid.

45 RG 18, vol. 3280, file 1920-HQ-681-G-4 (2), crime report, 13 February 1922.

46 RG 18, vol. 3821, file 1920-HQ-681-G-4 (Supp. A), statement by "Kutchuk,"
    10 February 1922.

47 RG 18, vol. 3280, file 1920-HQ-681-G-4 (2), crime report, 13 February 1922.

48 Friedland, *A Century of Criminal Justice*, 237. Until the British House of Lords
    case of Woolmington v DPP, the onus was on the accused to satisfy the jury of
    his or her innocence.

49 RG 18, vol. 3280, file 1920-HQ-681-G-4 (2). The quote from the coroner's report
    appears in the crime report dated 13 February 1922. As noted earlier, the mis-
    take in Nuqallaq's alias is repeated in all official documents. Nuqallaq's other
    name was Qiugaarjuk, not Ki-wat-soo.

50 RG 18, vol. 3281, file 1920-HQ-681-G-4 (Supp. A). Copies of all the documentation
    are on file, including the "Information to Hold Inquest," "Warrant to Constable
    to Summon Jury," the "Coroner's Oath," the "Inquisition," and the signed
    testimonies of each witness.

51 National Archives of Manitoba / HBC Archives, Pond Inlet Post Number: B.465, Reference Number: B.465/a/1–16, Post Journals 1921–1939, Reel 1MA54, entry date, 10 February 1922. Reference provided by Stéphane Cloutier.

52 Ibid., journal entry, 20 March 1922.

53 RG 18, vol. 3281, file 1920-HQ-681-G-4 (Supp. B). The statements taken after the preliminary hearings appear in RG 18, vol. 3280, file 1920-HQ-681-G-4 (2).

54 RG 18, vol. 3280, file 1920-HQ-81-G-4 (2), crime report, 13 April 1922.

55 Ibid. statement by "Nahkahdagbe" and covering memo regarding a suggestion to send the bill to Janes's executors, 7 June 1922.

56 RG 18, vol. 3280, file 1920-HQ-81-G-4 (2), crime report, 13 April 1922. There is no detailed description of the disease, and hence no way of knowing whether this was a form of rabies or distemper. An obscure reference to "a neurologic type" of disease affecting sled dogs in the NWT during the 1920s might suggest a form of rabies: see Charleton and Tabel, "Epizootiology of Rabies in Canada," 301–5. The most celebrated case of canine distemper disease in the high Arctic was at Cumberland Sound in the early 1960s, which wiped out two-thirds of the area's dog population. See Duffy, "The Cumberland Sound Dog Disease."

57 RG 18, vol. 3281, file 1920-HQ-681-G-4 (Supp. B), statement by "Qamaniq," 28 April 1922. His testimony would be submitted in the preliminary hearing as evidence for the defence, but is not mentioned in Joy's report on the hearings.

58 RG 18, vol. 3280, file 1920-HQ-681-G-4 (2), report on "Effects of the Late Robert Janes," 18 May 1922.

59 Ibid. See memos and crime reports from May through to June 1922.

60 Referred to in police reports as an "adopted son," Kijuapik was Nuqallaq's son from his first marriage, thus "adopted" by Ataguttiaq (information from Philippa Ootoowak, librarian at Pond Inlet, 30 March 2001).

61 RG 18, vol. 3280, file 1920-HQ-681-G-4 (2), "Crime Report re: Noo-kud-lah, Eskimo. Murder of Robert Janes at Baffin Land," 10 July 1922.

62 Ibid., crime report, 22 July 1922.

63 RG 18, vol. 3281, file 1920-HQ-681-G-4 (Supp. B), statement by "Edineyah," 11 July 1921.

64 Ibid.

65 Ibid.

66 Ibid., statement by "Ahtootahloo," 10 July 1922.

67 Ibid.

68 Ibid., statement by "Kutchuk," 10 July 1922.

69 Ibid., statement by "Oo-took- ito," 18 July 1922.

70 Ibid.

71 Ibid.

72 Ibid.

73 RG 18, vol. 3280, file 1920-HQ-681-G-4 (2), crime report, 22 July 1921.

74 RG 18, vol. 3281, file 1920-HQ-681-G-4 (Supp. B), statement by "Oo-took-ito," 18 July 1922.

75 RG 18, vol. 3281, file 1920-HQ-681-G-4 (Supp. B), statement by "Nootakgagyuk," 28 April 1922.

76 Ibid., "Statement of the Accused" for "Noo-kud-lah," "Oo-roo-re-ung-nak," and "Ahteetah," 19 July 1922; also statutory declarations by "Amooahlik," "Penneloo," "Qamaniq," and "Munoo."

77 Ibid., statement by "Edineyah," 11 July 1922; also statement by "Oo-roo-re-ung-nak," 19 July 1922.

78 Ibid. See the preamble to each "Statement of the Accused" for "Noo-kud-lah," "Oo-reung-nak" and "Ah-tee-tah."

79 Ibid., "Statement of the Accused" for "Noo-kud-lah."

80 Ibid.

81 RG 18, vol. 3280, file 1920-HQ-681-G-4 (2), crime report, 22 July 1922.

82 RG 18, vol. 3281, file 1920-HQ-681-G-4 (Supp. B), statement by "Ahtooteuk," Nuqallaq's wife, 20 July 1922.

83 RG 18, vol. 3281, file 1920-HQ-681-G-4 (Supp. B), testimony by Wilfred Caron, 20 July 1922.

84 RCMP Annual Report for the Year Ending September 1922, 34.

85 McInnes Collection, audiotape, "My First Year at Pond Inlet."

86 RG 18, vol. 3280, file 1920-HQ-681-G-4 (2), crime report, 22 July 1922.

87 Ibid.

88 Lee, Policing the Top of the World, 127.

89 RG 18, vol. 3280, file 1920-HQ-681-G-4 (2), crime report, 22 July 1922.

90 RG 18, vol. 3281, file 1920-HQ-681-G-4 (Supp. B), "Statement of Prisoner Ahteetah," 24 July 1922.

91 Ibid., attached memo dated 9 August 1922.

92 RG 18, vol. 3280, file 1920-HQ-681-G-4 (2), memo, 4 August, 1922.

93 Ibid., crime report, 24 July 1922.

94 Ibid., "Memo to Officer Commanding, re: Prisoners Noo-kud-lah, Ahteetah and Oo-roo-re-ung-nak," 10 August 1922.

CHAPTER SIX

1 RG 85, vol. 556, file 982, correspondence, February 1922 through to July 22. Also MG 30 B 57, volume 1, file "Correspondence."

2 MG 30 B 57, vol. 1, file "Correspondence." The objective of the company is described in a memo by J.D. Craig to R.A. Gibson, deputy commissioner of the Northwest Territories, 7 March 1922. Attached was a letter from Alfred Tremblay to the minister of the Interior, 22 February 1922. The company charter had authorized a capital of $500,000.

3 RG 85, vol. 602. files 2502, pts. 1 and 2, Arctic Expedition reports and decoded messages for 1922 and 1923, from Commander J.D. Craig in files 2502 (1) and 2502 (2). See also file 2502 (2) for quote taken from a letter from the deputy minister of the Interior, W.W. Cory, to Prime Minister Mackenzie King, 5 July 1923.

4 McInnes Collection, audiotape of "First Trip to the Arctic" (recorded circa 1979) 5–7.

5 Ibid., audiotape of a speech by retired Major Robert Logan. McInnes also recalled the stench fifty years later when he taped recollections of his first voyage to the Arctic. See McInnes tape, "First Trip to the Arctic." Similar comments appear in the diary of W.H. Grant.

6 MG 30 B 129, vol. 1, Craig diary, entry 5 August 1922. This record group contains the diaries of both William Harold Grant and John Davidson Craig.

7 McInnes Collection, official RCMP "Diary of the Voyage on the CGS Arctic," 9 August 1922.

8 Speech quoted in "A Bit of Bernier" by Dr Gordon Smith, North 29, no. 2 (Summer 1982): 52–6. See also McInnes Collection, "Diary on Board the CGS Arctic," 30 July 1922.

9 McInnes Collection, audiotape, "First Trip to the Arctic," transcript pages 11–12.

10 William Harold Grant Papers, MG 30 B 129, Grant diary, entry 15 August 1922.

11 Ibid.

12 Ibid., entries for 15–18 August 1922.

13 Ibid., entry for 17 August 1922.

14 NAC, Photography Division, "Royal Canadian Mounted Police 1922 Expedition" (video ISN 33255).

15 MG 30 B 129, Grant diary, entries for 16–18 August 1922.

16 Lee, 26.

17 MG 30 B 129, Grant diary, entry for 18 August 1922.

18 RG 85, vol. 601, file 2502, pt. 1, "Report on the Arctic Expedition of 1922," by J.D. Craig. See also Canada's Arctic Islands: Log of the Canadian Expedition, 1922, 15–18.

19 McInnes Collection, transcript of audiotape "First Trip to the Arctic," 11.

20 MG 30 B 129, Grant diary, entry for 2 September 1922; and in same volume, J.D. Craig diary, entry for 8 September 1922.

21 MG 30 B 129, Grant diary, entry for 3 September 1922.

22 MG 30 B 68, Robert A. Logan Papers, vol. 1, "Report on Pond Inlet," 55.

23 Ibid., entry for 28 August 1922; see also the J.D. Craig diary in the same volume, entry for 28 August 1922.

24 RG 18, vol. 3181, file 1924-G-1323-4-24, Joy to Wilcox, 30 August 1922.

25 RG 18, vol. 3293, file 1922-HQ-681-G-5, report by Joy, 7 September 1922.

26 MG 30 B 129, Grant diary, entry for 6–7 September 1922.

27 RG 85, vol. 601, file 2502, "Canada's Arctic Islands: The CGS "ARCTIC" Expedition of 1922," appendix A.

28 McInnes Collection, audiotape, "First Trip to the Arctic," Unless noted otherwise, or in reference to quotations, the following stories of life at the police detachment were obtained from this taped recording.

29 Fetherstonhaugh, The Royal Canadian Mounted Police, 211.

30 Interview with former RCMP Constable Robert Christy (now deceased), November 1994.

31 McInnes Collection, audiotape,"First Trip to the Arctic," transcript pages 25–6.

32 Ibid., 27–8.

33 McInnes Collection, audiotape, "First Trip to the Arctic."

34 RG 18, vol. 3668, file 567–69 (3), "Patrol Report to Igloolik and Fury and Hecla Strait" by F. McInnes, 25 April 1923. Warnings that the Iglulingmiut might be hostile were recorded on the audiotape "First Trip to the Arctic."

35 RG 18, vol. 3668, file 567–69 (3), patrol report, 25 April 1923.

36 Ibid.

37 Mathiassen, *Material Culture of the Igloolik Eskimos*, 234–6, as cited in Christopher Trott, "The Rapture and the Rupture," 213.

38 RG 18, vol. 3668, file 567–69 (3), patrol report, 25 April 1923.

39 McInnes Collection, audiotape, "First Trip to the Arctic," transcript page 20.

40 Oyukuluk's story, in *We Don't Live in Snow Houses Now*, 31.

41 RG 18, vol. 3280, file 1920-HQ-681-G-4 (2), report, 20 March 1923.

42 RG 85, vol. 786, file 5997C, report by S/Sgt Joy to Officer Commanding, RCMP Headquarters, Ottawa, 26 May 1923.

43 Ibid., report of discussion with "Sinnikah," 17 August 1923. A third report of 24 September 1924 tells of Amoowalik finding the two missing bodies in the summer of 1923.

44 RG 18, vol. 3281, file 1920-HQ-681-G-4 (4), statements by "Toopingin" and "Ekepireyah" recorded by Corporal McInnes, both on 3 May 1923. These statements were not signed by an interpreter and do not appear among the statements included in the file that the court clerk delivered to the Department of Justice after the trial, according to the receipt from Biron for the documents he received from Joy, 1 September 1923.

45 Ibid., statement by "Toopingin," 3 May 1923.

46 McInnes Collection, audiotape, "First Year in the Arctic," transcript 28–9.

47 RG 18, vol. 3281, file 1920-HQ-681-G-4 (4), statement by "Ootoogek" (Paumi's wife), 8 August 1923.

48 Ibid., statement by "Mikootooee," 7 August 1923.

49 Ibid., statement by "Palmee," 9 August 1923.

50 In the summer of 1923 Corporal McInnes took a photograph of Aarjuaq following a successful hunt of snow geese (n.d.). The terrain is consistent with Bylot Island, whereas the size and colouring of the birds suggest a stage of development one might find in early August.

CHAPTER SEVEN

1 Compiled from Fetherstonhaugh, *The Royal Canadian Mounted Police*.

2 To accommodate the remote location and lack of communication, some contingency plan must have been agreed upon in advance.

3 RG 18, vol. 3280, file 1920-HQ-681-G-4 (3), Acting Commissioner Starnes to Deputy Minister of Justice E.L. Newcombe, 23 October 1922.

4 Ibid.

5 RG 85, vol. 601, file 2502 (1), "Report of the 1922 Arctic Expedition, 1922" by J. D. Craig, 21.

6 RG 85, vol. 602, file 2502 (2), Deputy Minister W.W. Cory to the Hon. W.L. Mackenzie King, 5 July 1923, plus follow-up correspondence in the same file.

7 RG 18, vol. 3280, file 1920-HQ-681-G-4 (3), Munn to Starnes, 7 November 1922; Bernier to Starnes, 2 December 1922.

8 Kenn Harper, "In Search of William Duval, Arctic Whaler and Trader," *Above and Beyond* (date unknown but circa early 1990s). Xerox copy provided by Rebecca Idlout Library, Pond Inlet.

9 RG 18, vol. 3280, file 1920-HQ-681-G-4 (3), Starnes to William Duval, 6 February 1923; Duval to Starnes, 12 February 1923.

10 Information supplied by Philip Goldring; source: Scott Polar Research Institute, MS 987/1/3.

11 RG 18, vol. 3280, file 1920-HQ-681-G-4 (3), Munn to Starnes, 7 November 1922.

12 Ibid., Ralph Parsons to Commissioner Starnes, 6 June 1923.

13 Ibid., Parsons to Starnes, 5 July 1923, confirming telephone call. Also telegrams from Craig, 6 July from Quebec, and to Craig from Assistant Deputy Minister Edwards to Craig, same day.

14 Munn (1932), 277. Munn complained about being put off at Port Burwell for six weeks, implying that it was the company's fault that he was delayed in reaching Pond Inlet. In fact, he would have been informed of the supply ship's schedule before he boarded the ship.

15 Roy, "L'Honorable Juge Louis-Alfred-Adhémar Rivet," 467.

16 RG 18, vol. 3280, file 1920-HQ-681-G-4 (3). Memo to Joy from the RCMP commissioner referring to F.X. Biron's anticipated appointment as the Crown prosecutor, 21 June 1923.

17 Ibid., memo to Justice, 29 June 1923, with clippings attached from the *Ottawa Citizen* and an unnamed French-language paper.

18 McInnes Collection, audiotape "My First Year in the Arctic." See McInnes's report on the voyage of the CGS *Arctic* in 1922. Evidently Mrs Craig accompanied her husband to Father Point the first year, but on that occasion she did get off the boat.

19 Price, "Remote Justice," 255n23.

20 RG 85, vol. 2138, file "CGS Arctic Logbook, 9 July – 4 October 1923"; also RG 85, vol. 601, file 2502, pt. 2, draft report of the 1923 expedition by J.D. Craig. Stéphane Cloutier reported that a diary of one of the crew members suggested that Caron had been deliberately "pushed." This is counter to other "eye-witness" accounts. Correspondence from Cloutier to the author, November 2000.

21 Griffin, "Now Baffin's Land Has an Eskimo Trial by Jury." Article based on the diaries of W.C. Earl, the wireless operator on the CGS *Arctic*.

22 French nickname provided by Stéphane Cloutier.

23 Claude Minotto, "Le frontière arctique du Canada: Les expéditions de Joseph-Elzéar Bernier 1895–1925." Minotto stated that Caron's body was found a week after his death in front of Montmagny, east of Levis, Quebec, and that Desmond O'Connell's body was found a few weeks later near Point-au-Pic. Reference supplied by Stéphane Cloutier.

24 RG 85, vol. 605, file 2502, pt. 2. Starnes to Joy, 21 June 1923.

25 The plan to have the prisoners and witnesses waiting at Button Point for the arrival of the court party was confirmed by Corporal Finley McInnes in the audiotape, "My First Trip to the Arctic," transcript page 29. This tape refers to a second tape covering the trial itself, but it was not in the collection inherited by his granddaughter. She recalls that some "government people" had visited her grandmother after McInnes's death and asked to look at his papers. This appears to be the only explanation for the missing tape, if indeed it ever existed.

26 Ibid., transcript page 30. Judge Rivet was not known for his sense of humour. Apparently in an attempt to lighten things up, Mrs Craig had the ship's carpenter cut a piece of wood to look like toast and had the cook place a poached egg on top for his breakfast. After struggling with his knife for a moment, and realizing it was only wood, the judge evidently pushed back his chair and immediately went to his state room where he remained for the rest of the day. This story was told to McInnes by an unidentified member of the crew.

27 RG 85, vol. 605, file 2502, pt. 2, memo from Craig to O.S. Finnie, 29 September 1923.

28 RG 85, vol. 601, file 2502, pt. 1, report on the 1922 Arctic Expedition by J.D. Craig, p. 21.

29 RG 85, vol. 602, file 2502, pt. 2, memo from Craig to Finnie, 29 September 1923, regarding the coded telegram sent 23 September 1923.

30 Ibid.; see also despatch no. 266; also copies of the coded telegrams and the decoded message, 29 September 1923.

31 Ibid.; see also despatch no. 266 to the governor general of Canada from Britain's Colonial Office, containing a translated excerpt from the *Berlingske Tidende*, 19 September 1923.

32 Ibid., personal report from Commander Craig to O.S. Finnie, director of the Northwest Territories and Yukon Branch, Department of the Interior.

33 Film clips held in the National Film Board Archives were transferred to video through the services of the Photographic Division of the National Archives of Canada (NPD). These included two versions of a black and white, edited film with subtitles, "RCMP Eastern Arctic Expedition – 1922" (ISN 132980 and ISN 33288). Neither has a proper title page, suggesting that they were not edited for public distribution. Portions of the footage taken in 1925, with same camera loaned by Fox News Films, were incorporated into a Fox Movietone News production (ISN 33255).

34 Canada, Department of the Interior, *Canada's Arctic Islands, Canadian Expeditions 1922–23–24–25–26*, 15–16.
35 Steele, *Policing the Arctic*, 238, citing excerpts from the RCMP *Annual Report for the Year Ending March 1924*.
36 *Canada's Arctic Islands* (1927), 17–23. This includes a description of the days spent exploring historical sites and other landmarks, from 12 August 1923 until arrival at Pond Inlet on 20 August (internal documents give the 21st as the arrival date). Also RG 85, vol. 601, file 2502, pt. 2. See the decoded telegram of 23 September 1923 for date of arrival at Eclipse Sound.
37 RG 18, vol. 3280, file 1920-HQ-681-G-4 (2), the trial summary prepared by Staff-Sergeant Joy (1 September 1923): 1.
38 *Toronto Star Weekly*, 3 November 1923.
39 RG 85, vol. 601, file 2502, pt. 2, preliminary report of the 1923 expedition to O.S. Finnie from J.D. Craig, 29 September 1923. Craig notes disappointing problems with the ship's wireless communications, p. 7.
40 Copland, *Livingstone of the Arctic*, 28.
41 Griffin, "Now Baffin's Land Has an Eskimo Murder Trial by Jury," 19–20. This article was based on the diaries of one of the jurors, W.C. Earl, the wireless operator.
42 RG 18, vol. 3280, file 1920-HQ-681-G-4 (2). The trial summary prepared by Staff-Sergeant Joy (1 September 1923) implied that the Crown prosecutor was assigned to translate for the jury, when he wrote that "the presiding Justice addressed the court through interpreter Duval for the information of the natives present, and the jury were addressed by Mr. Folardeau, [sic] counsel for the Crown." While it is possible that Joy might be referring to the Crown prosecutor's opening "address" to the jury, and not to a translation to the jury, the biography of Dr Livingstone clearly states that "the witnesses had to be interrogated in their own language, which had to be repeated in French and English" (Copland, *Livingstone of the Arctic*, 29). Similarly, jurors' notes left behind at the detachment were all written in French, suggesting that the five francophones were more comfortable in their first language (information from Robert Pilot Senior, a former RCMP officer stationed at Pond Inlet in the early 1950s, 5 April 2001).
43 RG 18, vol. 3280, file 1920-HQ-681-G-4 (3), crime report, 1 September 1923. Unless otherwise stated, the trial proceedings and related descriptions are taken from this summary by Staff-Sergeant Joy, with an addendum by Inspector Wilcox.
44 "Oyukuluk," Aatitaaq's son, clearly recalls that all the men in the front row were police in red tunics. See *We Don't Live in Snow Houses Now*, 31.
45 Alex Stevenson, 21.
46 According to former circuit court judges Jack Sissons and William Morrow, there was no Inuktitut word or phrase for the word "guilty" at the time they sat on the bench. See Finkler (1975), 19.
47 Canada, Department of the Interior, *Canada's Arctic Islands* (1927), 24.

48 RG 18, vol. 3280, file 1920-HQ-681-G-4 (3), crime report, 1 September 1923. Unless otherwise stated, the order of proceedings came from this report.

49 Canada, Department of the Interior, *Canada's Arctic Islands* (1927), 24.

50 Stevenson, "The Robert Janes Murder Trial," 22.

51 Based on explanations provided by Graham Price, QC, LLM, legal historian and former deputy judge for the NWT Court in the early 1990s. Any discrepancies appearing here are those of the author.

52 RG 18, vol. 3280, file 1920-HQ-681-G-4 (3). The proceedings were recorded in Joy's crime report, 1 September 1923. In court documents the names of the accused appear as Noo-kud-lah, Oo-roo-re-ung-nak, and Ah-tee-tah.

53 RG 18, vol. 3280, file 1920-HQ-681-G-4 (3), statement by "Oomee," 8 August 1923.

54 Stevenson, 22. Stevenson would not have had permission to use or quote from a document that was restricted, and thus he refers to the questioning in the abstract.

55 Pond Inlet Oral History Project, interview with Sam Arnakallak, 27 September 1994, who stated that his grandfather had told him that Uuttukuttuk ran away and hid during the trial.

56 Noah Piugaattuk, interview IE-041, 16 January 1989, Igloolik Inullariit Society, Igloolik Research Centre, Nunavut.

57 RG 18, vol. 3280, file 1920-HQ-681-G-4 (3), Joy's report on the trial; see also Stevenson, "The Robert Janes Murder Trial," 22.

58 RG 18, vol. 3280, file 1920-HQ-681-G-4 (3), statement by "Palmee," 9 August 1923.

59 Ibid. See statements by "Ekussah," 7 August 1923, "Toopingun," 3 May 1923, and "Ekepireyah," 3 May 1923.

60 Ibid. See statements by "Mikitooee," 7 August 1923, and "Ekepireyah," 3 May 1923; compared with RG 18, vol. 3280, file 1920-HQ-681-G-4 (supp. B), statements by "Ahtooteuk," 20 July 1922, and by "Kutchuk" 10 July 1922.

61 Longstreth, *The Silent Force*, 337; also see Copland, *Livingstone of the Arctic*, 29.

62 Pond Inlet Oral History Project: Sam Arnakallak was interviewed by his sister, Elisapee Ootoova (27 September 1994). Sam and Elisapee were Ataguttiaq's children, but Nuqallaq was not their father.

63 Interview with Martha Akumalik, 18 March 1994. Martha was aged eleven at the time and remembers being at the trial. The name of the person who intervened seemed vague in the original transcript, but the project coordinator, Lynn Cousins, has assured me that Martha was referring to Nuqallaq.

64 As cited in Stevenson, "The Robert Janes Murder Trial," 23.

65 Harper, "William Duval," 264.

66 RG 18, vol. 3280, file 1920-HQ-681-G-4 (3), crime report, 1 September 1923.

67 As described by juror W.C. Earl, in Griffin's *Toronto Star Weekly* article "Now Baffin's Land …" See also Stevenson, "Robert Janes Murder Trial," 22.

68 Ibid., crime report, 1 September 1923, addendum by C.E. Wilcox.

69 Edited film footage and unedited out-takes transferred to videotape for the National Archives photographic division (NPD) appear under the combined

title "Back to Baffin/Royal Canadian Mounted Police, 1922 Arctic Expedition" (video ISN 33255).

70 RG 18, vol. 3280, file 1920-HQ-681-G-4 (3). Certificates were dated 30 August 1923, but a covering memo by Joy indicated the examinations took place on 29 August.

71 Ibid, crime report, 1 September 1923. Note the addendum to Joy's report, signed by Inspector C.E. Wilcox.

72 Stevenson, "Robert Janes Murder Trial," 22.

73 *Toronto Star Weekly* (3 November 1923).

74 RG 18, vol. 3280, file 1920-HQ-681-G-4 (3), crime report, 1 September 1923, addendum to Joy's report, signed by C.E. Wilcox.

75 *Toronto Star Weekly* (3 November 1923). According to Joy's report, the jury returned with a verdict after only twenty minutes. See also RG 18, vol. 3280, file 1920-HQ-681-G-4 (3), crime report, 1 September 1923. Also see a report of the trial in *Canada's Arctic Islands* (1927), 23–4. It should be noted that at Alikomiak's trial on Herschel Island, it was reported that the jury had only been out for only eight minutes.

76 *Canada's Arctic Islands* (1927), 24; and RG 18, vol. 3280, file 1920-HQ-681-G-4 (3), crime report, 1 September 1923.

77 RG 18, vol. 3280, file 1920-HQ-681-G-4 (3), addendum to crime report, 1 September 1923, by C.E. Wilcox.

78 *Canada's Arctic Islands* (1927), 24.

79 *RCMP Annual Report for Year Ending September 30, 1923*, 34.

80 Steele, *Policing the Arctic*, 239.

81 Interview with Martha Akumalik, 4 June 1994, 6.

82 *Toronto Star Weekly* (3 November 1923).

83 RG 18, vol. 3280, file 1920-HQ-681-G-4 (1), Peter Freuchen to Inspector Frere, RCMP detachment, Chesterfield Inlet, 21 July 1923, received at headquarters on 7 September 1923.

84 Interview with Martha Akumalik, 18 March 1994.

85 RG 85, vol. 602, file 2502 (pt. 2), decoded telegram message, 28 September 1923.

86 Ibid, "Report on the CGS Arctic Expedition for 1923."

87 Robert Pilot Sr, former RCMP officer at Pond Inlet during the early 1950s, now mayor of Pembroke, Ontario, described the file containing the handwritten transcript and jurors' notes, and how it was often read by visitors. He believed that orders had gone out to the Arctic detachments to destroy all such papers sometime in the mid-1950s (discussion, 5 April 2001).

88 An author residing on Baffin Island claimed to have a copy of the trial transcript and provided me with a copy of the first and last page. It appeared to be a copy of the original handwritten draft, complete with spelling errors and other mistakes. He did not wish to share the full document, and even if he had, I knew that ethically it could not be used for research purposes without permission from the RCMP.

89 RG 18, vol. 3280, file 1920-HQ-681-G-4 (4), memo by A.H. Joy to his "Officer Commanding," 10 September 1923. Since his commanding officer, Inspector Wilcox, was present at the trial, it appears that Joy had written the report at his request.

90 *Toronto Star Weekly* (3 November 1923), 19.

91 Noah Piugaatuk, interview IE-041, Igloolik Inullariit Society, Igloolik Research Centre.

92 Interview with Elisapee Ootoova, March 1999, with Philip Paneak translating. Elisapee also said that her mother admitted she had been beaten on occasion but claimed that she probably deserved it. As a child, her son Sam Arnakallak had been told by his stepfather that Nuqallaq had beaten her (interview with Sam Arnakallak, 22 November 1994).

93 Atagutsiaq and Mary-Rousselière, "Eye-witness Account of Robert Janes's Murder": 5–1.

94 Isapee Qanguq, interview IE-144 (n.d.), Igloolik Inullariit Society, Igloolik Research Centre.

95 Munn, *Prairie Trails and Arctic By-ways*, 242.

96 Freuchen, *Vagrant Viking*, 188–90.

97 Longstreth, *The Silent Force*, 337–8.

CHAPTER EIGHT

1 RG 18, vol. 3293, file 1922-HQ-681-G-4 (4), report forwarded by Inspector Wilcox to RCMP Commissioner Starnes, 10 September 1923; O.S. Finnie to Starnes, 17 October 1923.

2 RG 85, vol. 602, file 2502, pt. 2, decoded telegram message, 28 September 1923. And on 3 October, a preliminary "Report on the CGS Arctic Expedition for 1923."

3 Stories by Anglican Bishop Lucas first appeared in the *Edmonton Journal* on 14 September 1923, then the next day in the *Calgary Herald*, 15 September 1923. These and other clippings may be found in RG 18, vol. 3295, file 1922-HQ-681-G-1 pt. 2 and pt. 6.

4 See the full story in the *Toronto Sunday World*, 21 October 1923.

5 "*Arctic* Comes Back with Strange Tales from the Frigid North," *Toronto Globe*, 6 October 1923.

6 Most clippings were obtained from RG 18, vol. 3280, file 1920-HQ-681-G-4 (4) and RG 85, vol. 602, file 2502, pt. 2. The first report appeared in the *Montreal Star*, 2 October 1923, "SS. ARCTIC SAFE AFTER BAD VOYAGE."

7 Compare stories in the *Quebec Chronicle* and *Quebec Telegraph* for 3–5 October 1923.

8 "Dramatic Account of Eskimo Murder Trial in Far Northland," *Quebec Telegraph*, 5 October 1923 (final edition).

9 Ibid.

10 Ibid.

11 Ibid.

12 RG 18, vol. 3297, file 1923-HQ-681-G-1 (Peeawahto) Correspondence: from Commissioner Starnes to Sir Joseph Pope, 9 June 1923; Pope to Starnes, 13 June 1923; Starnes to O.S. Finnie, 18 June 1923.

13 RG 18, vol. 3281, file 1920-HQ-681-G-4 (4), O.S. Finnie writing to W.W. Cory, deputy minister of the Interior, reporting on Judge Rivet's response to his inquiry, 10 November 1923.

14 Information on the history of the penitentiary was obtained from a variety of sources and personal information supplied by Elizabeth Bight at the Manitoba Provincial Archives. Sources include *Report of the Royal Commission to Investigate, Inquire into and Report upon Charges Preferred against Certain Officers and Guards connected with Stoney Mountain Penitentiary, 1897*, vol. 1 (Toronto: Micromedia, 1903); Cellard, *Punishment, Imprisonment and Reform in Canada*; Topping, *Canadian Penal Institutions*; and Zubrycki, *The Establishment of Canada's Penitentiary System*.

15 Zubrycki, *The Establishment of Canada's Penitentiary System*, 18; Cellard, *Punishment, Imprisonment, and Reform in Canada*, 11–15.

16 Topping, *Canadian Penal Institutions*, 36–43.

17 Ibid., 57.

18 Ibid., 25.

19 Ibid., 46–8. While it is apparent that Topping's book was supportive of the recent reforms undertaken at Canadian penitentiaries, to the best of my knowledge there is no contradictory evidence to suggest the descriptions are inaccurate.

20 Noah Piugaattuk, interview IE-041, 16 January 1989, Inuit Inullariit Society, Igloolik Research Institute, Nunavut.

21 Zubrycki, *The Establishment of Canada's Penitentiary System*, 69.

22 RG 18, vol. 3281, file 1920-HQ-681-G-4 (4), Henry Toke Munn to RCMP Commissioner Starnes, 6 February 1924.

23 Ibid. Cross-reference note from Penitentiaries Branch received by police headquarters, 7 March 1924.

24 Ibid., Warden W. Meighen to J.D. Clarke, 7 February 1924.

25 Ibid., Meighen to Clarke with attached note from the surgeon, 22 February 1924.

26 Ibid., Starnes to Superintendent of Penitentiaries W.S. Hughes, 1 October 1924; reply from Hughes to Starnes, 3 October 1924.

27 Ibid., J.J. McFadden, surgeon, to Warden Meighen, 9 November 1924.

28 Ibid., Warden Meighen to Superintendent of Penitentiaries W.S. Hughes, 10 November 1924.

29 Ibid., Finnie to Starnes, 4 December 1924; Wilcox to Starnes, 6 December 1924; and Starnes to Finnie, 10 December 1924; also related correspondence, 7 October 1924 through to January 1925. In deference to Wilcox's apparent hard-line position, he had no contact with Nuqallaq other than at the trial, as he was in Craig

Harbour at the time of his "house arrest" for the intervening year. He claimed that Joy had agreed with him, but there is no written record of any such concurrence. Under the circumstances it made no difference. Regardless, Nuqallaq would have contracted TB before he returned home.

30 Topping, 38.

31 Noah Piugaattuk, interview IE-041, 16 January 1989, Inuit Inullariit Society, Igloolik Research Institute, Nunavut.

32 Interview with Ningiuk Killiktee, Pond Inlet, 18 May 1998.

33 RG 18, vol. 3281, file 1920-HQ-681-G-4 (4), Inspector T. Dann to Commissioner Starnes, 31 March 1925.

34 Ibid., J.J. McFadden, surgeon, to Warden Meighen, 2 April 1925.

35 Ibid. Following protocol, the surgeon's report was forwarded to the Remission branch of the Department of Justice, which then forwarded a copy to Commissioner Starnes on 16 April 1925, who in turn passed on a copy to O.S. Finnie, the director of the NWT and Yukon Branch (who had originally requested information on Nuqallaq's health on 24 March, prompting the attempted visit by Inspector Mead of the RCMP). On 22 April, Finnie reported to Starnes that Superintendent D.C. Scott of Indian Affairs had taken the case in hand and was attempting to have the prisoner admitted to "Ninette Sanatorium" in Manitoba. Note that in 1925 responsibility for the Inuit was placed under the authority of the Indian Affairs Department.

36 Ibid., to Commissioner Starnes from the office of the secretary of state, 28 April 1923.

37 Ibid., Inspector Dann to Commissioner Starnes, 5 May 1923. The need for hospital treatment had been discussed by Dr L.D. Livingstone with officials of the Clemency branch of the Department of Justice, emphasizing his concern that if the prisoner did not receive "immediate medical attention, there was danger of his infecting the whole tribe with tuberculosis on his return."

38 Ibid., memo from Const. H.W. Chitty, forwarded with a note from Inspector Dann to Commissioner Starnes, 8 May 1925. Other memos, letters, and telegrams, 5–8 May, are too numerous to mention individually.

39 Grygier, A Long Way from Home, 4–10.

40 Ibid., 1–6; knowledge is also derived from the author's experience working at the Freeport Sanatorium in Preston, Ontario, in the late 1950s.

41 RG 18, vol. 3281, file 1920-HQ-681-G-4 (4), memos from 25 June to 7 July 1925.

42 According to Anna Ataguttiaq's daughter, there was no ring fitting this description in her mother's belongings. She remembered the Bible, however, and her mother saying that Nuqallaq had it with him in prison. Information provided by Elisapee Ootoova, Pond Inlet, October 1997.

43 RG 18, vol. 3281, file 1920-HQ-681-G-4 (4), telegram from Livingstone to O.S. Finnie, 25 June 1925.

44 RG 18, vol. 3281, file 1920-HQ-681-G-4 (4), Dr C. Laidlaw to Commissioner Starnes, 26 June 1925.

45 Noah Piugaattuk, interview IE-041, 16 January 1989, Inuit Inullariit Society, Igloolik Research Institute, Nunavut.

46 Richard Finnie, "Farewell Voyages: Bernier and the 'Arctic'," *The Beaver* (Summer 1974).

47 RG 18, vol. 3281, file 1920-HQ-681-G-4 (4), "Report Re: NOO-KOOD-LAH" by Dr Leslie Livingstone, 4 November 1925.

48 Finnie (1974).

49 RG 18, vol. 3281, file 1920-HQ-681-G-4 (4), "Report Re: NOO-KOOD-LAH."

50 Copland, *Livingstone of the Arctic*, 40.

51 RG 18, vol. 3281, file 1920-HQ-681-G-4 (4), "Report Re: NOO-KOOD-LAH"; also memo by Inspector Wilcox, 4 August 1925, aboard the CGS *Arctic*.

52 RG 19, vol. 3081, file 1920-HQ-681-G-4 (5), extract from messages received by North West Territories Branch from Haywood [sic] Steele forwarded to RCMP, Conso Press, 3 September 1925.

53 Unlike in 1923, they now had some form of wireless communication that had alerted the police to his pending arrival – at what point of time is not clear.

54 RG 19, vol. 3081, file 1920-HQ-681-G-4 (5), "Report Re: NOO-KOOD-LAH."

55 NAC, Audio-Visual Division, "Back to Baffin," black and white film with subtitles, copyright to the Museum of Science and Technology, permission received for a video copy. The agent for Fox News archival films, however, wanted to charge between U.S. $300 to $600 for a personal copy of their eleven-minute segment of the film.

56 McInnes Papers, report "Re: Noo-kud-lah, Eskimo prisoner," 30 June 1926. The list of rations given to Nookudlah appears in RG 85, vol. 786, file 5997C. Report by Corporal F. McInnes, 30 June 1926.

57 Interview with Martha Akumalik, 18 March 1994, page 30 of the transcripts.

58 When questioned about whether their mother, Ataguttiaq, had ever mentioned that Nuqallaq had tuberculosis, both Sam Arnakallak and Elisapee Ootoova responded negatively.

59 McInnes Collection, WC 2-A, vol. 1, file 9, a typed draft of a report on "Nookudluh" with hand-written corrections.

60 McInnes Papers, WC 2-A, vol. 1, file 10, "Pond Inlet," final report on "Nookudlah, Eskimo Prisoner," 30 June 1926.

61 Conversation with Sam Arnakallak, October 1997.

CHAPTER NINE

1 *RCMP Annual Report for the Year Ending September 1924*, 38.

2 RG 18, vol. 3668, file 567–69 (1), patrol report to Lancaster Sound and Prince Regent Inlet by S/Sgt Joy, 2 May 1924.

3 RG 18, vol. 786, file 5997C, memo "Re: Destitute Eskimo Innuteuk and Family" by Constable Must, 15 April 1924.

4 Bernier, *Master Mariner*, 384.

5 RG 18, vol. 3307, file HQ-1091-G-1, letter from O.S. Finnie to Commissioner Starnes, 25 January 1925.

6 Freuchen, *Arctic Adventure* (1936), 449–60. The same story is repeated in *Vagrant Vikings* (1953), 190–9. Compare this story with the official account by Therkel Mathiassen in his report on the expedition: *Report on the Fifth Thule Expedition 1921–24*, Vol. 1, no. 1 (Copenhagen: Glydendale Boghandel, Nordisk Forlag, 1945), 80–3.

7 Freuchen, *Arctic Adventure*, 437.

8 RG 85, vol. 786, file 5997B, "Contagious Diseases amongst the Eskimos,' by C.E. Wilcox, 23 September 1926. McInnes's original report was rewritten and signed by Inspector Wilcox after his arrival at Pond Inlet (McInnes Collection, WC2 – A/1/file 9).

9 WC 2 – A/1/file 9, "Infectious Disease amongst the Eskimo in the District of Pond Inlet," 8 June 1926. Handwritten copy dated May 3–7.

10 RG 18, vol. 3668, file 567–69 (1), "Patrol to Clyde River and Home Bay" by C.E. Wilcox, 9 June 1926. This and an earlier memo referred to a special report submitted on "sick Eskimos," but no such report was found in this file or in other police files.

11 When I mentioned to Anna Ataguttiaq's children, Sam Arnakallak and Elisapee Ootoova, that Nuqallaq had contracted tuberculosis, both expressed surprise, saying that they were sure their mother did not know or she would have told them.

12 Diubaldo, *The Government of Canada and the Inuit, 1900–1967*, 45.

13 Copland, *Livingstone of the Arctic*, 71–93.

14 "Banting Regrets Hudson Bay Use of the Eskimos," *Toronto Daily Star*, 8 September 1927, front page; see also follow-up article the next day.

15 RG 85, vol. 796, series C-1-a, file 6480, reel T-13300, 10 July 1929, O.S. Finnie to H.A. Stuart.

16 Ibid., James Lawlor to Secretary of the Interior J.M. Roberts, 3 December 1930; O.S. Finnie to Napier Moore, 23 December 1930. Copy of article on file, as well as the original draft.

17 Ibid., D.L. McKeand to Dr. H.A. Stuart, February 1932; Acting Chair of the Dominion Lands Branch to Dr. H.A. Stuart, 8 May 1934.

18 Walter Vanest, "The Death of Jennie Kanajuq: Tuberculosis, Religious Competition and Cultural Conflict in Coppermine, 1929–1931," *Études/Inuit/Studies* 15, no. 1 (1991): 75–104.

19 Grygier, *A Long Way from Home*, 58.

20 Ibid., 59.

21 RCMP postings in the eastern Arctic, 1922–1939, provided by Glenn Wright, at the time with the Historical Division of RCMP headquarters in Ottawa.

22 Greenland Inuit were hired from 1923 through to 1933, at which time Inuit from Pond Inlet were employed for five years after Craig Harbour reopened.

23 Mary-Rousselière, *Qidtlarssuaq*, 107.

24 Interview with Iggiannuguak Odak from Greenland, 19 May 1994.

25 Zaslow, "Administering…," 67–9; Diubaldo, *The Government of Canada and the Arctic*, 53–7.

26 Grant, *Sovereignty or Security?*, 17.

27 RG 18, vol. 3293, file 1922-HQ-681-G-5, report by Sergeant Joy, 13 April 1923.

28 McInnes Papers, Series A, box 1, file "Home Bay – Kevetuk Murders," testimony by "Kidlaapik," April 1924.

29 Interview with Timothy Kadloo, 18 August 1994.

30 In addition to comparison of detachment reports from Pond Inlet and Pangnirtung, this tendency was confirmed by my interpreter, Philip Paneak, originally from Clyde River and with connections to families in the Cumberland Sound region.

31 McInnes Papers, file "Kevetuk Murders," reports by Corporal McInnes, 19 and 22 April 1924.

32 Pitseolak and Eber, *People from Our Side*, 43, 68–9. See also Grant, "Religious Fanaticism at Leaf River, Ungava – 1931": 159–88.

33 McInnes Papers. Notes in Corporal McInnes's pocket diary relate to the murder investigation.

34 Ibid.

35 White, "Hector Pitchforth, 1886–1937," 267.

36 McInnes Papers, file "Kevetuk Murders," patrol report by Corporal McInnes, 19 April 1924.

37 *Royal Canadian Mounted Police Annual Report for 1927* (Ottawa: King's Printer, 1928), 66. Extracts from patrol report are by Constable J. Murray. Also see Copland, *Livingstone of the Arctic*, 78–9.

38 Story by Elisapee Kanangmaq Ahlooloo in *We Don't Live in Snow Houses Now*, 33.

39 Information provided by Philip Paneak of Pond Inlet.

40 RG 18, vol. 3307, file 1924-HQ-1091-G2, Joy to Wilcox, 11 February 1925. See also "Synopsis of Reports," prepared by O.S. Finnie with covering letter, 24 February 1925.

41 Ibid., Wilcox to Commissioner Starnes, 11 February 1925.

42 Ibid., "Synopsis of Reports Received, 1924–1925," prepared by O.S. Finnie with covering letter, 24 February 1925.

43 Parsons and Janes, *The King of Baffin Island*, 84.

44 RG 18, vol. 3307, file 1924-HQ-1091-G2, Corporal Timbury to Commanding Officer, 10 September 1926; same file, O.S. Finnie to Starnes, 20 November 1926.

45 RG 18, vol. 3313, file 1925-HQ-180-C-2, Report by Sgt. J.E.F. Wight, 5 July 1926. See also statement by John Hayward, same date.

46 RG 85, vol. 786, file 5997C, receipts and reports on "destitute rations," Pond Inlet, 30 June 1927, along with related correspondence with the Department of Indian Affairs.

47 RG 85, vol. 1044, file 540–3 (1), report by Corporal J. Petty, 1 June 1926.

48 Interview with Joanasie Arreak, taped and translated by Philip Paneak, February 1998; also interview with Timothy Kadloo, 14 August 1994; and general discussion with elders participating in the oral history project, May 1998, Philip Paneak translating.

49 Oosten, Laugrand, and Rasing, eds., *Perspectives on Traditional Law*, 1.

50 Ibid., 43 and 53.

51 Interview with Martha Akumalik, 18 March 1994; confirmed in general discussion with elders, May 1998. Martha believed that the individual in question was responsible for the death of her husband.

52 See the RCMP annual reports for the years ending 31 March 1927 and 31 March 1928.

53 Interview with Sam Arnakallak, 27 September 1994.

54 Grant, *Sovereignty or Security?*, 19–42; also personal research into government publications, films, and photographic materials.

55 For example, interview with Sam Arnakallak, 27 September 1994.

56 Interview with Ningiuk Killiktee, 18 May 1994.

57 Interview with Timothy Kadloo, 18 August 1994.

58 Interview with Sam Arnakallak, 28 April 1994.

59 Interview with Sam Arnakallak, 27 September 1994.

60 Interview with Ningiuk Killiktee, 18 May 1994.

61 Taped interview, 9 November 1995, with former Constable Robert Christy, stationed at Pond Inlet from 1932–34; also the notebooks in the McInnes Collection covering the period when Corporal McInnes was in charge of the Pond Inlet detachment, 1924–25. These are particularly informative about the value of goods and food purchased for use at the detachment.

62 Interview with Ningiuk Killiktee, 18 May 1994.

63 Interview with Timothy Kadloo, 18 August 1994.

64 Interview with Sam Arnakallak, 27 September 1994.

65 Interview with Letia Kyak, 13 July 1994.

66 Interview with Joanasie Arreak, 17 May 1994.

67 Interview with Sam Arnakallak, 28 April 1994.

68 Taped interview with former RCMP Constable Robert Christy, 9 November 1995.

69 McInnes made numerous notes in the back of his diary related to payment of specific items from the store in return for *kamiik*, mitts, and other skin clothing (McInnes Collection).

70 Interview with former Constable Robert Christy, November 1995.

71 Kyak, whose natural father was Wilfred Caron, spent his formative years at the Pond Inlet detachment, where his mother and stepfather were employed by the police (personal information from his widow, Letia Kyak, and his daughter, Martha Kyak).

72 McInnes Papers, Series A, box 1, file 15, "Purchasing of Articles from Hudson's Bay Company at Pangnirtung," report to RCMP Commissioner from Corporal McInnes, 22 June 1934.

73 McInnes Papers, Series C, box 3, file 3, from Corporal Finley McInnes's personal notebook (not paginated) circa 1924–34. He was posted to Pond Inlet from 1922 to 1923 and from 1924 to 1926.

74 Interview with Sam Arnakallak, 27 September 1994.

75 Ibid.

76 "Ahlooloo's Story," *We Don't Live in Snow Houses*, 26.

77 Brody, *The Other Side of Eden*, 218–19.

CHAPTER TEN

1   Diamond Jenness, for instance, refers to the Inuit becoming "Wards of the Police," whereas Morris Longstreth talks of the "immemorial ethic of conquest."

2   Morrison, "Canadian Sovereignty and the Inuit of the Central and Eastern Arctic," 254–8.

3   MG 30 B57, vol. 1, file "Dispatches 1874–1923," Lord Carnarvon to Lord Dufferin, governor-general of Canada, 30 April 1874.

4   Steele, *Policing the Arctic*, 239.

5   "Oyukuluk's Story," *We Don't Live in Snow Houses*, 3.

6   Personal discussion with Elisapee Ootoova, May 1997.

7   Atagutsiaq and Mary-Rousselière, "Eye-witness Account of Robert Janes's Murder," 5–9.

8   Taped interview with Anna Ataguttiaq by Father Guy Mary-Rousselière (1974), loaned to the author by Ataguttiaq's daughter, Elisapee Ootoova, and translated by Philip Paneak, February 1998. The story published by Father Mary is slightly longer, but the substance is the same. For purposes here, it was more appropriate to include the shorter version.

9   Atagutsiaq and Mary-Rousselière, "Eye-Witness Account" of Robert Janes's Murder, 9.

10 Jenness, *Eskimo Administration II*, 46.

11 Copland, *Livingstone of the Arctic*, 71. Livingstone suggests that there were a number of similar cases; also see the account of a murder/suicide at Home Bay in the early 1930s in Steele, 348.

12 *RCMP Annual Report for the Year Ending September 1932*, 100.

13 *RCMP Annual Report* (1934). See report on the patrol to Imigin, 1 June 1934.

14 *RCMP Annual Report for 1932*, 36. Also see RG 18, vol. 3663, file G567–56 (1), report, 5 February 1938, and attachment 26 October 1938.

15 RG 18, vol. 3663, file G567–56 (1). As an example, see the report by Cpl. McBeth, 25 September 1935.

16 RG 18, acc. 85–96/048, vol. 32, file G-804–1A (4), report on 1939 Eastern Arctic Patrol by R.A. Marriott, historian (11–14).

17 Taped interview with Jaco Evic at Pangnirtung, 12 August 1998.

18 RG 18, Acc 85–86/048, vol. 32, file G-804–1A (4), report by R.A. Marriott, "Eastern Arctic Patrol, 1939."

19 RG 85, vol. 1879, file 540–1 (2), T.L. Cory to R.A. Gibson, 22 June 1945.

20 Eber, *Images of Justice*, 139–49.

21 RG 85, vol. 1879, file 540–1 (2), J.G. Wright to R.A. Gibson, 10 January 1947.

22 Bell, "Coping with Crime in Nunavut," 13.

EPILOGUE

1 Grygier, *A Long Way from Home*, xxi.

2 Interview with Ningiuk Killiktee, 18 May 1994.

3 Harrington, "A. H. Joy (1887–1932)," 223–5.

4 Steele, *Policing the Arctic*, 339. McBeth returned to Pond Inlet twice after his original posting in 1928, whereas McInnes returned to both Pond Inlet and Pangnirtung following his initial assignments at both posts (information provided by the RCMP historical division, Ottawa).

5 Fetherstonhaugh, *The Royal Canadian Mounted Police*, 241.

6 Steele, *Policing the Arctic*, 339 and 247; photo of the plane at 340.

7 Roy, "L'Honorable Juge Louis-Alfred-Adhémar Rivet," 467.

8 Finnie, "Farewell Voyages."

9 Diamond Jenness, *Eskimo Administration*, 47.

10 White, "Henry Toke Munn," 74.

11 Interview with Martha Akumalik, 18 March 1994, transcript page 29–30; also interview with Sam Arnakallak, 27 September 1994; and group discussions with the elders.

12 Interview with Sam Arnakallak, 27 September 1994.

13 Interview with Robert Christy, November 1995.

14 RG 18, vol. 3668, file 567–69 (1), "Patrol to Arctic Bay and Return…." by Constable A.E. Fisher, 1 April 1936; other stories told by the elders and the Pond Inlet librarian, Philippa Ootoowak.

15 "Oyukuluk's Story," in *We Don't Live in Snow Houses*, 31.

16 Price, *The Howling Arctic*, 86–8.

17 Interview with Elisapee Ootoova, Jarick Oosten, and Frédéric Laugrand, eds., *Interviewing Inuit Elders: Introduction* (Iqaluit: Nunavut Arctic College, 1999).

18 Atagutsiaq and Mary-Rousselière, edited comments in "Eye-Witness of Robert Janes's Murder," 10.

19 Sissons, *Judge of the Far North*. The territorial administration was responsible for paying the fees for legal counsel, interpreters, witnesses, jurors, and the jury guard, and thus often delegated these tasks in eastern trials to individuals available on the Eastern Arctic Patrol. See Graham, "Remote Justice," 219–21.

20 Morrow, *Northern Justice*, 202.

21 Eber, *Images of Justice*: 131–4; Price "Remote Justice," 265n119. Graham cites Judge Morrow's "List of Jury Verdicts in the Northwest Territories" (1970), *Rex v. Shooyook*.

22 Eber, *Images of Justice*, 28.
23 Morrow, *Northern Justice*, xxii.

APPENDIX ONE

1 Stevenson, "The Robert Janes Murder Trial." In addition to a few minor inaccuracies, the major error was his assertion that Nuqallaq died while at Stony Mountain Penitentiary. It is difficult to believe that Stevenson would not have known where and why Nuqallaq died, yet he was not the first to imply ignorance. Bernier, in his autobiography, *Master Mariner*, describes the trial and Nuqallaq being sentenced to Stony Mountain Penitentiary but states that it was only for two years, not ten. Similarly, his detailed description of the CGS *Arctic*'s last voyage in 1925 makes no reference to Nuqallaq being on board, suggesting that either censorship rules were invoked or it was a matter of personal discretion. Either way, the public would not be informed that Nuqallaq had returned home with tuberculosis and died shortly after.
2 Göttschalk, "The Historian and the Historical Document."
3 Discussion with Cornelius Nutarak, an elder at Pond Inlet, with Martha Kyak translating, June 2000.
4 Brody, *The Other Side of Eden*, 39.
5 Laugrand, Oosten, and Trudel, *Memory and History in Nunavut*. See also the edited volumes by Jarich Oosten, Frédéric Laugrand, and William Rasing listed in the bibliography.

Bibliography

PRIMARY SOURCES

ARCHIVAL RECORDS AND GOVERNMENT REPORTS

National Archives of Canada (NAC)

Government Records
Record Group 13 (Department of Justice)
Record Group 15 (Department of the Interior)
Record Group 18 (RCMP papers)
Record Group 85 (Northern Affairs Program)
Record Group 42 (Department of Marine and Fisheries)

Manuscript Division
MG 30 B 6, Captain J.E. Bernier Collection.
MG 30 B 33, Albert Peter Low Collection
MG 30 B 34, Leonard T. Jackman Papers
MG 30 B 35, Fabien Vanasse-Vertefeuille Papers
MG 30 B 57, J.D. Craig Papers
MG 30 B 68, R.A. Logan Papers
MG 30 B 129, William Harold Grant Papers
MG 30 B 139, Edward Macdonald Diary
MG 30 E 169, J.D. Harkin Papers
MG 30 E 362, Thomas Henry Tredgold Collection

Photographic Division
Photographs from the Northern Affairs Collection, including the J.D. Craig, Richard Finnie, L.T. Burwash, W.H. Grant, T.H. Tredgold, and J.E. Bernier Collections. Also film footage by J.E. Bernier, R. Tass, and George Valiquette.

National Archives of Manitoba/Hudson's Bay Company Archives
  Hudson's Bay Company Post Journal, B. 465 for Pond Inlet, 1921–39
  Photographic Division

Northwest Territories Archives, Yellowknife
  Alex Stevenson and Dr Leslie Livingstone Papers
  Photographic Division: Collections related to the eastern Arctic, 1906–39.

Roman Catholic Diocese of Churchill-Hudson Bay Archives
  Photographs from Pond Inlet, 1929–39

Royal Canadian Mounted Police Headquarters, Ottawa, Historical Division
  RCMP Photo Collection and Annual Reports 1920–39.

UNPUBLISHED ORAL HISTORY TRANSCRIPTS

Anna Ataguttiaq. Taped interview with Father Guy Mary-Rousselière, 1974. Loaned
  to the author by owner, Elisapee Ootoova (Ataguttiaq's daughter); translated by
  Philip Paniaq.
Igloolik Inullariit Society, Igloolik Research Centre, Nunavut. Transcripts of oral
  history interviews with Noah Piugaattuk, Isapee Qanguk, and Titus Uyarasuk
Pangnirtung Oral History Project (author's research). Eleven tapes and transcripts
  of interviews with Inuit elders, March 1995.
Pond Inlet Oral History Project (author's portion). Ten tapes and transcripts of interviews with Inuit elders, 1994–98.

PRIVATE COLLECTIONS

Christy, Robert (1911–97). Photographs of former RCMP constable at Pond Inlet,
  1932–34; taped interview, 28 November 1994, permission to author.
MacGregor, William (1901–84). Photograph collection of former RCMP constable
  posted at Pond Inlet and Pangnirtung, 1922–24, courtesy his son, W.L. MacGregor.
McInnes, Finley (1894–1978). Private collection of papers, photographs, diaries,
  notes, maps, Inuit sketches, reports, clippings, correspondence and audiotapes of
  a former RCMP corporal stationed at Pond Inlet and Pangnirtung from 1922–26.
  The collection has been preserved and catalogued, and is temporarily housed at
  Trent University pending deposit in an archival repository selected by his granddaughter, Andrea Williams.

SECONDARY SOURCES

Anaviapik, Simon. "Early Days in Mittimatalik," Inuktitut 72 (1990): 47–58.
Atagutsiaq, Anna, and Guy Mary-Rousselière. "Eye-Witness Account of Robert
  Janes's Murder," Eskimo 36 (Fall-Winter 1988–89): 5–1.
Backhouse, Constance. Colour-Coded: A Legal History of Racism in Canada, 1900–1950.
  Toronto: University of Toronto Press 1999.

Bailey, Victor, ed. *Policing and Punishment in Nineteenth Century Britain*. New Brunswick, N.J.: Rutgers University Press 1981.

Balicki, Asen. *The Nestlik Eskimo*. New York: Garden City 1970.

Beahen, William. "The Arctic Islands – The RCMP and 100 Years of Canadian Sovereignty." In Donovan T. Saul, ed. *Red Serge and Stetsons: A Hundred Years of Mounties' Memories*. Victoria, B.C.: Horsdal and Schubert 1993.

Bell, Jim. "Coping with Crime in Nunavut." *Nunatsiaq News* 29, no. 29 (3 August 2001): 13.

Bernier, J.E. *Master Mariner and Arctic Explorer*. Ottawa: Le Droit 1939.

– *Report on the Dominion of Canada Government Expedition to the Arctic Islands and Hudson Strait on the D.G.S. "Arctic," 1908–1909*. Ottawa: Department of Marine and Fisheries, Government Printing Bureau 1910.

– *Report on the Dominion Government Expedition to Arctic Islands and the Hudson Strait on Board the C.G.S. "Arctic" 1906–1907*. Ottawa: Department of Marine and Fisheries, C.H. Parmelee 1909.

Birket-Smith, Kaj. *The Eskimos*. London: Methuen 1936.

Boas, Franz. *The Central Eskimo*. 1888. Reprint, Lincoln: University of Nebraska Press 1964.

Brody, Hugh. *The Other Side of Eden: Hunters, Farmers and the Shaping of the World*. Vancouver: Douglas & McIntyre 2000.

– *Living Arctic: Hunters of the Canadian North*. Vancouver: Douglas & McIntyre 1987.

– *The Peoples' Land: Whites and the Eastern Arctic*. Harmondsworth, England: Penguin 1975.

Canada. *Report of the Royal Commission to Investigate, Inquire into and Report upon Charges Preferred against Certain Officers and Guards Connected with Stoney Mountain Penitentiary, 1897–1903*. Vol. 1. Toronto: Micromedia.

Canada, Department of Marine and Fisheries. *Report on the Expedition to Hudson Bay and Cumberland Gulf in the Steamship "Diana" under the Command of William Wakeham*. Ottawa: Queen's Printer 1898.

– *Report on the Dominion Government Expedition to the Northern Waters and Arctic Archipelago of the D.G.S. "Arctic" in 1910*. Ottawa: King's Printer 1911.

Canada, Department of the Interior. *Canada's Arctic Islands: Log of Canadian Expedition, 1922*. Ottawa: King's Printer 1923.

– *Canada's Arctic Islands: Canadian Expeditions, 1922–23–24–25–26*. Ottawa: King's Printer 1927.

– *Canada's Eastern Arctic: Its History, Resources, Population and Administration*. Ottawa: King's Printer 1934.

Canada, Sessional Papers. *Annual Reports of the Royal North West Mounted Police*. Ottawa: King's Printer 1911–19.

– *Annual Reports of the Royal Canadian Mounted Police* (ending 30 September). Ottawa: King's Printer 1920–39.

Carrigan, D. Owen. *Crime and Punishment in Canada*. Toronto: McClelland & Stewart 1991.

Cellard, André. *Punishment, Imprisonment and Reform in Canada, from New France to the Present*. CHA Historical Booklet No. 60. Ottawa: Canadian Historical Association 2000.

Choque, Charles. *Guy Mary-Rousselière, 1913–1994*. Montreal: Mediaspaul 1998.

Coates, K.S., and W.R. Morrison. "'To Make These Tribes Understand': The Trial of Alikomiak and Tatamigana." *Arctic* 51, no. 3 (September 1998) 220–30.

Cockburn, J. S., ed. *Crime in England, 1550–1800*. London: Methuen and Co. 1977.

Cooke, Alan, and Clive Holland. *The Exploration of Northern Canada, 500 to 1920: A Chronology*. Toronto: Arctic History Press 1978.

Condon, Richard. *Inuit Behaviour and Seasonal Change: A Study of Behavioral Ecology in the Central Canadian Arctic*. Ann Arbor, Michigan: University of Michigan Press 1983.

Copland, Dudley. *Coplalook*. Winnipeg: Watson and Dwyer 1985.

– *Livingstone of the Arctic*. Lancaster, Ont.: Canadian Century Publishers 1976.

Cowan, Susan, ed. *We Don't Live in Snow Houses Now*. Ottawa: Canadian Arctic Producers 1976.

Damas, David. "Shifting Relations in the Administration of Inuit: The Hudson's Bay Company and the Canadian Government." *Études/Inuit/Studies* 17, no. 2 (1993): 5–28.

Damas, David, ed. *Handbook of North American Indians*. Vol. 5: *Arctic*. Washington: Smithsonian Institute 1984.

Davis, Richard, ed. *Lobsticks and Stone Cairns: Human Landmarks in the Arctic*. Calgary: University of Calgary Press 1996.

Diubaldo, Richard J. *The Government of Canada and the Inuit, 1900–1967*. Ottawa: Indian and Northern Affairs 1985.

– *Stefansson and the Canadian Arctic Expedition*. Montreal and Kingston: McGill-Queen's University Press 1978.

Dorion-Robitaille, Yolande. *Captain J.E. Bernier's Contribution to Canadian Sovereignty in the Arctic*. Ottawa: Indian and Northern Affairs 1978.

Eber, Dorothy Harley. *Images of Justice: A Legal History of the North*. Montreal and Kingston: McGill-Queen's University Press 1997.

– "Interpreting the Law: The Arctic's Unsung Linguistic Geniuses." *Arctic Circle* (Summer 1992): 14–19.

– *When the Whalers Were Up North*. Montreal and Kingston: McGill-Queen's University Press 1989.

Fetherstonhaugh, F. C. *The Royal Canadian Mounted Police*. New York: Carrick and Evans 1938.

Finkler, H. W. *Inuit and the Administration of Criminal Justice in the Northwest Territories: The Case of Frobisher Bay*. Ottawa: Supply and Services 1976.

Finnie, Richard. "Joseph Elzéar Bernier (1852–1934)." *Arctic* 39 (September 1986): 272. Reprinted in Richard Davis, ed., *Lobsticks and Stone Cairns* (Calgary: Arctic Institute of North America 1996).

– "Farewell Voyages: Bernier and the 'Arctic.'" *The Beaver* (Summer 1974): 44–54.

Fleming, Archibald Lang. *Archibald the Arctic*. New York: Appleton-Century-Crofts 1956.

– *Perils of the Polar Pack: The Adventures of the Reverend E.W.T. Greenshields of Black-lead Island, Baffin Island*. Toronto: Missionary Society of the Church of England in Canada 1932.

– *Dwellers in Arctic Night*. London: Society for the Propagation of the Gospel in Foreign Parts 1928.

Flint, Maurice S. *Operation Canon*. London: The Bible Churchmen's Missionary Society 1949.

Fortune, Robert. *The Health of the Eskimos: A Bibliography, 1857–1967*. Hanover, N.H.: Dartmouth College Libraries Publication 1969.

Freuchen, Peter. *Book of the Eskimos*. New York: World Publishing 1961.

– *Vagrant Viking*. New York: Julian Messner Inc. 1953.

– *Arctic Adventure: My Life in the Frozen North*. New York: Farrar & Rinehart 1935.

Friedland, Martin L. *A Century of Criminal Justice: Perspectives on the Development of Canadian Law*. Toronto: Carswell Legal Publications 1984.

George, Jane. "Kapitaikallak's Abiding Legacy." *Nunatsiaq News* 29, no. 39 (22 October 2001): 16–17.

Goldring, Philip. "Inuit Economic Responses to Euro-American Contacts: Southeast Baffin Island, 1824–1940." In Kenneth S. Coates and William R. Morrison, eds., *Interpreting Canada's North*, 252–77. Toronto: Copp Clark Pitman 1989.

– "Religion, Missions, and Native Culture." *Journal of the Canadian Church Historical Society* 26, no. 2 (1986): 146–72.

Göttschalk, Louis. "The Historian and the Historical Document." In Louis Göttschalk, Clyde Kluckhohn, and Robert Angell, *The Use of Personal Documents in History, Anthropology, and Sociology*, 3–78. New York: Social Science Research Council 1948.

Graburn, N.H. "Eskimo Law in Light of Self- and Group-Interest." In *Law and Society Review* 4 no. 1 (August 1969): 45–60.

Grant, Shelagh D. "Sovereignty, Justice, and the Inuit of Eastern Canada, 1920–1925." In *Proceedings of the International Congress on the History of the Arctic and Sub-Arctic Regions*. Reykjavik: University of Iceland Press 2001.

– "Writing Inuit History: Challenges and Rewards," in Kerry Abel and Ken S. Coates eds. *Northern Visions: New Perspectives on the North in Canadian History*. Peterborough: Broadview Press 2001.

– "Imagination and Spirituality: Written Narratives and the Oral Tradition." In John Moss, ed. *Echoing Silence: Papers on Arctic Narratives*. Ottawa: University of Ottawa Press 1997.

– "Canadian Justice and the Inuit of the Eastern Arctic." Paper presented at the Law of the Musk-Ox, Law of the Buffalo conference at the University of Calgary, 5 April 1997.

– "Religious Fanaticism at Leaf Bay, Ungava – 1931," *Études/Inuit/Studies* 21, nos. 1/2 (1997).

– *Sovereignty or Security: Government Policy in the Canadian North, 1936–1950.* Vancouver: University of British Columbia Press 1988.

Griffin, Fred G. "Now Baffin's Land Has an Eskimo Murder Trial by Jury," *Toronto Star Weekly* (3 November 1923), 19–20.

Grygier, Patricia Sandiford. *A Long Way From Home: The Tuberculosis Epidemic among the Inuit.* Montreal/Kingston: McGill-Queen's University Press 1994.

Hall, Charles Francis. *Life with the Esquimaux: A Narrative of Arctic Experience in Search of Survivors of Sir John Franklin's Expedition.* 1867. Reprint, Edmonton: Hurtig Publishers 1971.

– *Narrative of a Second Expedition made by Charles F. Hall: Voyage to Repulse Bay, Sledge Journey to the Straits of Hecla and Fury, and to King William's Island, and Residence Among the Eskimoes During the Years 1864–1869.* J.E. Nourse, ed. Washington: U.S. Government Printing Office 1879.

Hallendy, Norman. "The Last Known Traditional Inuit Trial on Southwest Baffin Island in the Canadian Arctic." Background Paper No. 2, *Places of Power and Objects of Veneration in the Canadian Arctic,* for the World Archaeological Congress III (August 1991).

Harper, Kenn. "Writing in Inuktitut: An Historical Perspective." In *North: Landscape of the Imagination.* Rev. ed. Ottawa: National Library of Canada 1998.

– "In Search of William Duval, Arctic Trader, *Above and Beyond* (circa 1995).

– "William Duval (1858–1931)." in Richard Davis ed., *Lobsticks and Stone Cairns: Human Landmarks in the Arctic,* 263–4. Calgary: University of Calgary Press 1996.

– "Pangnirtung." *Inuktitut* (Spring 1985): 18–36.

Harring, Sidney. *White Man's Law: Native People in Nineteenth-Century Canadian Jurisprudence.* Toronto: Published for the Osgoode Society for Canadian Legal History by University of Toronto Press 1998.

– "The Rich Men of the Country: Canadian Law in the Land of the Copper Inuit, 1914–1930." *Ottawa Law Review,* 1989.

Hoebel, E. Adamson. *The Law of the Primitive Man: A Study in Comparative Legal Dynamics.* Cambridge: Harvard University Press 1954.

Jenness, Diamond. *The People of the Twilight.* Chicago: University of Chicago Press 1929.

– *Eskimo Administration II: Canada.* Paper No. 14. Montreal: AINA 1967.

Keenleyside, Anne. "Euro-American Whaling in the Canadian Arctic: Its Effects on Eskimo Health." *Arctic Anthropology* 27, no. 1 (1990) 1–19.

Kemp, Vernon. *Without Fear, Favour or Affection.* Toronto: Longmans 1958.

Kemp, William B. "Baffinland Eskimo." David Damas, ed. *Handbook of North American Indians,* Vol. 5: *Arctic,* 463–75. Washington: Smithsonian Institute 1984.

King, W.F. *Report upon the Title of Canada to the Islands North of the Mainland of Canada.* Ottawa: Government Printing Bureau 1905.

Laugrand, Frédéric. "Le mythe comme instrument de mémoire. Rémoration et interprétation d'un extrait de la Genese par un ainé inuit de la Terre de Baffin." *Études/Inuit/Studies* 23, nos. 1–2 (1999) 91–116.

– *"Le siqqitiq*: Rénouvellement religieux et premier rituel de conversion chez les Inuit du nord de la Terre de Baffin." *Études/Inuit/Studies*. 21, nos. 1–2 (1997): 101–40.

Laugrand, Frédéric, Jarich Oosten, and François Trudel. *Memory and History in Nunavut: Representing Tuurngait*. Iqaluit: Nunavut Arctic College 2000.

Lee, Herbert Patrick. *Policing the Top of the World*. London: John Lane 1928.

Longstreth, T. Morris. *The Silent Force: Scenes from the Life of the Mounted Police in Canada*. New York: Century 1927.

Low, A.P. *Report on the Dominion Government Expedition to Hudson Bay and the Arctic Islands on Board the D.G.S. Neptune, 1903–1904*. Ottawa: Government Printing Bureau 1906.

Lubbock, Basil. *The Arctic Whalers*. 2nd ed. Glasgow: Brown, Son and Ferguson 1937.

MacEachern, Alan. "Edward Macdonald's Arctic Diary, 1910–1911," *The Island Magazine* 46 (Fall/Winter 1999): 30–40.

Mackinnon, C.S. "Canada's Eastern Arctic Patrol 1922–68." *Polar Record* 27, no. 161 (1991): 93–101.

MacLeod, R.C. *The North-West Mounted Police and Law Enforcement, 1873–1905*. Toronto: University of Toronto Press 1976.

MacLeod, R.C., ed. *Lawful Authority: Readings on the History of Criminal Justice in Canada*. Toronto: Copp Clark Pitman 1988.

Markham, A.H. *A Whaling Cruise to Baffin's Bay and the Gulf of Boothia. And an Account of the Rescue of the Crew of the Polaris*. 2nd ed. London: Sampson Low, Marston, Low and Searle 1875.

Martin, Constance. *Search for the Blue Goose: J. Dewey Soper – The Arctic Adventures of a Canadian Naturalist*. Calgary: Bayeux Arts and Arctic Institute of North America 1995.

Mary-Rousselière, Guy, OMI. "Eskimo Toponymy of Pond Inlet." Unpublished manuscript, n.d. Copy on file in the Rebecca Idlout Library in Pond Inlet.

– "Igarjuaq." Unpublished manuscript, n.d.

– *Qitdlarssuaq: The Story of a Polar Migration*. Winnipeg: Wuerz Publishing 1991.

– with Anna Atagutsiaq. "Eye-Witness Account to Janes's Murder." *Eskimo* (Fall/Winter 1988–89): 3–7.

– with Anna Atagutsiaq. "The Tuniit Invented Automatic Harpoon, Shared Seal Gun Invention." *Eskimo* (Fall/Winter 1986–87): 3–9.

– "Factors Affecting Human Occupation of the Land in the Pond Inlet Region from Prehistorical to Contemporary Times." *Eskimo* 41, no. 28 (Fall/Winter 1984–85).

– "Iglulik," in David Damas, ed. *Handbook of North American Indians*. Vol. 5: *Arctic*, 431–46. Washington: Smithsonian Institute 1984.

– "Mittima's Grave." *Eskimo* 75 (Summer 1967): 13–15.

Mathiassen, Therkel. *Material Culture of the Iglulik Eskimos: Report of the Fifth Thule Expedition, 1921–1924*. Vol. 6, no. 1. Copenhagen: Glydendal 1928.

– *Archaeology of the Central Eskimo: Report of the Fifth Thule Expedition, 1921–1924*. Vol. 4, nos. 1–2. Copenhagen: Glydendal 1927.

Matthiasson, John S. *Living on the Land: Change among the Inuit of Baffin Island*. Peter-borough, Ont.: Broadview Press 1992.

Maxwell, Maureau S. "Pre-Dorset and Dorset Prehistory of Canada." David Damas, ed. In *Handbook of North American Indians*. Vol. 5: *Arctic*, 359–68. Washington: Smithsonian Institute 1984.

McClintock, F. Leopold. *The Voyage of the "Fox" in the Arctic Seas, in Search of Sir John Franklin and His Companions*. London: John Murray 1881.

McGhee, Robert. "Thule Prehistory of Canada." David Damas, ed. In *Handbook of North American Indians*. Vol. 5: *Arctic*, 369–7. Washington: Smithsonian Institute 1984.

– *Canadian Arctic Prehistory*. Ottawa: Canadian Museum of Civilization 1990.

– *Ancient People of the Arctic*. Vancouver: University of British Columbia Press 1996.

Millward, A.E. *Southern Baffin Island: An Account of Exploration, Investigation and Settlement during the Past Fifty Years*. Ottawa: Department of the Interior 1930.

Minotto, Claude. "Le frontière arctique du Canada: Les expéditions de Joseph-Elzéar Bernier 1895–1925." Master's thesis, McGill University, Montreal 1975.

Montague, Sydney R. *North to Adventure*. New York: National Travel Club 1939.

Morice, Adrian G. *Thawing Out the Eskimo*. Boston: Society for the Propagation of the Faith 1943.

Morrison, David, and Georges-Hébert Germain. *Inuit: Glimpses of an Arctic Past*. Ottawa: Canadian Museum of Civilization 1995.

Morrison, William R. *True North: The Yukon and Northwest Territories*. Toronto: Oxford University Press 1998.

– "Canadian Sovereignty and the Inuit of the Central and Eastern Arctic." *Études/Inuit/Studies* 10 nos. 1 and 2 (Autumn 1986): 245–59.

– *Showing the Flag: The Mounted Police and Canadian Sovereignty in the North, 1894–1925*. Vancouver: University of British Columbia Press 1985.

– *Under the Flag: Canadian Sovereignty and the Native People in Northern Canada*. Ottawa: Indian and Northern Affairs 1984.

Morrow, W.H., ed. *Northern Justice: The Memoirs of Justice William G. Morrow*. Toronto: University of Toronto Press 1995.

Moyles, R.G. *British Law and Arctic Men: The Celebrated 1917 Trials of Sinnisiak and Uluksuk, First Inuit Tried under White Man's Law*. Saskatoon: Western Producer Prairie Books 1979.

Munn, Henry Toke. *Prairie Trails and Arctic By-ways*. London: Hurst and Blackett 1932.

– *Tales of the Eskimo*. London: W. & R. Chambers 1926.

Nungak, Zebedee. "Fundamental Values, Norms and Concepts of Justice – Inuit of Nunavik." In *Aboriginal Peoples and the Justice System*, Royal Commission on Aboriginal Peoples, Ottawa 1993.

Oosten, Jarich, and Frédéric Laugrand, eds. *Interviewing the Elders: Introduction*. Iqaluit: Nunavut Arctic College 1999.

– *The Transition to Christianity*. Inuit Perspectives on the 20th Century Series, No. 1. Iqaluit: Nunavut Arctic College 1999.

Oosten, Jarich, Frédéric Laugrand, and William Rasing, eds. *Perspectives on Traditional Law.* Interviewing Inuit Elders Series, No. 2. Iqaluit: Nunavut Arctic College 1999.

Parry, William. *Journal of a Voyage for the Discovery of a Northwest Passage from the Atlantic to the Pacific: Performed in the Years 1819–20.* London: John Murray 1821.

Parsons, John, and Burton K. Janes. *The King of Baffin Land: W. Ralph Parsons, Last Fur Trade Commissioner of the Hudson's Bay Company.* St John's, Nfld.: Creative Publishers 1996.

Patenaude, Alan L. "The Administration of Justice in Canada's Northwest Territories, 1870–1990: A Case Study in Colonialism and Social Change." Master's thesis, Simon Fraser University, Burnaby, B.C. 1990.

– "Whose Law? Whose Justice? Two Conflicting Systems of Law and Justice in Canada's Northwest Territories." Honours thesis, Simon Fraser University. Courtesy Northern Justice Society Resources 1989.

Pilot, Robert S. "Lazaroosie Kyak (1919–1976)." In Richard Davis, ed. *Lobsticks and Stone Cairns: Human Landmarks in the Arctic,* 269–71. Calgary: University of Calgary Press 1996.

Pitseolak, Peter, and Dorothy Harley Eber. *People from Our Side.* Kingston/Montreal: McGill-Queen's University Press 1993.

Pospisil, Leopold J. *Anthropology of Law: A Comparative Theory.* New Haven: HRAF Press 1964.

Price, Graham. "The North," *Manitoba Law Journal* 23, no. 1/2 (1995): 352–78.

– "The King v. Alikomiak." In Dale Gibson and W. Lesley Pue, eds., *Glimpses of Canadian Legal History,* 213. Winnipeg: Legal Research Institute of the University of Manitoba 1991.

– "Remote Justice: The Stipendiary Magistrates Court of the Northwest Territories." LL Master's thesis, University of Manitoba 1986.

Price, Ray. *The Howling Arctic: The Remarkable People Who Made Canada Sovereign in the Farthest North.* Toronto: Peter Martin Associates 1970.

Rasing, W.C.E. *"Too Many People" – Order and Nonconformity in Iglulingmiut Social Process.* Nijmegen, Netherlands: Recht and Samenleving 1994.

Rasmussen, Knud. *Across Arctic America.* New York: G.P. Putnam's Sons 1927.

Robertson, D.S. *To the Arctic with the Mounties.* Toronto: Macmillan Company of Canada 1934.

Ross, John. *A Voyage of Discovery, Made under the Orders of the Admiralty, in His Majesty's Ships Isabella and Alexander, for the Purpose of Exploring Baffin's Bay, and Inquiring into the Probability of a Northwest Passage.* London: John Murray 1819.

– *Narrative of a Second Voyage in Search of a North-West Passage, and of a Residence in the Arctic Regions During the Years 1829, 1830, 1831, 1832, 1833.* London: A.W. Webster 1835.

Ross, W. Gillies. *This Distant and Unsurveyed Country: A Woman's Winter at Baffin Island, 1857–1858.* Montreal and Kingston: McGill-Queen's University Press 1996.

– "The Use and Misuse of Historical Photographs: A Case Study from Hudson Bay, Canada," *Arctic Anthropology* 27, no. 2 (1990): 93–112.

- "Whaling, Inuit and the Arctic Islands." In Coates and Morrison, eds, *Interpreting Canada's North*, 235–51. Toronto: Copp Clark Pitman 1989.
- *Arctic Whalers Icy Seas: Narratives of the Davis Strait Whale Fishery.* Toronto: Irwin Publishing 1985.
- *An Arctic Whaling Diary: The Journal of Captain George Comer in Hudson Bay, 1903–1905.* Toronto: University of Toronto Press 1984.
Rowley, Graham. *Cold Comfort: My Love Affair with the Arctic.* Montreal and Kingston: McGill-Queen's University Press 1996.
Rowley, Susan. "Frobisher Miksanut: Inuit Accounts of the Frobisher Voyages." In William W. Fitzhugh and Jacqueline S. Olin, eds., *Archeology of the Frobisher Voyages*, 27–40. Washington: Smithsonian Institute 1993.
Roy, Pierre-Georges. "L'Honorable Juge Louis-Alfred-Adhémar Rivet." In *Les Juges de la province de Québec*. Québec: Le Service des Archives du Gouvernment de la Province de Québec 1933.
Ryan, Joan. *Doing Things the Right Way: Dene Traditional Justice in Lac La Martre, N.W.T.* Calgary: University of Calgary Press/Arctic Institute of North America 1995.
Schledermann, Peter. *Voices in Stone: A Personal Journey into the Past.* Calgary: Arctic Institute of North America 1996.
- *Crossroads to Greenland: 3000 Years of Prehistory in the Eastern High Arctic.* Calgary: Arctic Institute of North America 1990.
Shepard, R.J. and S. Itoh, eds. *Circumpolar Health: Proceedings of the Third International Symposium, Yellowknife, NWT.* Toronto: University of Toronto Press 1976.
Sissons, Jack. *Judge of the Far North: The Memoirs of Jack Sissons.* Toronto: McClelland & Stewart 1968.
Smandych, Russell C., et al. *Canadian Criminal Justice History: An Annotated Bibliography.* Toronto: University of Toronto Press 1987.
Smith, Gordon W. "A Bit of Bernier." *North* 24, no. 2 (Summer 1982): 52–7.
- *Territorial Sovereignty in the Canadian North: A Historical Outline of the Problem.* Report for the Department of Northern Affairs and National Resources, Ottawa: Queen's Printer 1963.
Soper, J. Dewey. *Canadian Arctic Recollections: Baffin Island 1923–1931.* Saskatoon: Institute for Northern Studies, University of Saskatoon 1981.
Stager, J.S., and Harry Swain. *Canada North: Journey to the High Arctic.* New Brunswick, N.J.: Rutgers University Press 1992.
Steele, Harwood. *Policing the Arctic: The Story of the Conquest of the Arctic by the Royal Canadian (Formerly North-West) Mounted Police.* Toronto: Ryerson Press 1935.
Stevenson, Alex. "The Robert Janes Murder Trial at Pond Inlet." *The Beaver* (Autumn 1973): 16–23.
Stevenson, Marc G. *Inuit, Whalers and Cultural Persistence: Structure in Cumberland Sound and Central Inuit Social Organization.* Toronto: Oxford University Press 1997.

Stuart, Hugh A. "Arctic Patrol: A Dramatic Pen Picture of the Canadian Medical Man in Action in the Far North." *Maclean's* (15 March 1931).

Sullivan, Alan. "When God Came to the Belchers." *Queen's Quarterly* 51, no. 2 (1944): 14–28.

Sutherland, Patricia D. "Strands of Culture Contact: Dorset-Norse Interactions in the Canadian Eastern Arctic." In Martin Appelt, Joel Berglund, and Hans Christian Güllov, eds., *Identities and Cultural Contacts in the Arctic: Proceedings from a Conference at the Danish National Museum, Copenhagen*. Copenhagen: The Danish National Museum and Danish Polar Center 2000.

Sutherland, Patricia D., and Robert McGhee. *Lost Visions, Forgotten Dreams: Life and Art of the Ancient Arctic People*. Ottawa: Canadian Museum of Civilization 1996.

Tester, Frank, and Peter Kulchyski. *Tammarniit (Mistakes): Inuit Relocation in the Eastern Arctic*. Vancouver: University of British Columbia Press 1994.

Topping, C.W. *Canadian Penal Institutions*. Toronto: Ryerson Press 1929.

Tremblay, Alfred. *Cruise of the Minnie Maud: Arctic Seas and Hudson Bay, 1912–13*. Quebec City: The Arctic Exchange and Publishing Company 1921.

Trott, Christopher G. "The Rapture and the Rupture: Religious Change amongst the Inuit of North Baffin Island." *Études/Inuit/Studies* 21, nos. 1–2 (1997): 209–28.

Trudel, François. "Autobiographies, mémoire et histoire: Jalons de recherche chez les Inuit." *Études/Inuit/Studies* 23, nos. 1–2 (1999): 145–72.

van den Steenhoven, Gert. *Legal Concepts among the Netsilik Eskimos of Pelly Bay*. Ottawa: Department of Northern Affairs and Natural Resources 1959.

Vanest, Walter J. "The Death of Jennie Kanajuq: Tuberculosis, Religious Competition and Cultural Conflict in Coppermine, 1929–31." *Études/Inuit/Studies* 15, no. 1 (1991): 75–104.

Vaughan, Richard. *The Arctic: A History*. London: Alan Sutton 1994.

Wachowich, Nancy. *Sagiyuq: Stories from the Lives of Three Inuit Women*, in collaboration with Apphia Agalakti Awa, Rhoda Kaujak Katsak, and Sandra Pikujak Katsak. Montreal/Kingston: McGill-Queen's University Press 1999.

Wakeham, William. *Report of the Expedition to Hudson Bay and Cumberland Gulf in the Steamship "Diana" under the Command of William Wakeham in the Year 1897*. Ottawa: Queen's Printer 1898.

Weissling, Lee E. "Inuit Life in the Eastern Arctic, 1922–1942: Change as Recorded by the RCMP." *Canadian Geographer* 35, no. 1 (1991): 59–69.

Wenzel, George. "Clyde River Historical Notes," Department of Geography, McGill University 1996.

– *Clyde Inuit Adaptation and the Organization of Subsistence*. Museum of Man, Mercury Series, Ethnology Service Paper 77. Ottawa: Government of Canada 1980.

White, Gavin. "Hector Pitchforth (1886–1927)." In Richard Davis, ed., *Lobsticks and Stone Cairns: Human Landmarks in the Arctic*. Calgary: University of Calgary Press 1996.

– "Henry Toke Munn (1864–1952)." *Arctic* 37, no. 1 (March 1984): 74–5.

– "Scottish Traders to Baffin Island, 1910–1930." *Maritime History* 5, no. 1 (1977).

Zaslow, Morris. "Administering the Arctic Islands, 1880–1940: Policemen, Missionaries, Fur Traders." In Morris Zaslow ed., *A Century of Canada's Arctic Islands: 1880–1990*. Ottawa: Royal Society of Canada 1981.

Zubrycki, Richard M. *The Establishment of Canada's Penitentiary System: Federal Correctional Policy, 1867–1900*. Toronto: University of Toronto Press 1980.

Index

Page numbers in italics refer to illustrations or maps.